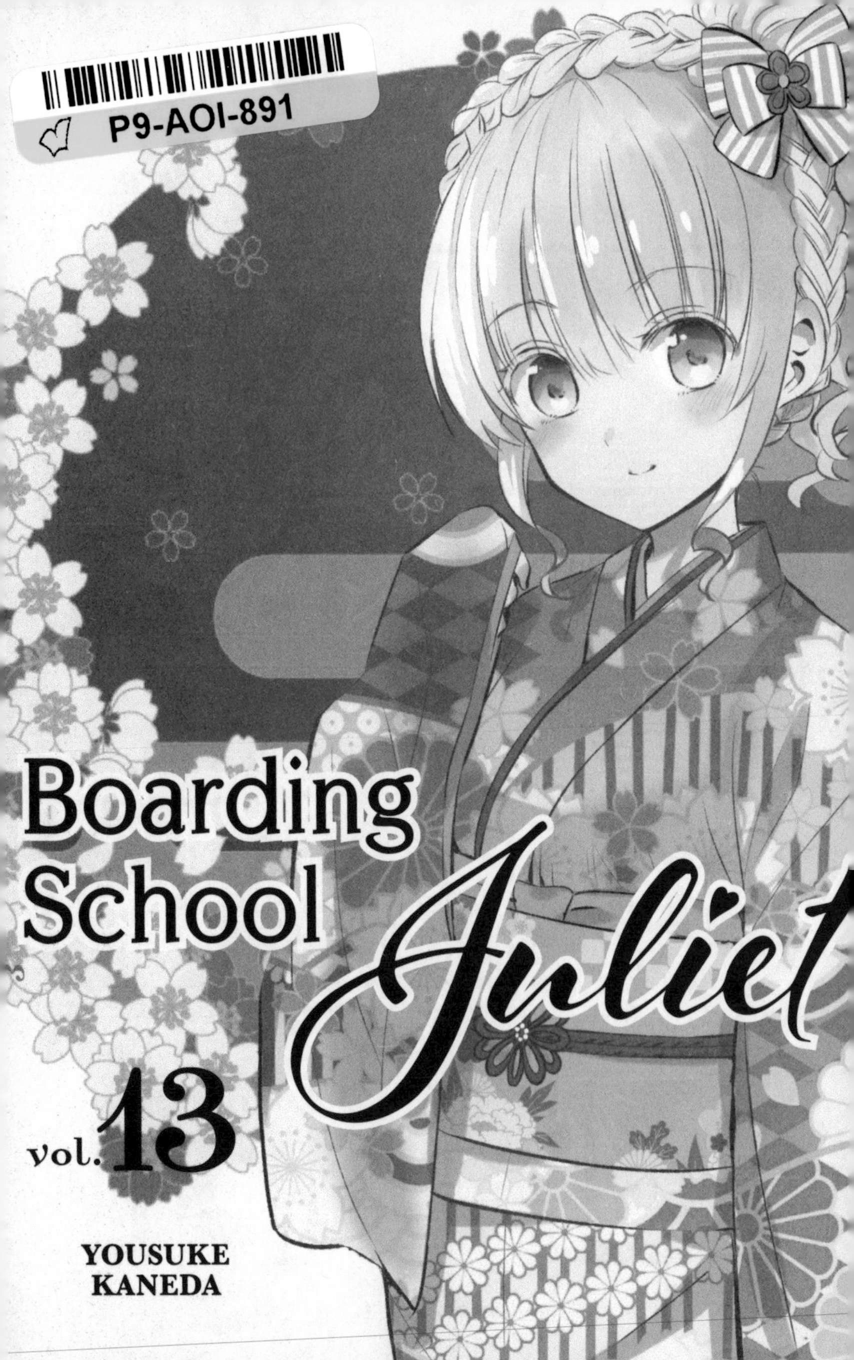



# Boarding School Juliet

vol. 13

YOUSUKE KANEDA

# THE PLAYERS

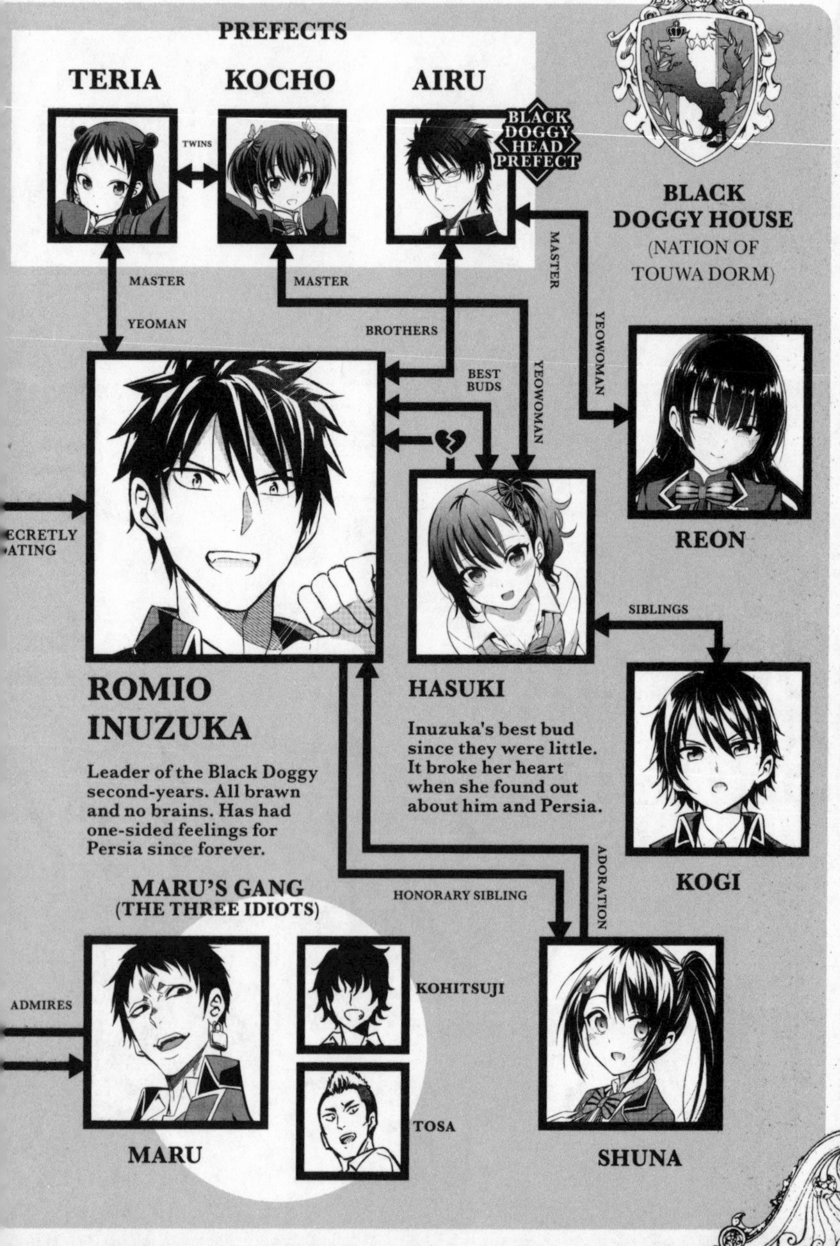
PREFECTS
TERIA
KOCHO
AIRU
TWINS
BLACK DOGGY HEAD PREFECT
BLACK DOGGY HOUSE
(NATION OF TOUWA DORM)
MASTER
MASTER
MASTER
YEOMAN
BROTHERS
BEST BUDS
YEOWOMAN
YEOWOMAN
REON
ECRETLY
ATING
SIBLINGS
ROMIO INUZUKA
Leader of the Black Doggy second-years. All brawn and no brains. Has had one-sided feelings for Persia since forever.
HASUKI
Inuzuka's best bud since they were little. It broke her heart when she found out about him and Persia.
KOGI
ADORATION
HONORARY SIBLING
MARU'S GANG
(THE THREE IDIOTS)
ADMIRES
KOHITSUJI
TOSA
MARU
SHUNA

# BOARDING SCHOOL JULIET

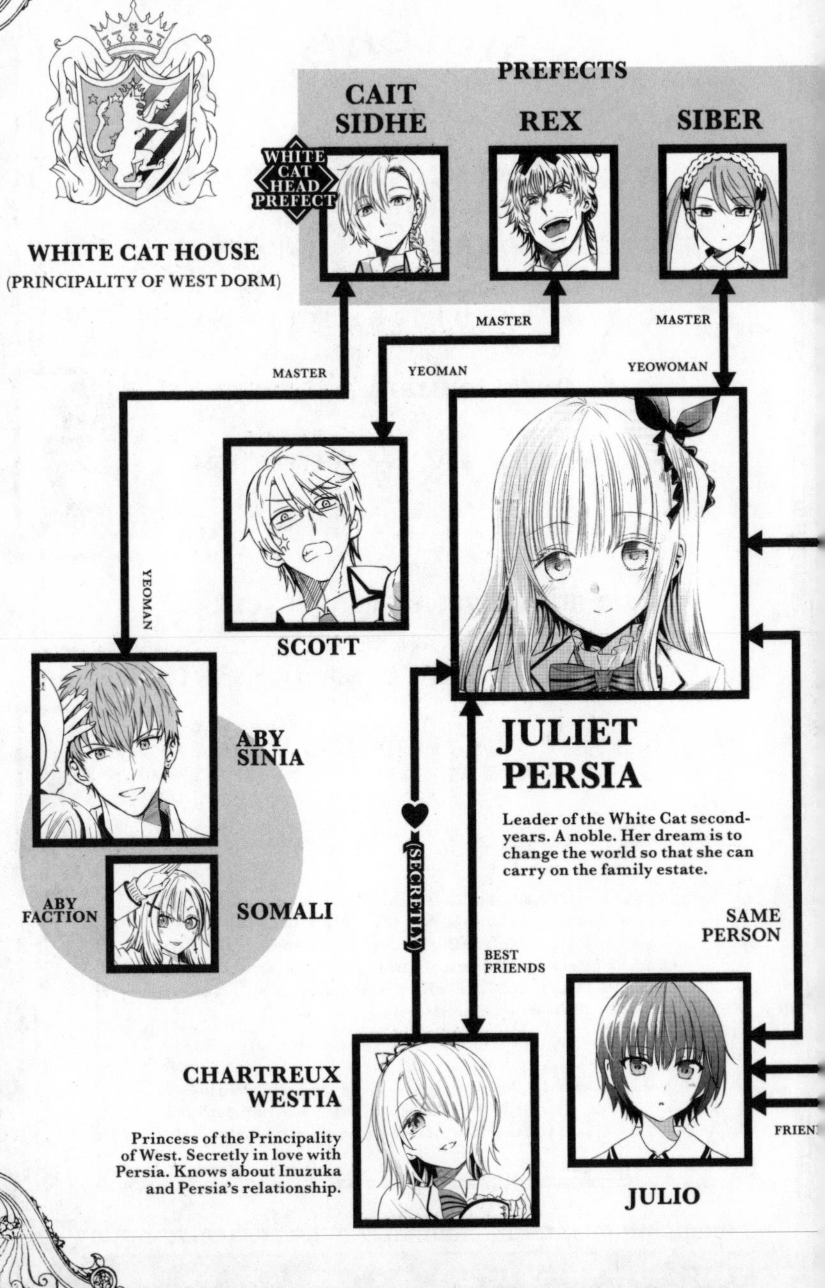

WHITE CAT HOUSE
(PRINCIPALITY OF WEST DORM)
PREFECTS
CAIT SIDHE
WHITE CAT HEAD PREFECT
REX
SIBER
MASTER
MASTER
YEOMAN
MASTER
YEOWOMAN
YEOMAN
SCOTT
ABY SINIA
SOMALI
ABY FACTION
SECRETLY
BEST FRIENDS
JULIET PERSIA
Leader of the White Cat second-years. A noble. Her dream is to change the world so that she can carry on the family estate.
SAME PERSON
CHARTREUX WESTIA
Princess of the Principality of West. Secretly in love with Persia. Knows about Inuzuka and Persia's relationship.
JULIO

# contents

## story

At boarding school Dahlia Academy, attended by students from two feuding countries, one first-year longs for a forbidden love. His name: Romio Inuzuka, leader of the Black Doggy House first-years. The apple of his eye: Juliet Persia, leader of the White Cat House first-years. It all begins when Inuzuka confesses his feelings to her. This is Inuzuka and Persia's star-crossed, secret love story...

Now second-years, Inuzuka and Persia are both running for prefect with intentions of knocking down the wall between the dorms—and Election Day has finally arrived. But Reon, the candidate who has pledged to divide the Black Doggies and the White Cats, has caught the secret couple in a devious trap, and revealed their relationship to the entire student body!!

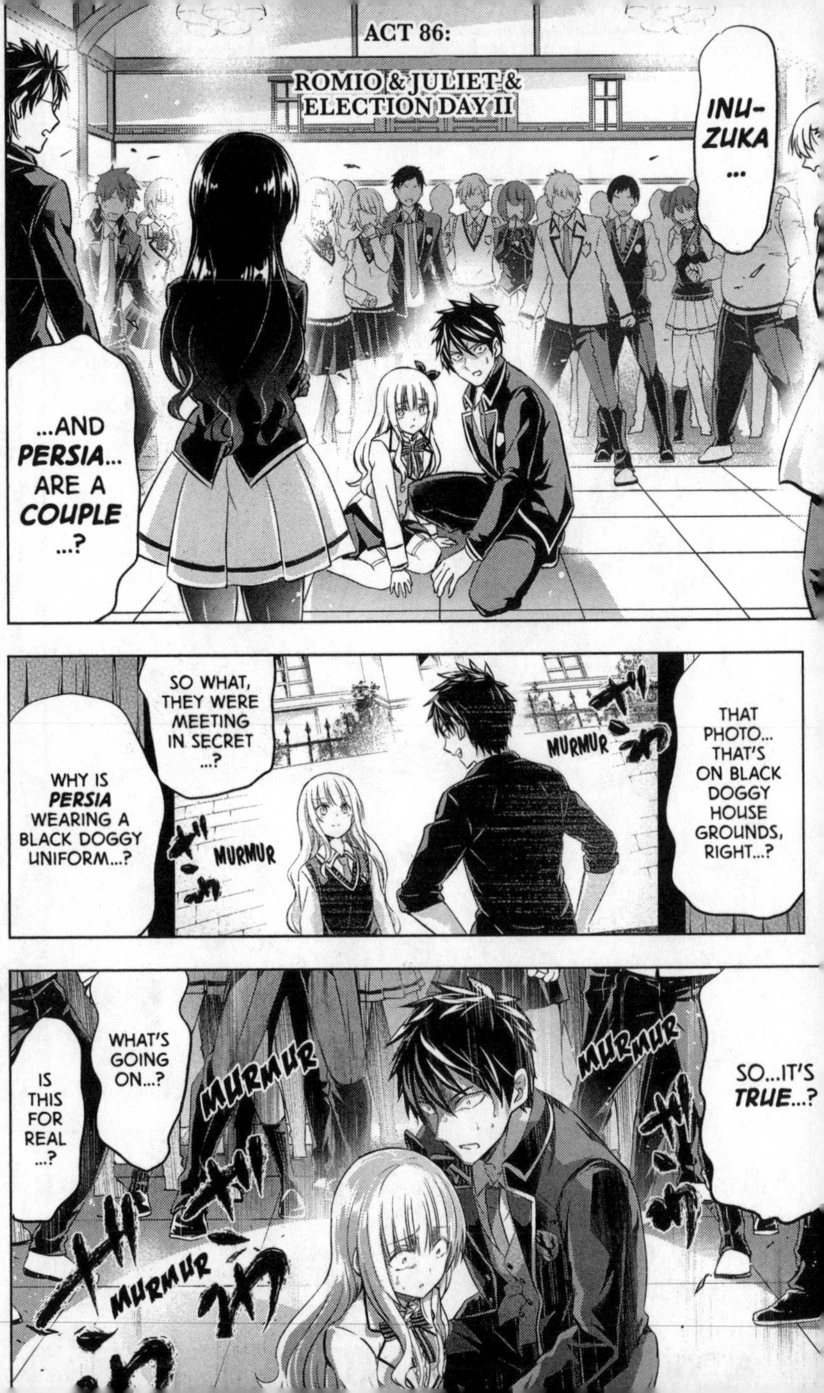
ACT 86:
ROMIO & JULIET & ELECTION DAY II
INU-ZUKA...
...AND PERSIA... ARE A COUPLE...?
THAT PHOTO... THAT'S ON BLACK DOGGY HOUSE GROUNDS, RIGHT...?
MURMUR
SO WHAT, THEY WERE MEETING IN SECRET...?
WHY IS PERSIA WEARING A BLACK DOGGY UNIFORM...?
MURMUR
SO...IT'S TRUE...?
MURMUR
MURMUR
WHAT'S GOING ON...?
IS THIS FOR REAL...?
MURMUR

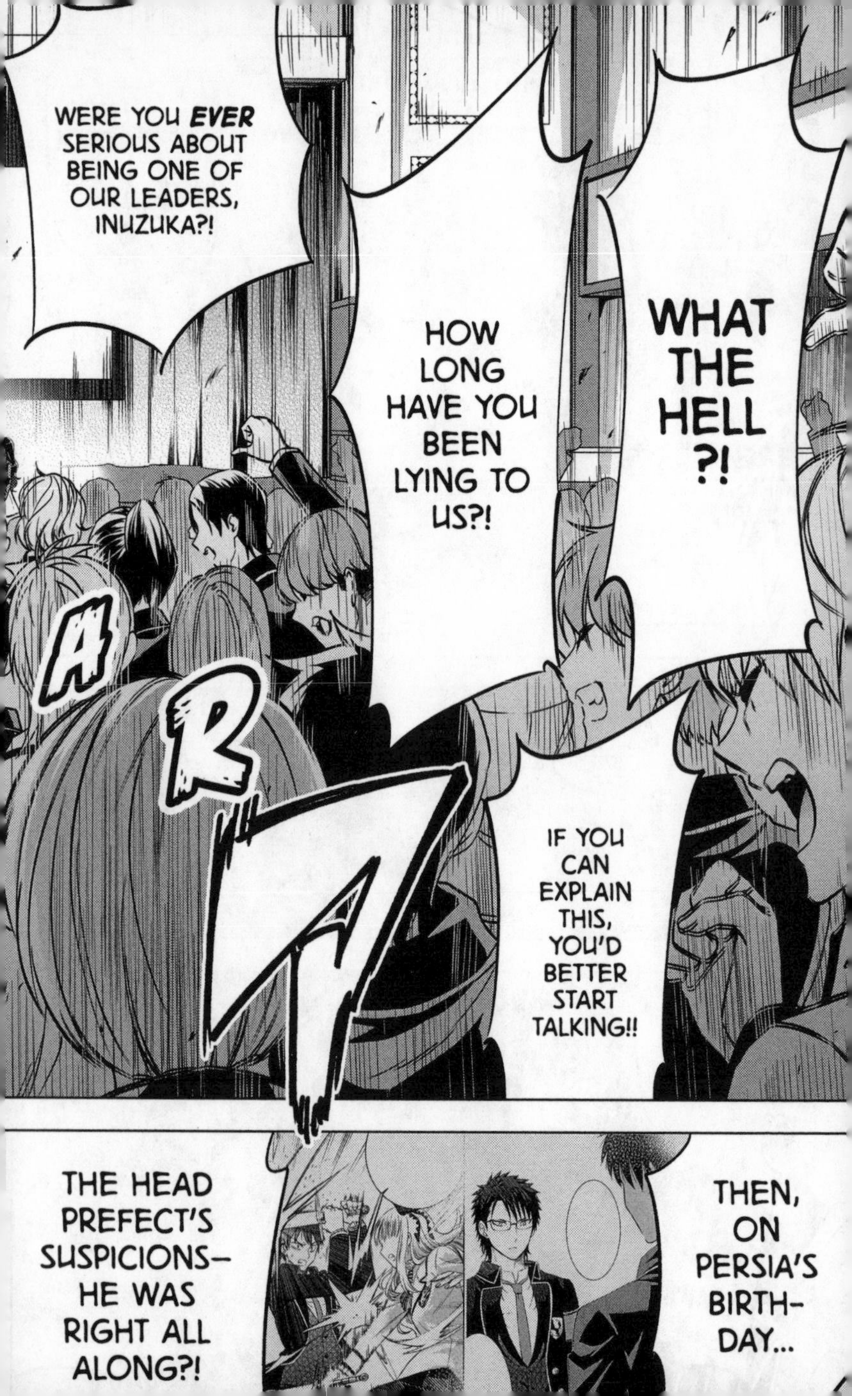

WHAT THE HELL?!
HOW LONG HAVE YOU BEEN LYING TO US?!
WERE YOU *EVER* SERIOUS ABOUT BEING ONE OF OUR LEADERS, INUZUKA?!
IF YOU CAN EXPLAIN THIS, YOU'D BETTER START TALKING!!
AR
THEN, ON PERSIA'S BIRTH-DAY...
THE HEAD PREFECT'S SUSPICIONS— HE WAS RIGHT ALL ALONG?!

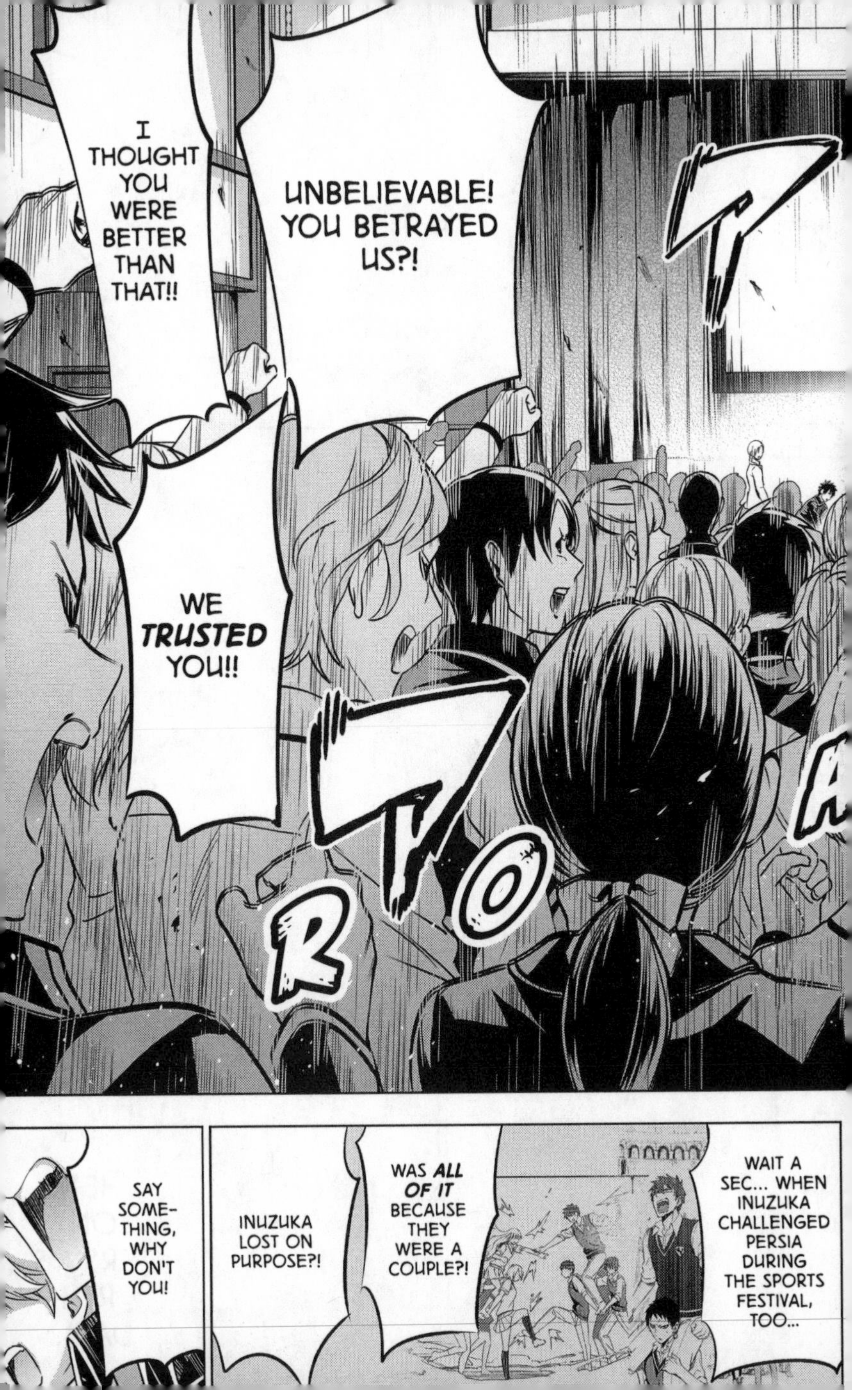
UNBELIEVABLE! YOU BETRAYED US?!
I THOUGHT YOU WERE BETTER THAN THAT!!
WE TRUSTED YOU!!
WAIT A SEC... WHEN INUZUKA CHALLENGED PERSIA DURING THE SPORTS FESTIVAL, TOO...
WAS ALL OF IT BECAUSE THEY WERE A COUPLE?!
INUZUKA LOST ON PURPOSE?!
SAY SOME-THING, WHY DON'T YOU!

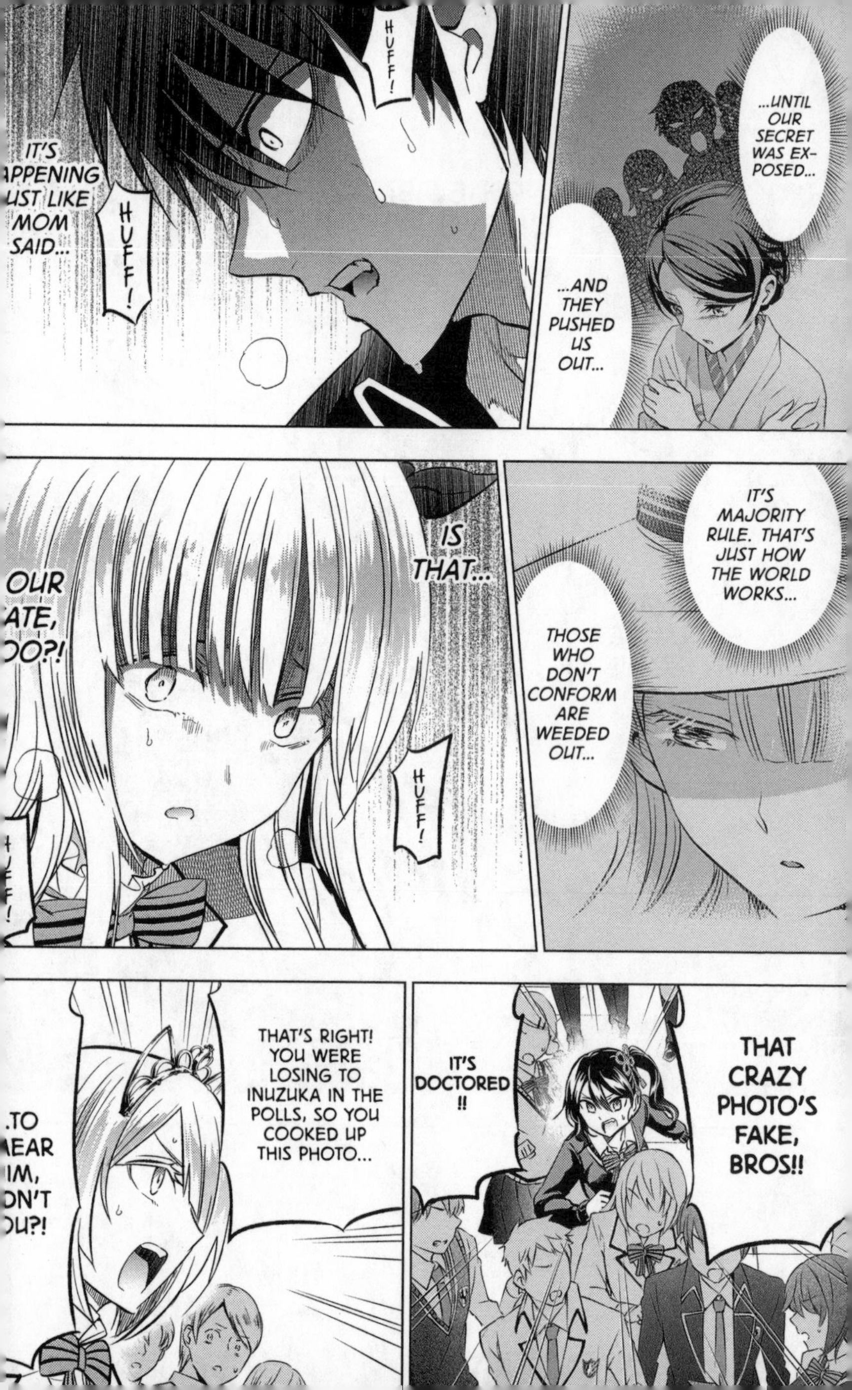
...UNTIL OUR SECRET WAS EXPOSED...
...AND THEY PUSHED US OUT...
HUFF!
IT'S PPENING UST LIKE MOM SAID...
HUFF!
IT'S MAJORITY RULE. THAT'S JUST HOW THE WORLD WORKS...
THOSE WHO DON'T CONFORM ARE WEEDED OUT...
IS THAT...
OUR ATE, OO?!
HUFF!
THAT CRAZY PHOTO'S FAKE, BROS!!
IT'S DOCTORED!!
THAT'S RIGHT! YOU WERE LOSING TO INUZUKA IN THE POLLS, SO YOU COOKED UP THIS PHOTO...
.TO EAR IM, ON'T OU?!

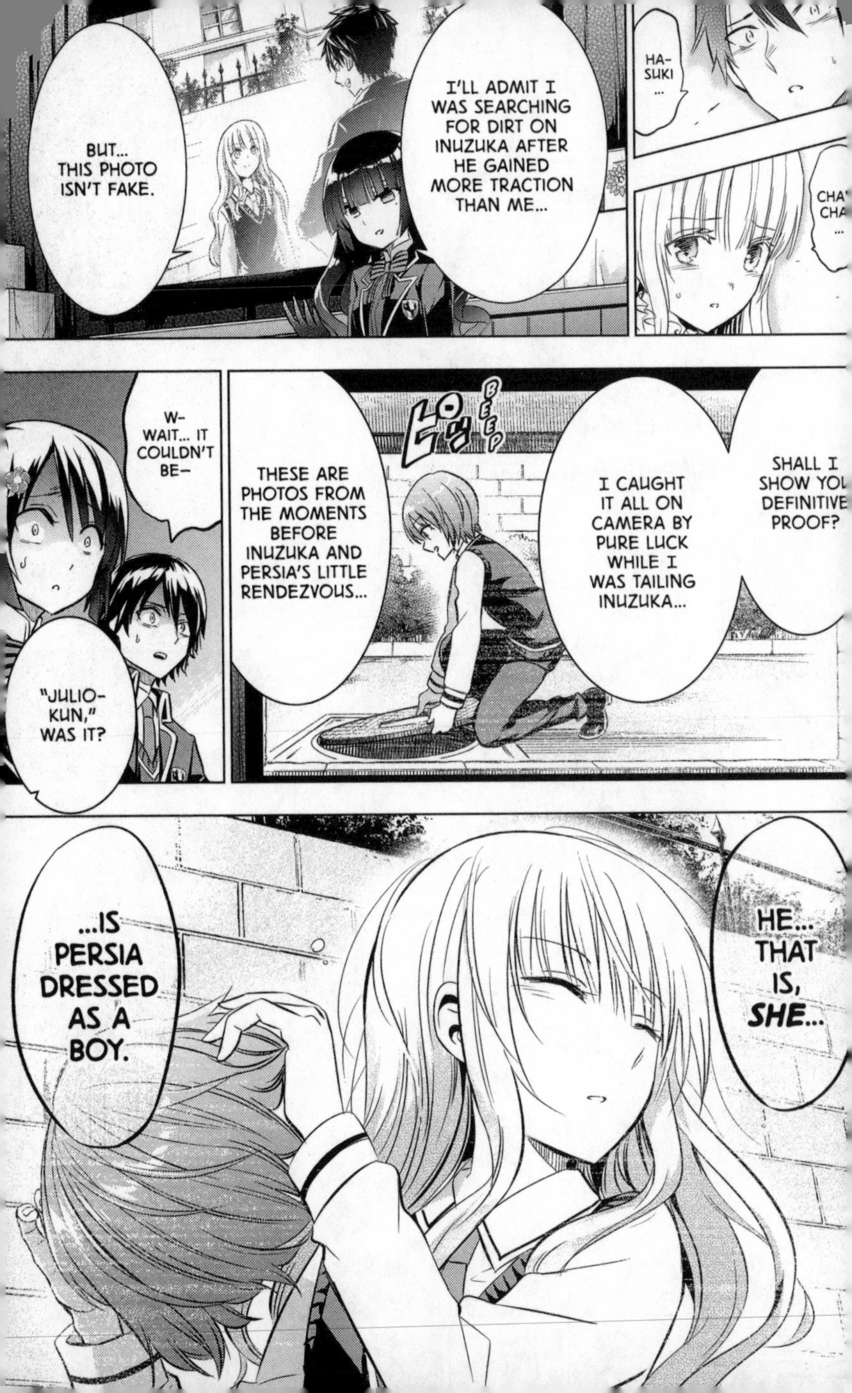
HA-SUKI...
CHA CHA...
I'LL ADMIT I WAS SEARCHING FOR DIRT ON INUZUKA AFTER HE GAINED MORE TRACTION THAN ME...
BUT... THIS PHOTO ISN'T FAKE.
SHALL I SHOW YO DEFINITIVE PROOF?
I CAUGHT IT ALL ON CAMERA BY PURE LUCK WHILE I WAS TAILING INUZUKA...
BEEP
THESE ARE PHOTOS FROM THE MOMENTS BEFORE INUZUKA AND PERSIA'S LITTLE RENDEZVOUS...
W-WAIT... IT COULDN'T BE–
"JULIO-KUN," WAS IT?
HE... THAT IS, SHE...
...IS PERSIA DRESSED AS A BOY.

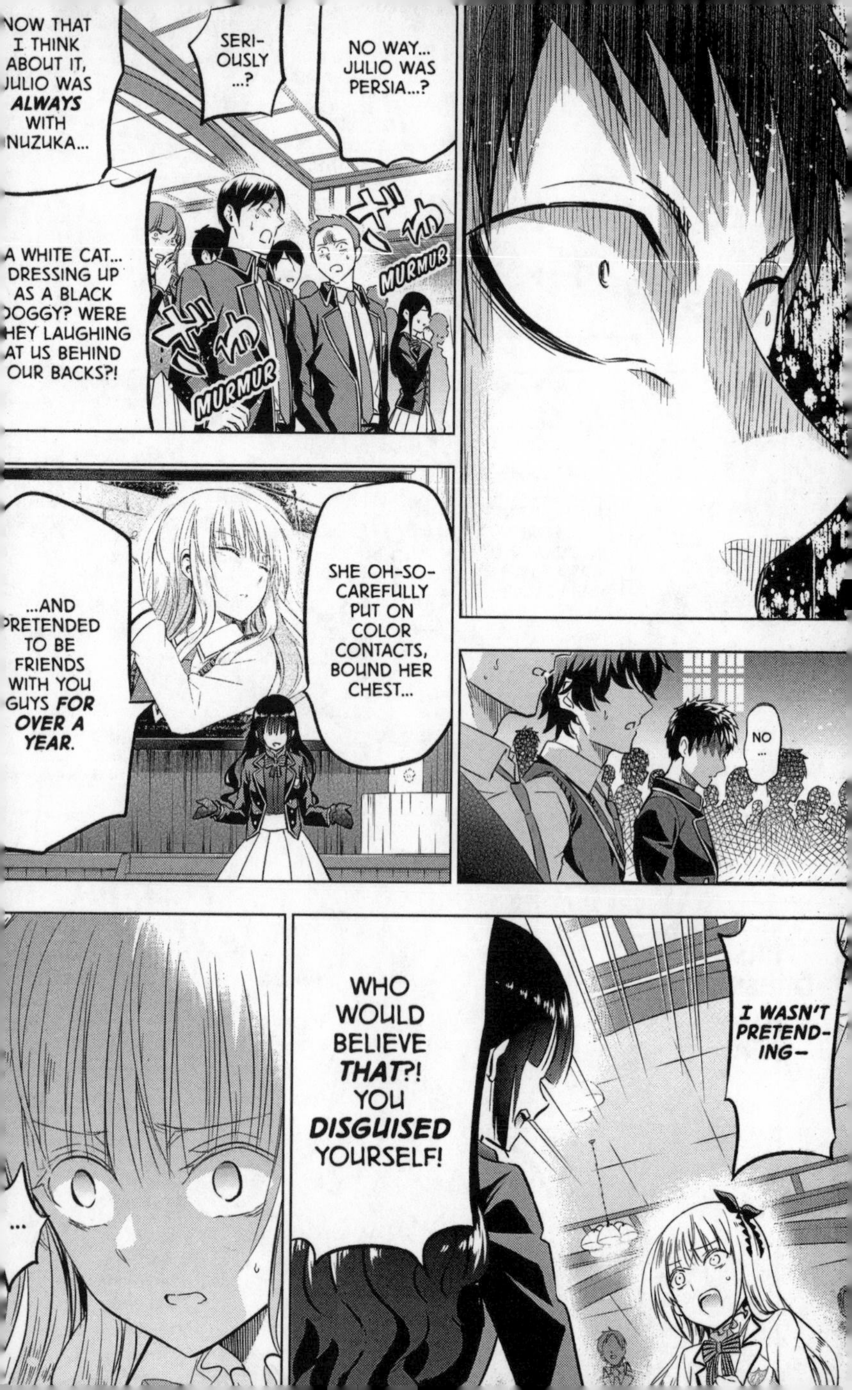
NO WAY... JULIO WAS PERSIA...?
SERI-OUSLY ...?
NOW THAT I THINK ABOUT IT, JULIO WAS **ALWAYS** WITH NUZUKA...
ざわ
MURMUR
ざわ
MURMUR
A WHITE CAT... DRESSING UP AS A BLACK DOGGY? WERE HEY LAUGHING AT US BEHIND OUR BACKS?!
SHE OH-SO-CAREFULLY PUT ON COLOR CONTACTS, BOUND HER CHEST...
...AND PRETENDED TO BE FRIENDS WITH YOU GUYS **FOR OVER A YEAR.**
NO ...
**I WASN'T PRETEND-ING–**
WHO WOULD BELIEVE **THAT**?! YOU **DISGUISED** YOURSELF!
...

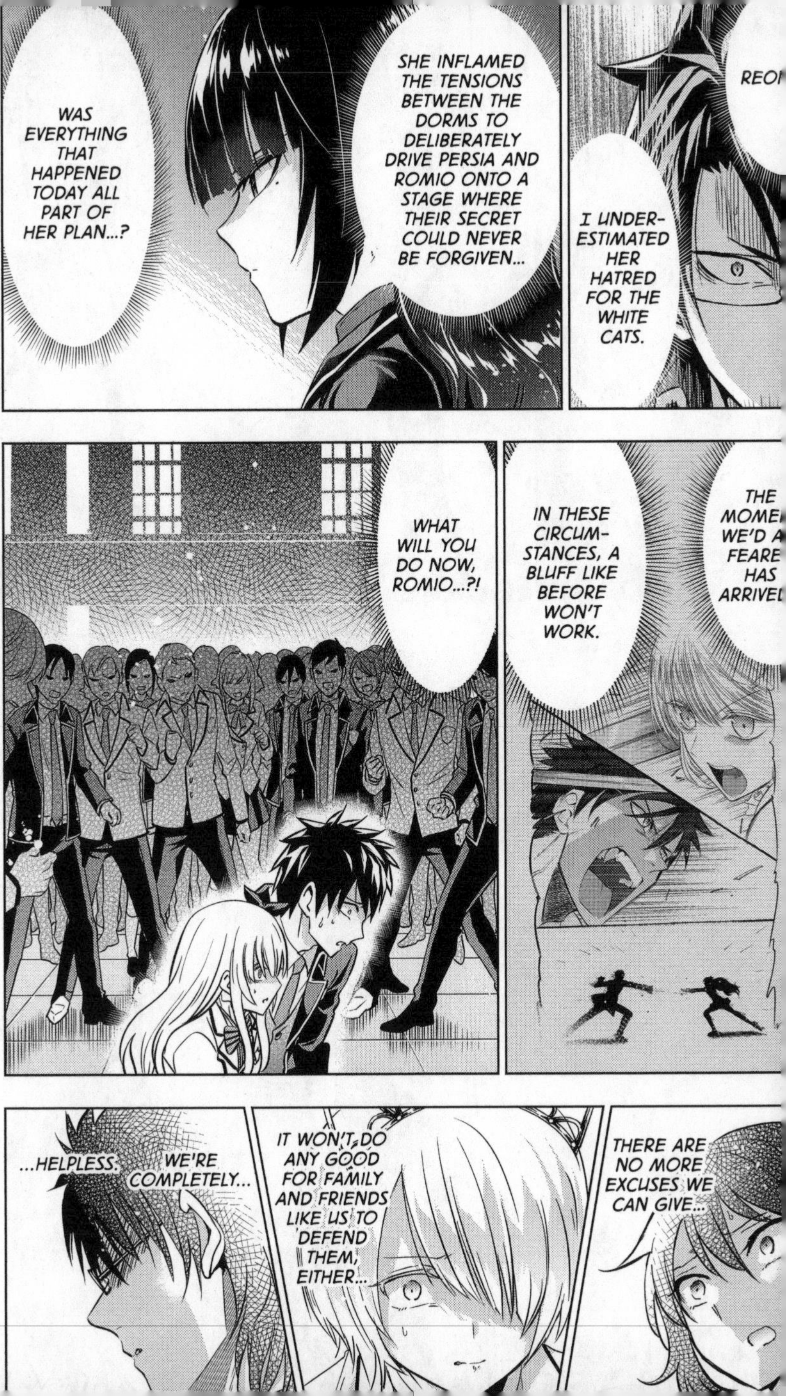
REO
I UNDER-ESTIMATED HER HATRED FOR THE WHITE CATS.
SHE INFLAMED THE TENSIONS BETWEEN THE DORMS TO DELIBERATELY DRIVE PERSIA AND ROMIO ONTO A STAGE WHERE THEIR SECRET COULD NEVER BE FORGIVEN...
WAS EVERYTHING THAT HAPPENED TODAY ALL PART OF HER PLAN...?
THE MOME WE'D A FEARE HAS ARRIVE
IN THESE CIRCUM-STANCES, A BLUFF LIKE BEFORE WON'T WORK.
WHAT WILL YOU DO NOW, ROMIO...?!
THERE ARE NO MORE EXCUSES WE CAN GIVE...
IT WON'T DO ANY GOOD FOR FAMILY AND FRIENDS LIKE US TO DEFEND THEM, EITHER...
WE'RE COMPLETELY...
...HELPLESS.

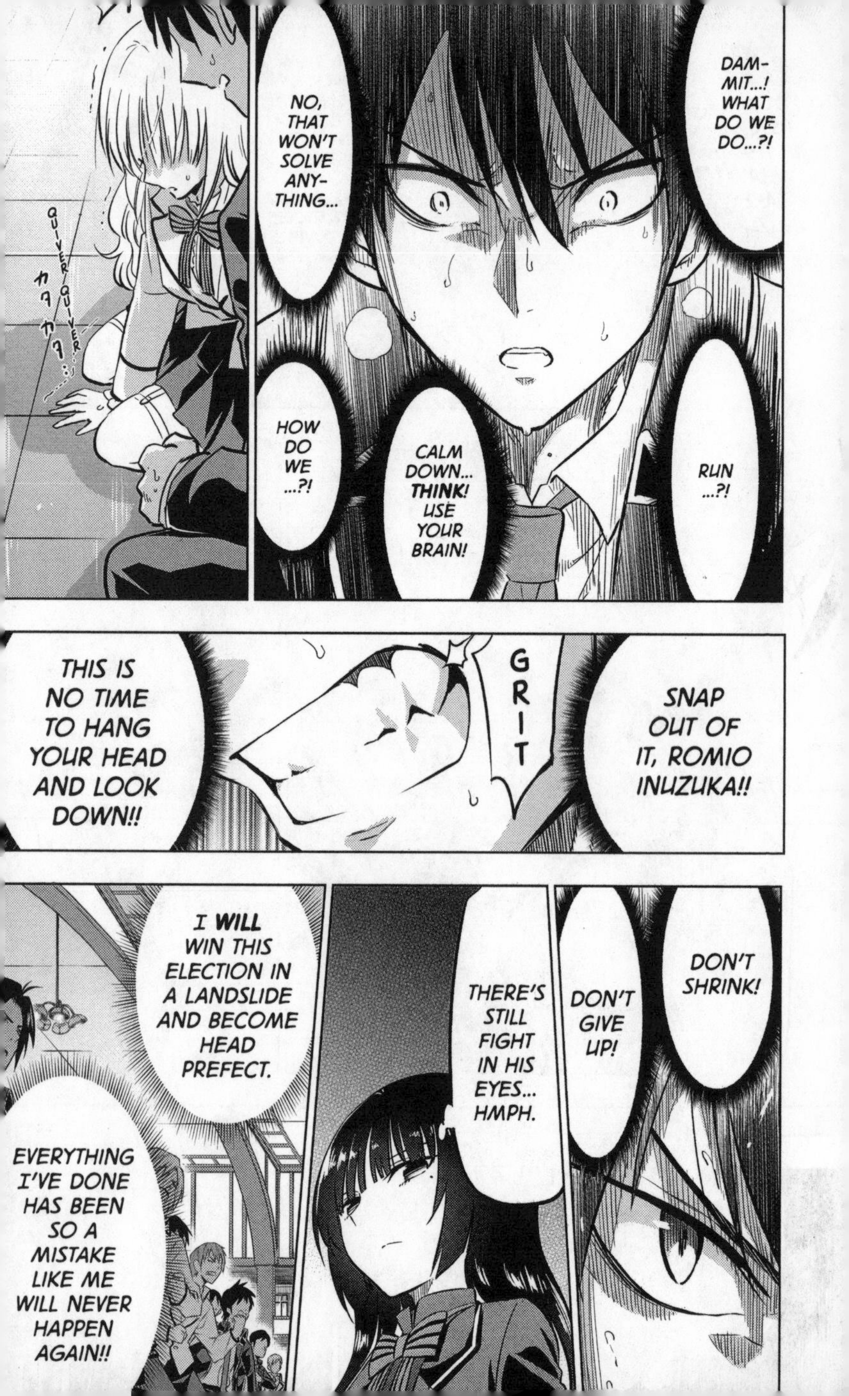
DAM-MIT...! WHAT DO WE DO...?!
RUN ...?!
NO, THAT WON'T SOLVE ANY-THING...
CALM DOWN... **THINK!** USE YOUR BRAIN!
HOW DO WE ...?!
QUIVER QUIVER
カタカタ
SNAP OUT OF IT, ROMIO INUZUKA!!
GRIT
THIS IS NO TIME TO HANG YOUR HEAD AND LOOK DOWN!!
DON'T SHRINK!
DON'T GIVE UP!
THERE'S STILL FIGHT IN HIS EYES... HMPH.
I **WILL** WIN THIS ELECTION IN A LANDSLIDE AND BECOME HEAD PREFECT.
EVERYTHING I'VE DONE HAS BEEN SO A MISTAKE LIKE ME WILL NEVER HAPPEN AGAIN!!

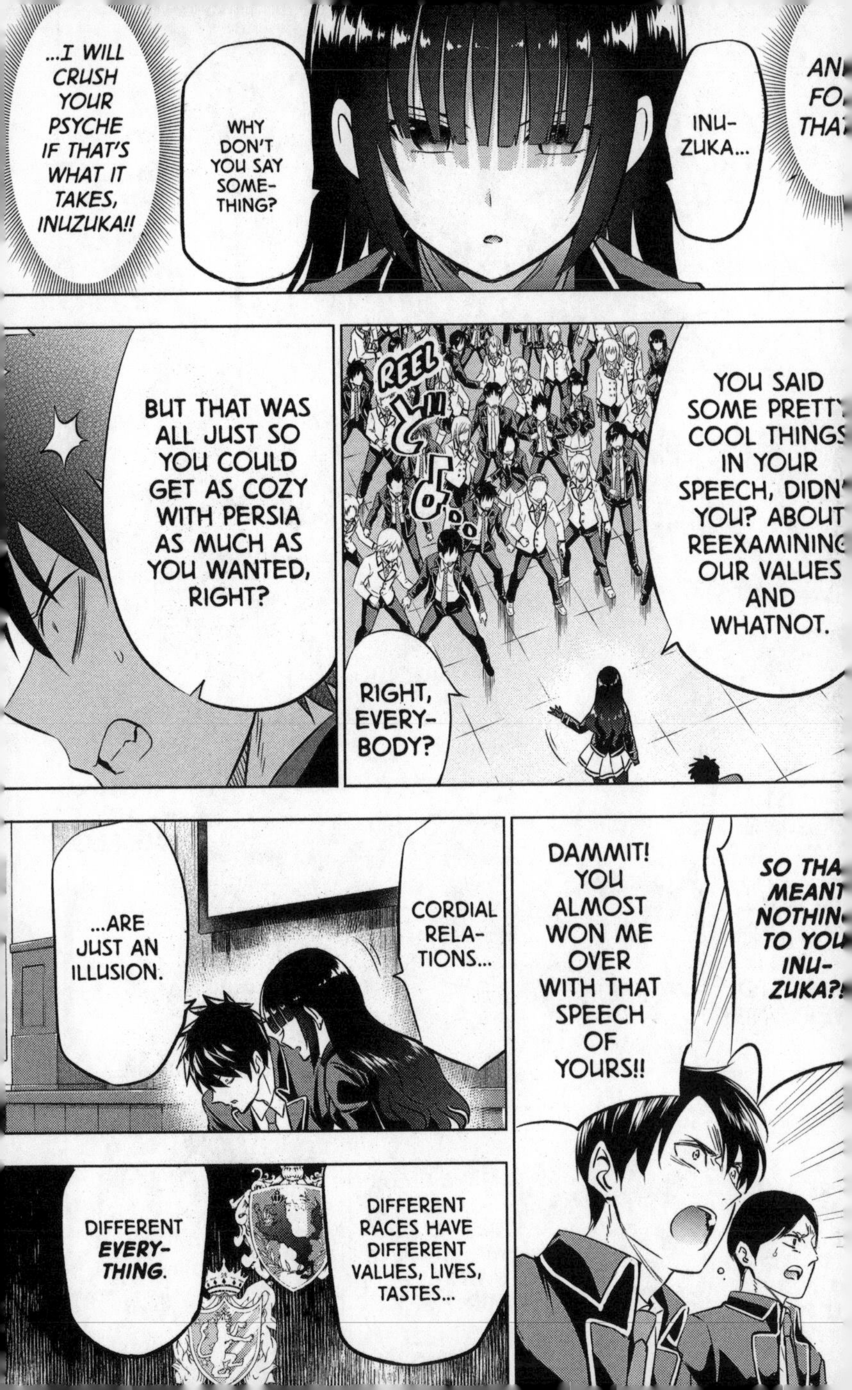
INU-ZUKA...
WHY DON'T YOU SAY SOME-THING?
...I WILL CRUSH YOUR PSYCHE IF THAT'S WHAT IT TAKES, INUZUKA!!
YOU SAID SOME PRETTY COOL THINGS IN YOUR SPEECH, DIDN'T YOU? ABOUT REEXAMINING OUR VALUES AND WHATNOT.
REEL
RIGHT, EVERY-BODY?
BUT THAT WAS ALL JUST SO YOU COULD GET AS COZY WITH PERSIA AS MUCH AS YOU WANTED, RIGHT?
SO THAT MEANT NOTHING TO YOU INU-ZUKA?!
DAMMIT! YOU ALMOST WON ME OVER WITH THAT SPEECH OF YOURS!!
CORDIAL RELA-TIONS...
...ARE JUST AN ILLUSION.
DIFFERENT RACES HAVE DIFFERENT VALUES, LIVES, TASTES...
DIFFERENT *EVERY-THING*.

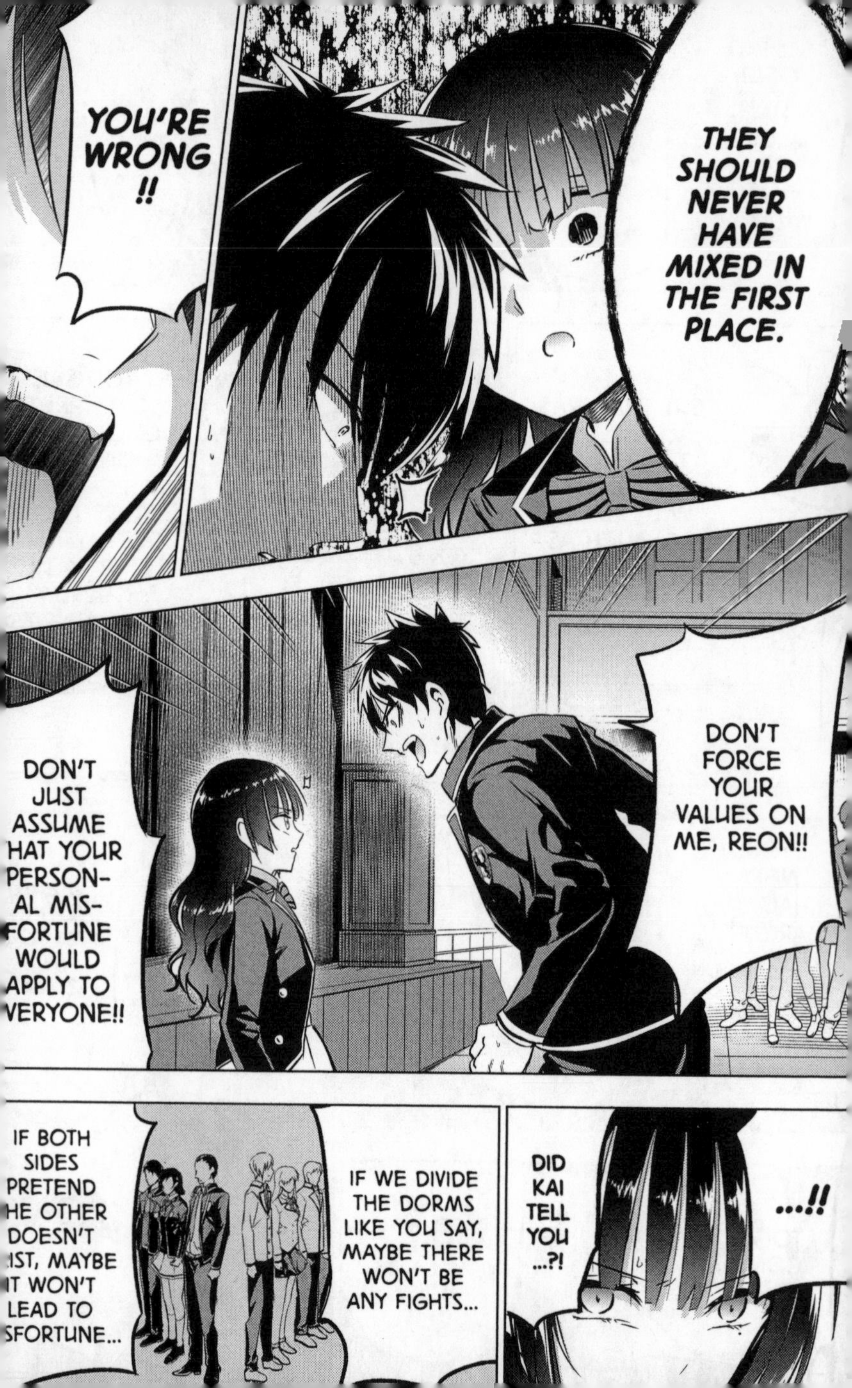
THEY SHOULD NEVER HAVE MIXED IN THE FIRST PLACE.
YOU'RE WRONG !!
DON'T FORCE YOUR VALUES ON ME, REON!!
DON'T JUST ASSUME HAT YOUR PERSON-AL MIS-FORTUNE WOULD APPLY TO VERYONE!!
...!!
DID KAI TELL YOU ...?!
IF WE DIVIDE THE DORMS LIKE YOU SAY, MAYBE THERE WON'T BE ANY FIGHTS...
IF BOTH SIDES PRETEND HE OTHER DOESN'T IST, MAYBE IT WON'T LEAD TO SFORTUNE...

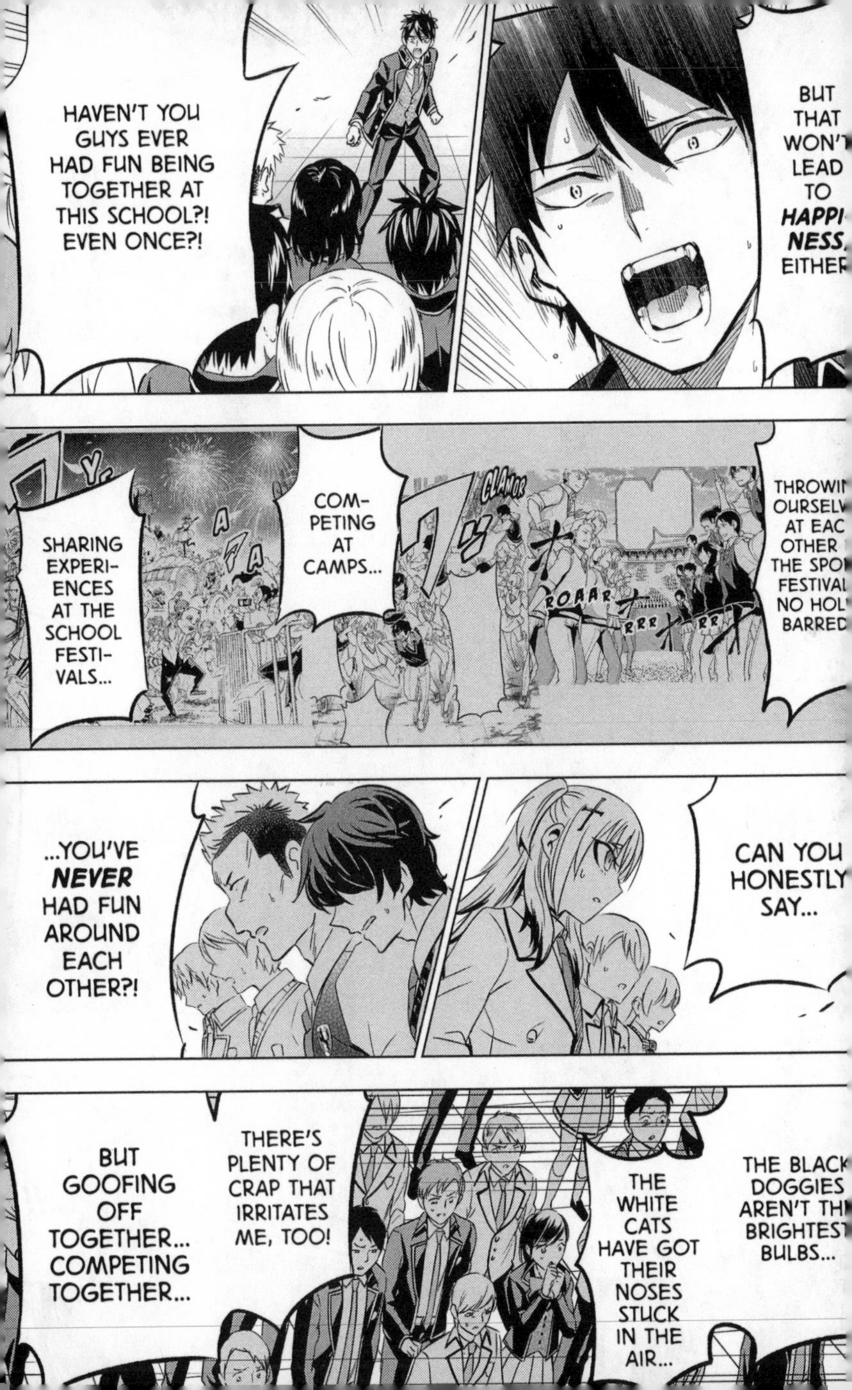
BUT THAT WON'T LEAD TO HAPPINESS, EITHER
HAVEN'T YOU GUYS EVER HAD FUN BEING TOGETHER AT THIS SCHOOL?! EVEN ONCE?!
THROWIN OURSELV AT EAC OTHER THE SPO FESTIVAL NO HOL BARRED
ROOAAR
RRR
RRR
CLAMOR
COM-PETING AT CAMPS...
YAAA
SHARING EXPERI-ENCES AT THE SCHOOL FESTI-VALS...
CAN YOU HONESTLY SAY...
...YOU'VE NEVER HAD FUN AROUND EACH OTHER?!
THE BLACK DOGGIES AREN'T THE BRIGHTEST BULBS...
THE WHITE CATS HAVE GOT THEIR NOSES STUCK IN THE AIR...
THERE'S PLENTY OF CRAP THAT IRRITATES ME, TOO!
BUT GOOFING OFF TOGETHER... COMPETING TOGETHER...

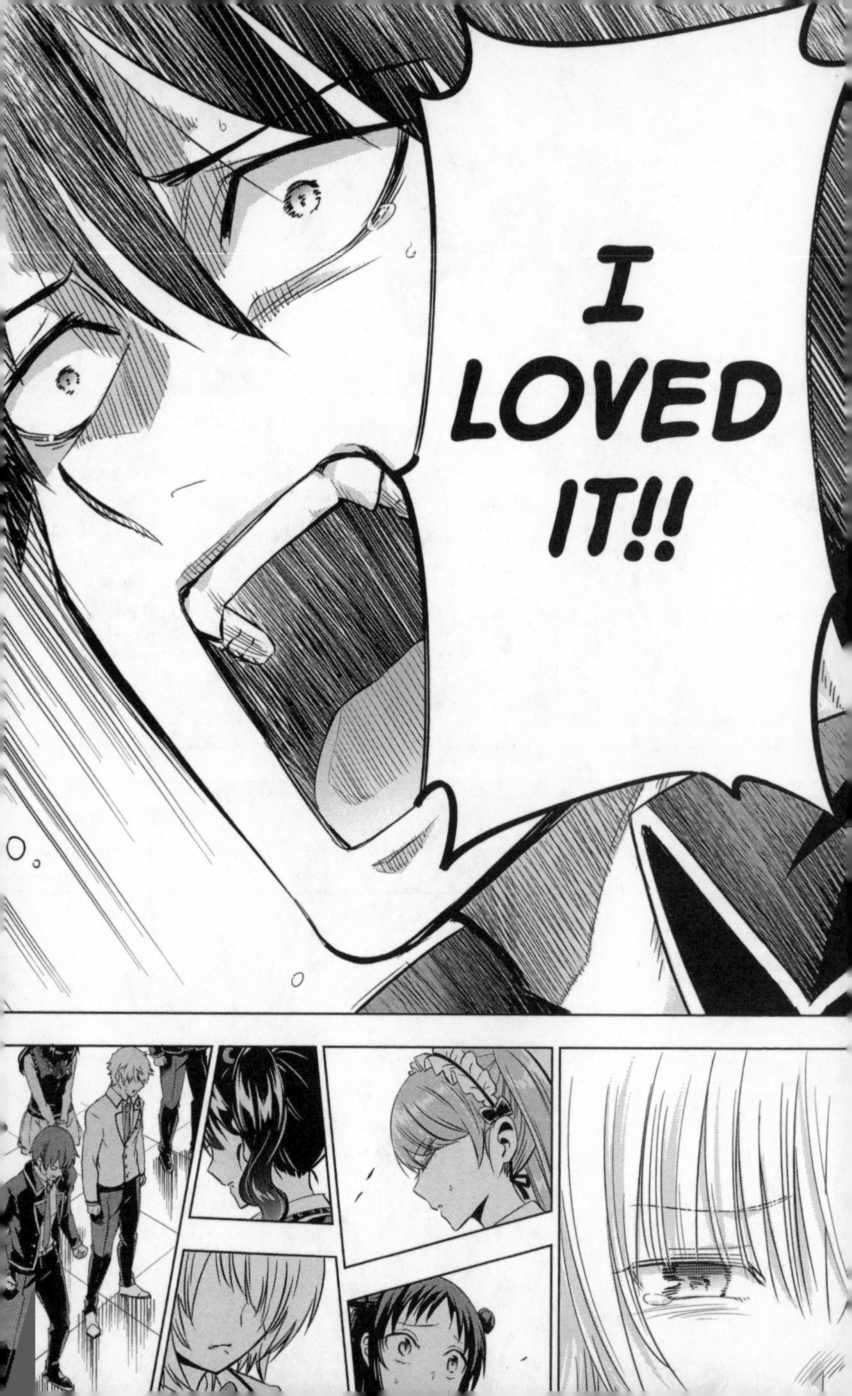
I LOVED IT!!

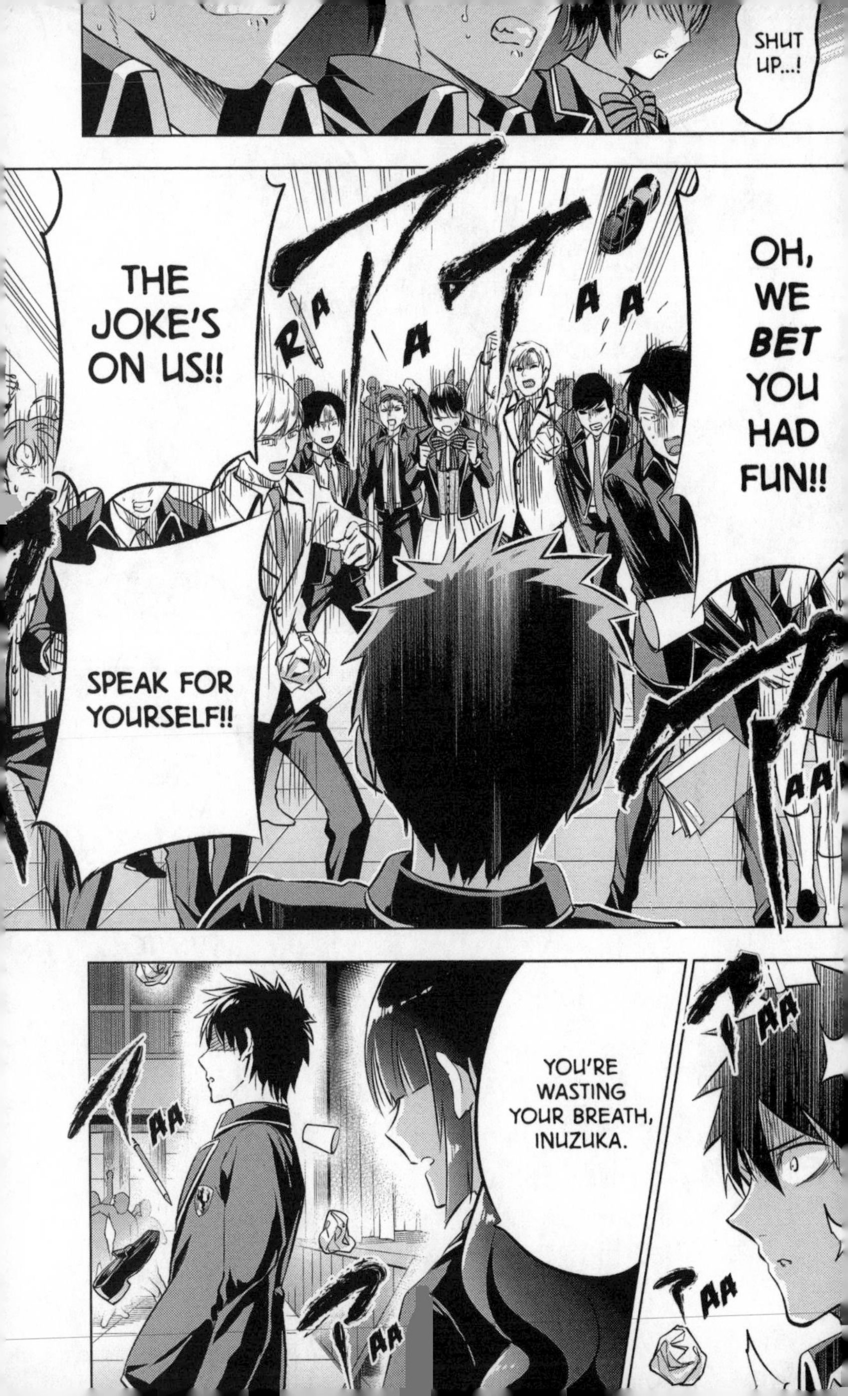
SHUT UP...!
OH, WE *BET* YOU HAD FUN!!
RAAAA
THE JOKE'S ON US!!
AA
SPEAK FOR YOURSELF!!
AA
AA
YOU'RE WASTING YOUR BREATH, INUZUKA.
AA
AA

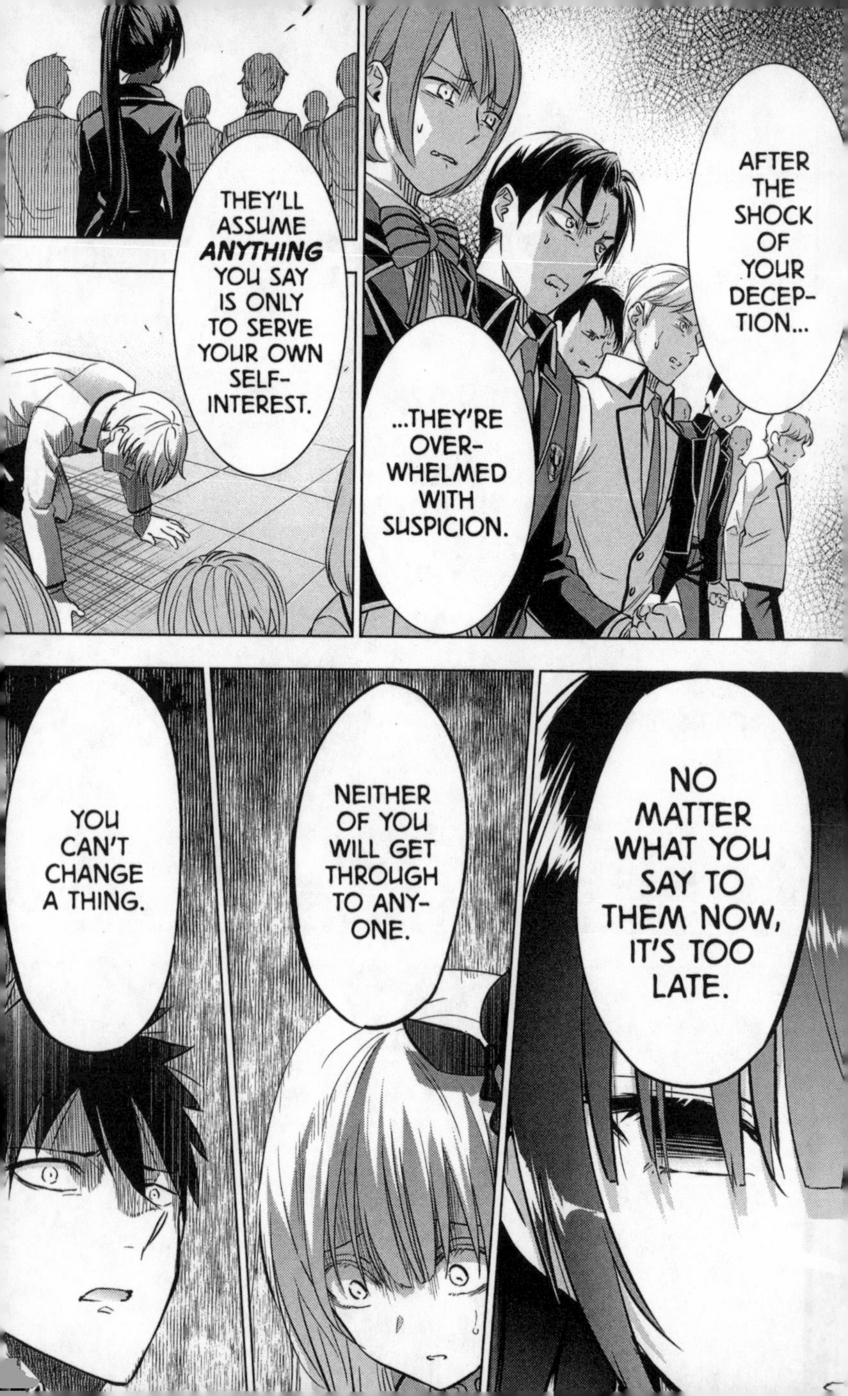
AFTER THE SHOCK OF YOUR DECEPTION...
...THEY'RE OVERWHELMED WITH SUSPICION.
THEY'LL ASSUME *ANYTHING* YOU SAY IS ONLY TO SERVE YOUR OWN SELF-INTEREST.
NO MATTER WHAT YOU SAY TO THEM NOW, IT'S TOO LATE.
NEITHER OF YOU WILL GET THROUGH TO ANYONE.
YOU CAN'T CHANGE A THING.

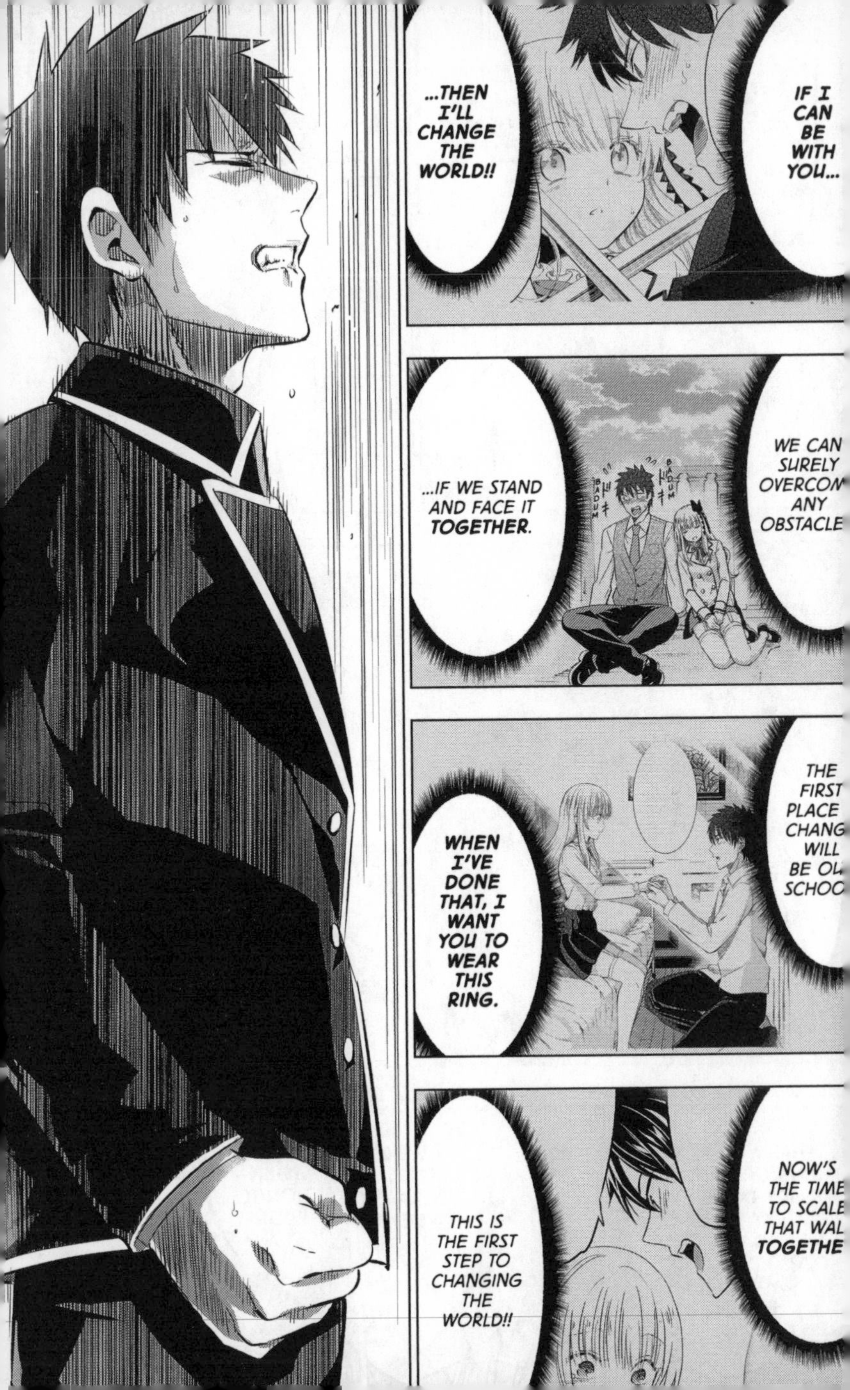
IF I CAN BE WITH YOU...
...THEN I'LL CHANGE THE WORLD!!
WE CAN SURELY OVERCOM ANY OBSTACLE
BADUM
BADUM
...IF WE STAND AND FACE IT TOGETHER.
THE FIRST PLACE CHANG WILL BE OU SCHOO
WHEN I'VE DONE THAT, I WANT YOU TO WEAR THIS RING.
NOW'S THE TIME TO SCALE THAT WAL TOGETHE
THIS IS THE FIRST STEP TO CHANGING THE WORLD!!

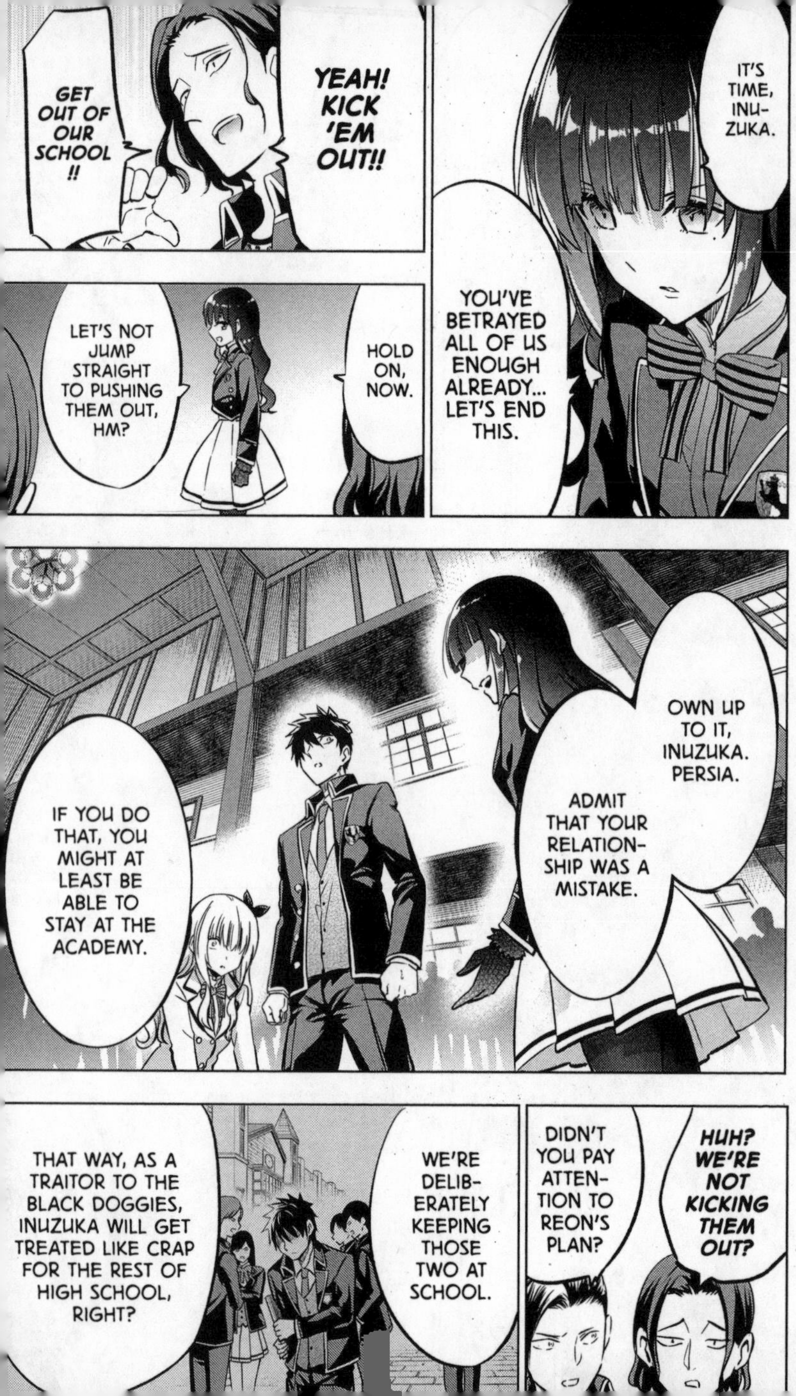
IT'S TIME, INU-ZUKA.
YOU'VE BETRAYED ALL OF US ENOUGH ALREADY... LET'S END THIS.
YEAH! KICK 'EM OUT!!
GET OUT OF OUR SCHOOL!!
HOLD ON, NOW.
LET'S NOT JUMP STRAIGHT TO PUSHING THEM OUT, HM?
OWN UP TO IT, INUZUKA. PERSIA.
ADMIT THAT YOUR RELATION-SHIP WAS A MISTAKE.
IF YOU DO THAT, YOU MIGHT AT LEAST BE ABLE TO STAY AT THE ACADEMY.
HUH? WE'RE NOT KICKING THEM OUT?
DIDN'T YOU PAY ATTEN-TION TO REON'S PLAN?
WE'RE DELIB-ERATELY KEEPING THOSE TWO AT SCHOOL.
THAT WAY, AS A TRAITOR TO THE BLACK DOGGIES, INUZUKA WILL GET TREATED LIKE CRAP FOR THE REST OF HIGH SCHOOL, RIGHT?

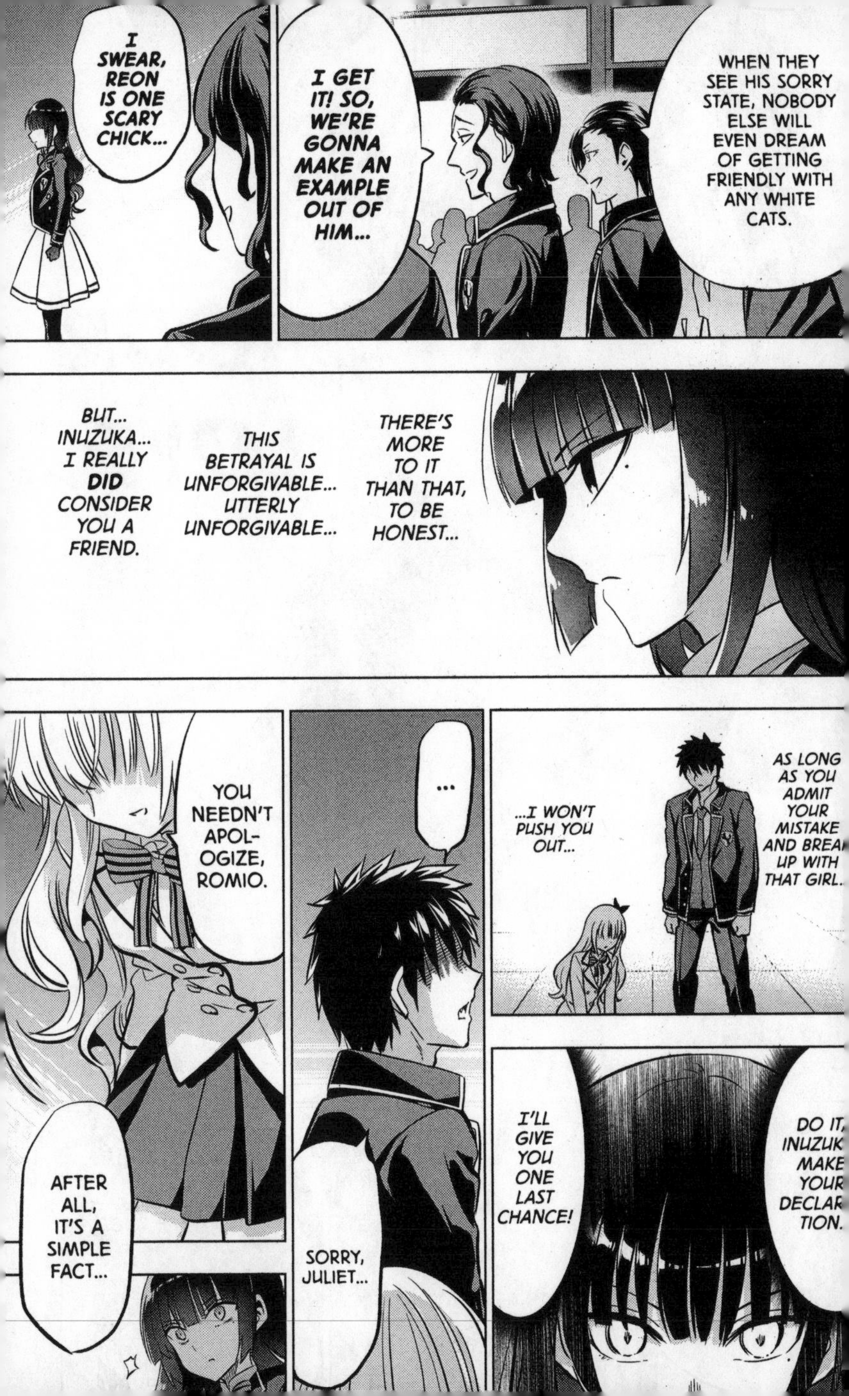

WHEN THEY SEE HIS SORRY STATE, NOBODY ELSE WILL EVEN DREAM OF GETTING FRIENDLY WITH ANY WHITE CATS.
I GET IT! SO, WE'RE GONNA MAKE AN EXAMPLE OUT OF HIM...
I SWEAR, REON IS ONE SCARY CHICK...
THERE'S MORE TO IT THAN THAT, TO BE HONEST...
THIS BETRAYAL IS UNFORGIVABLE... UTTERLY UNFORGIVABLE...
BUT... INUZUKA... I REALLY **DID** CONSIDER YOU A FRIEND.
AS LONG AS YOU ADMIT YOUR MISTAKE AND BREA UP WITH THAT GIRL...
...I WON'T PUSH YOU OUT...
DO IT, INUZUK MAKE YOUR DECLAR TION.
I'LL GIVE YOU ONE LAST CHANCE!
...
SORRY, JULIET...
YOU NEEDN'T APOLOGIZE, ROMIO.
AFTER ALL, IT'S A SIMPLE FACT...

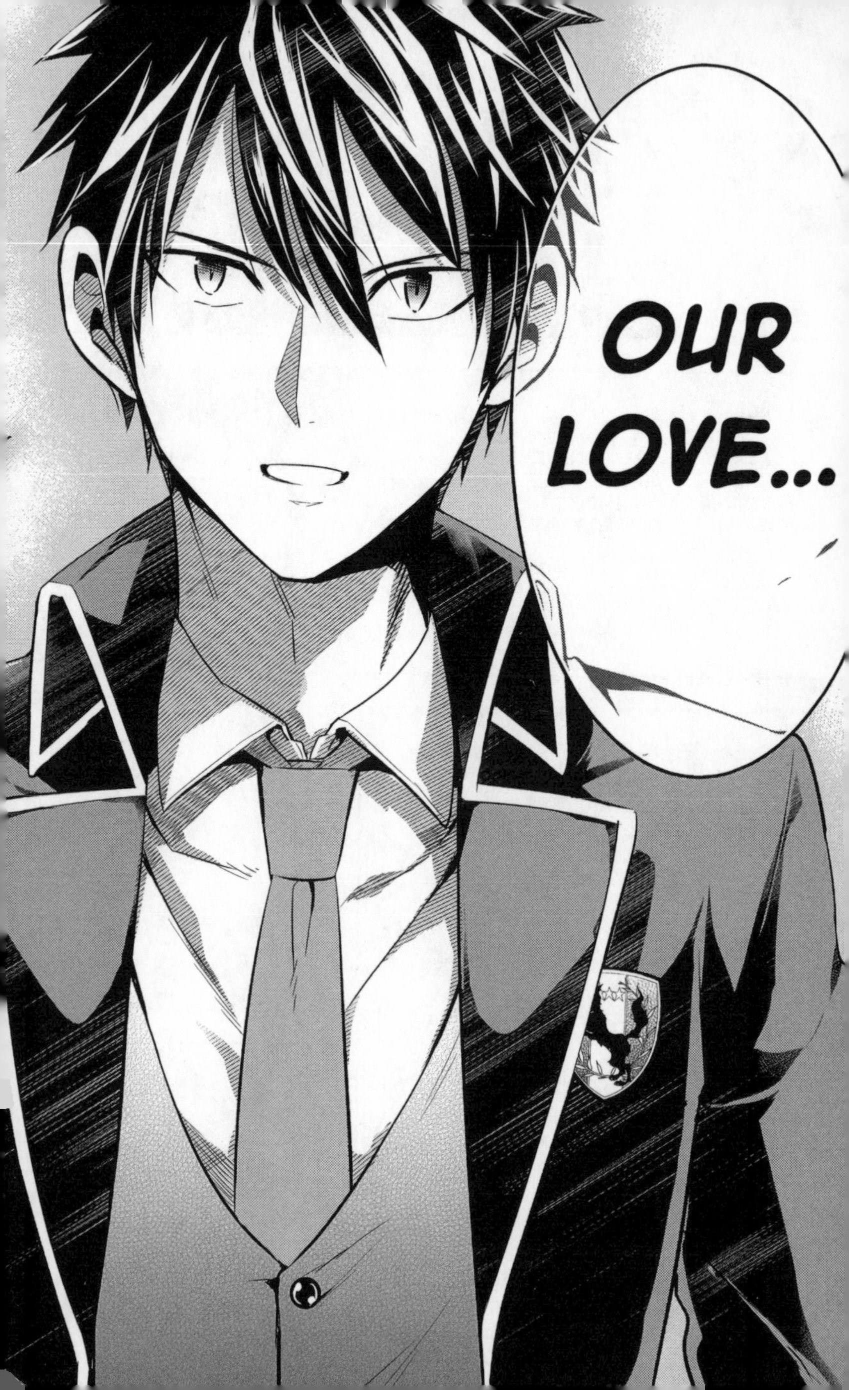
OUR LOVE...

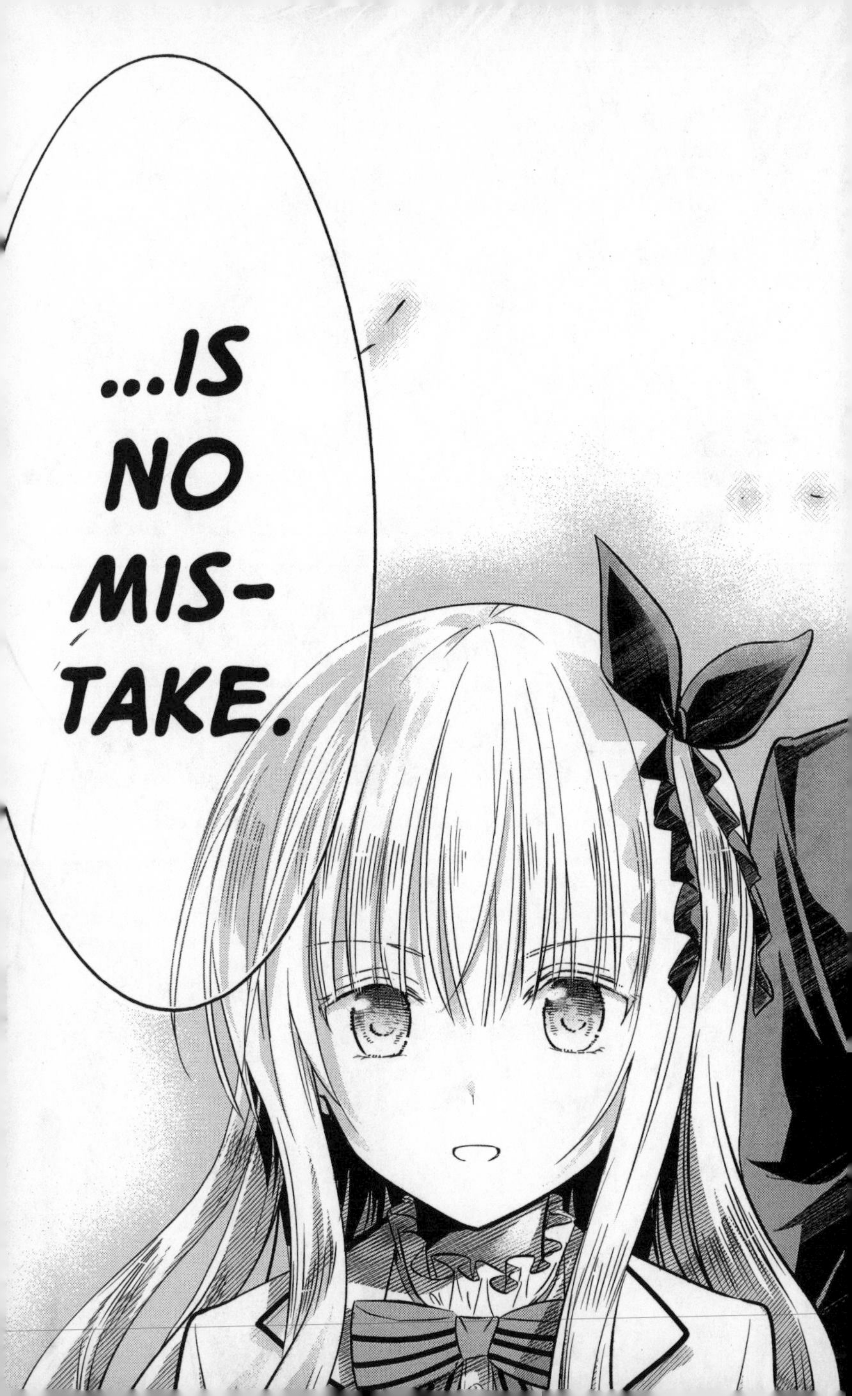
...IS NO MIS-TAKE.

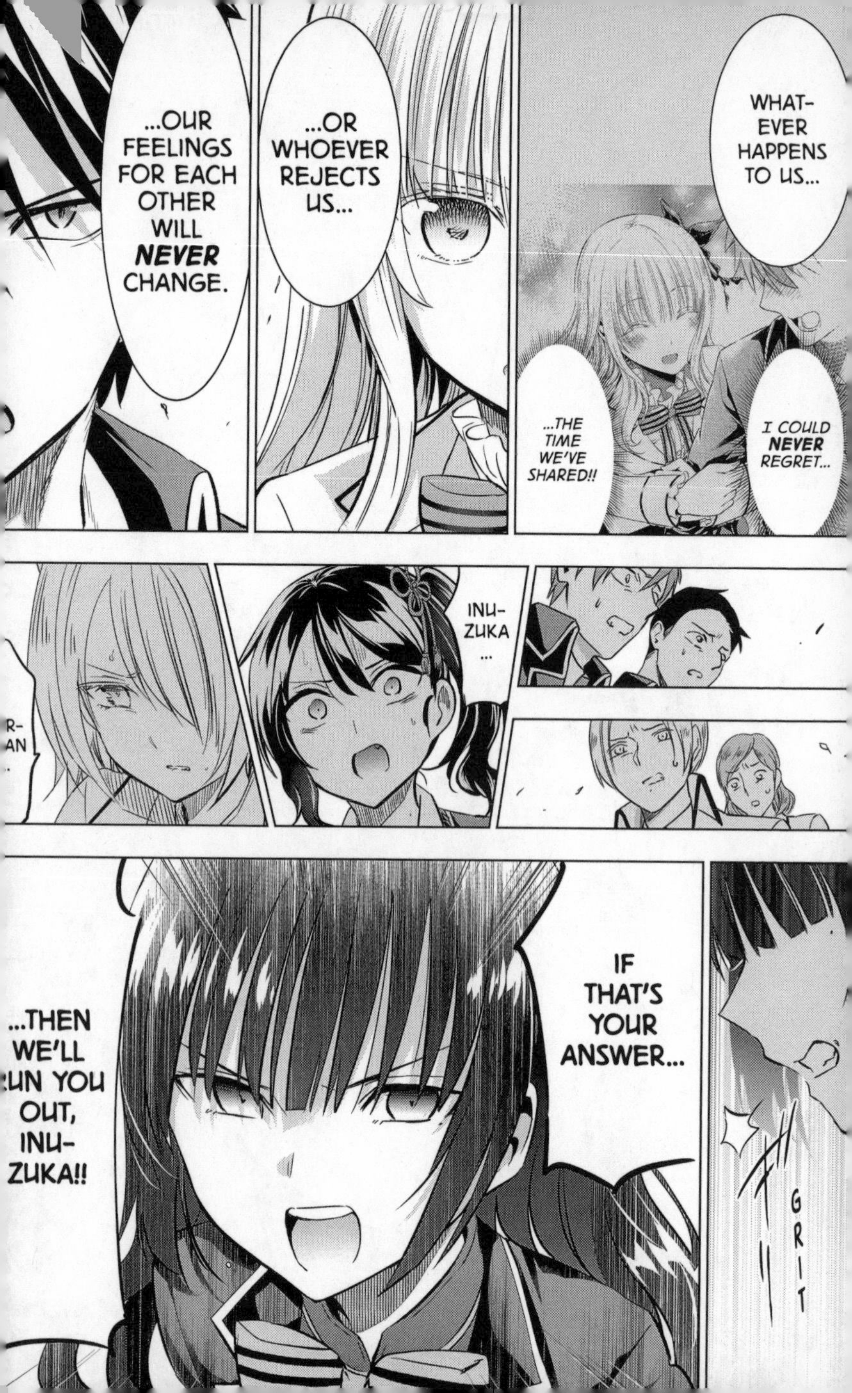
WHAT-EVER HAPPENS TO US...
I COULD NEVER REGRET...
...THE TIME WE'VE SHARED!!
...OR WHOEVER REJECTS US...
...OUR FEELINGS FOR EACH OTHER WILL NEVER CHANGE.
INU-ZUKA ...
GRIT
IF THAT'S YOUR ANSWER...
...THEN WE'LL RUN YOU OUT, INU-ZUKA!!

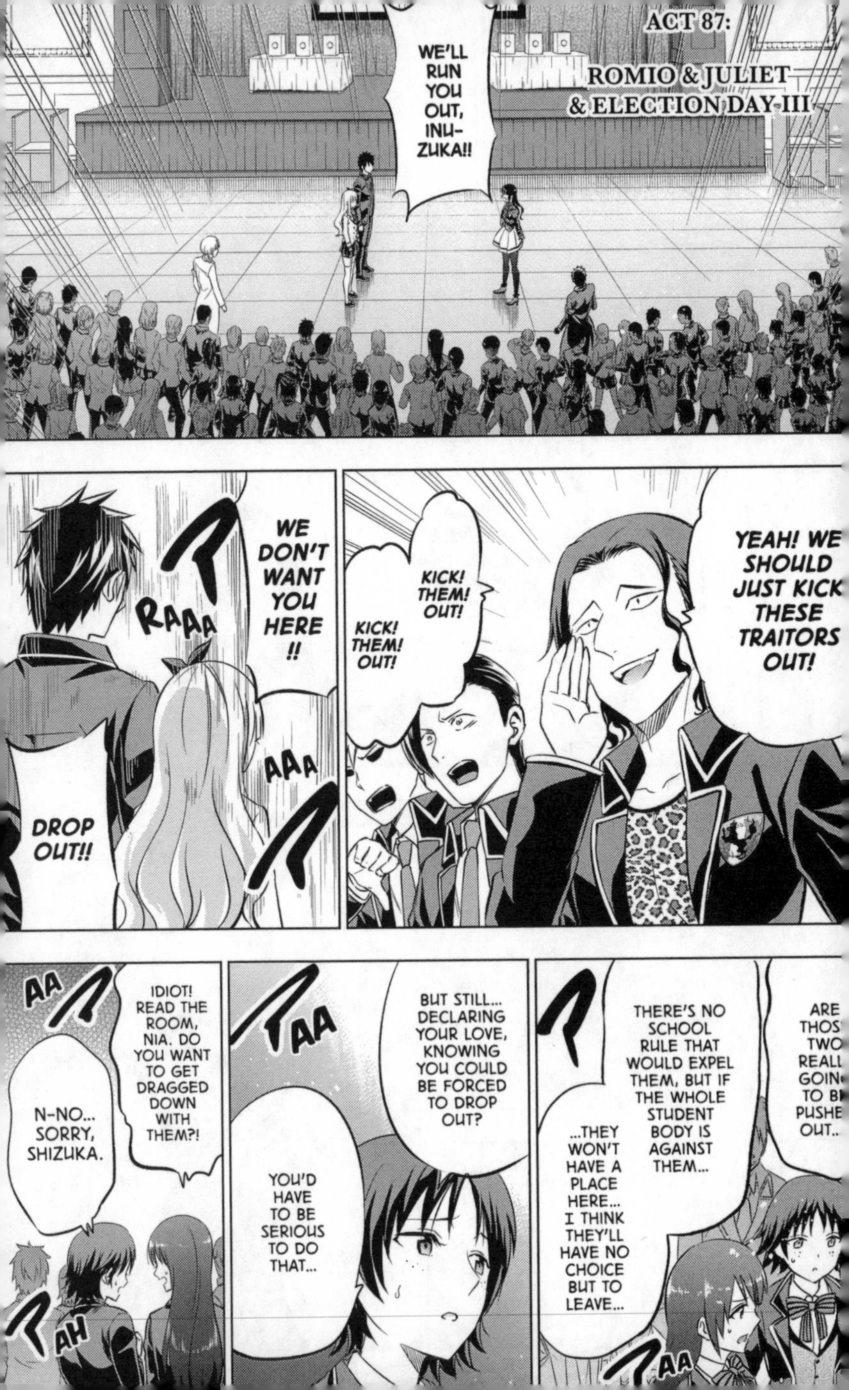
ACT 87:
ROMIO & JULIET & ELECTION DAY III
WE'LL RUN YOU OUT, INU-ZUKA!!
YEAH! WE SHOULD JUST KICK THESE TRAITORS OUT!
KICK! THEM! OUT!
KICK! THEM! OUT!
WE DON'T WANT YOU HERE!!
RAAA
AAA
DROP OUT!!
ARE THOS TWO REALL GOIN TO B PUSHE OUT...
THERE'S NO SCHOOL RULE THAT WOULD EXPEL THEM, BUT IF THE WHOLE STUDENT BODY IS AGAINST THEM...
...THEY WON'T HAVE A PLACE HERE... I THINK THEY'LL HAVE NO CHOICE BUT TO LEAVE...
AA
BUT STILL... DECLARING YOUR LOVE, KNOWING YOU COULD BE FORCED TO DROP OUT?
YOU'D HAVE TO BE SERIOUS TO DO THAT...
AA
AA
IDIOT! READ THE ROOM, NIA. DO YOU WANT TO GET DRAGGED DOWN WITH THEM?!
N-NO... SORRY, SHIZUKA.
AH

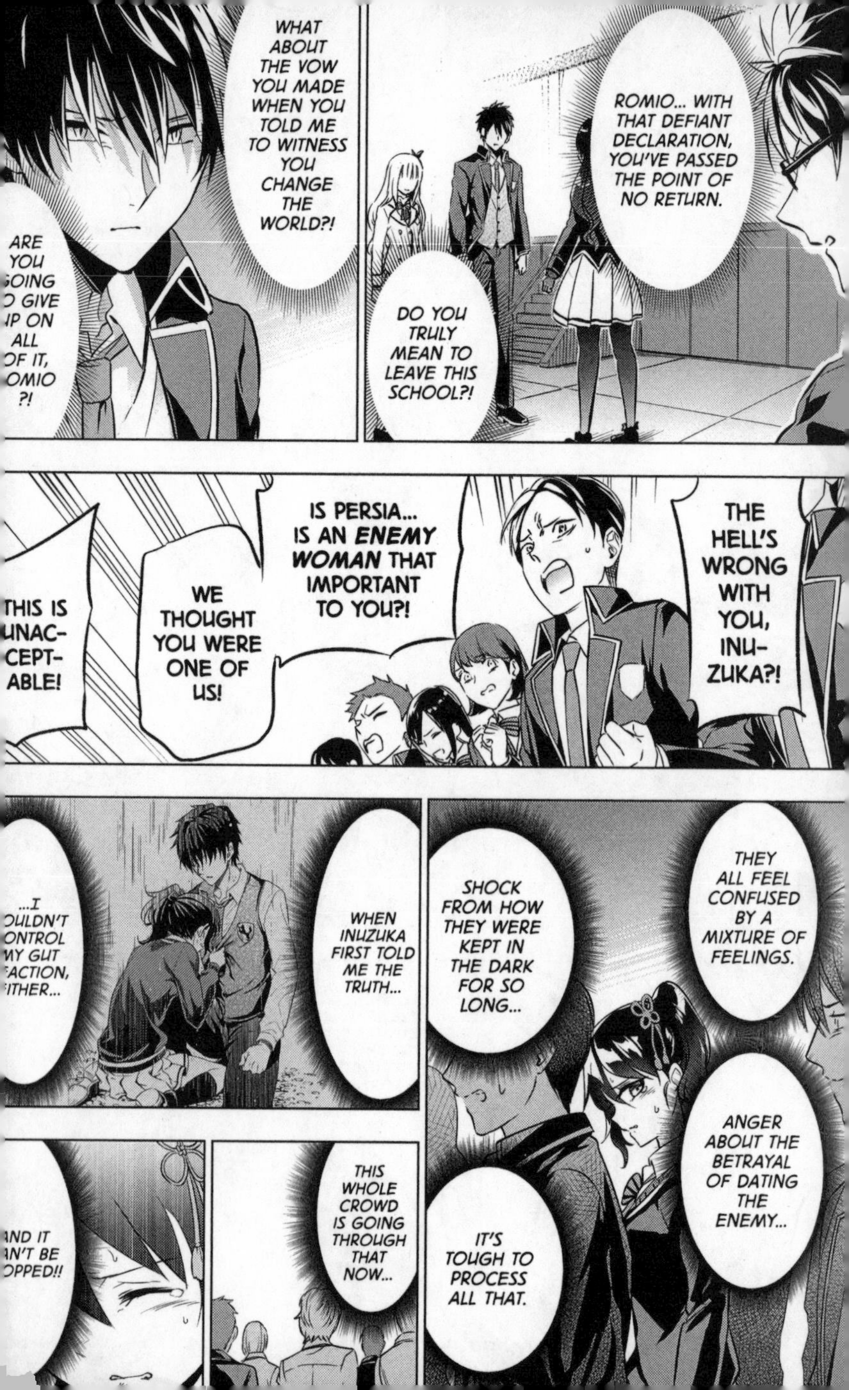
ROMIO... WITH THAT DEFIANT DECLARATION, YOU'VE PASSED THE POINT OF NO RETURN.
DO YOU TRULY MEAN TO LEAVE THIS SCHOOL?!
WHAT ABOUT THE VOW YOU MADE WHEN YOU TOLD ME TO WITNESS YOU CHANGE THE WORLD?!
ARE YOU OING GIVE P ON ALL OF IT, OMIO ?!
THE HELL'S WRONG WITH YOU, INU-ZUKA?!
IS PERSIA... IS AN *ENEMY WOMAN* THAT IMPORTANT TO YOU?!
WE THOUGHT YOU WERE ONE OF US!
THIS IS NAC-CEPT-ABLE!
THEY ALL FEEL CONFUSED BY A MIXTURE OF FEELINGS.
SHOCK FROM HOW THEY WERE KEPT IN THE DARK FOR SO LONG...
ANGER ABOUT THE BETRAYAL OF DATING THE ENEMY...
IT'S TOUGH TO PROCESS ALL THAT.
WHEN INUZUKA FIRST TOLD ME THE TRUTH...
...I OULDN'T ONTROL MY GUT ACTION, ITHER...
THIS WHOLE CROWD IS GOING THROUGH THAT NOW...
ND IT N'T BE OPPED!!

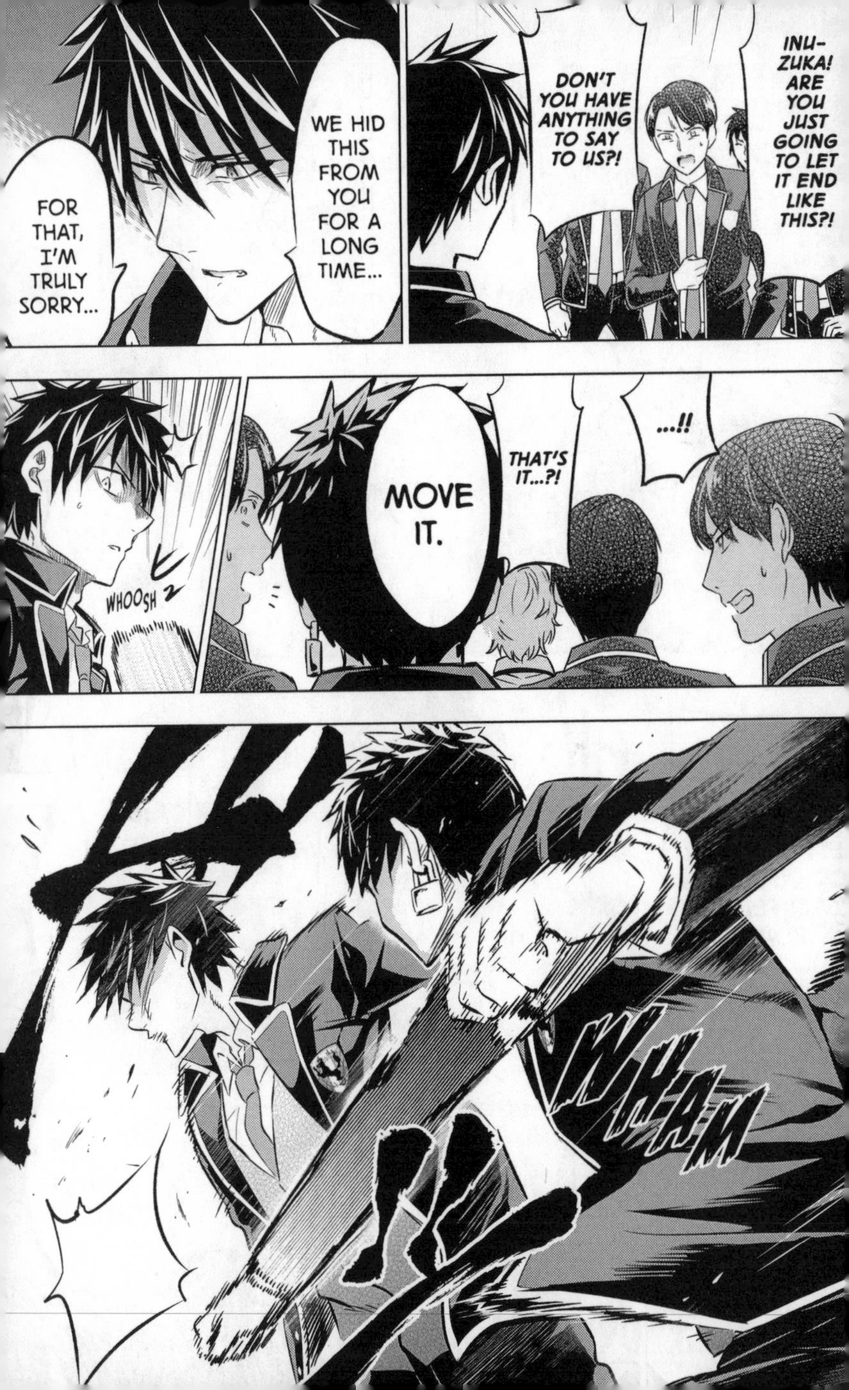
INU-ZUKA! ARE YOU JUST GOING TO LET IT END LIKE THIS?!
DON'T YOU HAVE ANYTHING TO SAY TO US?!
WE HID THIS FROM YOU FOR A LONG TIME...
FOR THAT, I'M TRULY SORRY...
...!!
THAT'S IT...?!
MOVE IT.
WHOOSH
WHAM

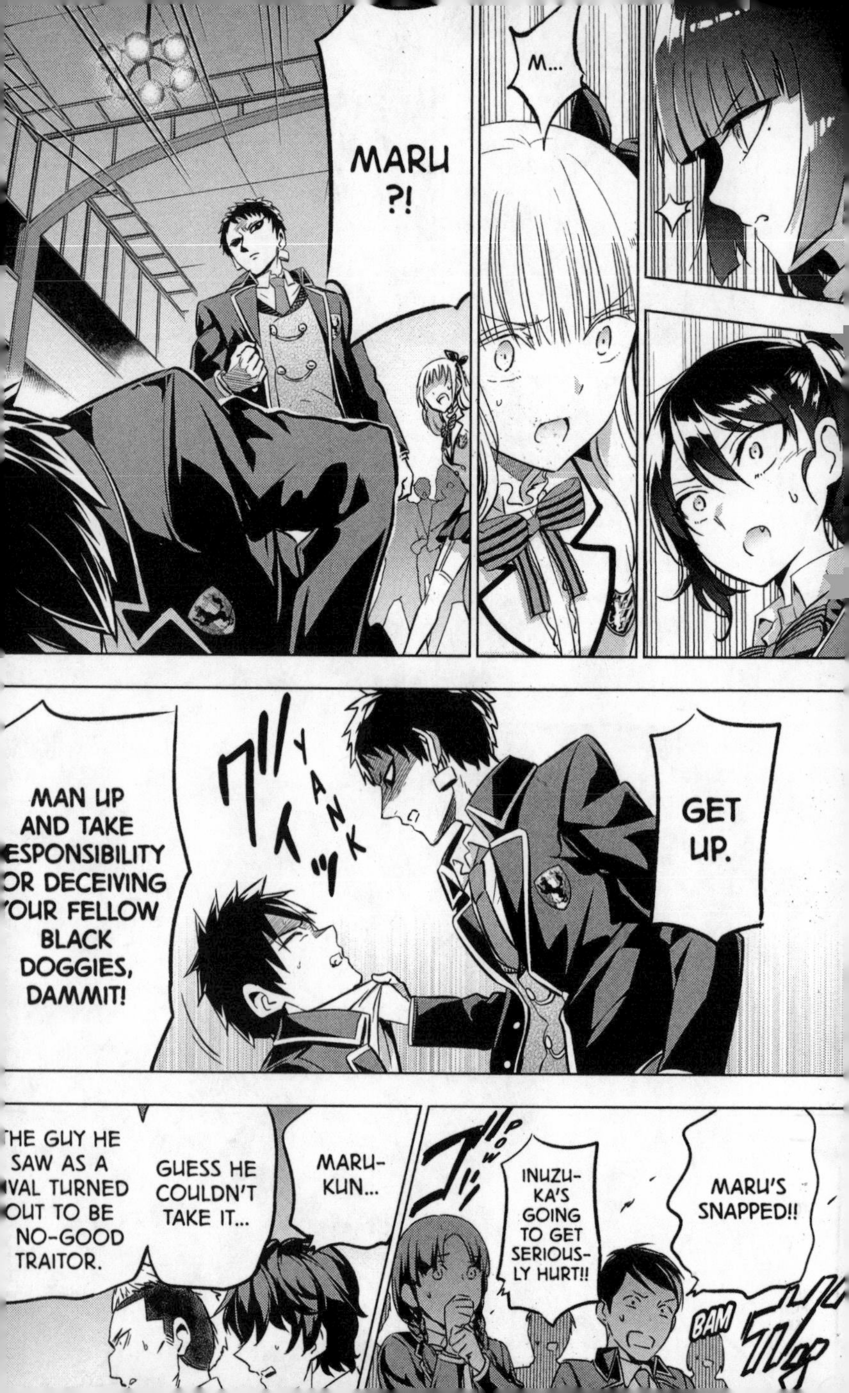
M...
MARU ?!
GET UP.
YANK
MAN UP AND TAKE ESPONSIBILITY OR DECEIVING OUR FELLOW BLACK DOGGIES, DAMMIT!
MARU'S SNAPPED!!
BAM
INUZU-KA'S GOING TO GET SERIOUS-LY HURT!!
POW
MARU-KUN...
GUESS HE COULDN'T TAKE IT...
HE GUY HE SAW AS A VAL TURNED OUT TO BE NO-GOOD TRAITOR.

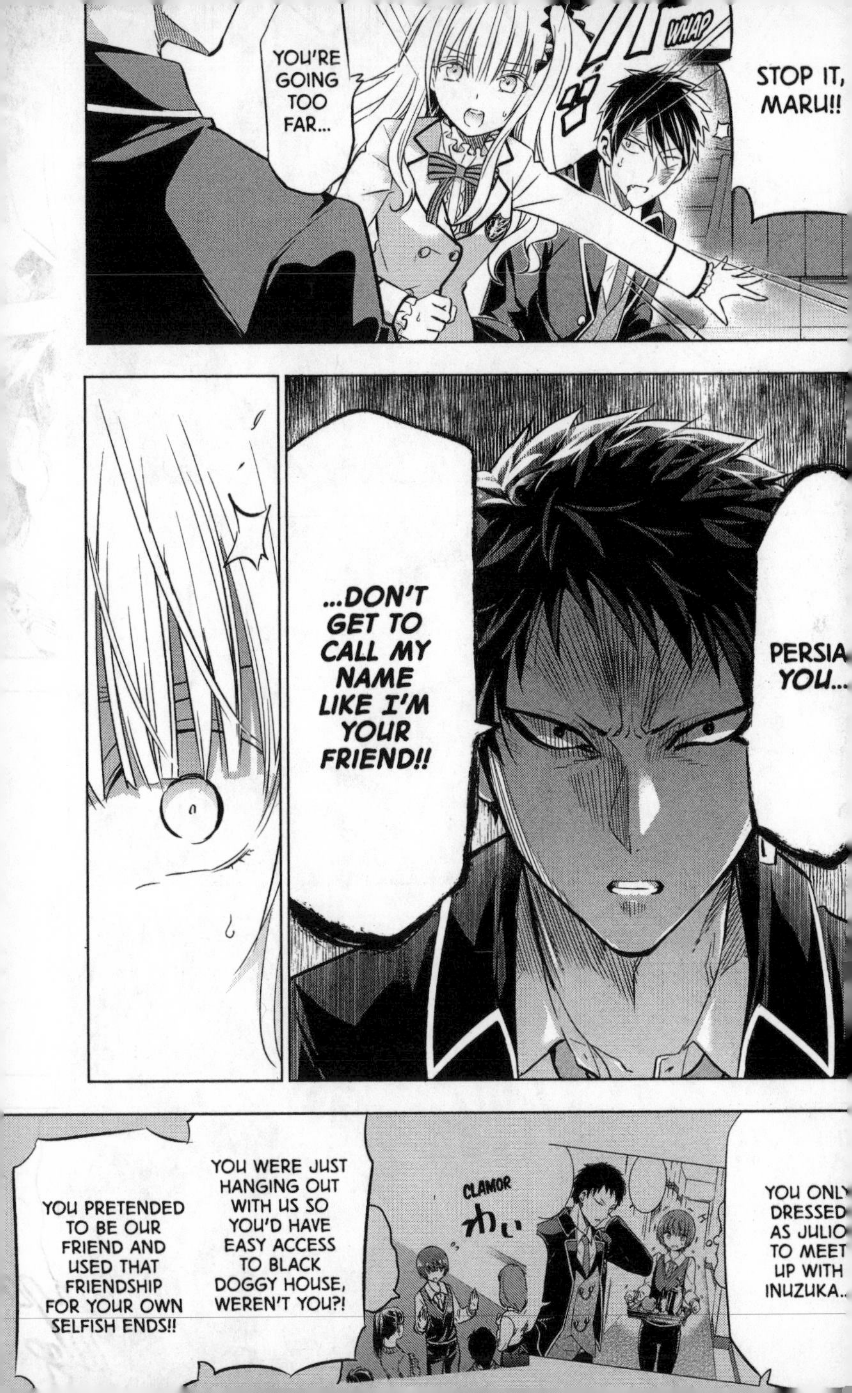
WHAP
STOP IT, MARU!!
YOU'RE GOING TOO FAR...
PERSIA YOU...
...DON'T GET TO CALL MY NAME LIKE I'M YOUR FRIEND!!
YOU ONLY DRESSED AS JULIO TO MEET UP WITH INUZUKA..
CLAMOR
わい
YOU WERE JUST HANGING OUT WITH US SO YOU'D HAVE EASY ACCESS TO BLACK DOGGY HOUSE, WEREN'T YOU?!
YOU PRETENDED TO BE OUR FRIEND AND USED THAT FRIENDSHIP FOR YOUR OWN SELFISH ENDS!!

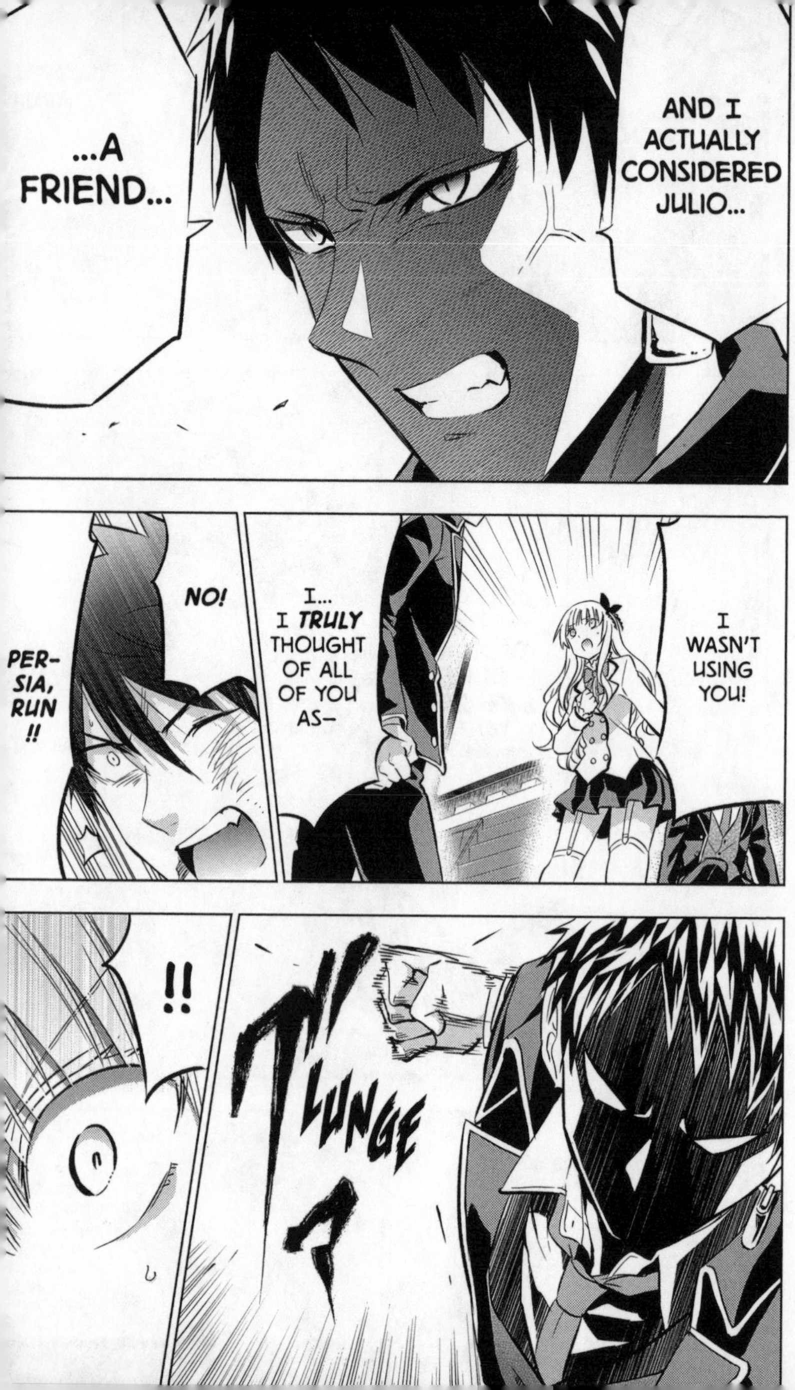
AND I ACTUALLY CONSIDERED JULIO...
...A FRIEND...
I WASN'T USING YOU!
I... I *TRULY* THOUGHT OF ALL OF YOU AS—
NO!
PER-SIA, RUN!!
LUNGE
!!

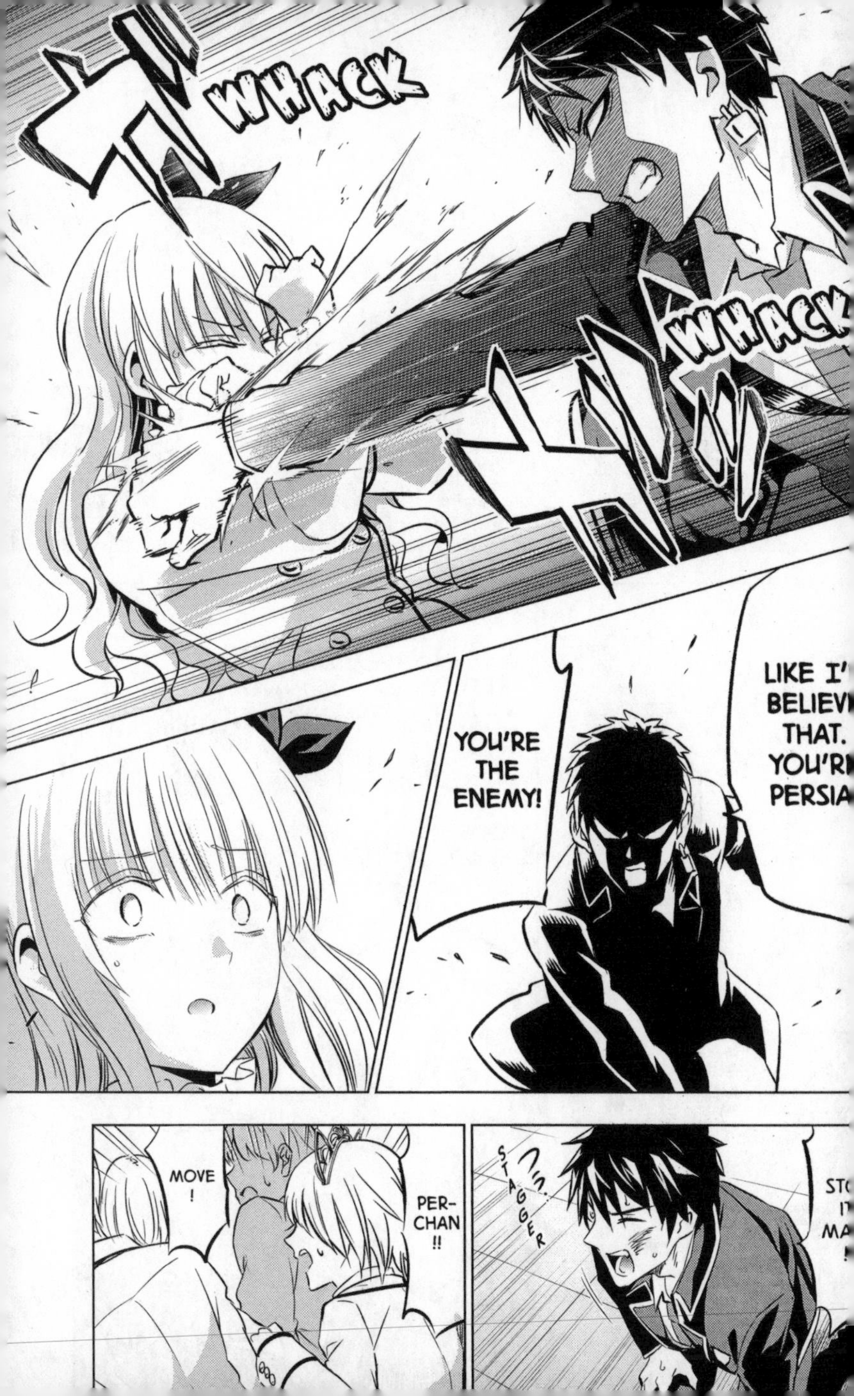
WHACK
WHACK
LIKE I' BELIEV THAT. YOU'R PERSIA
YOU'RE THE ENEMY!
STAGGER
STO IT MA !
PER-CHAN !!
MOVE !

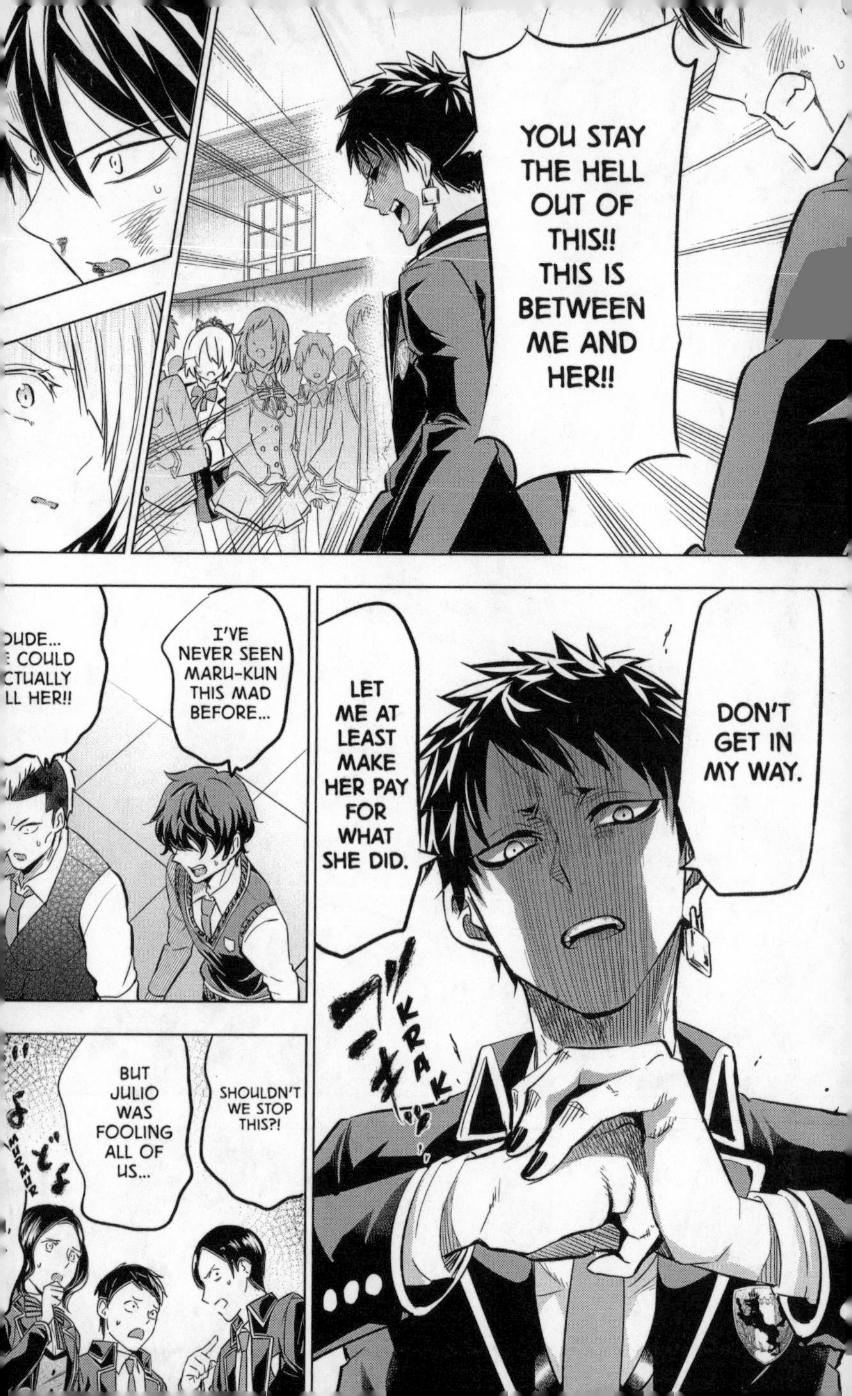
YOU STAY THE HELL OUT OF THIS!! THIS IS BETWEEN ME AND HER!!
DON'T GET IN MY WAY.
LET ME AT LEAST MAKE HER PAY FOR WHAT SHE DID.
KRAK
I'VE NEVER SEEN MARU-KUN THIS MAD BEFORE...
UDE... COULD CTUALLY LL HER!!
SHOULDN'T WE STOP THIS?!
BUT JULIO WAS FOOLING ALL OF US...
MURMUR

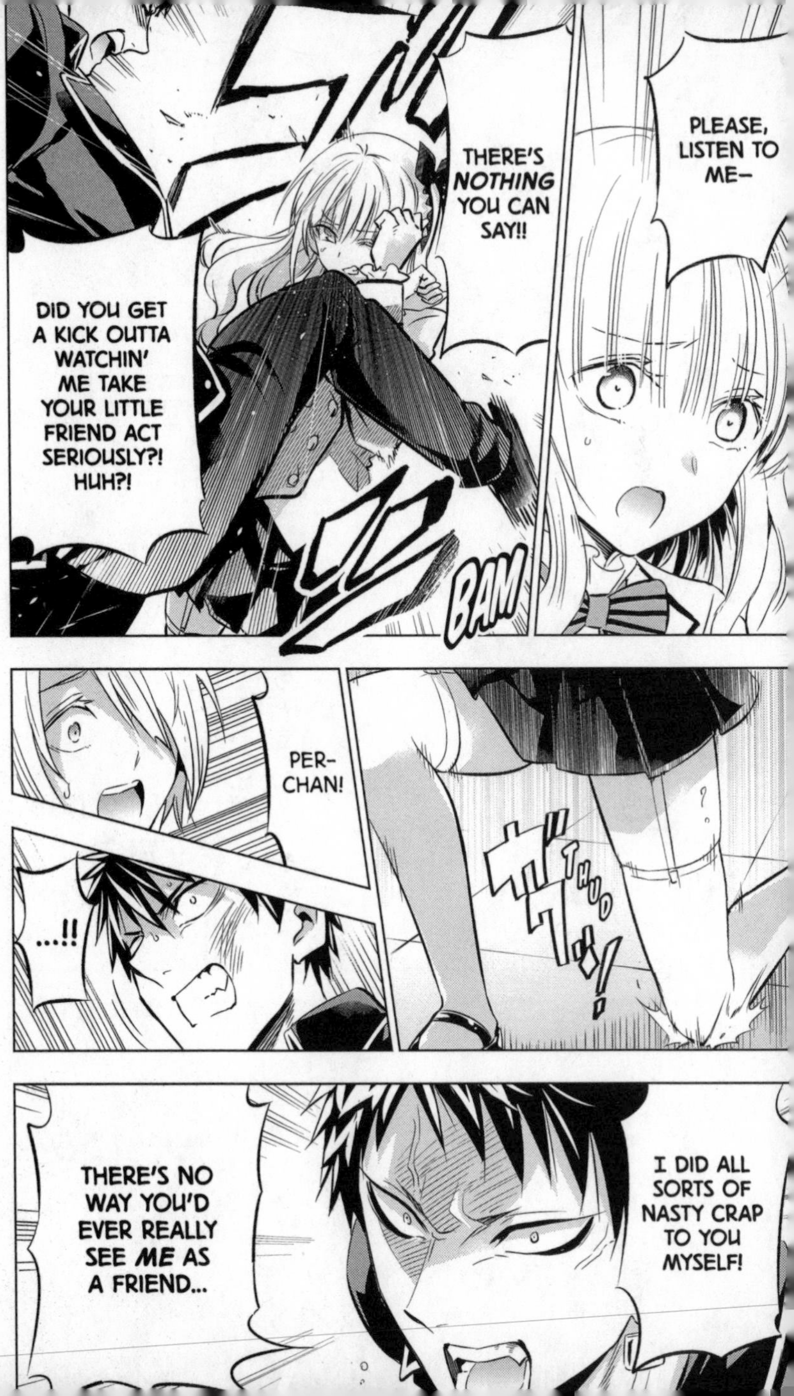
PLEASE, LISTEN TO ME—
THERE'S *NOTHING* YOU CAN SAY!!
DID YOU GET A KICK OUTTA WATCHIN' ME TAKE YOUR LITTLE FRIEND ACT SERIOUSLY?! HUH?!
BAM
THUD
PER-CHAN!
...!!
I DID ALL SORTS OF NASTY CRAP TO YOU MYSELF!
THERE'S NO WAY YOU'D EVER REALLY SEE *ME* AS A FRIEND...

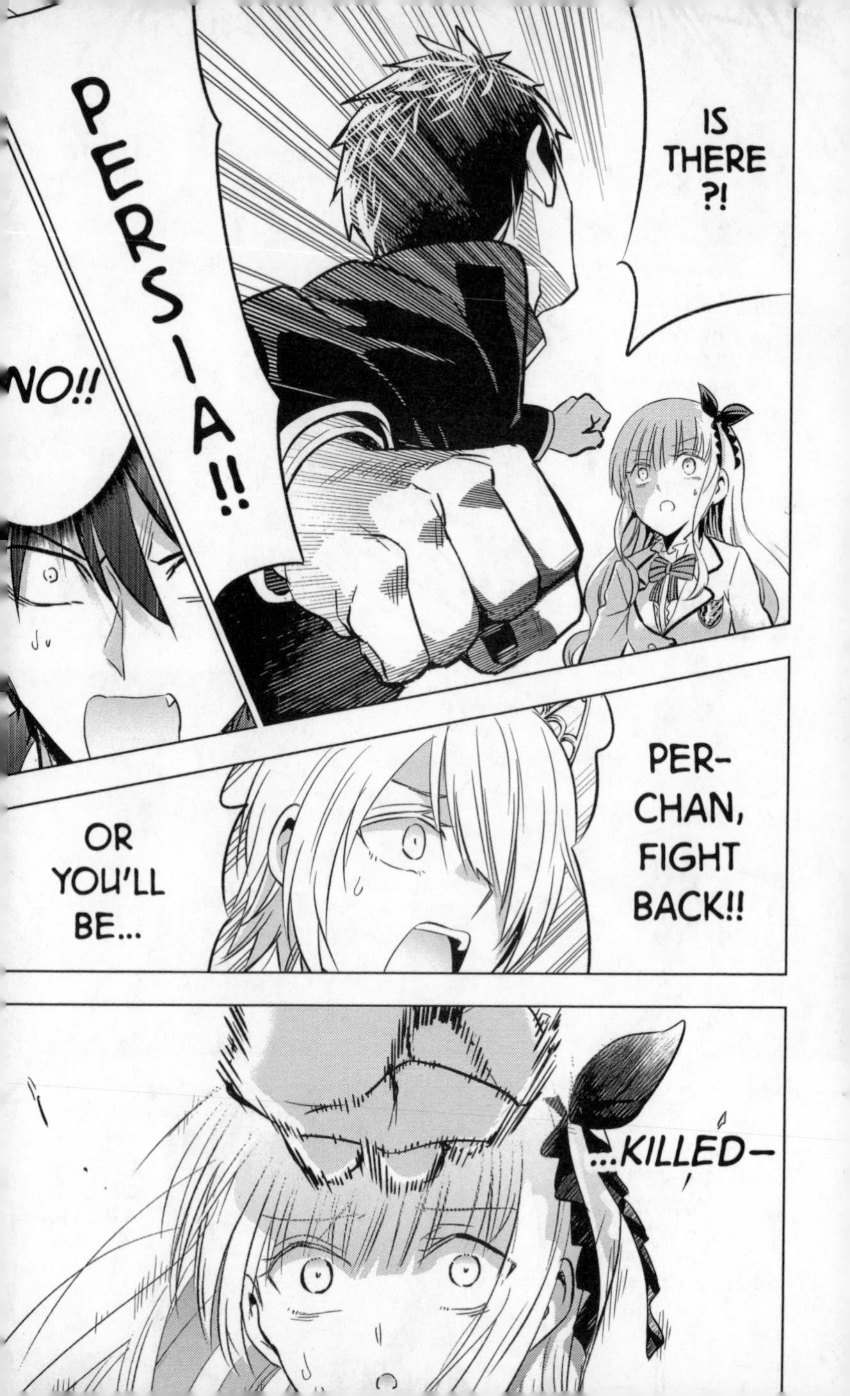
IS THERE ?!
PERSIA!!
NO!!
PER-CHAN, FIGHT BACK!!
OR YOU'LL BE...
...KILLED—

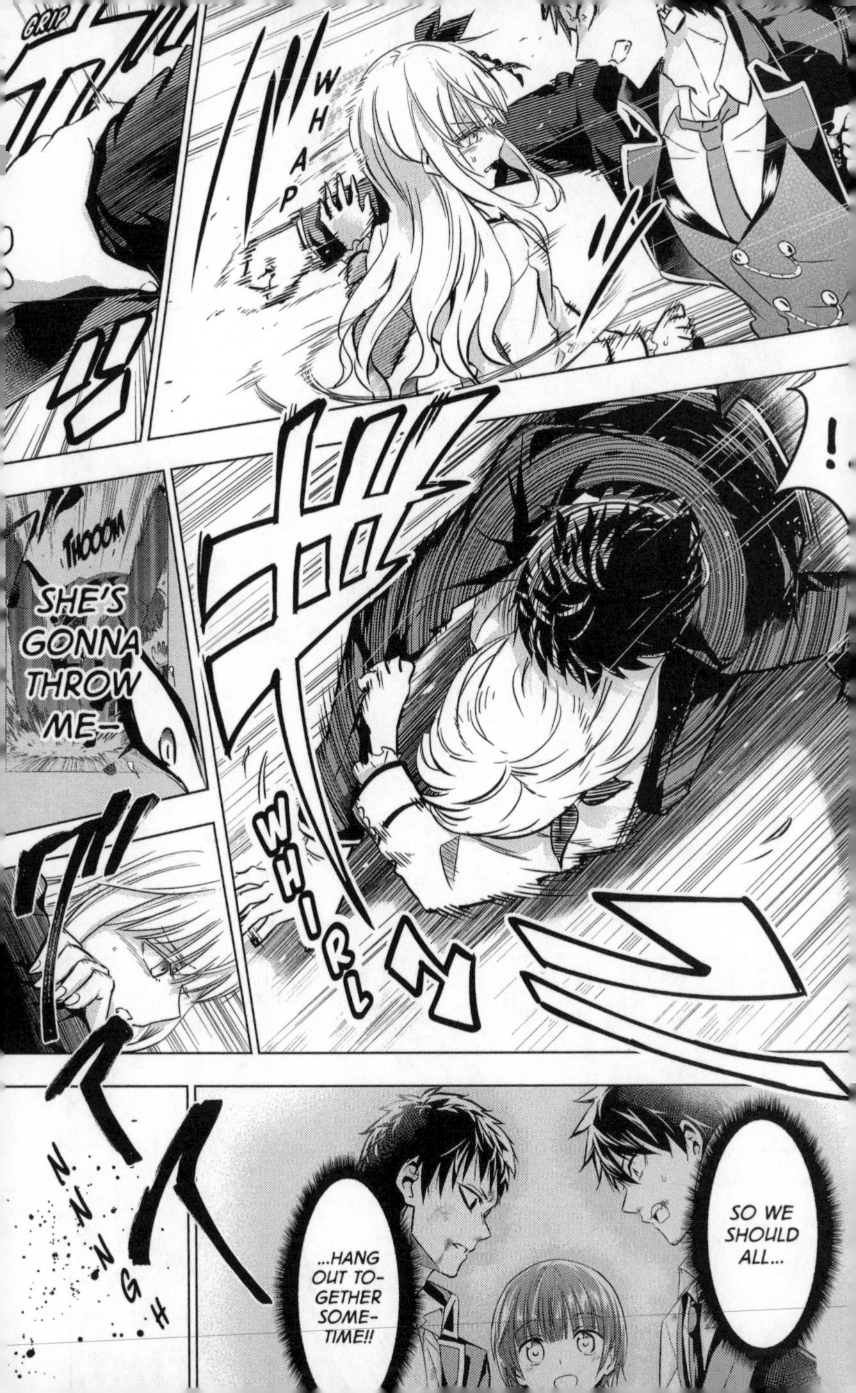
WHAP
GRIP
!
WHIRL
THOOOM
SHE'S GONNA THROW ME—
SO WE SHOULD ALL...
...HANG OUT TO-GETHER SOME-TIME!!
NNNNGH

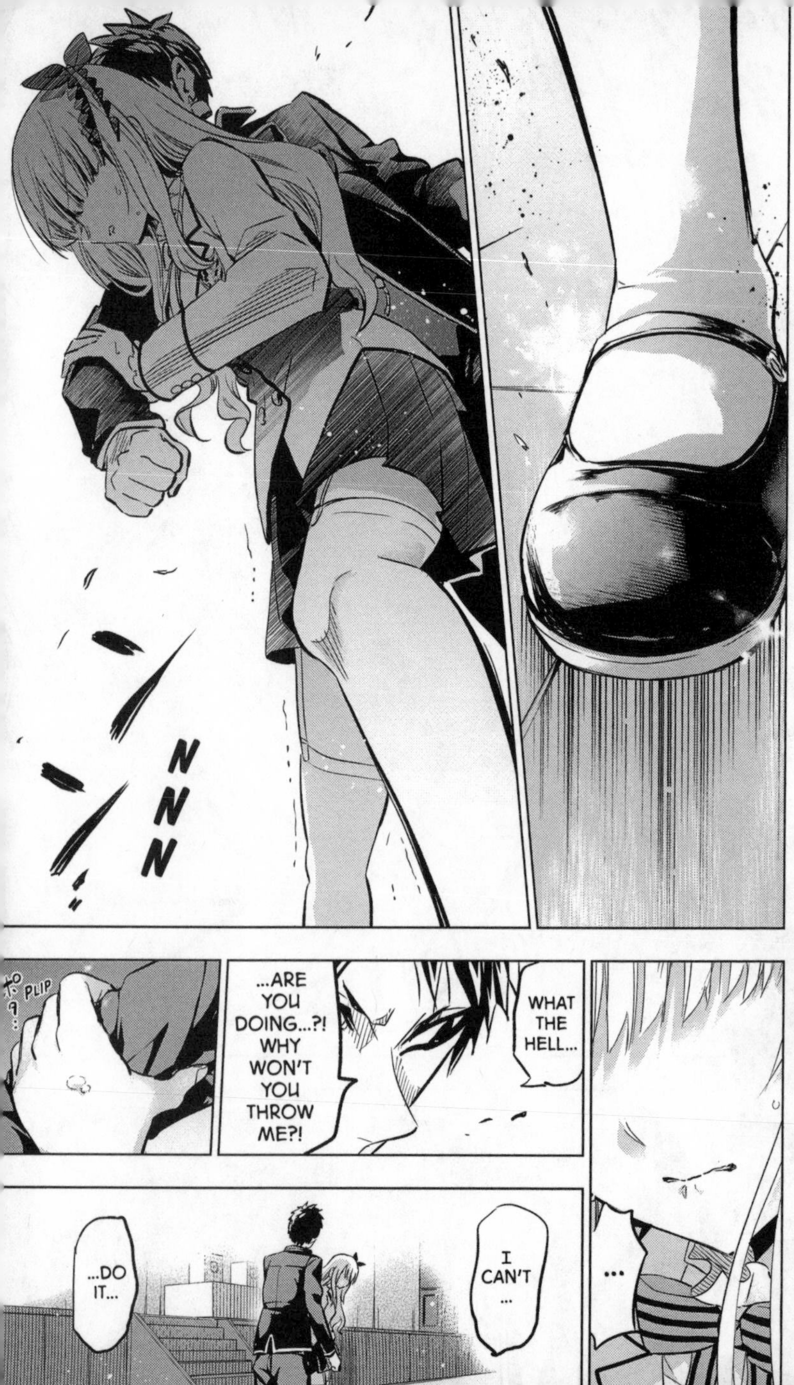
NNN
WHAT THE HELL...
...ARE YOU DOING...?! WHY WON'T YOU THROW ME?!
PLIP
...
I CAN'T ...
...DO IT...

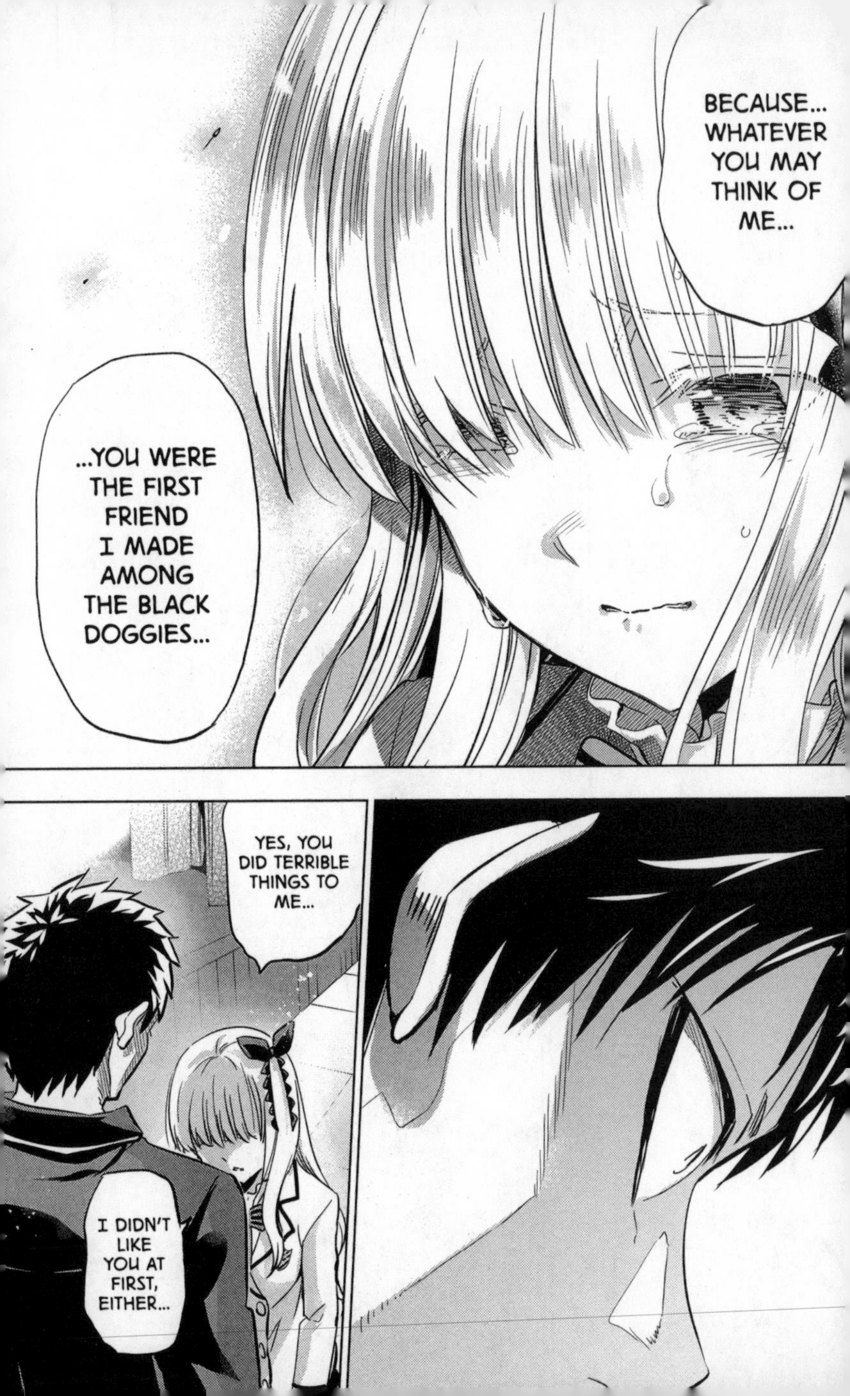
BECAUSE... WHATEVER YOU MAY THINK OF ME...
...YOU WERE THE FIRST FRIEND I MADE AMONG THE BLACK DOGGIES...
YES, YOU DID TERRIBLE THINGS TO ME...
I DIDN'T LIKE YOU AT FIRST, EITHER...

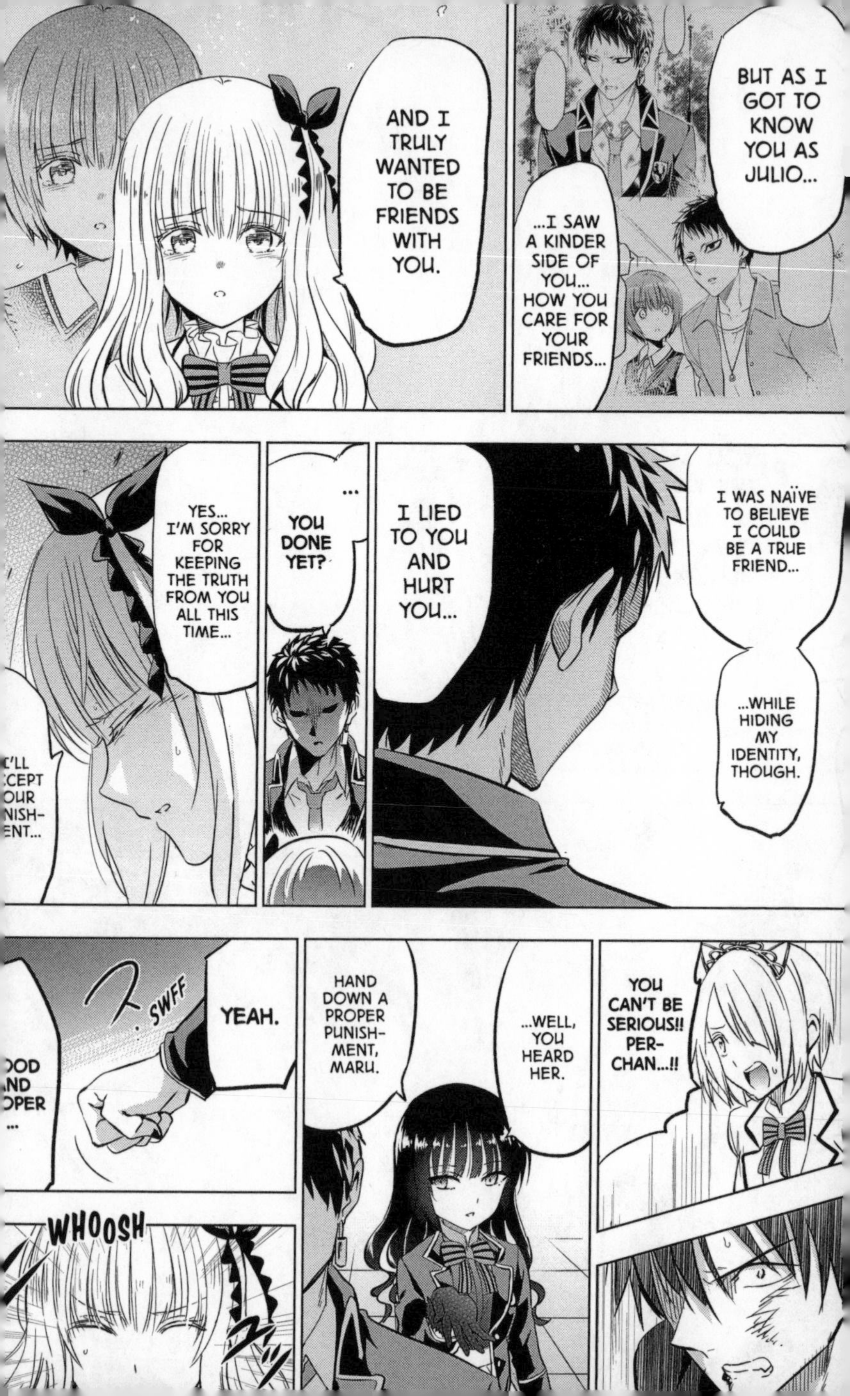
BUT AS I GOT TO KNOW YOU AS JULIO...
...I SAW A KINDER SIDE OF YOU... HOW YOU CARE FOR YOUR FRIENDS...
AND I TRULY WANTED TO BE FRIENDS WITH YOU.
I WAS NAÏVE TO BELIEVE I COULD BE A TRUE FRIEND...
...WHILE HIDING MY IDENTITY, THOUGH.
I LIED TO YOU AND HURT YOU...
...
YOU DONE YET?
YES... I'M SORRY FOR KEEPING THE TRUTH FROM YOU ALL THIS TIME...
YOU CAN'T BE SERIOUS!! PER-CHAN...!!
...WELL, YOU HEARD HER.
HAND DOWN A PROPER PUNISHMENT, MARU.
YEAH.
SWFF
WHOOSH

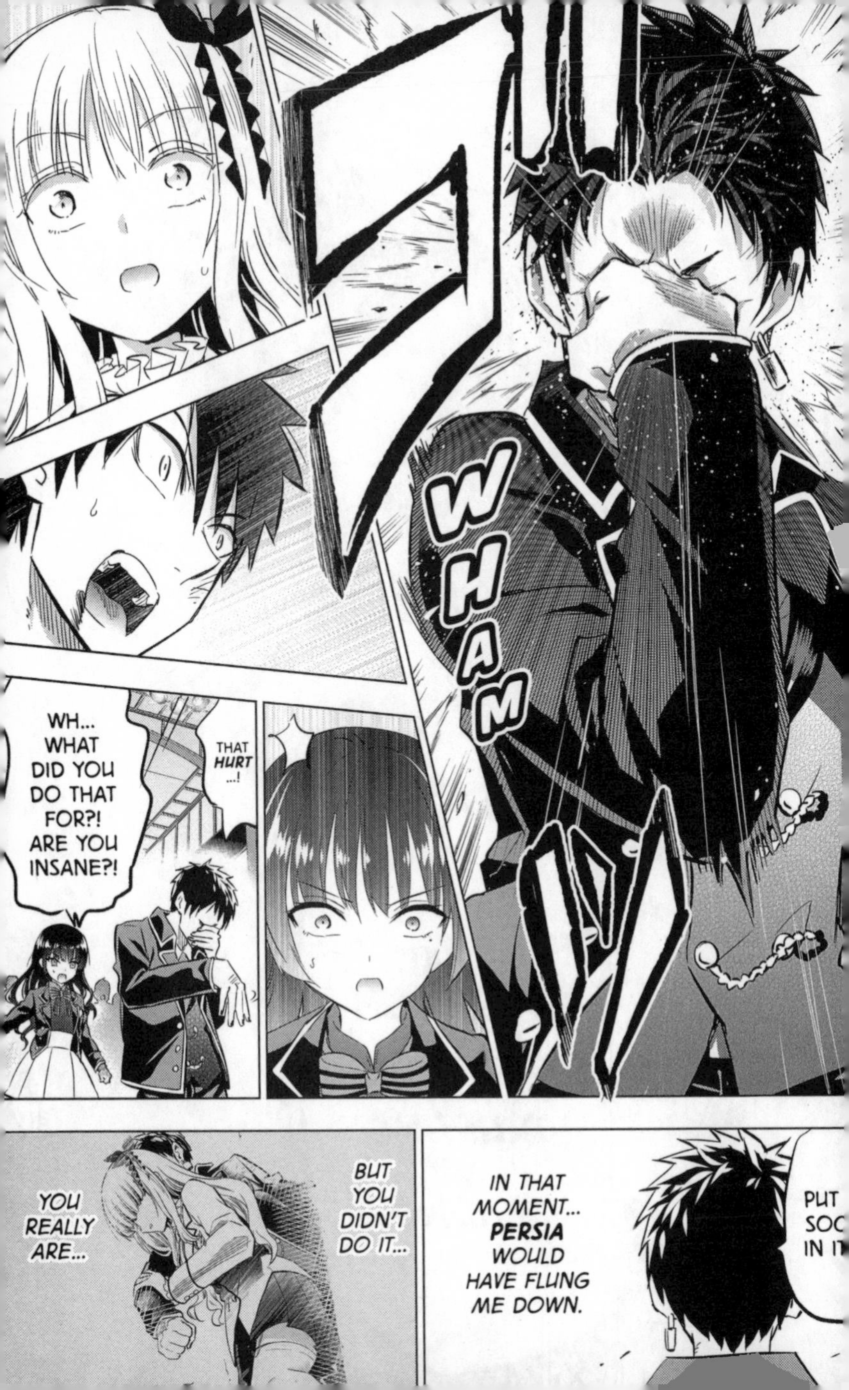
WHAM
THAT HURT ...!
WH... WHAT DID YOU DO THAT FOR?! ARE YOU INSANE?!
PUT SOC IN IT
IN THAT MOMENT... PERSIA WOULD HAVE FLUNG ME DOWN.
BUT YOU DIDN'T DO IT...
YOU REALLY ARE...

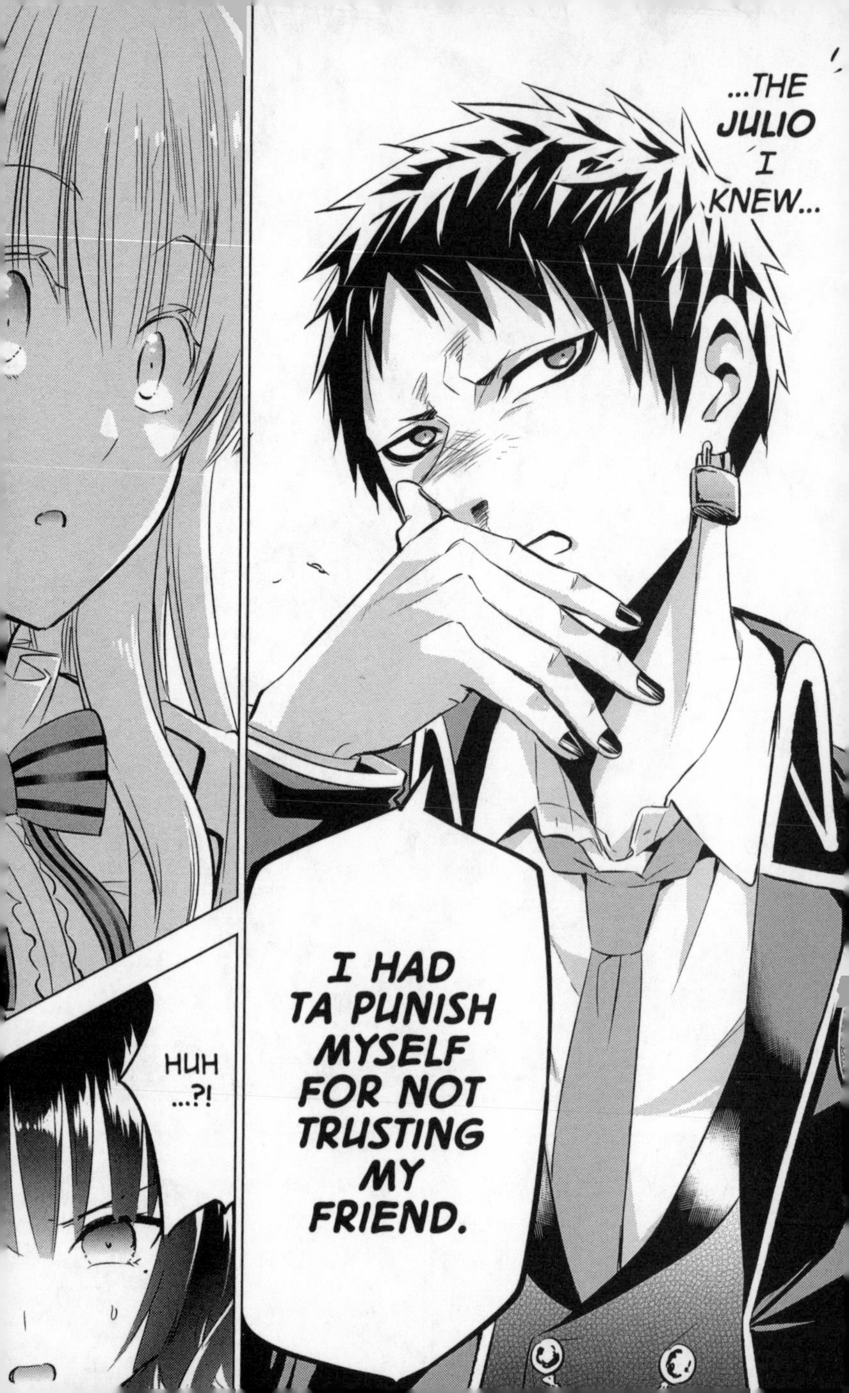
...THE JULIO I KNEW...
I HAD TA PUNISH MYSELF FOR NOT TRUSTING MY FRIEND.
HUH ...?!

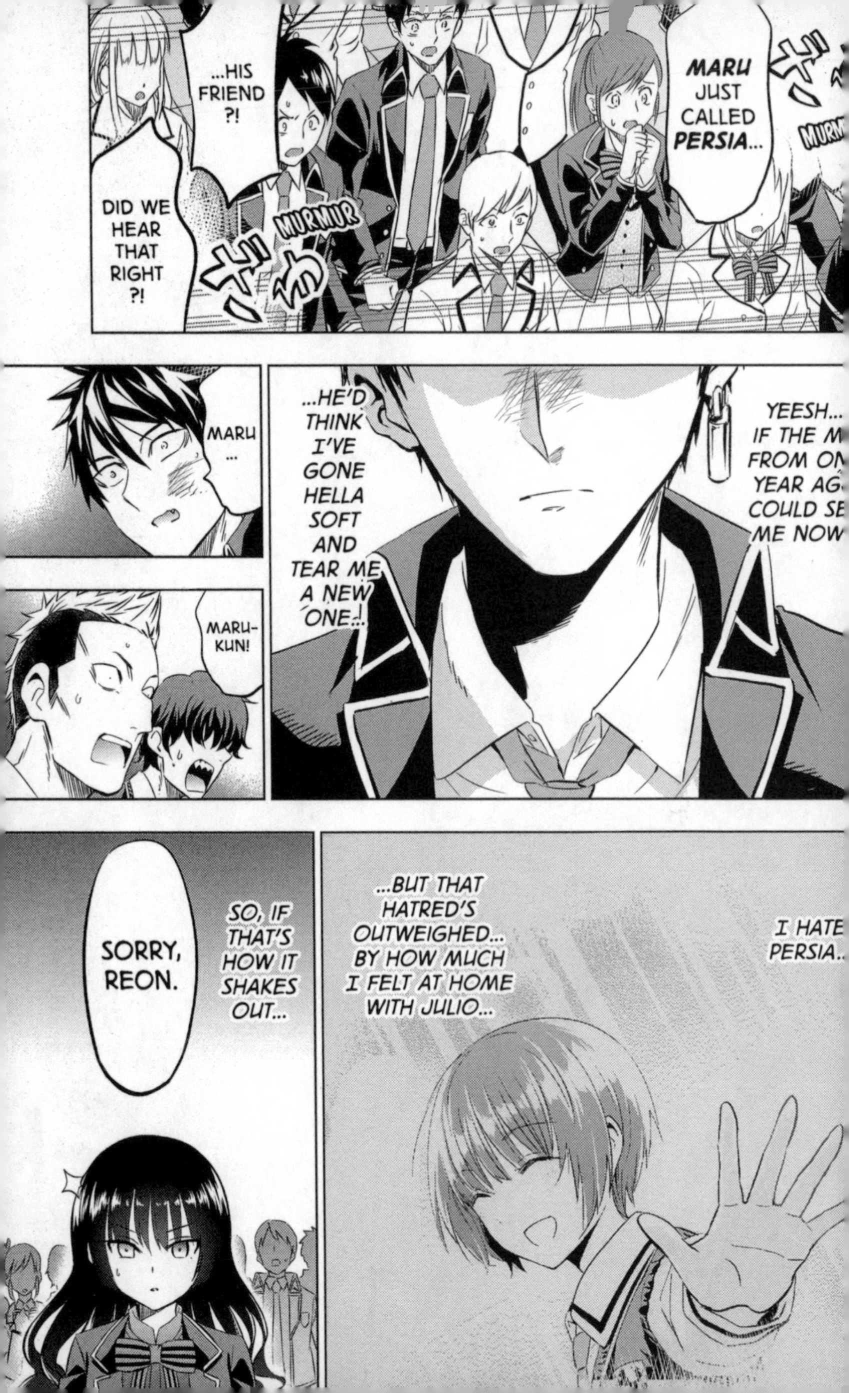
ザ
MURM
MARU JUST CALLED PERSIA...
...HIS FRIEND?!
DID WE HEAR THAT RIGHT?!
MURMUR
ザわ
YEESH... IF THE M FROM ON YEAR AG COULD SE ME NOW
...HE'D THINK I'VE GONE HELLA SOFT AND TEAR ME A NEW ONE..!
MARU...
MARU-KUN!
I HATE PERSIA...
...BUT THAT HATRED'S OUTWEIGHED... BY HOW MUCH I FELT AT HOME WITH JULIO...
SO, IF THAT'S HOW IT SHAKES OUT...
SORRY, REON.

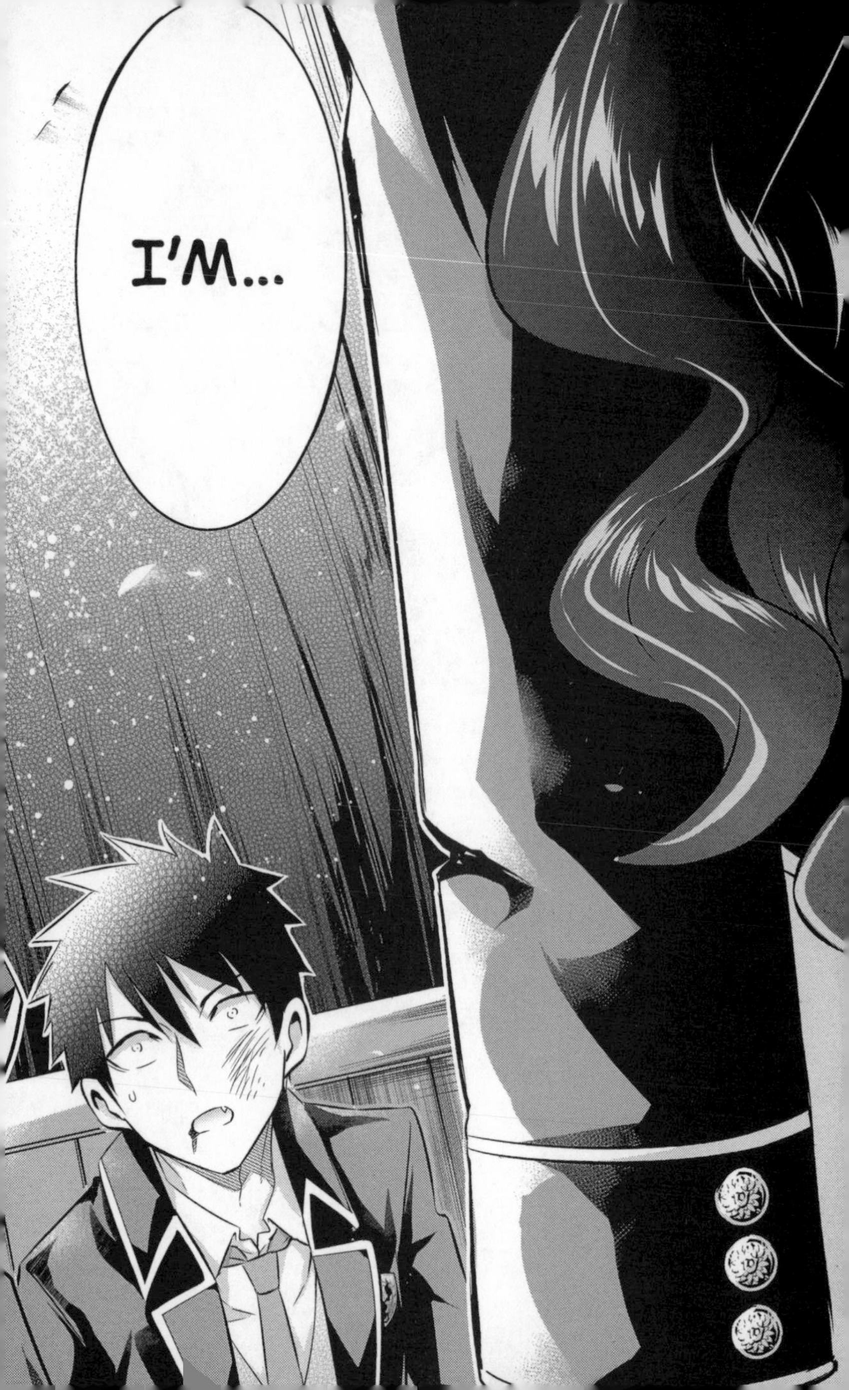
I'M...

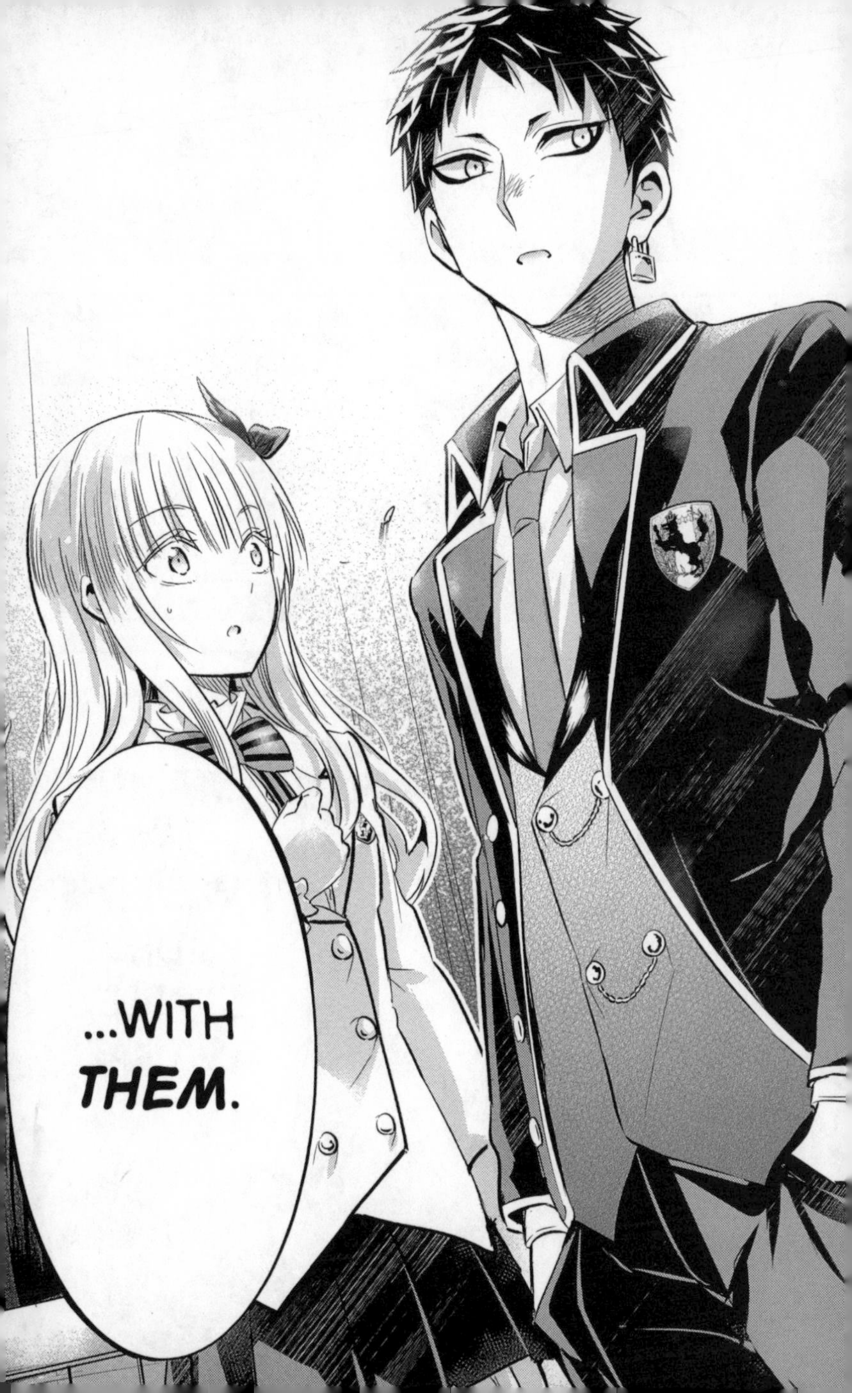
...WITH THEM.

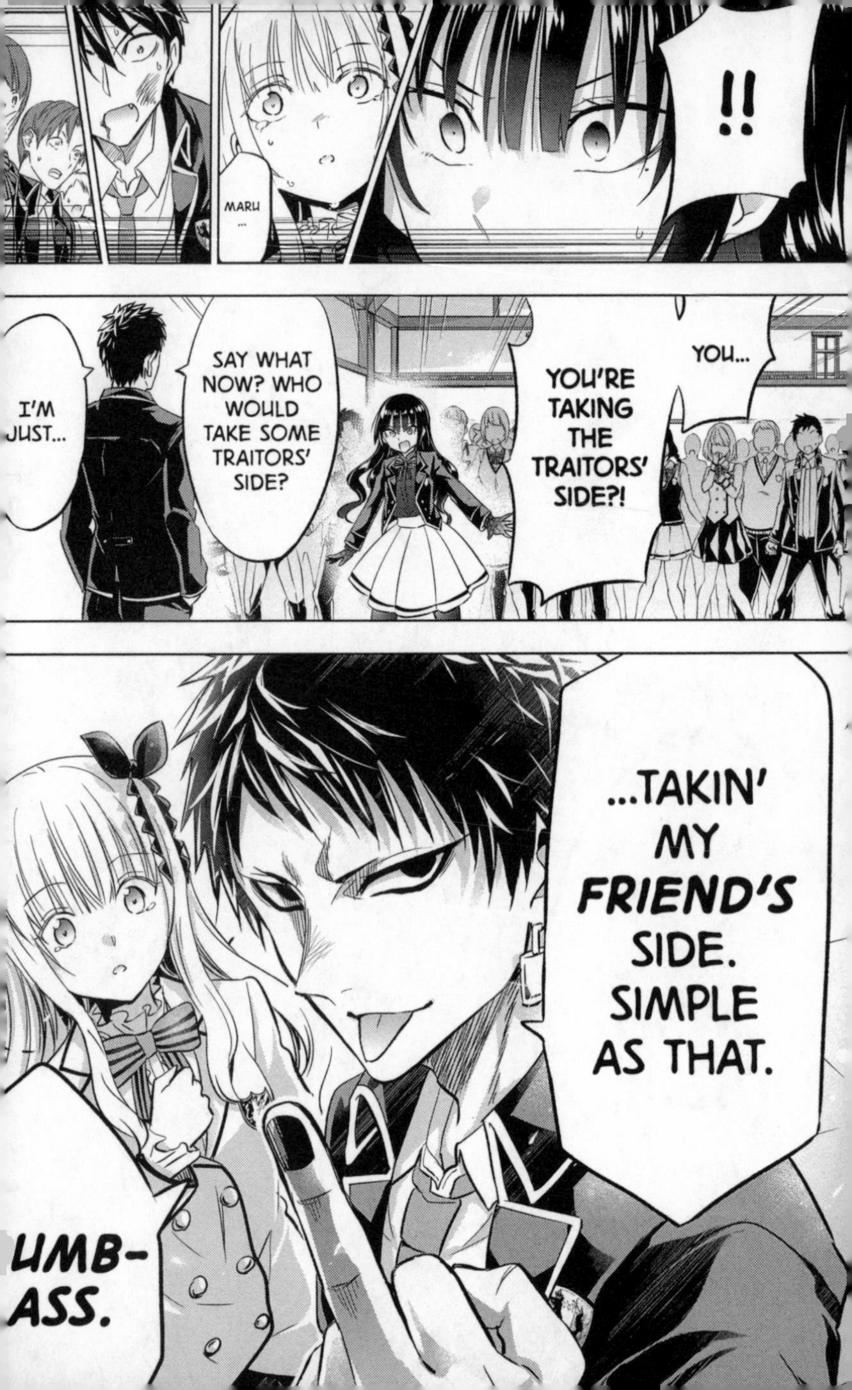
!!
MARU...
YOU...
YOU'RE TAKING THE TRAITORS' SIDE?!
SAY WHAT NOW? WHO WOULD TAKE SOME TRAITORS' SIDE?
I'M JUST...
...TAKIN' MY FRIEND'S SIDE. SIMPLE AS THAT.
UMB-ASS.

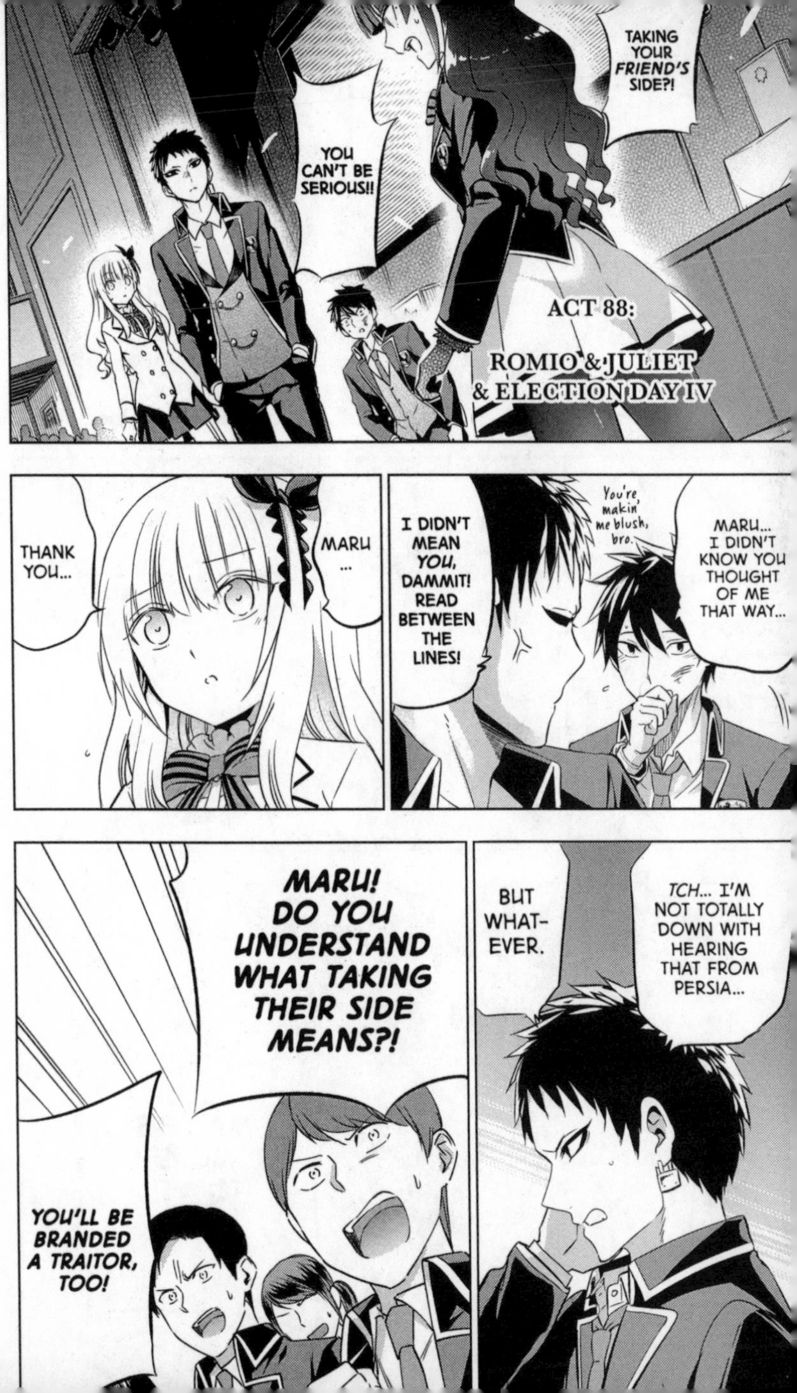
TAKING YOUR *FRIEND'S* SIDE?!
YOU CAN'T BE SERIOUS!!
ACT 88:
ROMIO & JULIET & ELECTION DAY IV
MARU... I DIDN'T KNOW YOU THOUGHT OF ME THAT WAY...
You're makin' me blush, bro.
I DIDN'T MEAN *YOU*, DAMMIT! READ BETWEEN THE LINES!
MARU ...
THANK YOU...
*TCH*... I'M NOT TOTALLY DOWN WITH HEARING THAT FROM PERSIA...
BUT WHAT-EVER.
MARU! DO YOU UNDERSTAND WHAT TAKING THEIR SIDE MEANS?!
YOU'LL BE BRANDED A TRAITOR, TOO!

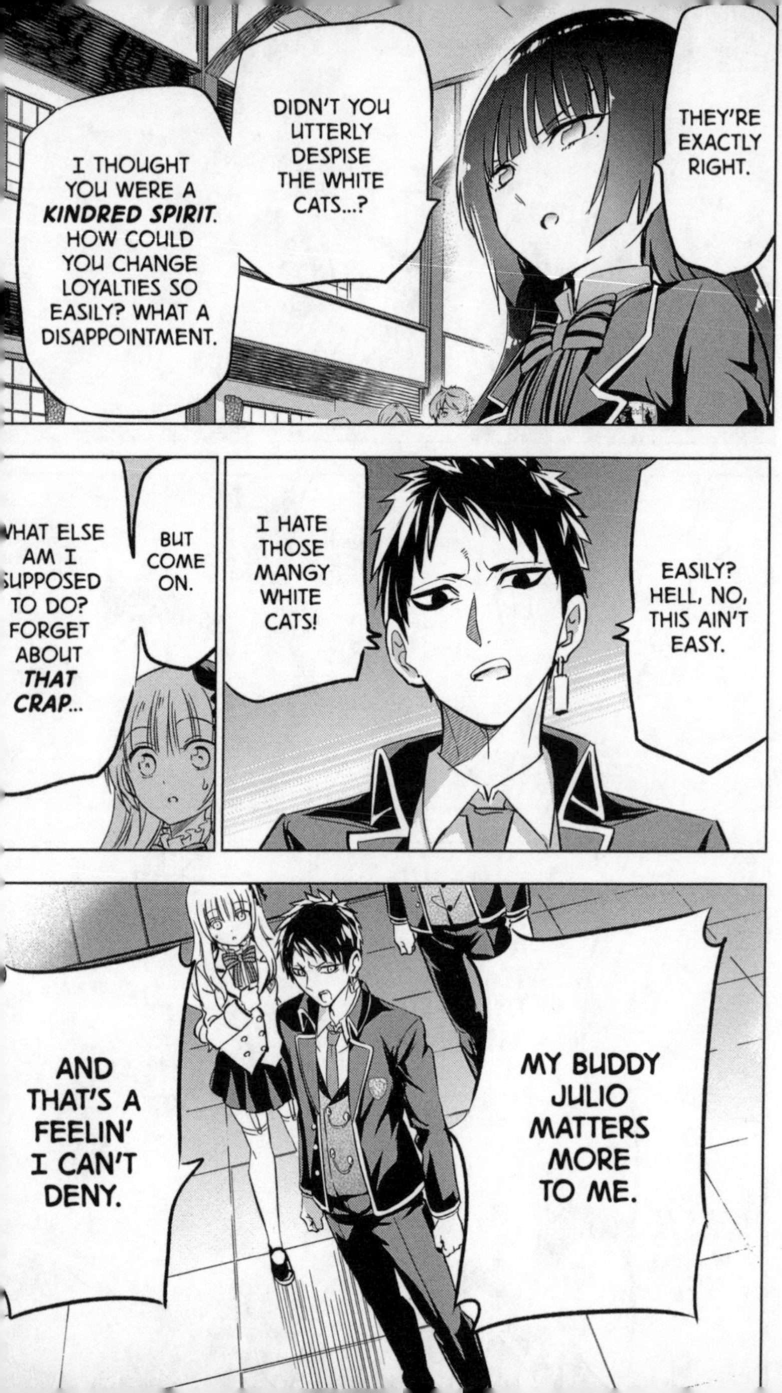
THEY'RE EXACTLY RIGHT.
DIDN'T YOU UTTERLY DESPISE THE WHITE CATS...?
I THOUGHT YOU WERE A ***KINDRED SPIRIT***. HOW COULD YOU CHANGE LOYALTIES SO EASILY? WHAT A DISAPPOINTMENT.
EASILY? HELL, NO, THIS AIN'T EASY.
I HATE THOSE MANGY WHITE CATS!
BUT COME ON.
WHAT ELSE AM I SUPPOSED TO DO? FORGET ABOUT ***THAT CRAP***...
MY BUDDY JULIO MATTERS MORE TO ME.
AND THAT'S A FEELIN' I CAN'T DENY.

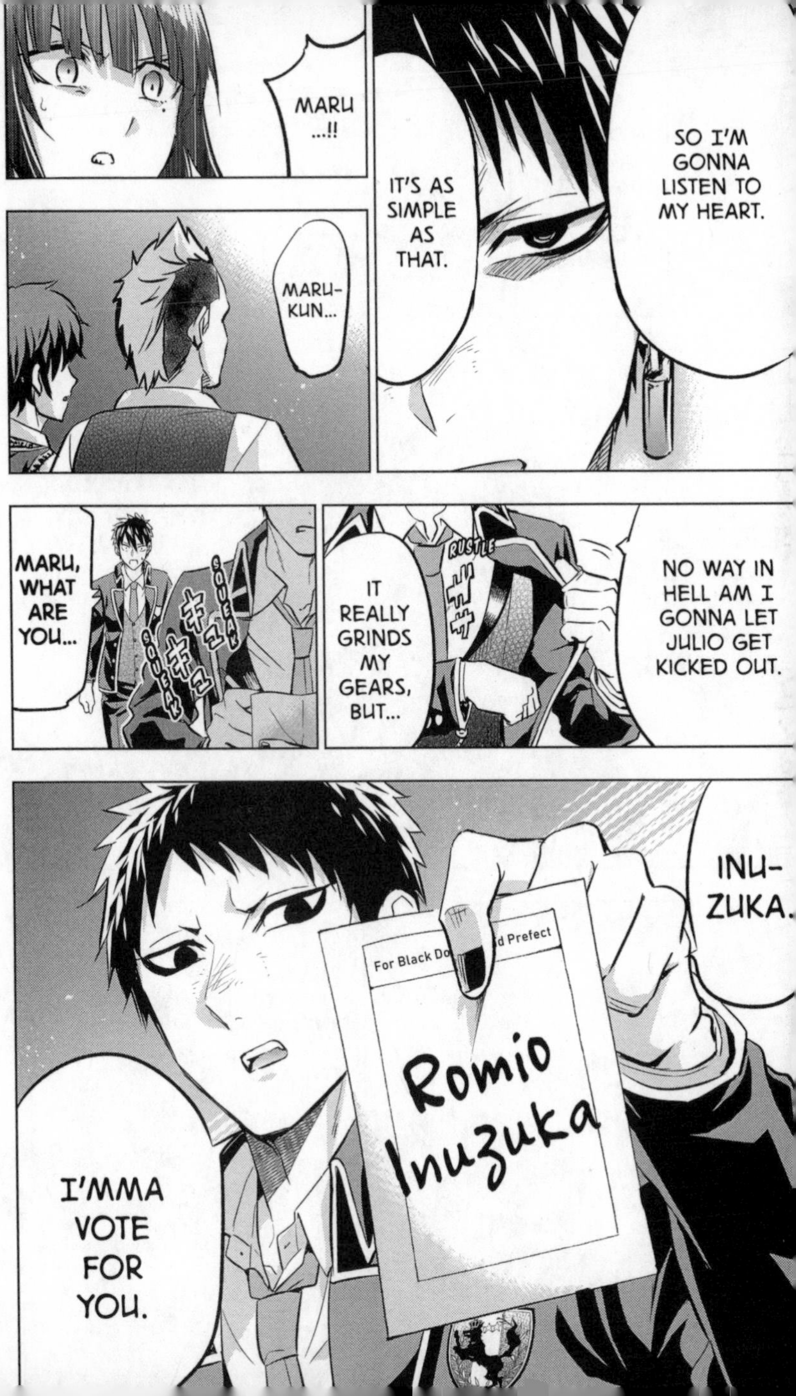

SO I'M GONNA LISTEN TO MY HEART.
IT'S AS SIMPLE AS THAT.
MARU ...!!
MARU-KUN...
NO WAY IN HELL AM I GONNA LET JULIO GET KICKED OUT.
RUSTLE
IT REALLY GRINDS MY GEARS, BUT...
SQUEAK
SQUEAK
MARU, WHAT ARE YOU...
INU-ZUKA.
Romio Inuzuka
I'MMA VOTE FOR YOU.

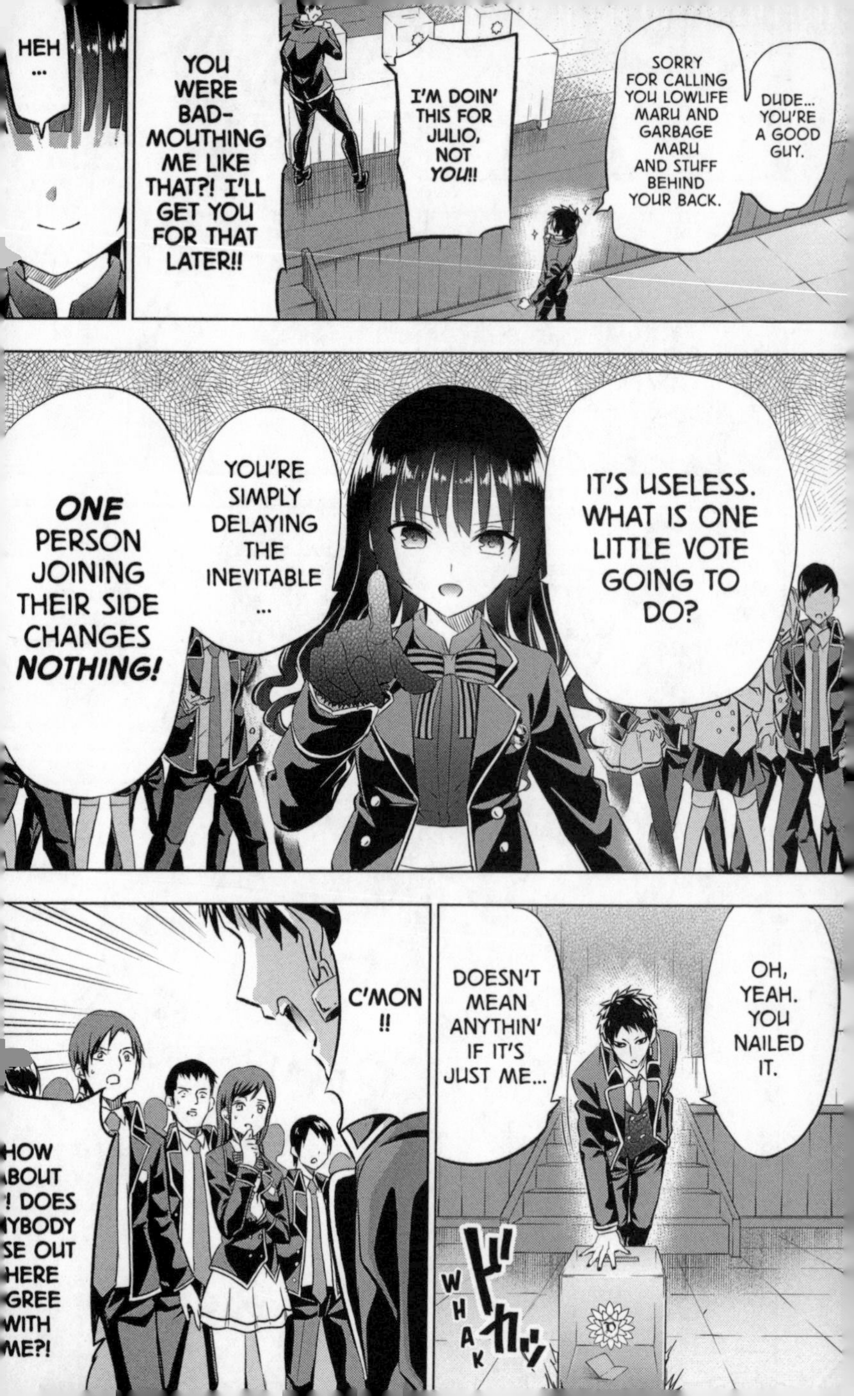
DUDE... YOU'RE A GOOD GUY.
SORRY FOR CALLING YOU LOWLIFE MARU AND GARBAGE MARU AND STUFF BEHIND YOUR BACK.
I'M DOIN' THIS FOR JULIO, NOT *YOU*!!
YOU WERE BAD-MOUTHING ME LIKE THAT?! I'LL GET YOU FOR THAT LATER!!
HEH ...
IT'S USELESS. WHAT IS ONE LITTLE VOTE GOING TO DO?
YOU'RE SIMPLY DELAYING THE INEVITABLE ...
***ONE*** PERSON JOINING THEIR SIDE CHANGES ***NOTHING!***
OH, YEAH. YOU NAILED IT.
DOESN'T MEAN ANYTHIN' IF IT'S JUST ME...
WHAK
C'MON !!
HOW BOUT ! DOES YBODY SE OUT HERE GREE WITH ME?!

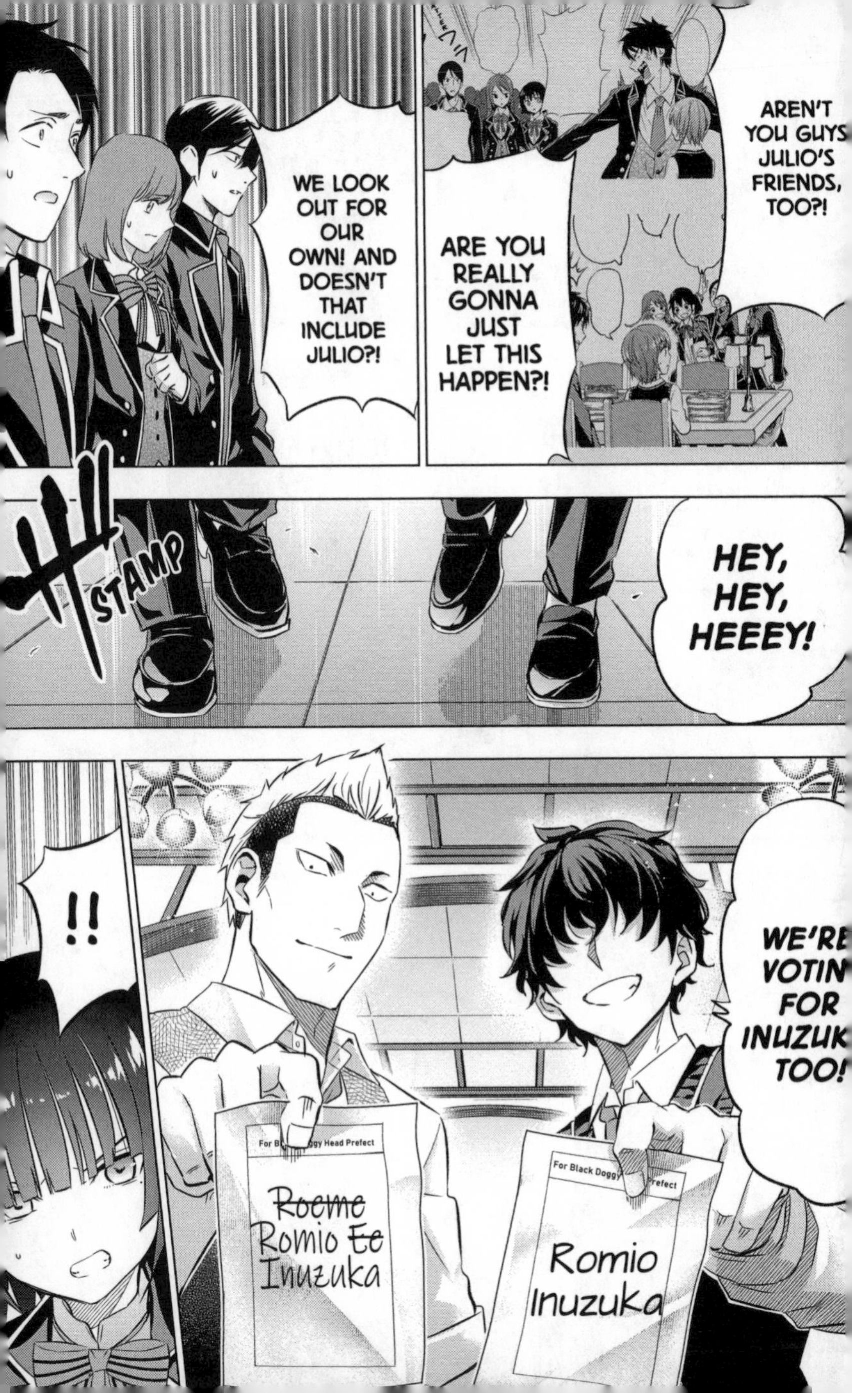
AREN'T YOU GUYS JULIO'S FRIENDS, TOO?!
ARE YOU REALLY GONNA JUST LET THIS HAPPEN?!
WE LOOK OUT FOR OUR OWN! AND DOESN'T THAT INCLUDE JULIO?!
HEY, HEY, HEEEY!
STAMP
WE'RE VOTIN FOR INUZUK TOO!
For Black Doggy Prefect
Romio Inuzuka
Head Prefect
~~Roeme~~ Romio ~~Ee~~ Inuzuka
!!

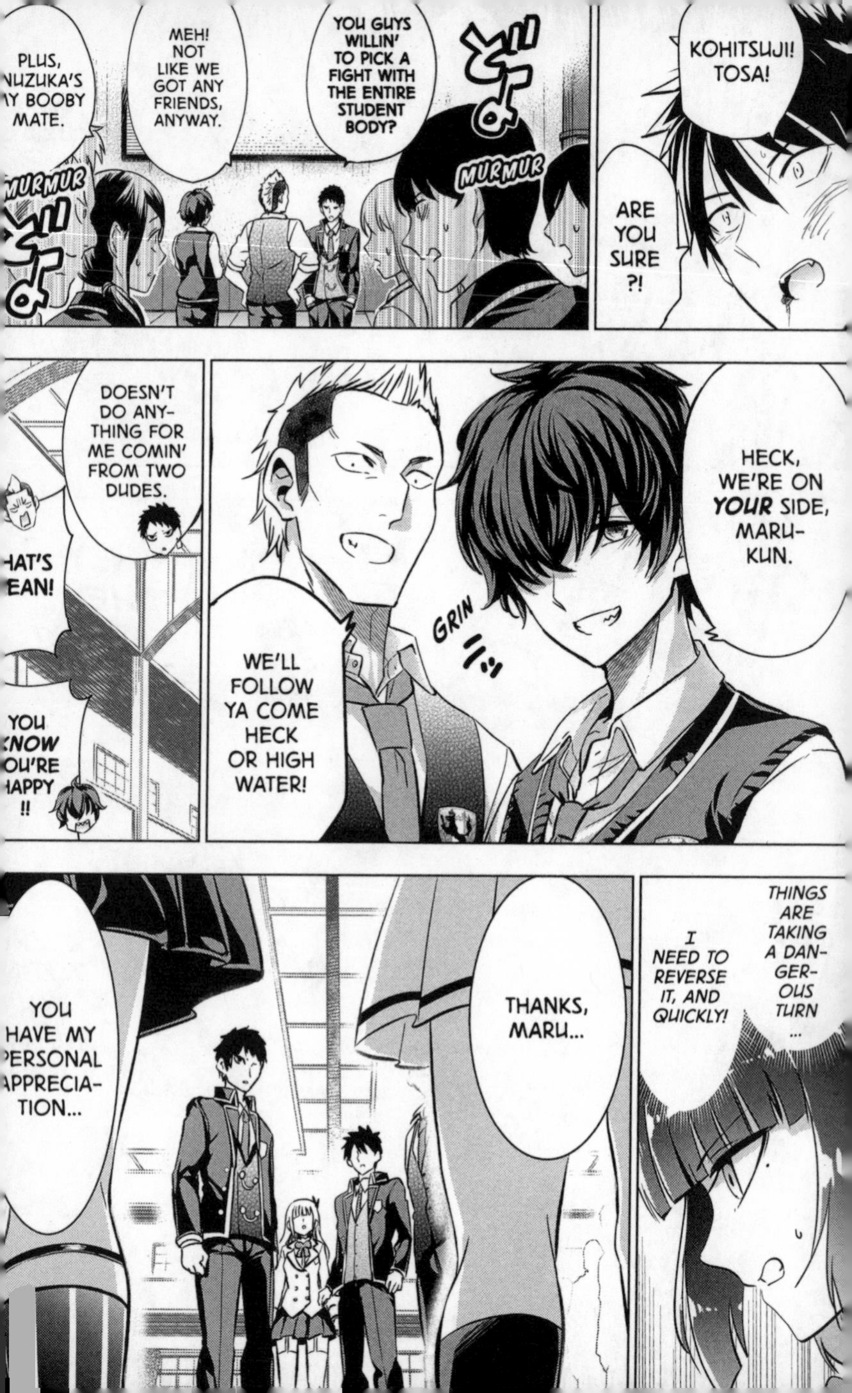

KOHITSUJI! TOSA!
ARE YOU SURE ?!
YOU GUYS WILLIN' TO PICK A FIGHT WITH THE ENTIRE STUDENT BODY?
どよ
MURMUR
MEH! NOT LIKE WE GOT ANY FRIENDS, ANYWAY.
PLUS, NUZUKA'S Y BOOBY MATE.
MURMUR
どよ
HECK, WE'RE ON YOUR SIDE, MARU-KUN.
GRIN
ニッ
WE'LL FOLLOW YA COME HECK OR HIGH WATER!
DOESN'T DO ANYTHING FOR ME COMIN' FROM TWO DUDES.
HAT'S EAN!
YOU NOW OU'RE HAPPY !!
THINGS ARE TAKING A DANGEROUS TURN ...
I NEED TO REVERSE IT, AND QUICKLY!
THANKS, MARU...
YOU HAVE MY ERSONAL PPRECIATION...

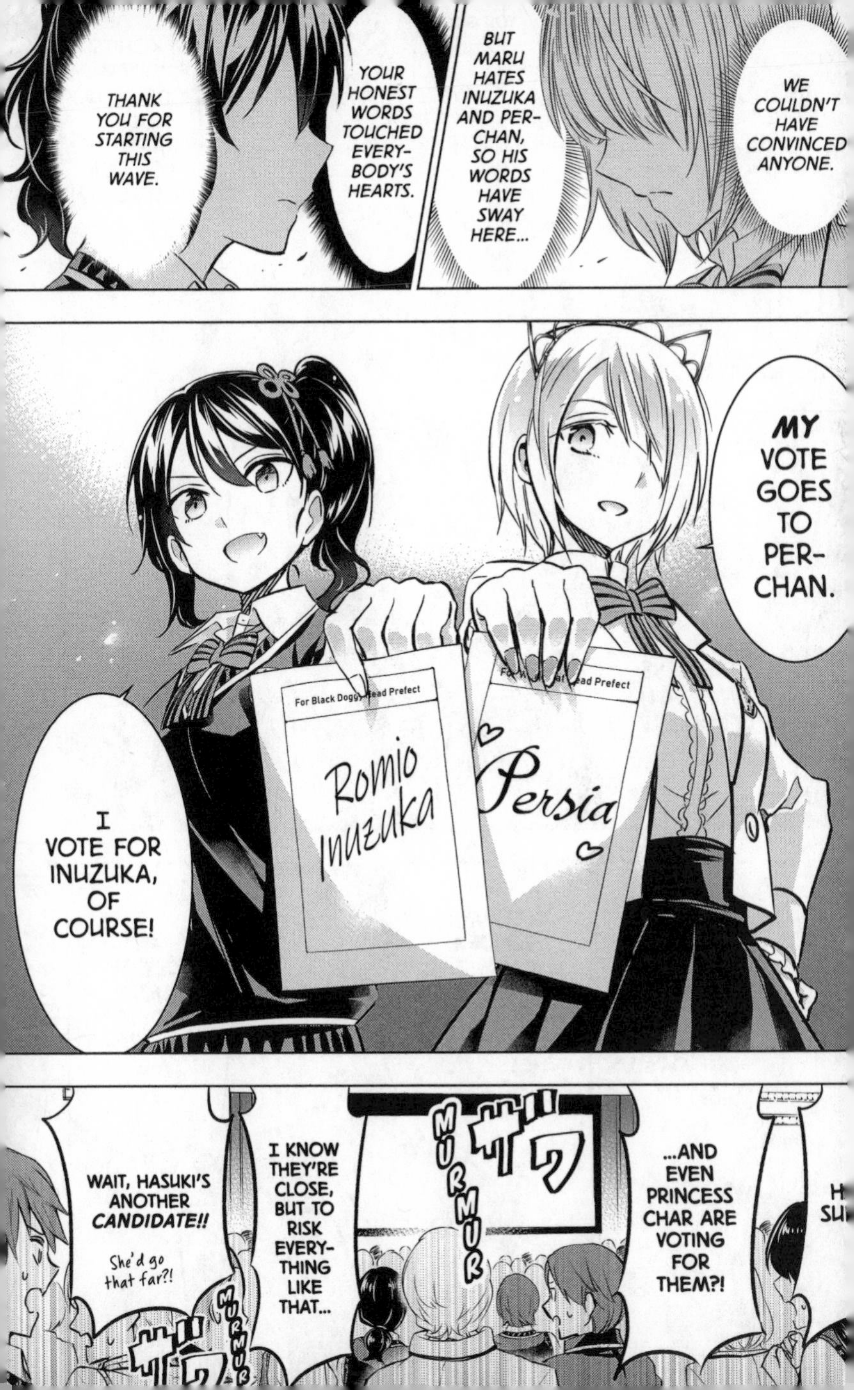
WE COULDN'T HAVE CONVINCED ANYONE.
BUT MARU HATES INUZUKA AND PER-CHAN, SO HIS WORDS HAVE SWAY HERE...
YOUR HONEST WORDS TOUCHED EVERY-BODY'S HEARTS.
THANK YOU FOR STARTING THIS WAVE.
MY VOTE GOES TO PER-CHAN.
Persia
Romio Inuzuka
I VOTE FOR INUZUKA, OF COURSE!
...AND EVEN PRINCESS CHAR ARE VOTING FOR THEM?!
MURMUR
I KNOW THEY'RE CLOSE, BUT TO RISK EVERY-THING LIKE THAT...
WAIT, HASUKI'S ANOTHER CANDIDATE!!
She'd go that far?!
MURMUR

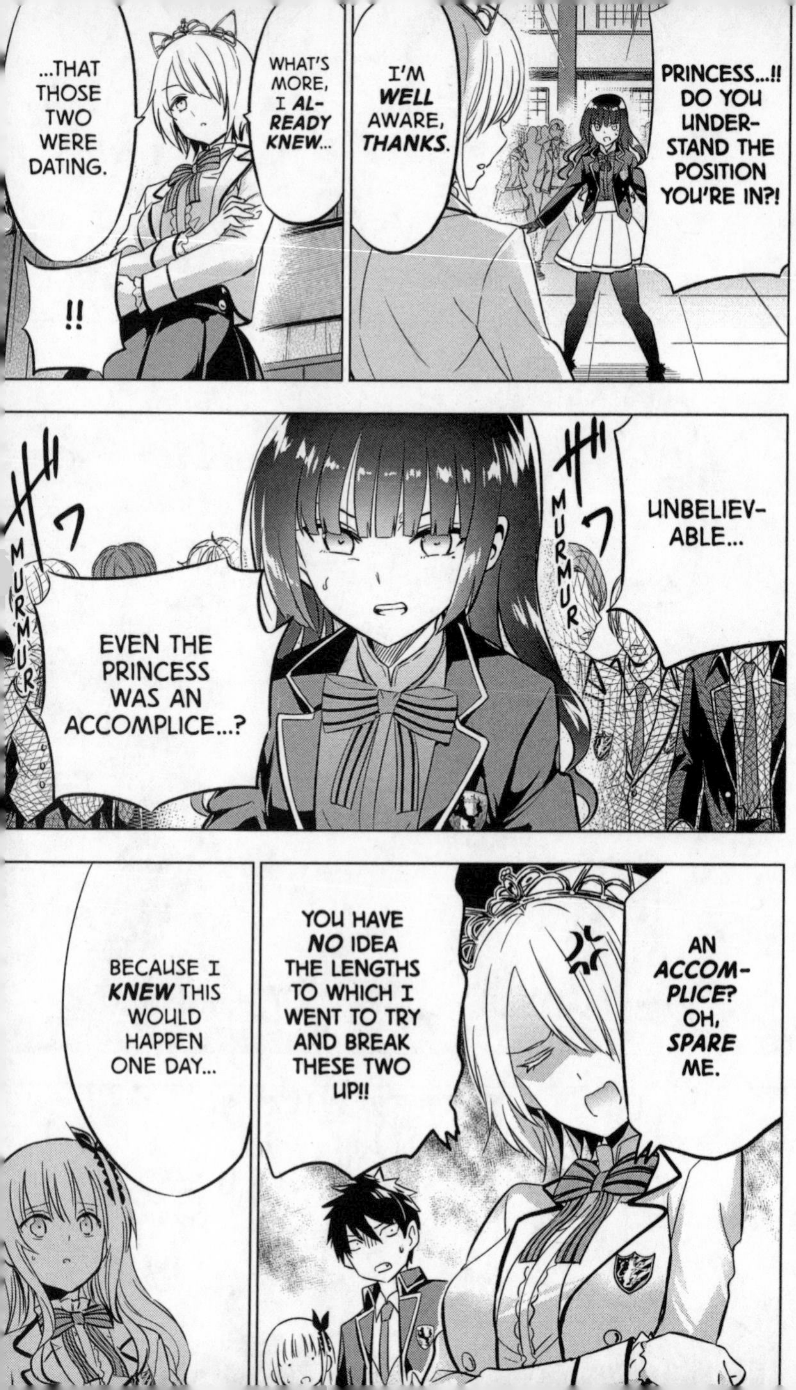
PRINCESS...!! DO YOU UNDERSTAND THE POSITION YOU'RE IN?!
I'M WELL AWARE, THANKS.
WHAT'S MORE, I ALREADY KNEW...
...THAT THOSE TWO WERE DATING.
!!
MURMUR
UNBELIEVABLE...
MURMUR
EVEN THE PRINCESS WAS AN ACCOMPLICE...?
AN ACCOMPLICE? OH, SPARE ME.
YOU HAVE NO IDEA THE LENGTHS TO WHICH I WENT TO TRY AND BREAK THESE TWO UP!!
BECAUSE I KNEW THIS WOULD HAPPEN ONE DAY...

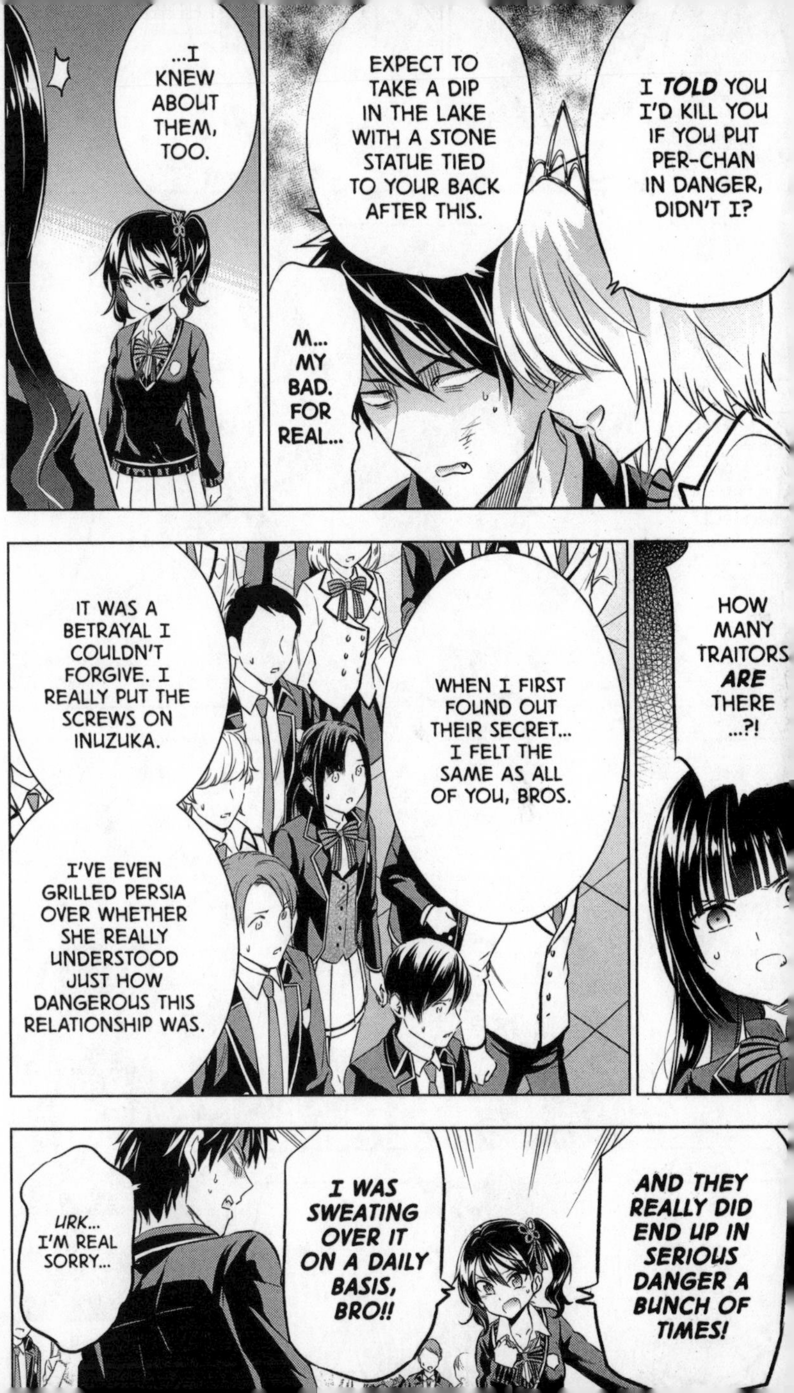
I *TOLD* YOU I'D KILL YOU IF YOU PUT PER-CHAN IN DANGER, DIDN'T I?
EXPECT TO TAKE A DIP IN THE LAKE WITH A STONE STATUE TIED TO YOUR BACK AFTER THIS.
M... MY BAD. FOR REAL...
...I KNEW ABOUT THEM, TOO.
HOW MANY TRAITORS *ARE* THERE ...?!
WHEN I FIRST FOUND OUT THEIR SECRET... I FELT THE SAME AS ALL OF YOU, BROS.
IT WAS A BETRAYAL I COULDN'T FORGIVE. I REALLY PUT THE SCREWS ON INUZUKA.
I'VE EVEN GRILLED PERSIA OVER WHETHER SHE REALLY UNDERSTOOD JUST HOW DANGEROUS THIS RELATIONSHIP WAS.
AND THEY REALLY DID END UP IN SERIOUS DANGER A BUNCH OF TIMES!
I WAS SWEATING OVER IT ON A DAILY BASIS, BRO!!
URK... I'M REAL SORRY...

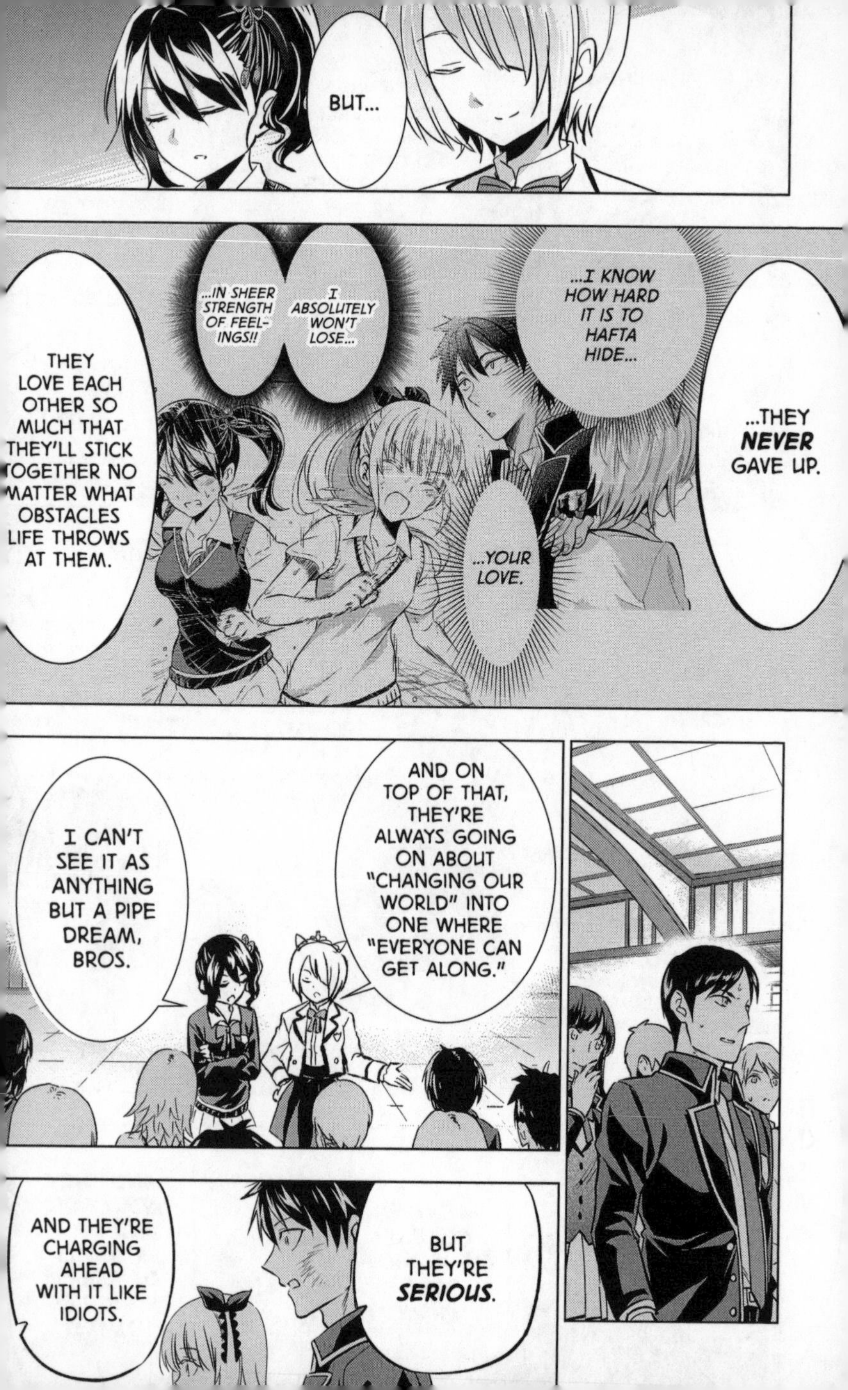
BUT...
...THEY NEVER GAVE UP.
...I KNOW HOW HARD IT IS TO HAFTA HIDE...
...YOUR LOVE.
I ABSOLUTELY WON'T LOSE...
...IN SHEER STRENGTH OF FEEL-INGS!!
THEY LOVE EACH OTHER SO MUCH THAT THEY'LL STICK TOGETHER NO MATTER WHAT OBSTACLES LIFE THROWS AT THEM.
AND ON TOP OF THAT, THEY'RE ALWAYS GOING ON ABOUT "CHANGING OUR WORLD" INTO ONE WHERE "EVERYONE CAN GET ALONG."
I CAN'T SEE IT AS ANYTHING BUT A PIPE DREAM, BROS.
BUT THEY'RE SERIOUS.
AND THEY'RE CHARGING AHEAD WITH IT LIKE IDIOTS.

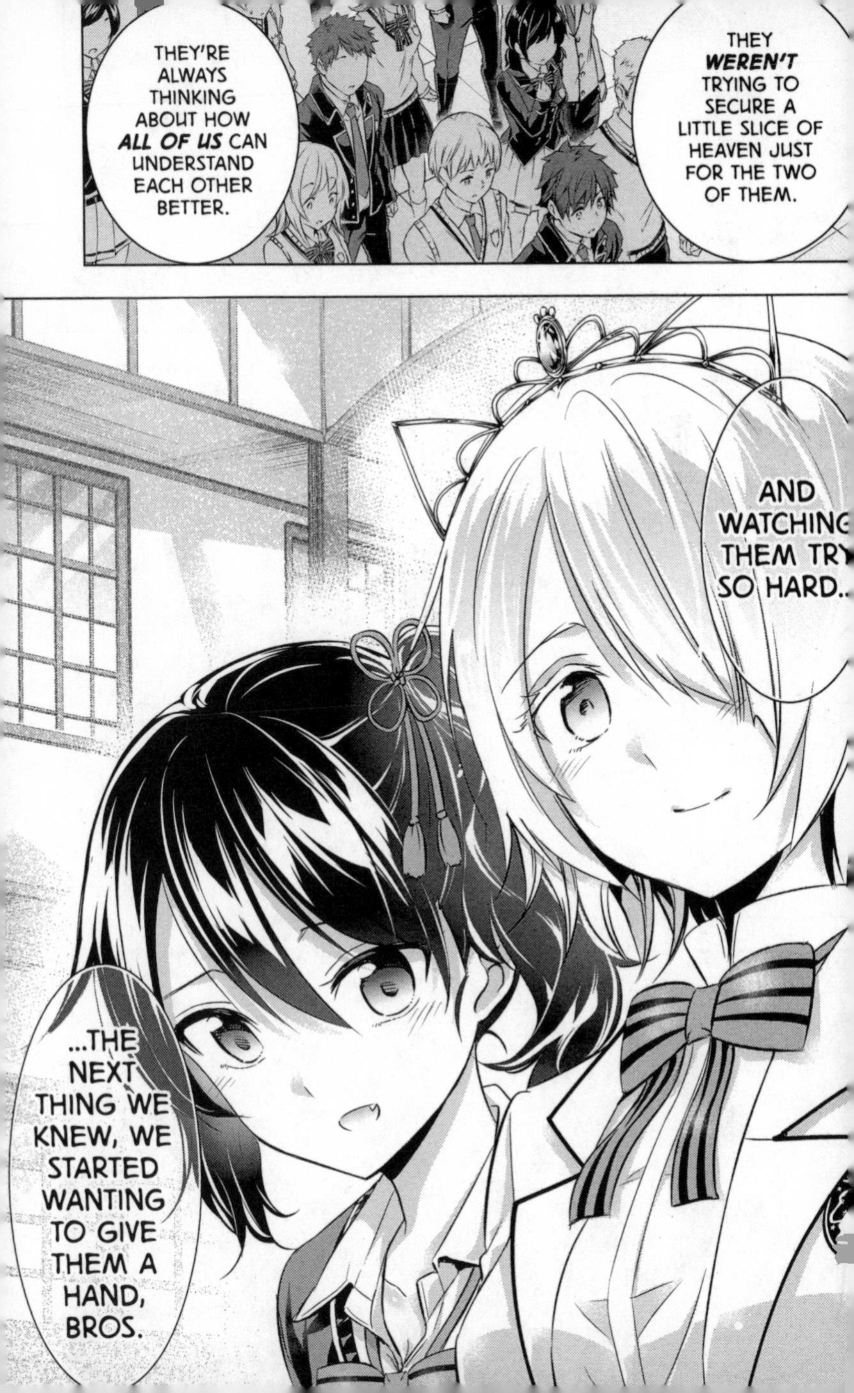
THEY WEREN'T TRYING TO SECURE A LITTLE SLICE OF HEAVEN JUST FOR THE TWO OF THEM.
THEY'RE ALWAYS THINKING ABOUT HOW ALL OF US CAN UNDERSTAND EACH OTHER BETTER.
AND WATCHING THEM TRY SO HARD...
...THE NEXT THING WE KNEW, WE STARTED WANTING TO GIVE THEM A HAND, BROS.

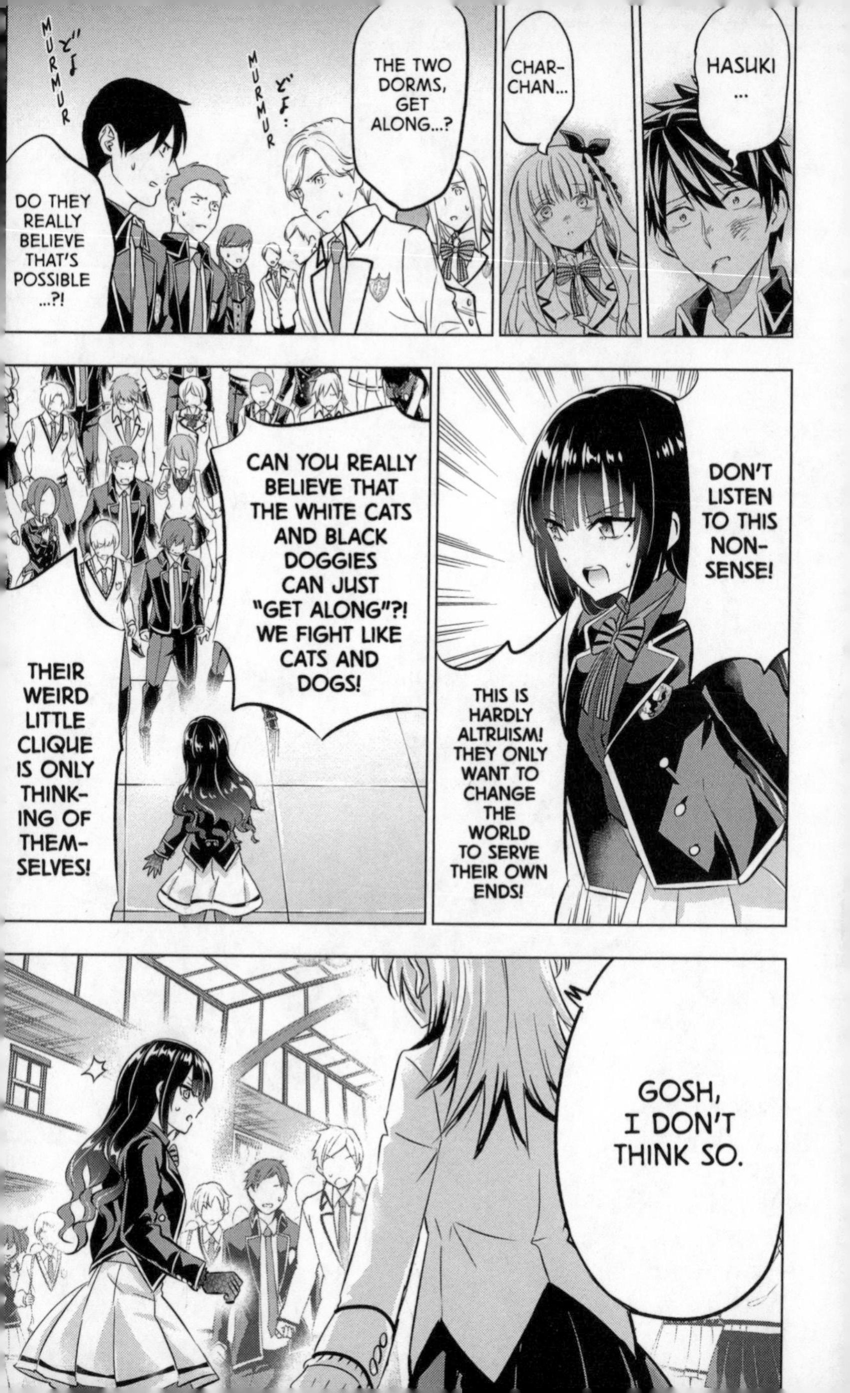
HASUKI ...
CHAR-CHAN...
THE TWO DORMS, GET ALONG...?
MURMUR
MURMUR
DO THEY REALLY BELIEVE THAT'S POSSIBLE ...?!
DON'T LISTEN TO THIS NON-SENSE!
THIS IS HARDLY ALTRUISM! THEY ONLY WANT TO CHANGE THE WORLD TO SERVE THEIR OWN ENDS!
CAN YOU REALLY BELIEVE THAT THE WHITE CATS AND BLACK DOGGIES CAN JUST "GET ALONG"?! WE FIGHT LIKE CATS AND DOGS!
THEIR WEIRD LITTLE CLIQUE IS ONLY THINKING OF THEMSELVES!
GOSH, I DON'T THINK SO.

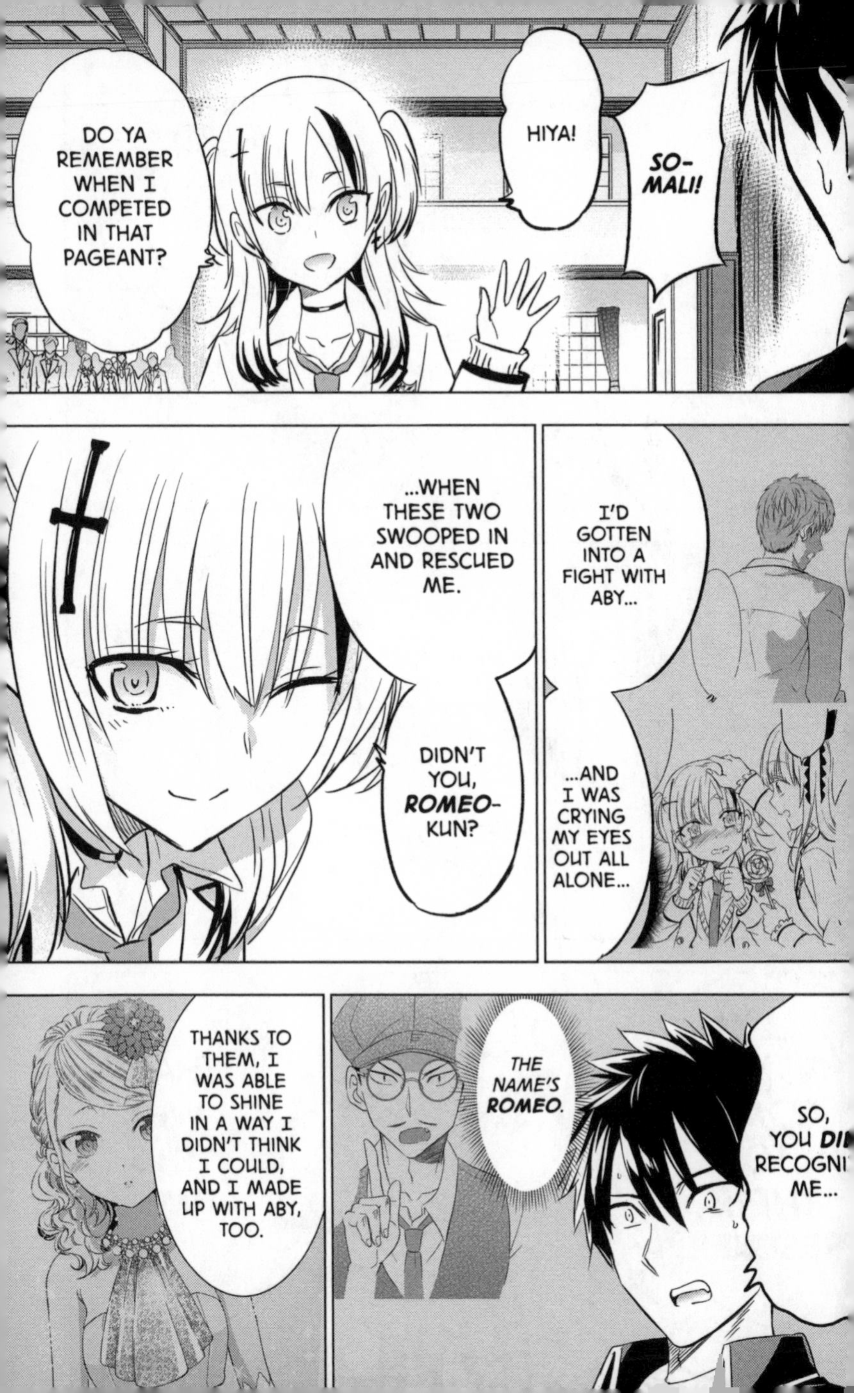
SO-MALI!
HIYA!
DO YA REMEMBER WHEN I COMPETED IN THAT PAGEANT?
I'D GOTTEN INTO A FIGHT WITH ABY...
...AND I WAS CRYING MY EYES OUT ALL ALONE...
...WHEN THESE TWO SWOOPED IN AND RESCUED ME.
DIDN'T YOU, ROMEO-KUN?
SO, YOU DI RECOGNI ME...
THE NAME'S ROMEO.
THANKS TO THEM, I WAS ABLE TO SHINE IN A WAY I DIDN'T THINK I COULD, AND I MADE UP WITH ABY, TOO.

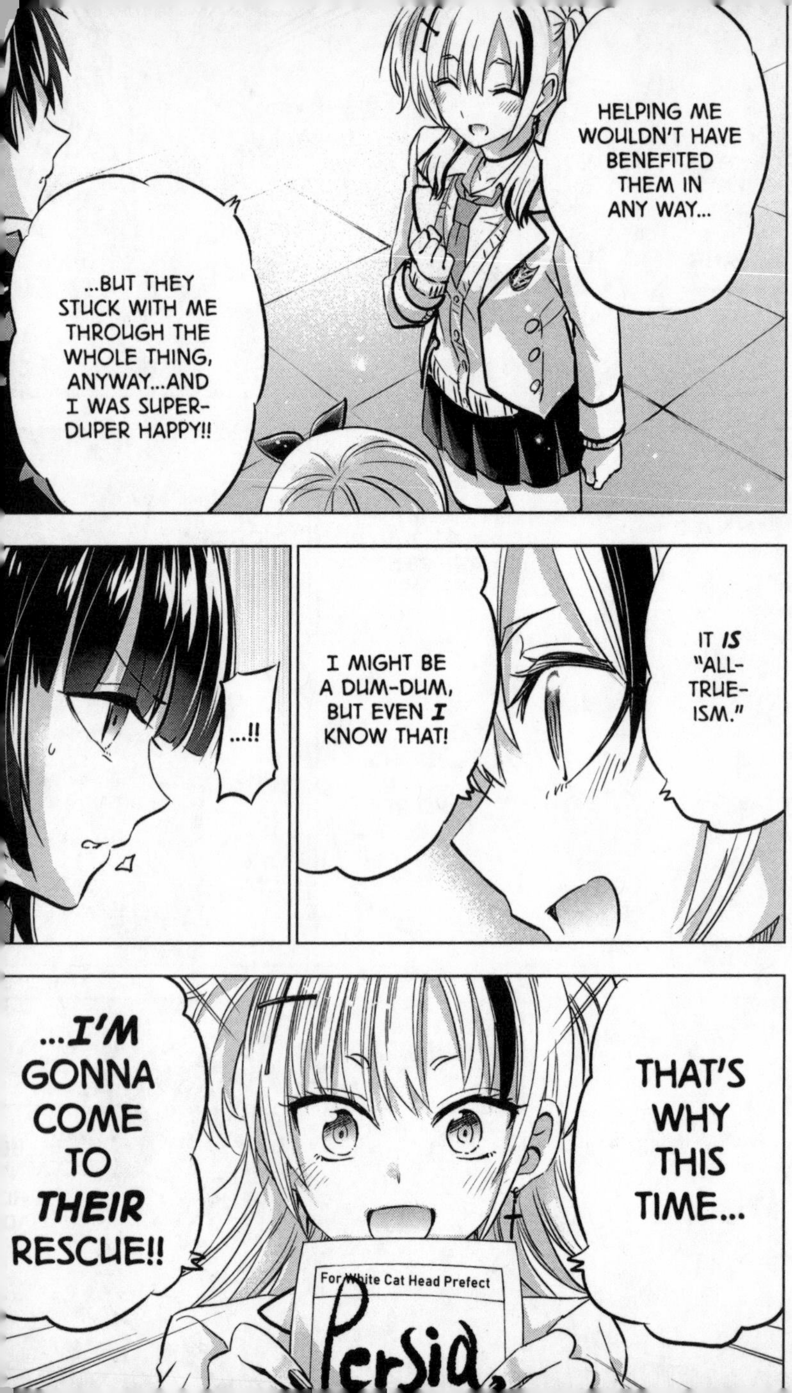
HELPING ME WOULDN'T HAVE BENEFITED THEM IN ANY WAY...
...BUT THEY STUCK WITH ME THROUGH THE WHOLE THING, ANYWAY...AND I WAS SUPER-DUPER HAPPY!!
IT *IS* "ALL-TRUE-ISM."
I MIGHT BE A DUM-DUM, BUT EVEN *I* KNOW THAT!
...!!
THAT'S WHY THIS TIME...
...*I'M* GONNA COME TO *THEIR* RESCUE!!
For White Cat Head Prefect
Persia,

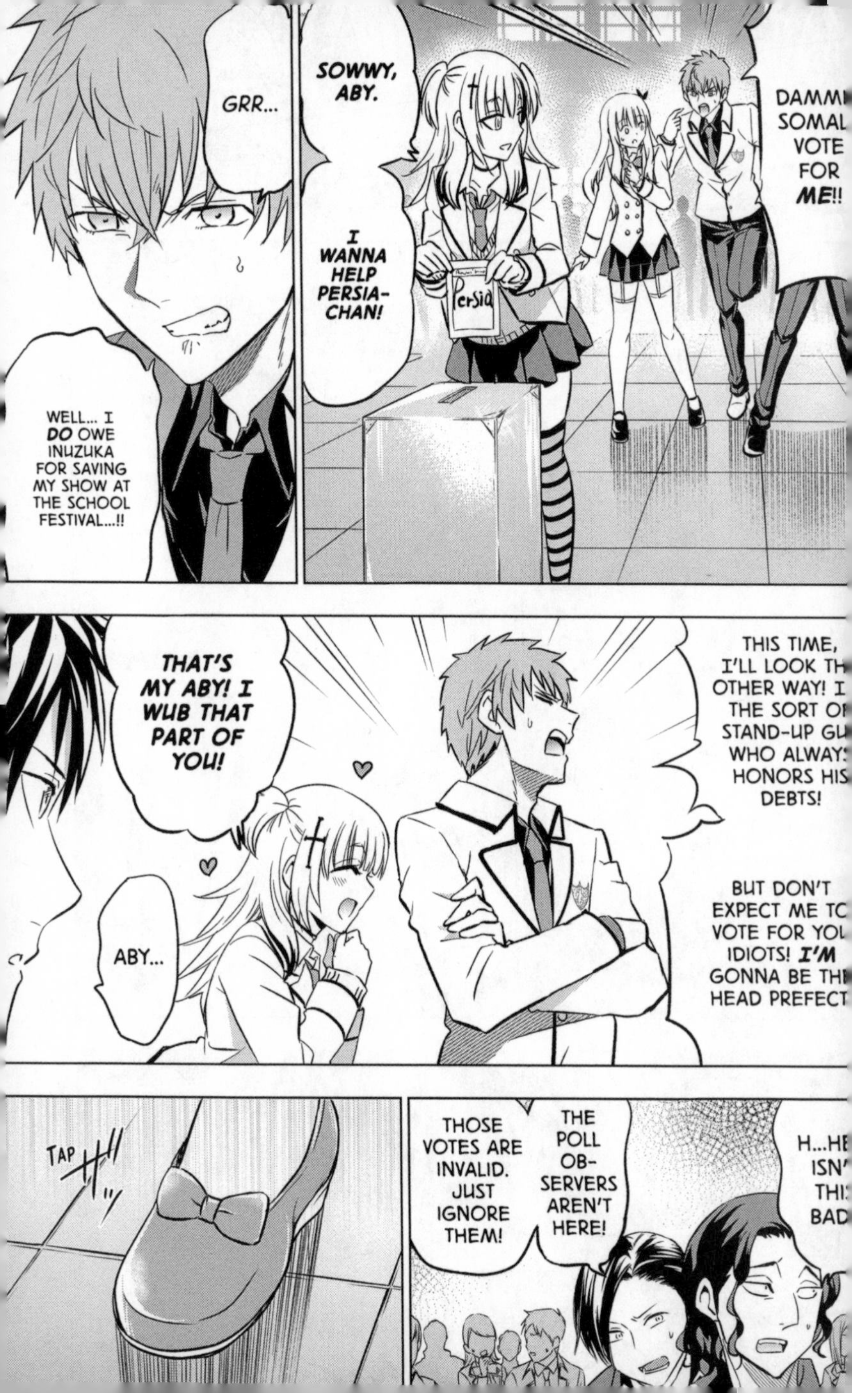
DAMM SOMAL VOTE FOR ME!!
SOWWY, ABY.
I WANNA HELP PERSIA-CHAN!
Persia
GRR...
WELL... I DO OWE INUZUKA FOR SAVING MY SHOW AT THE SCHOOL FESTIVAL...!!
THIS TIME, I'LL LOOK TH OTHER WAY! I THE SORT OF STAND-UP GU WHO ALWAY HONORS HIS DEBTS!
BUT DON'T EXPECT ME TO VOTE FOR YO IDIOTS! I'M GONNA BE TH HEAD PREFECT
THAT'S MY ABY! I WUB THAT PART OF YOU!
ABY...
H...HE ISN' THI BAD
THE POLL OB-SERVERS AREN'T HERE!
THOSE VOTES ARE INVALID. JUST IGNORE THEM!
TAP

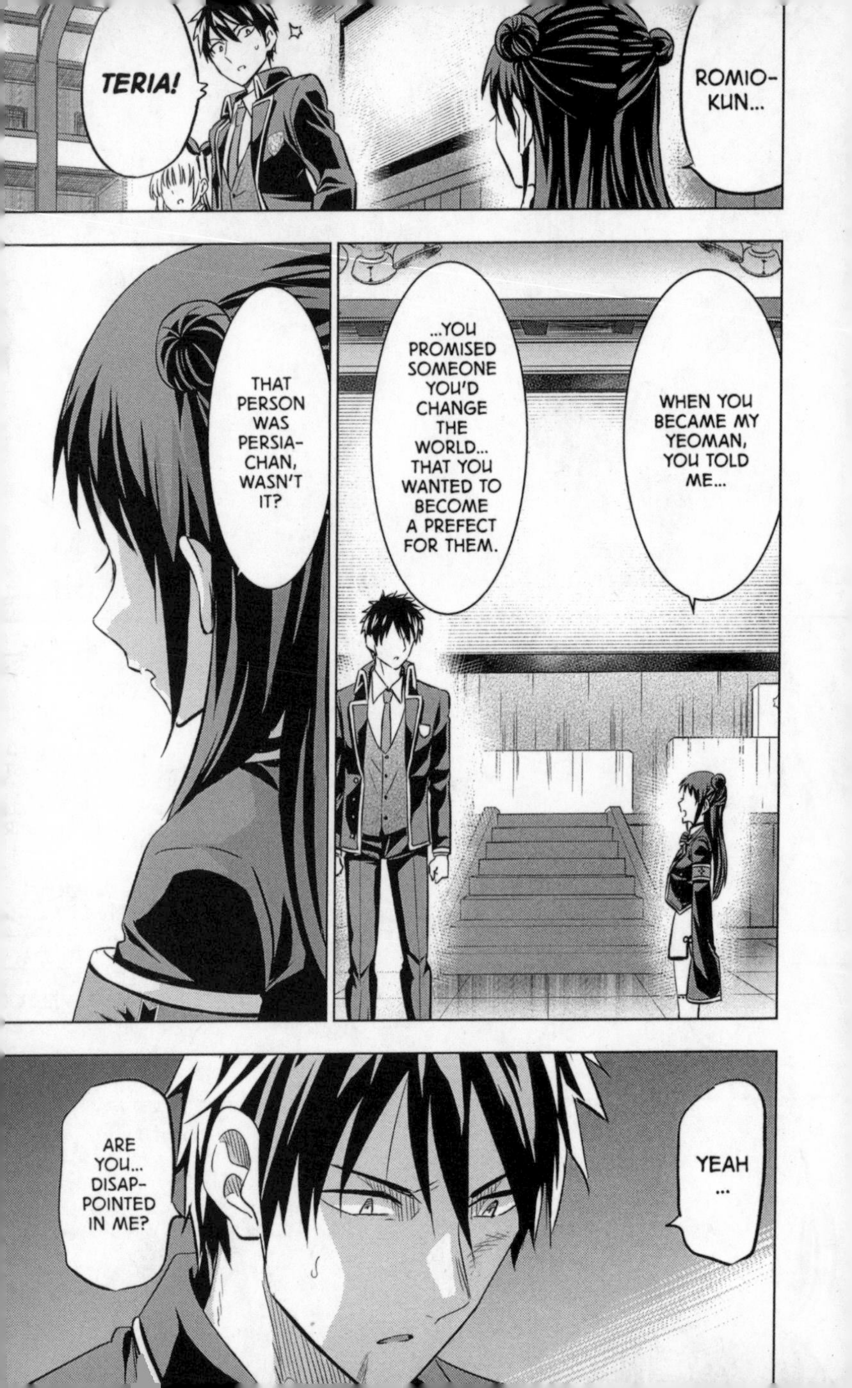
ROMIO-KUN...
TERIA!
WHEN YOU BECAME MY YEOMAN, YOU TOLD ME...
...YOU PROMISED SOMEONE YOU'D CHANGE THE WORLD... THAT YOU WANTED TO BECOME A PREFECT FOR THEM.
THAT PERSON WAS PERSIA-CHAN, WASN'T IT?
YEAH ...
ARE YOU... DISAP-POINTED IN ME?

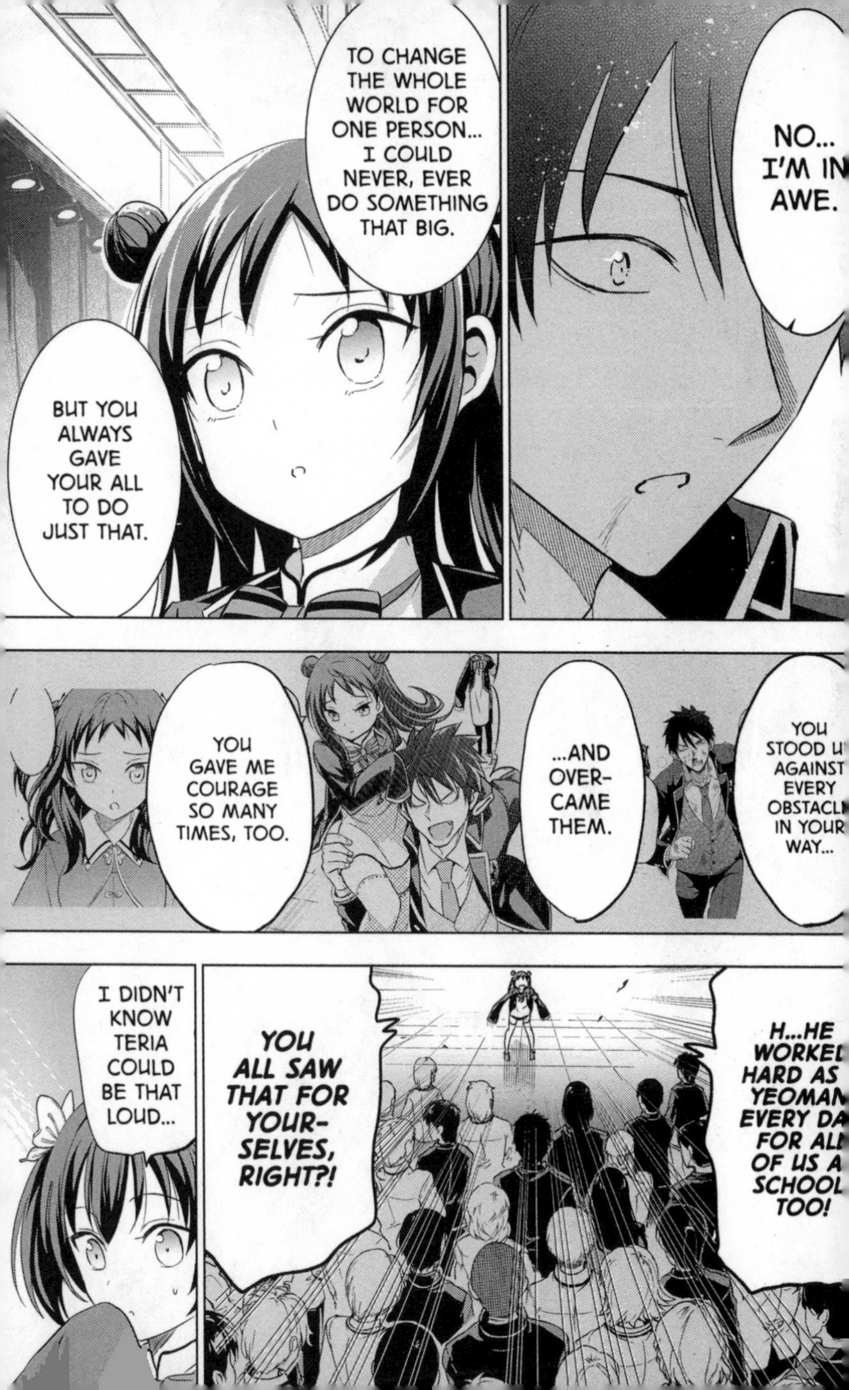
NO... I'M IN AWE.
TO CHANGE THE WHOLE WORLD FOR ONE PERSON... I COULD NEVER, EVER DO SOMETHING THAT BIG.
BUT YOU ALWAYS GAVE YOUR ALL TO DO JUST THAT.
YOU STOOD U AGAINST EVERY OBSTACL IN YOUR WAY...
...AND OVER-CAME THEM.
YOU GAVE ME COURAGE SO MANY TIMES, TOO.
H...HE WORKE HARD AS YEOMAN EVERY DA FOR AL OF US A SCHOOL TOO!
YOU ALL SAW THAT FOR YOUR-SELVES, RIGHT?!
I DIDN'T KNOW TERIA COULD BE THAT LOUD...

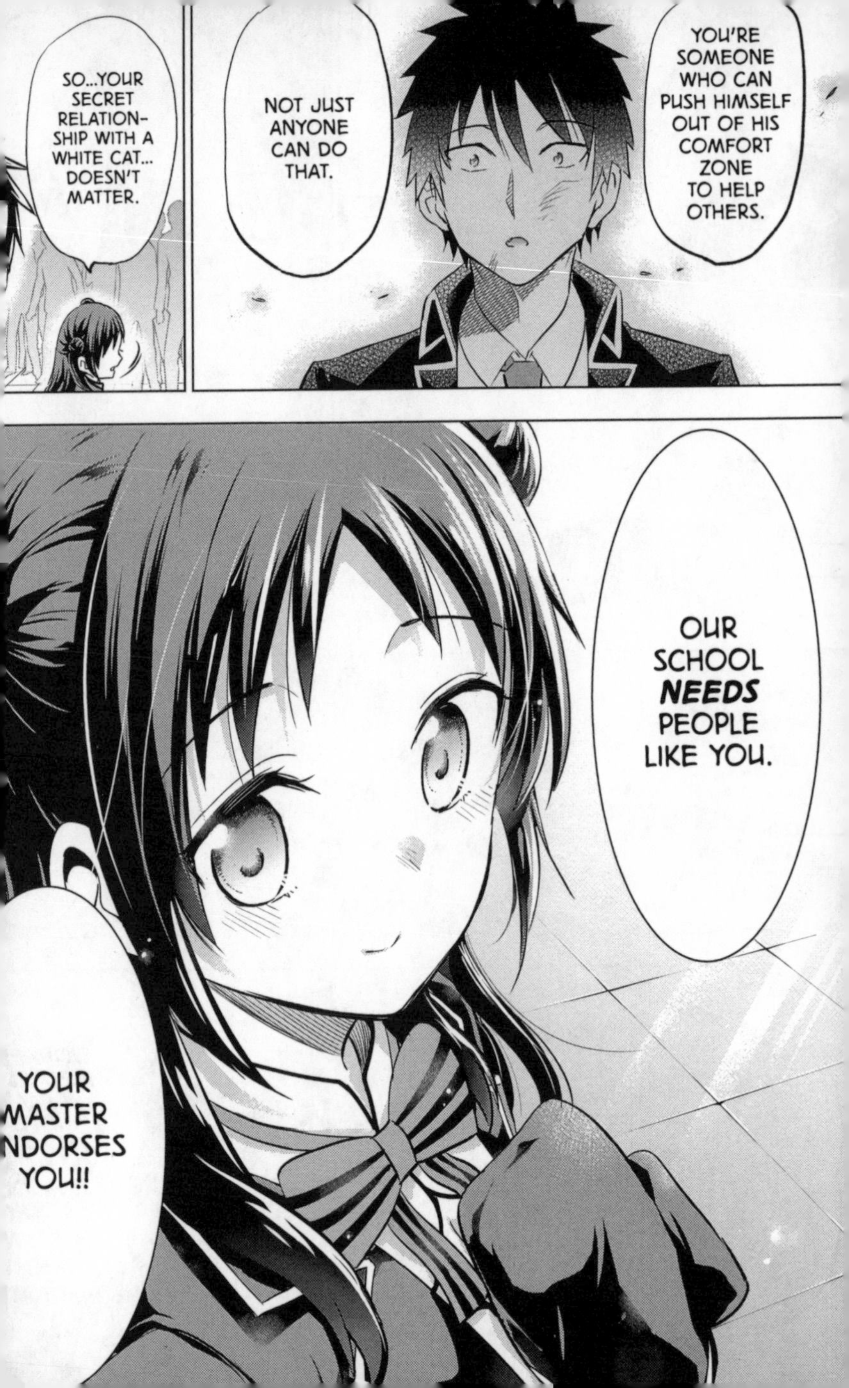
YOU'RE SOMEONE WHO CAN PUSH HIMSELF OUT OF HIS COMFORT ZONE TO HELP OTHERS.
NOT JUST ANYONE CAN DO THAT.
SO...YOUR SECRET RELATION-SHIP WITH A WHITE CAT... DOESN'T MATTER.
OUR SCHOOL ***NEEDS*** PEOPLE LIKE YOU.
YOUR MASTER NDORSES YOU!!

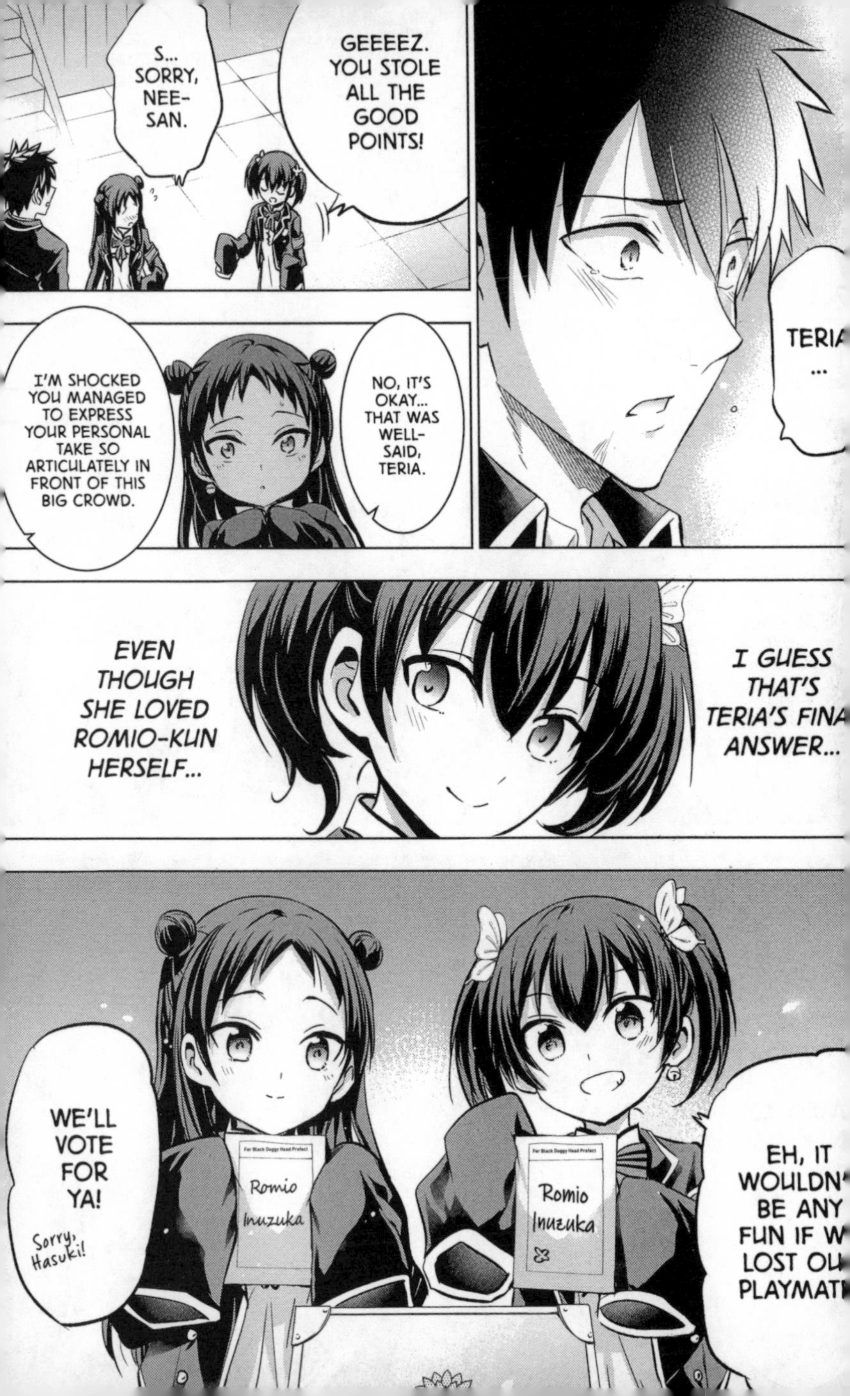
TERIA ...
GEEEEZ. YOU STOLE ALL THE GOOD POINTS!
S... SORRY, NEE-SAN.
NO, IT'S OKAY... THAT WAS WELL-SAID, TERIA.
I'M SHOCKED YOU MANAGED TO EXPRESS YOUR PERSONAL TAKE SO ARTICULATELY IN FRONT OF THIS BIG CROWD.
I GUESS THAT'S TERIA'S FINA ANSWER...
EVEN THOUGH SHE LOVED ROMIO-KUN HERSELF...
EH, IT WOULDN' BE ANY FUN IF W LOST OU PLAYMAT
For Black Doggy Head Prefect
Romio Inuzuka
WE'LL VOTE FOR YA!
Sorry, Hasuki!
For Black Doggy Head Prefect
Romio Inuzuka

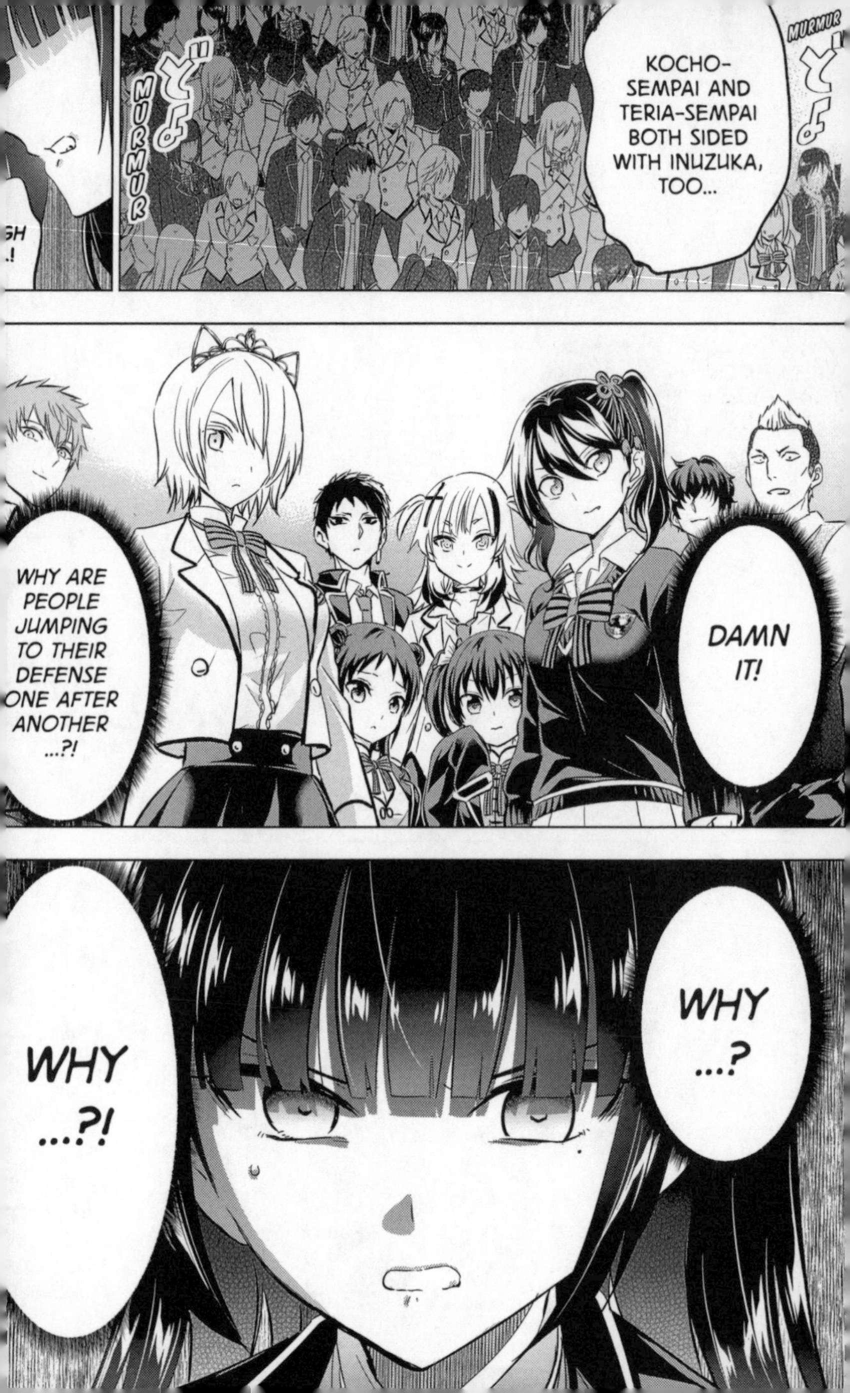
MURMUR
KOCHO-SEMPAI AND TERIA-SEMPAI BOTH SIDED WITH INUZUKA, TOO...
MURMUR
DAMN IT!
WHY ARE PEOPLE JUMPING TO THEIR DEFENSE ONE AFTER ANOTHER ...?!
WHY ...?
WHY ...?!

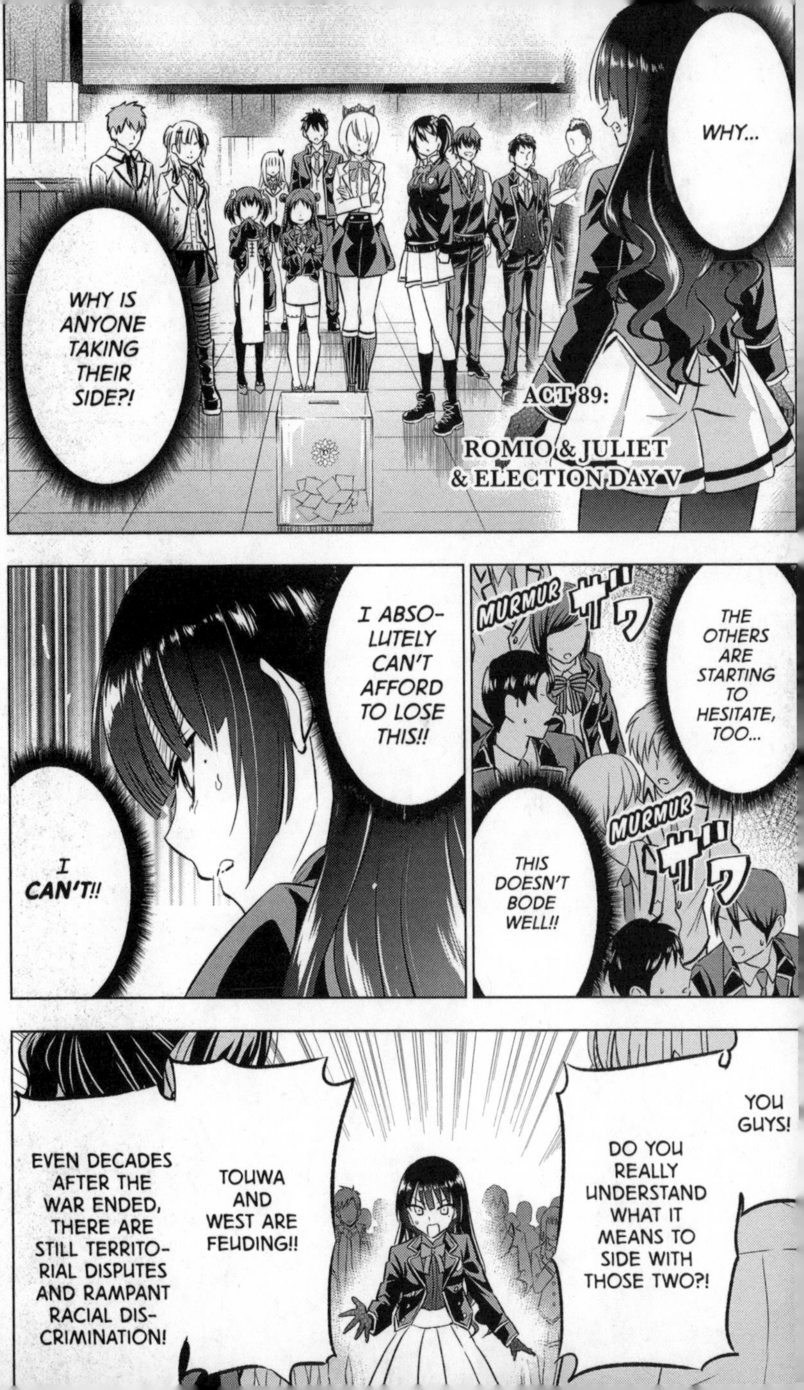
WHY...
WHY IS ANYONE TAKING THEIR SIDE?!
ACT 89:
ROMIO & JULIET & ELECTION DAY V
MURMUR ザワ
THE OTHERS ARE STARTING TO HESITATE, TOO...
THIS DOESN'T BODE WELL!!
MURMUR ザワ
I ABSOLUTELY CAN'T AFFORD TO LOSE THIS!!
I CAN'T!!
YOU GUYS!
DO YOU REALLY UNDERSTAND WHAT IT MEANS TO SIDE WITH THOSE TWO?!
TOUWA AND WEST ARE FEUDING!!
EVEN DECADES AFTER THE WAR ENDED, THERE ARE STILL TERRITORIAL DISPUTES AND RAMPANT RACIAL DISCRIMINATION!

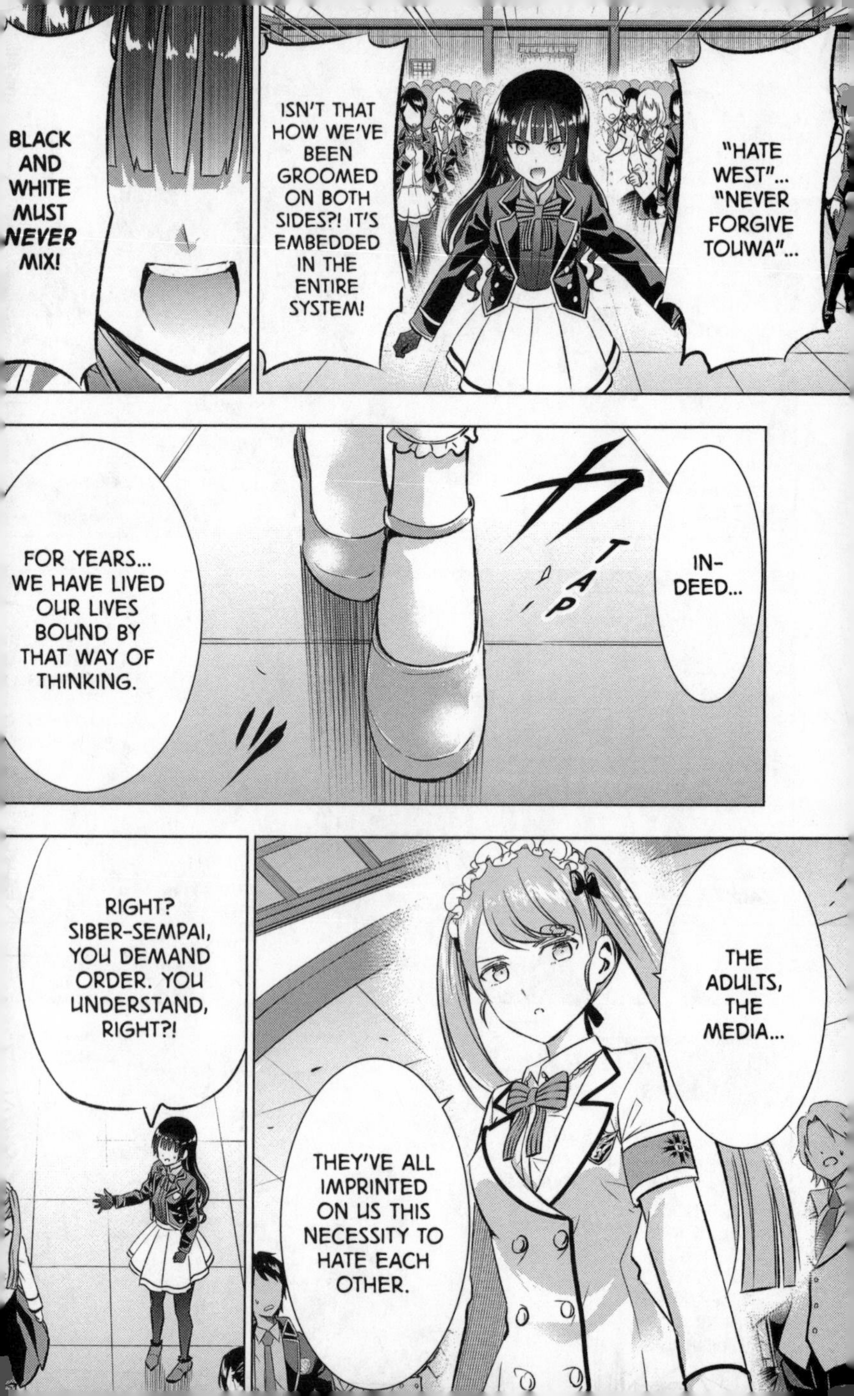
"HATE WEST"... "NEVER FORGIVE TOUWA"...
ISN'T THAT HOW WE'VE BEEN GROOMED ON BOTH SIDES?! IT'S EMBEDDED IN THE ENTIRE SYSTEM!
BLACK AND WHITE MUST NEVER MIX!
IN-DEED...
TAP
FOR YEARS... WE HAVE LIVED OUR LIVES BOUND BY THAT WAY OF THINKING.
THE ADULTS, THE MEDIA...
THEY'VE ALL IMPRINTED ON US THIS NECESSITY TO HATE EACH OTHER.
RIGHT? SIBER-SEMPAI, YOU DEMAND ORDER. YOU UNDERSTAND, RIGHT?!

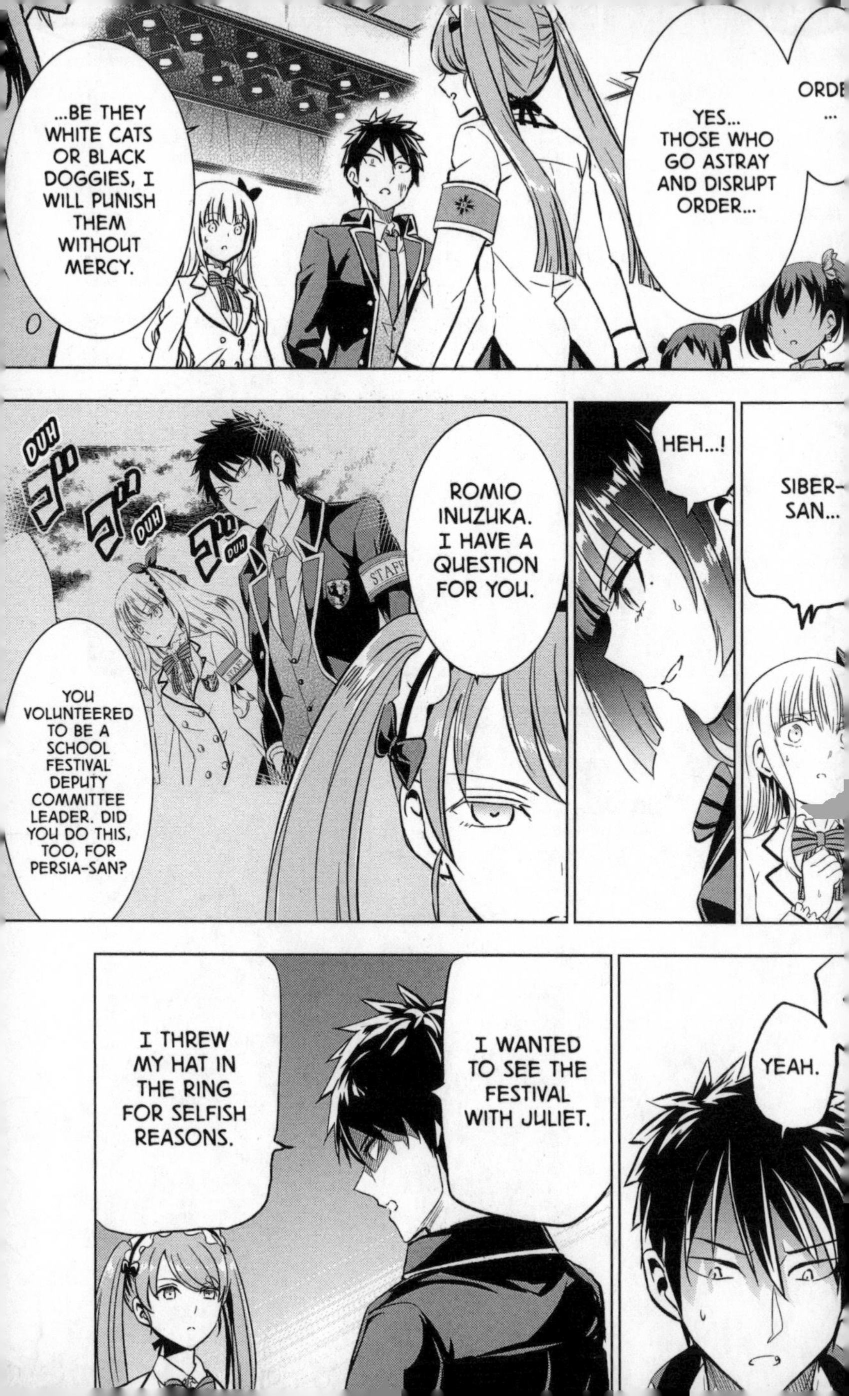
ORDE ...
YES... THOSE WHO GO ASTRAY AND DISRUPT ORDER...
...BE THEY WHITE CATS OR BLACK DOGGIES, I WILL PUNISH THEM WITHOUT MERCY.
SIBER-SAN...
HEH...!
ROMIO INUZUKA. I HAVE A QUESTION FOR YOU.
DUH
DUH
DUH
YOU VOLUNTEERED TO BE A SCHOOL FESTIVAL DEPUTY COMMITTEE LEADER. DID YOU DO THIS, TOO, FOR PERSIA-SAN?
YEAH.
I WANTED TO SEE THE FESTIVAL WITH JULIET.
I THREW MY HAT IN THE RING FOR SELFISH REASONS.

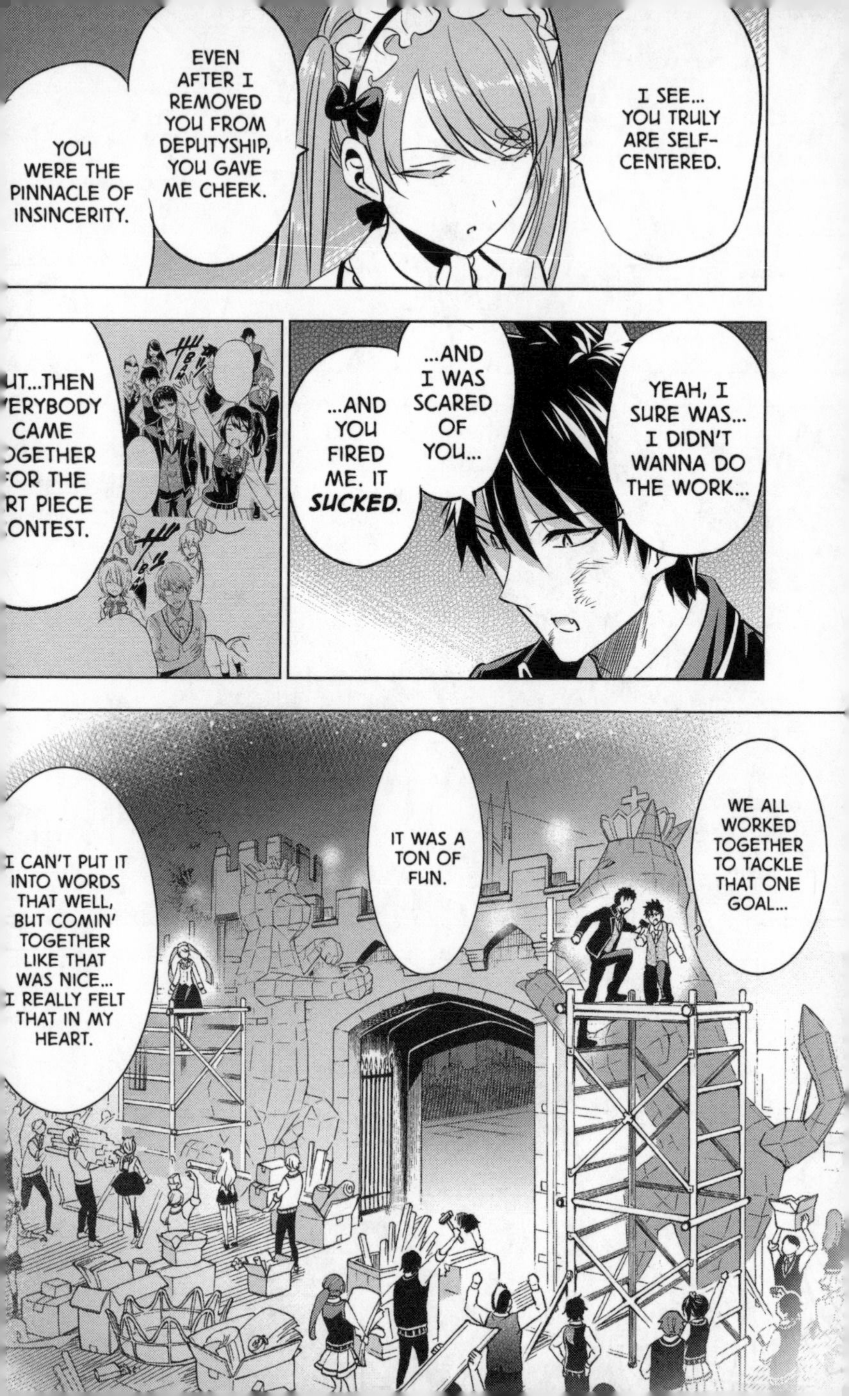
I SEE... YOU TRULY ARE SELF-CENTERED.
EVEN AFTER I REMOVED YOU FROM DEPUTYSHIP, YOU GAVE ME CHEEK.
YOU WERE THE PINNACLE OF INSINCERITY.
YEAH, I SURE WAS... I DIDN'T WANNA DO THE WORK...
...AND I WAS SCARED OF YOU...
...AND YOU FIRED ME. IT *SUCKED.*
UT...THEN ERYBODY CAME OGETHER FOR THE RT PIECE ONTEST.
WE ALL WORKED TOGETHER TO TACKLE THAT ONE GOAL...
IT WAS A TON OF FUN.
I CAN'T PUT IT INTO WORDS THAT WELL, BUT COMIN' TOGETHER LIKE THAT WAS NICE... I REALLY FELT THAT IN MY HEART.

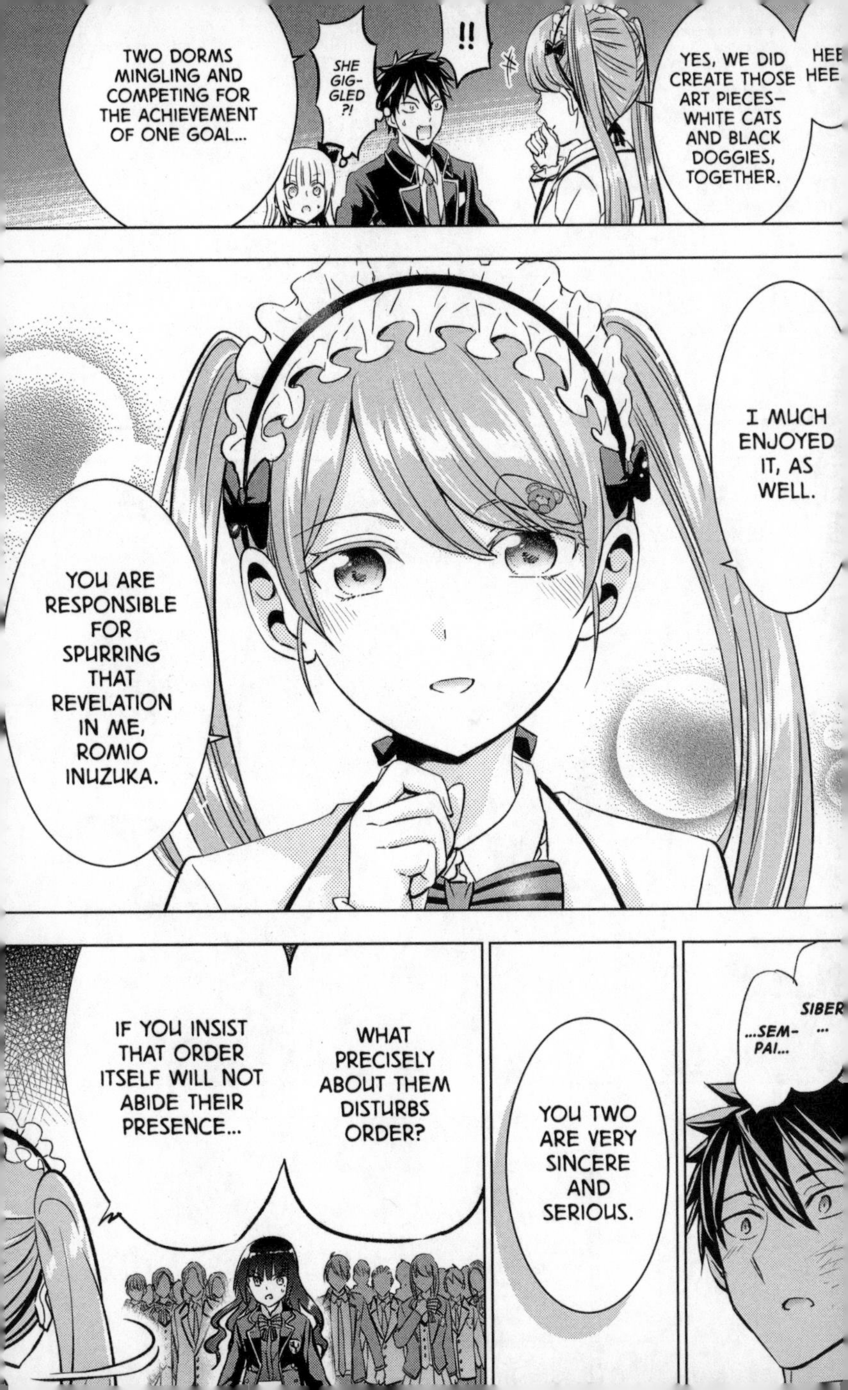
HEE HEE
YES, WE DID CREATE THOSE ART PIECES—WHITE CATS AND BLACK DOGGIES, TOGETHER.
!!
SHE GIGGLED ?!
TWO DORMS MINGLING AND COMPETING FOR THE ACHIEVEMENT OF ONE GOAL...
I MUCH ENJOYED IT, AS WELL.
YOU ARE RESPONSIBLE FOR SPURRING THAT REVELATION IN ME, ROMIO INUZUKA.
SIBER ...
...SEM-PAI...
YOU TWO ARE VERY SINCERE AND SERIOUS.
WHAT PRECISELY ABOUT THEM DISTURBS ORDER?
IF YOU INSIST THAT ORDER ITSELF WILL NOT ABIDE THEIR PRESENCE...

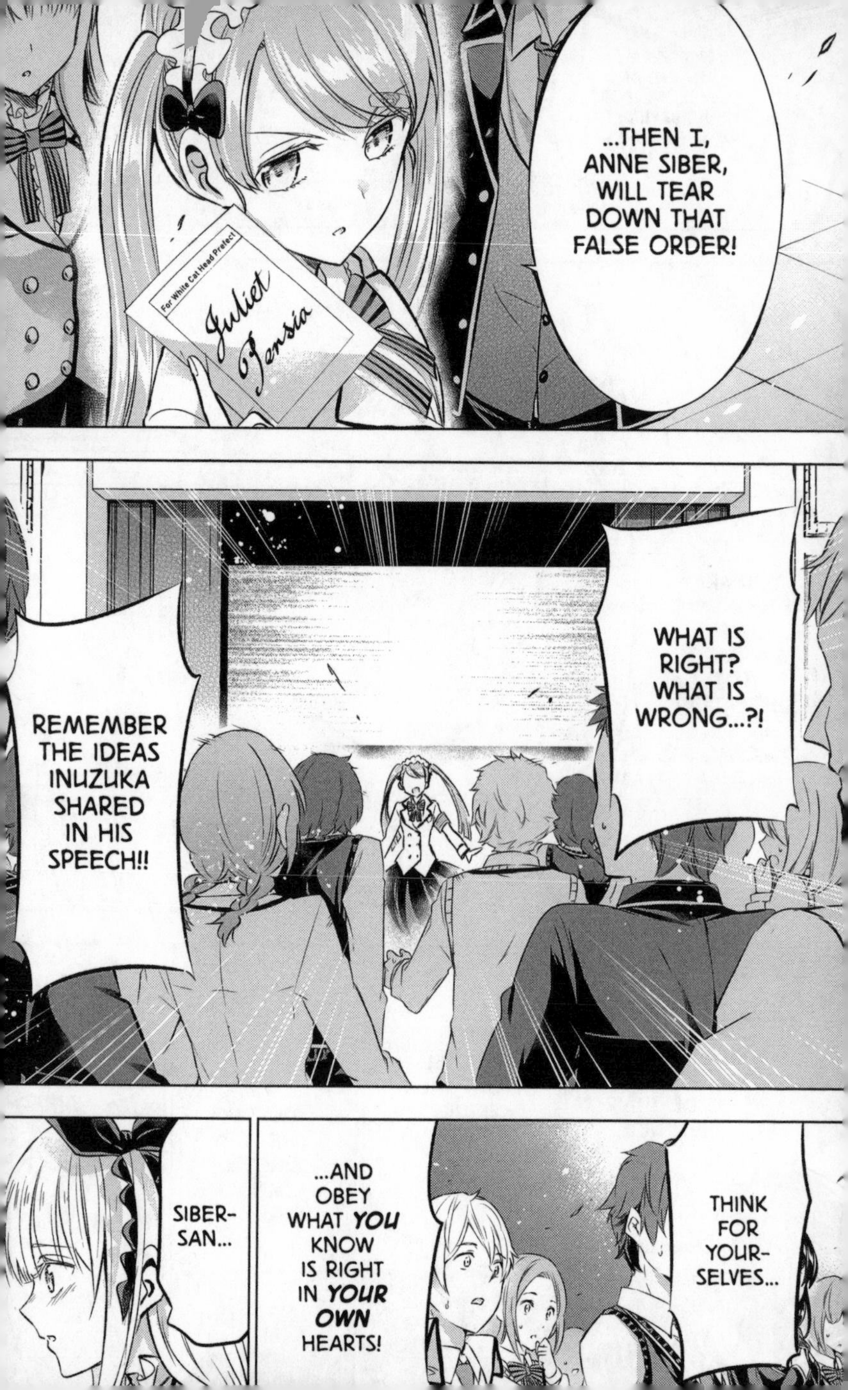
...THEN I, ANNE SIBER, WILL TEAR DOWN THAT FALSE ORDER!
For White Cat Head Prefect
Juliet Persia
WHAT IS RIGHT? WHAT IS WRONG...?!
REMEMBER THE IDEAS INUZUKA SHARED IN HIS SPEECH!!
THINK FOR YOUR-SELVES...
...AND OBEY WHAT *YOU* KNOW IS RIGHT IN *YOUR OWN* HEARTS!
SIBER-SAN...

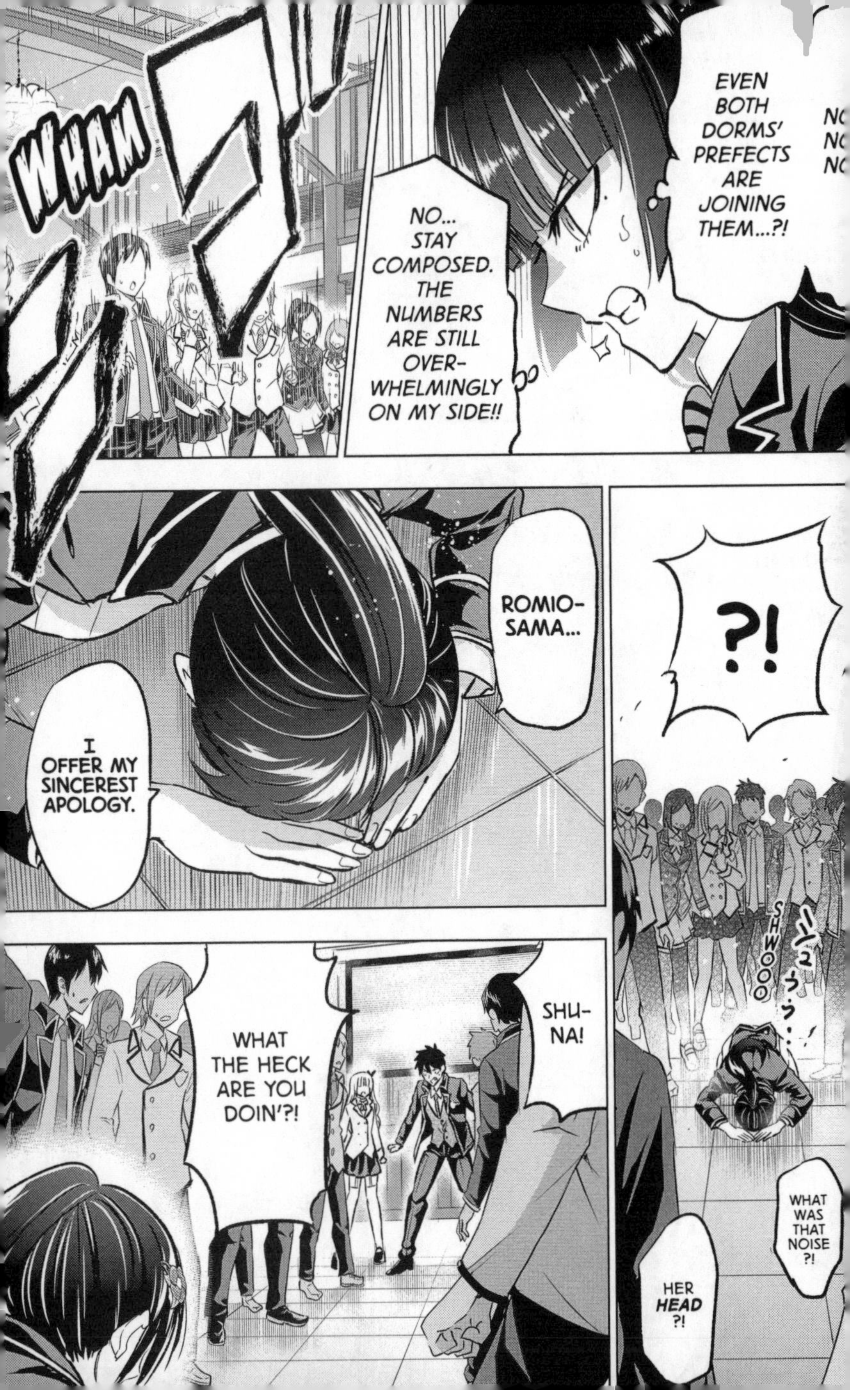
EVEN BOTH DORMS' PREFECTS ARE JOINING THEM...?!
NO... STAY COMPOSED. THE NUMBERS ARE STILL OVER-WHELMINGLY ON MY SIDE!!
WHAM
?!
SHWOOO
WHAT WAS THAT NOISE ?!
HER HEAD ?!
ROMIO-SAMA...
I OFFER MY SINCEREST APOLOGY.
SHU-NA!
WHAT THE HECK ARE YOU DOIN'?!

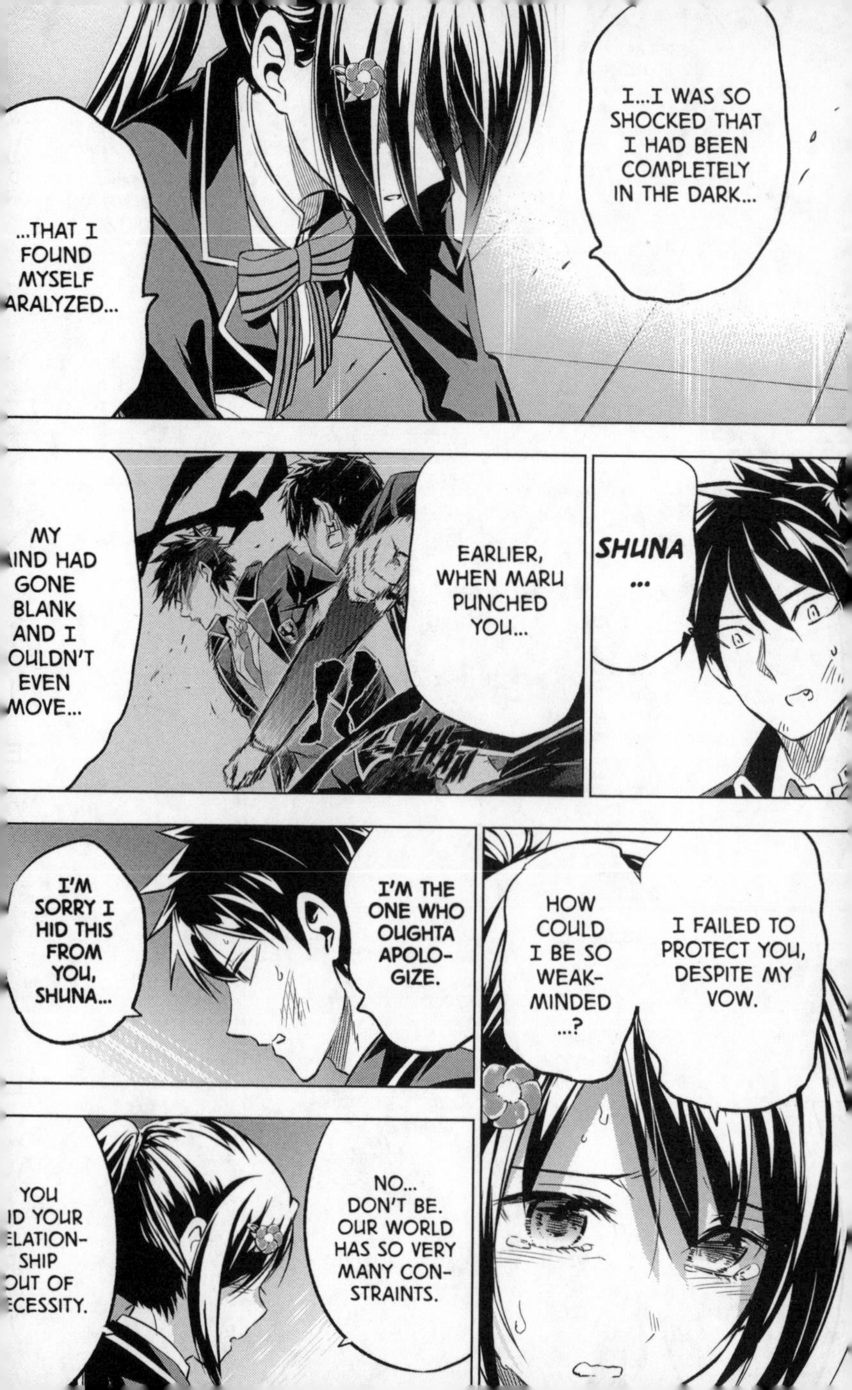
I...I WAS SO SHOCKED THAT I HAD BEEN COMPLETELY IN THE DARK...
...THAT I FOUND MYSELF ARALYZED...
SHUNA ...
EARLIER, WHEN MARU PUNCHED YOU...
MY IND HAD GONE BLANK AND I OULDN'T EVEN MOVE...
I FAILED TO PROTECT YOU, DESPITE MY VOW.
HOW COULD I BE SO WEAK-MINDED ...?
I'M THE ONE WHO OUGHTA APOLO-GIZE.
I'M SORRY I HID THIS FROM YOU, SHUNA...
NO... DON'T BE. OUR WORLD HAS SO VERY MANY CON-STRAINTS.
YOU ID YOUR ELATION-SHIP UT OF ECESSITY.

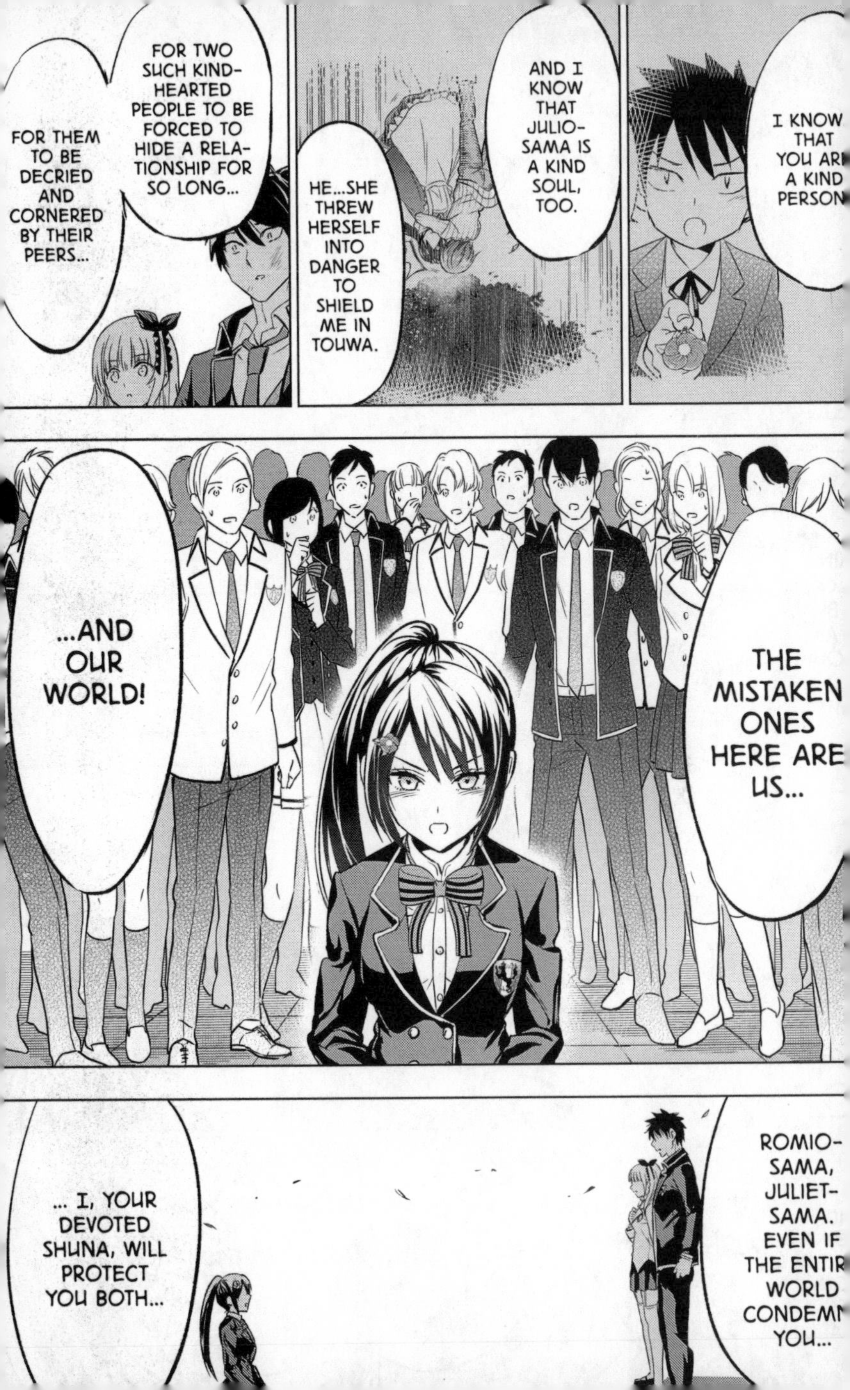
I KNOW THAT YOU AR A KIND PERSON
AND I KNOW THAT JULIO-SAMA IS A KIND SOUL, TOO.
HE...SHE THREW HERSELF INTO DANGER TO SHIELD ME IN TOUWA.
FOR TWO SUCH KIND-HEARTED PEOPLE TO BE FORCED TO HIDE A RELA-TIONSHIP FOR SO LONG...
FOR THEM TO BE DECRIED AND CORNERED BY THEIR PEERS...
THE MISTAKEN ONES HERE ARE US...
...AND OUR WORLD!
ROMIO-SAMA, JULIET-SAMA. EVEN IF THE ENTIR WORLD CONDEMN YOU...
... I, YOUR DEVOTED SHUNA, WILL PROTECT YOU BOTH...

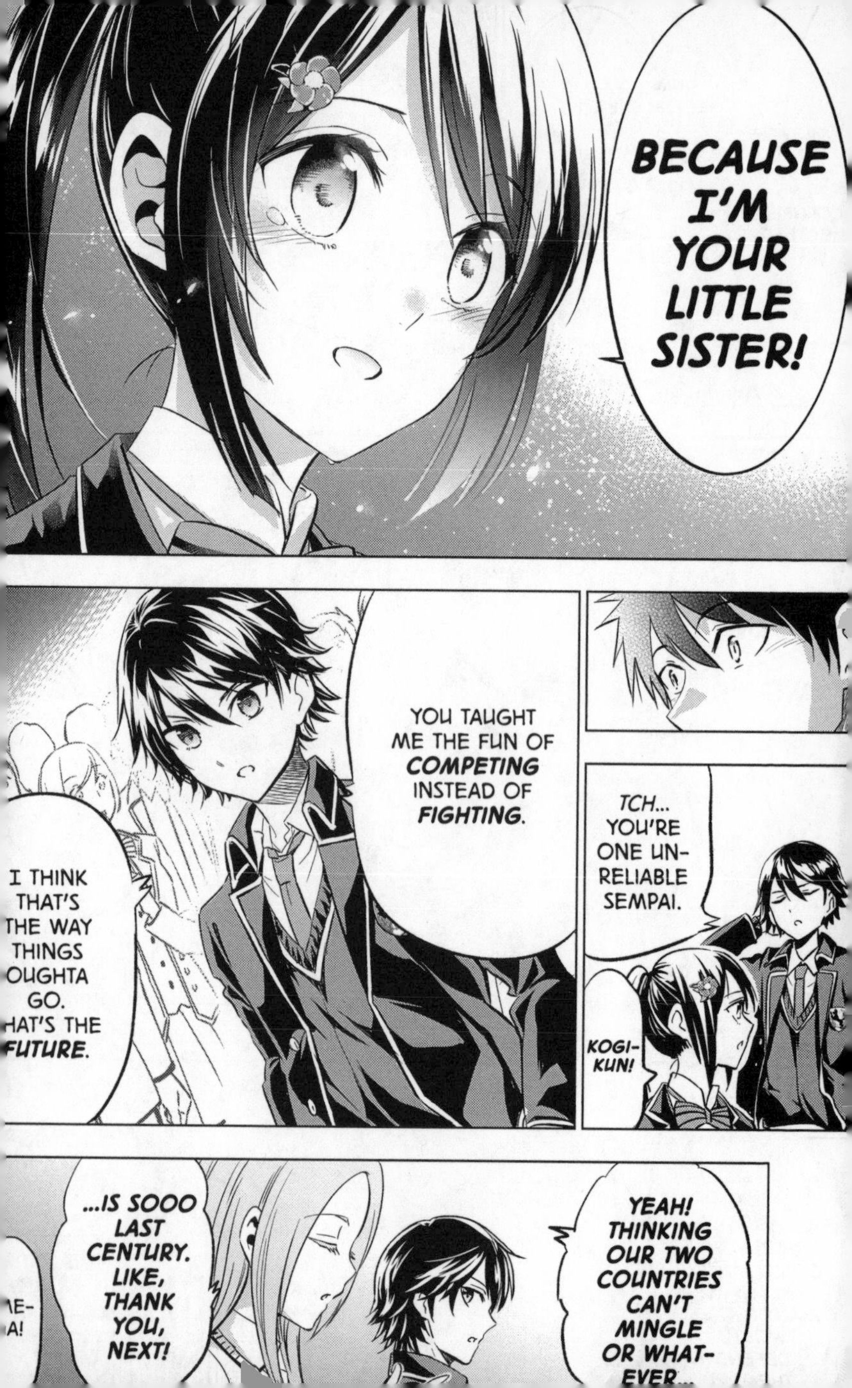
BECAUSE I'M YOUR LITTLE SISTER!
TCH... YOU'RE ONE UN-RELIABLE SEMPAI.
KOGI-KUN!
YOU TAUGHT ME THE FUN OF COMPETING INSTEAD OF FIGHTING.
I THINK THAT'S THE WAY THINGS OUGHTA GO. HAT'S THE FUTURE.
YEAH! THINKING OUR TWO COUNTRIES CAN'T MINGLE OR WHAT-EVER...
...IS SOOO LAST CENTURY. LIKE, THANK YOU, NEXT!

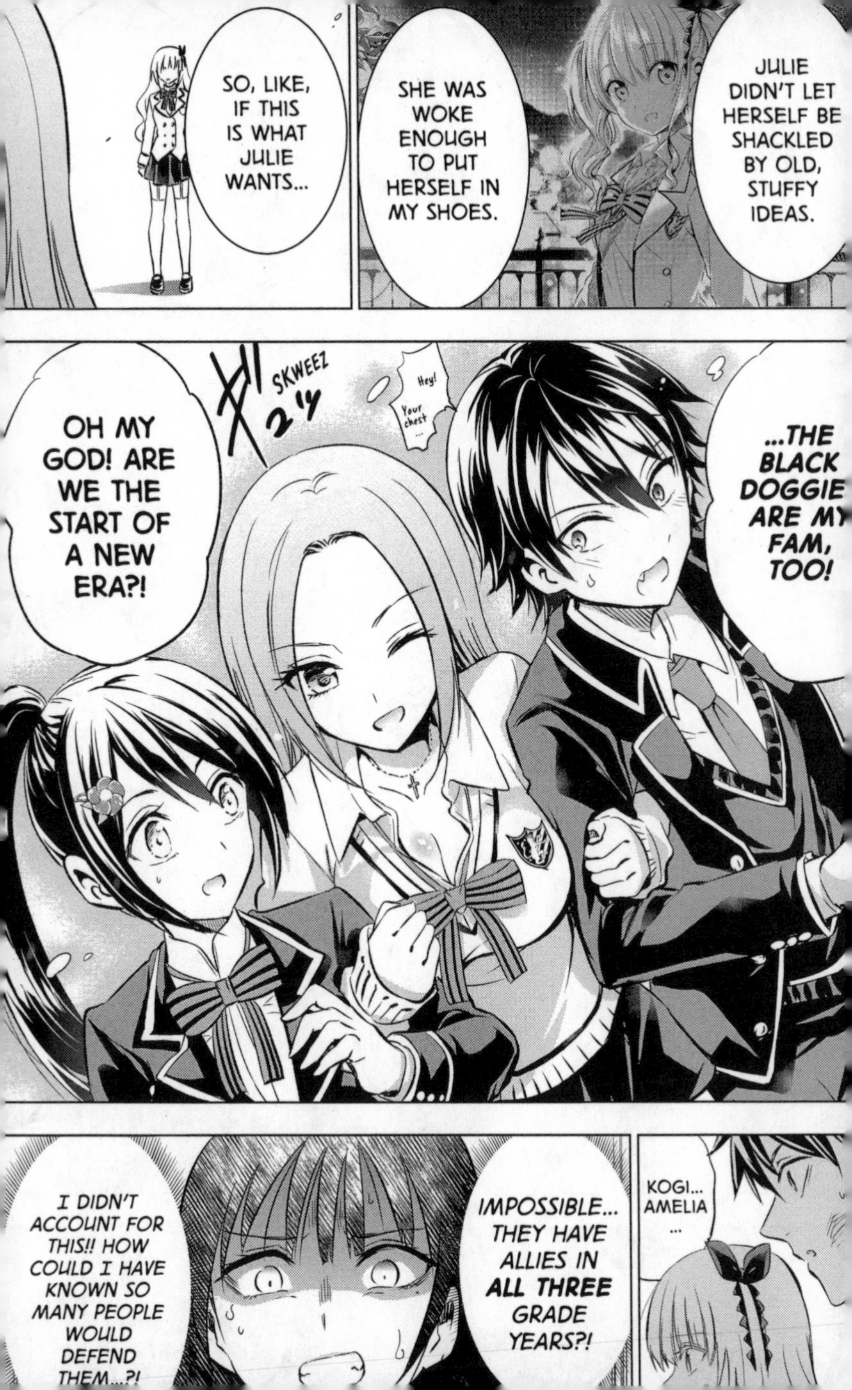
JULIE DIDN'T LET HERSELF BE SHACKLED BY OLD, STUFFY IDEAS.
SHE WAS WOKE ENOUGH TO PUT HERSELF IN MY SHOES.
SO, LIKE, IF THIS IS WHAT JULIE WANTS...
...THE BLACK DOGGIE ARE MY FAM, TOO!
Hey! Your chest ...
SKWEEZ
OH MY GOD! ARE WE THE START OF A NEW ERA?!
KOGI... AMELIA ...
IMPOSSIBLE... THEY HAVE ALLIES IN ALL THREE GRADE YEARS?!
I DIDN'T ACCOUNT FOR THIS!! HOW COULD I HAVE KNOWN SO MANY PEOPLE WOULD DEFEND THEM...?!

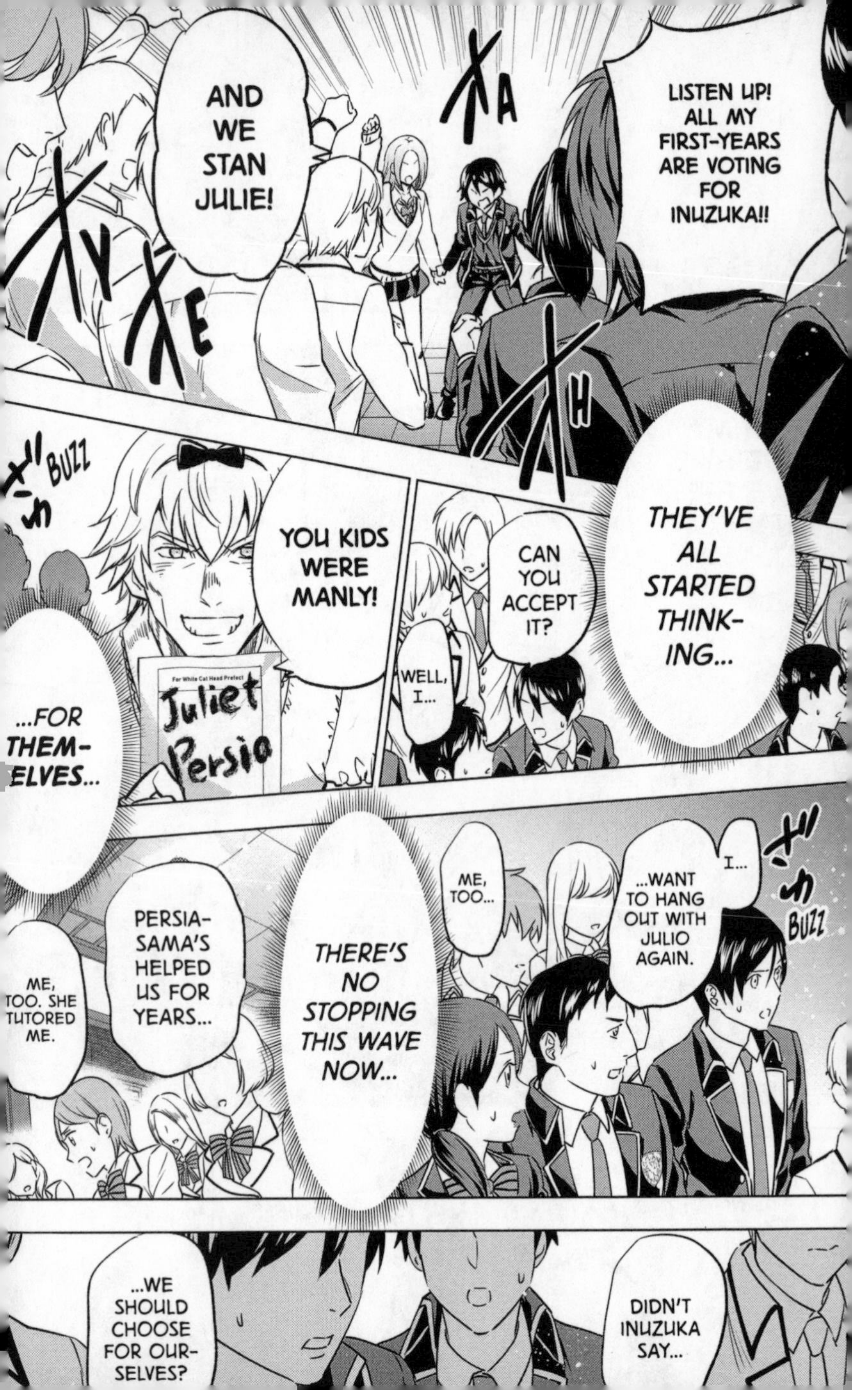
LISTEN UP! ALL MY FIRST-YEARS ARE VOTING FOR INUZUKA!!
A
H
AND WE STAN JULIE!
Y
E
THEY'VE ALL STARTED THINKING...
CAN YOU ACCEPT IT?
WELL, I...
BUZZ
YOU KIDS WERE MANLY!
For White Cat Head Prefect
Juliet Persia
...FOR THEMSELVES...
BUZZ
I...
...WANT TO HANG OUT WITH JULIO AGAIN.
ME, TOO...
THERE'S NO STOPPING THIS WAVE NOW...
PERSIA-SAMA'S HELPED US FOR YEARS...
ME, TOO. SHE TUTORED ME.
DIDN'T INUZUKA SAY...
...WE SHOULD CHOOSE FOR OURSELVES?

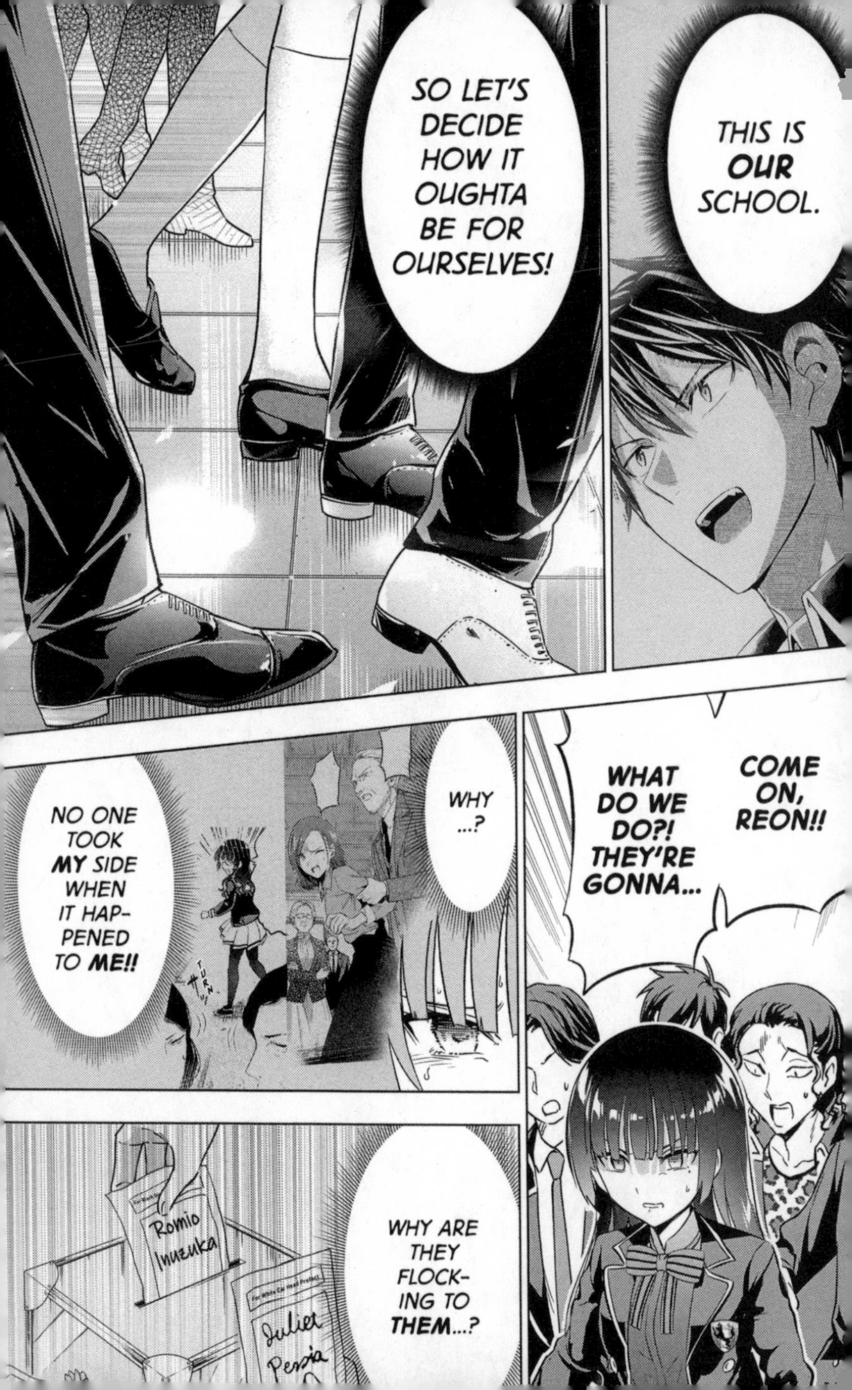
THIS IS OUR SCHOOL.
SO LET'S DECIDE HOW IT OUGHTA BE FOR OURSELVES!
COME ON, REON!!
WHAT DO WE DO?! THEY'RE GONNA...
WHY ...?
NO ONE TOOK MY SIDE WHEN IT HAPPENED TO ME!!
TURN
WHY ARE THEY FLOCKING TO THEM...?
Romio Inuzuka
Juliet Persia

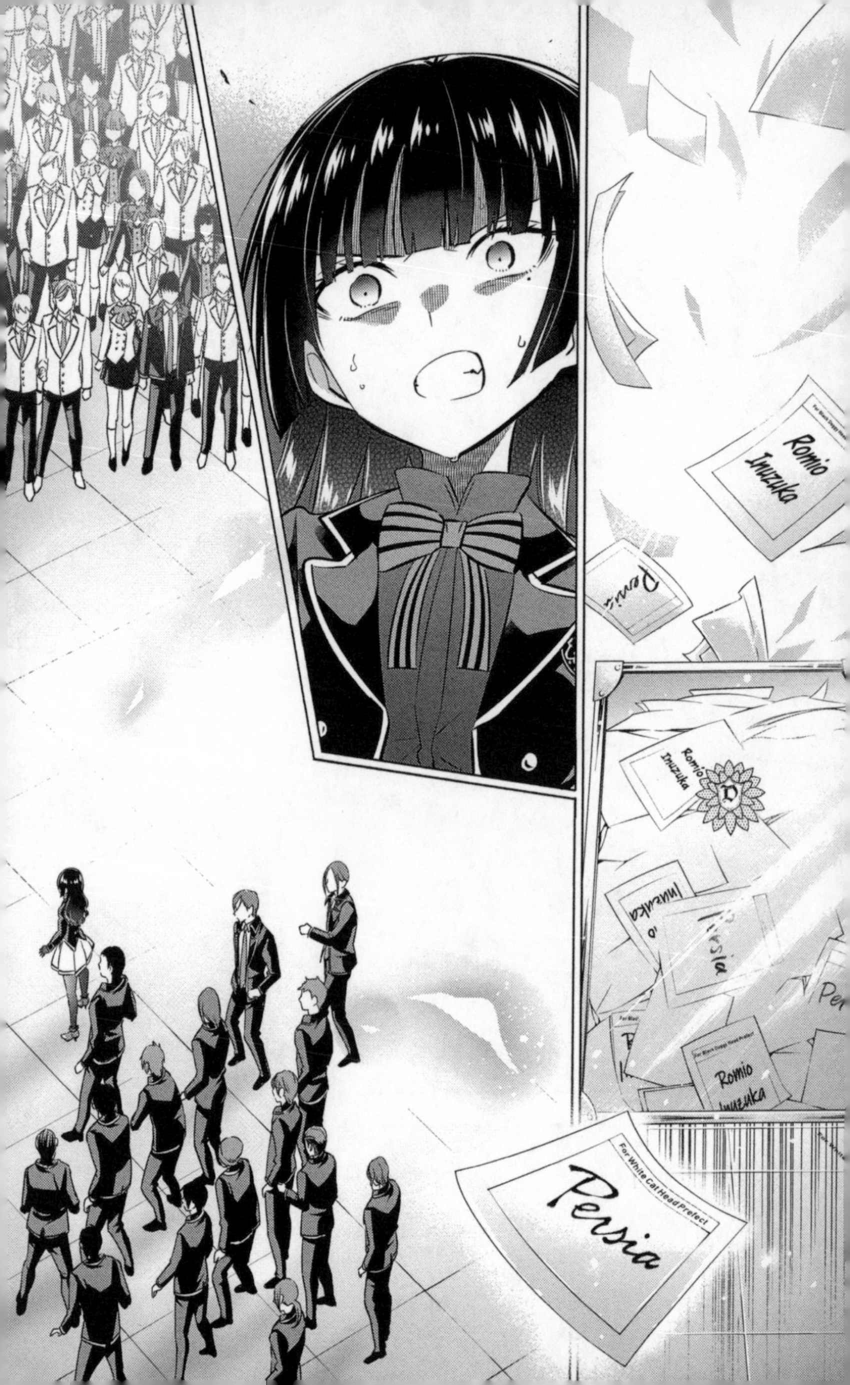

Romio Inuzuka
Persia
Romio Inuzuka
Inuzuka
Persia
Romio Inuzuka
For White Cat Head Prefect
Persia

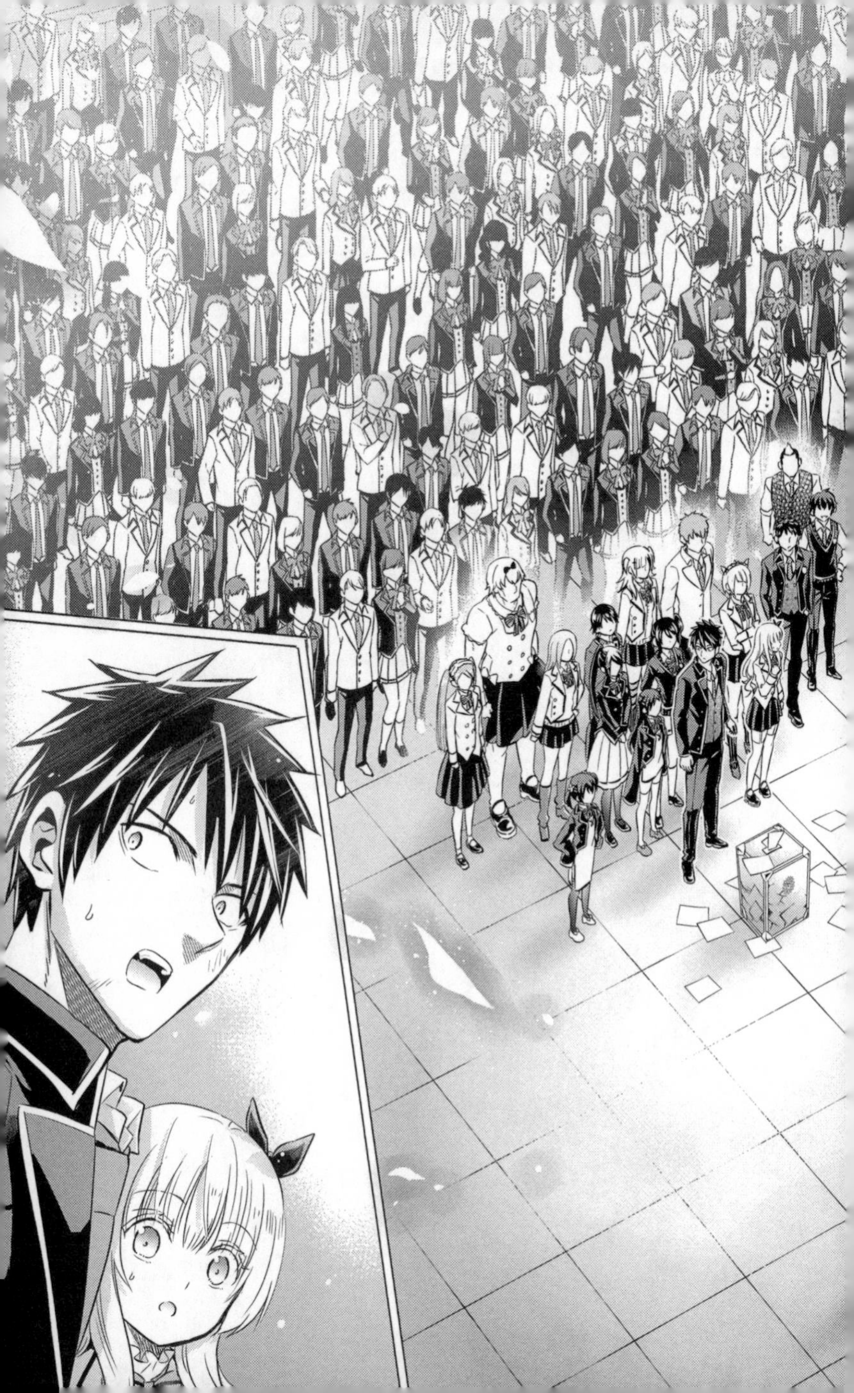

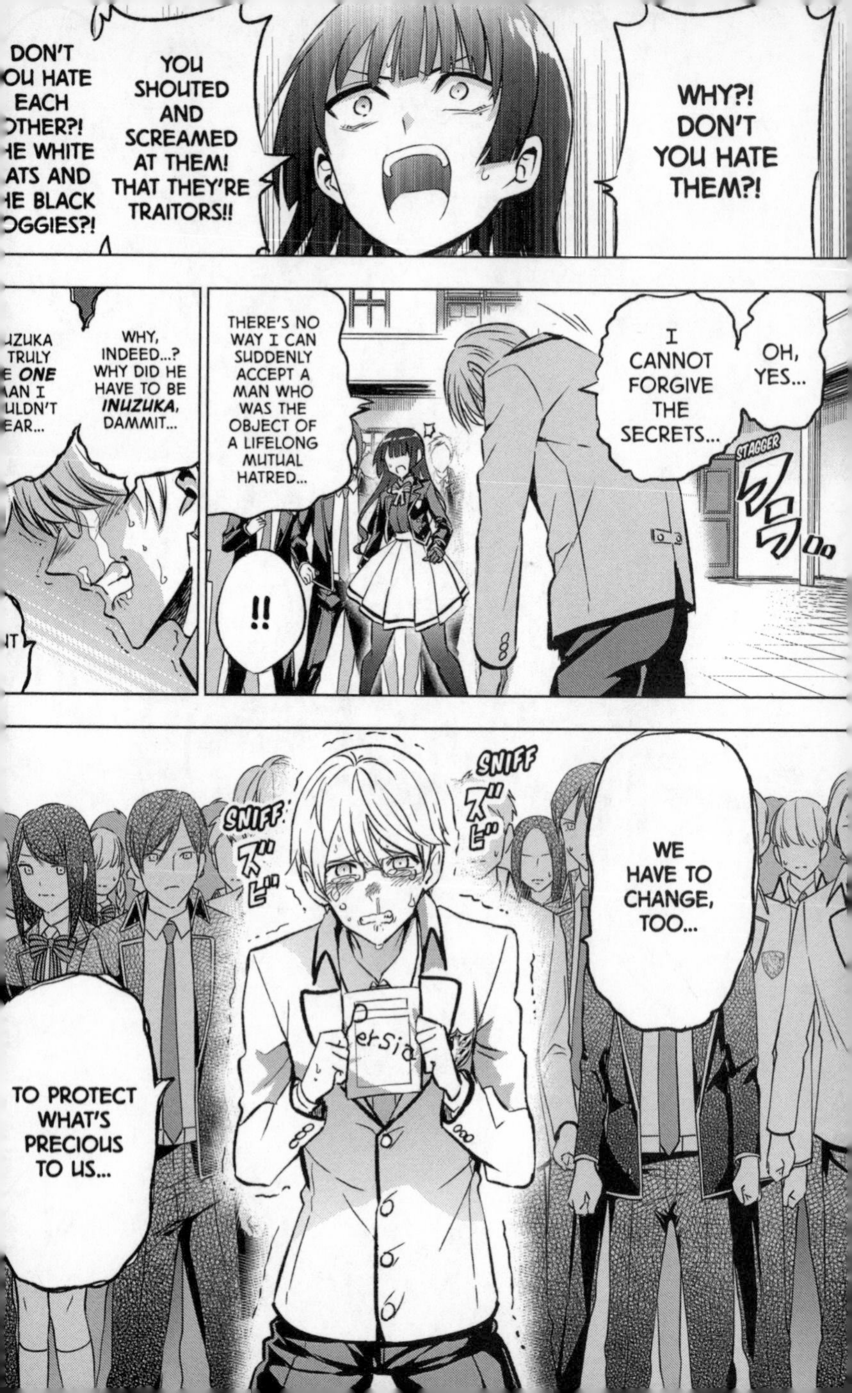
WHY?! DON'T YOU HATE THEM?!
YOU SHOUTED AND SCREAMED AT THEM! THAT THEY'RE TRAITORS!!
DON'T OU HATE EACH OTHER?! HE WHITE ATS AND HE BLACK OGGIES?!
OH, YES...
I CANNOT FORGIVE THE SECRETS...
STAGGER
THERE'S NO WAY I CAN SUDDENLY ACCEPT A MAN WHO WAS THE OBJECT OF A LIFELONG MUTUAL HATRED...
!!
WHY, INDEED...? WHY DID HE HAVE TO BE *INUZUKA*, DAMMIT...
IZUKA TRULY E *ONE* AN I ULDN'T EAR...
IT
WE HAVE TO CHANGE, TOO...
SNIFF
SNIFF
TO PROTECT WHAT'S PRECIOUS TO US...

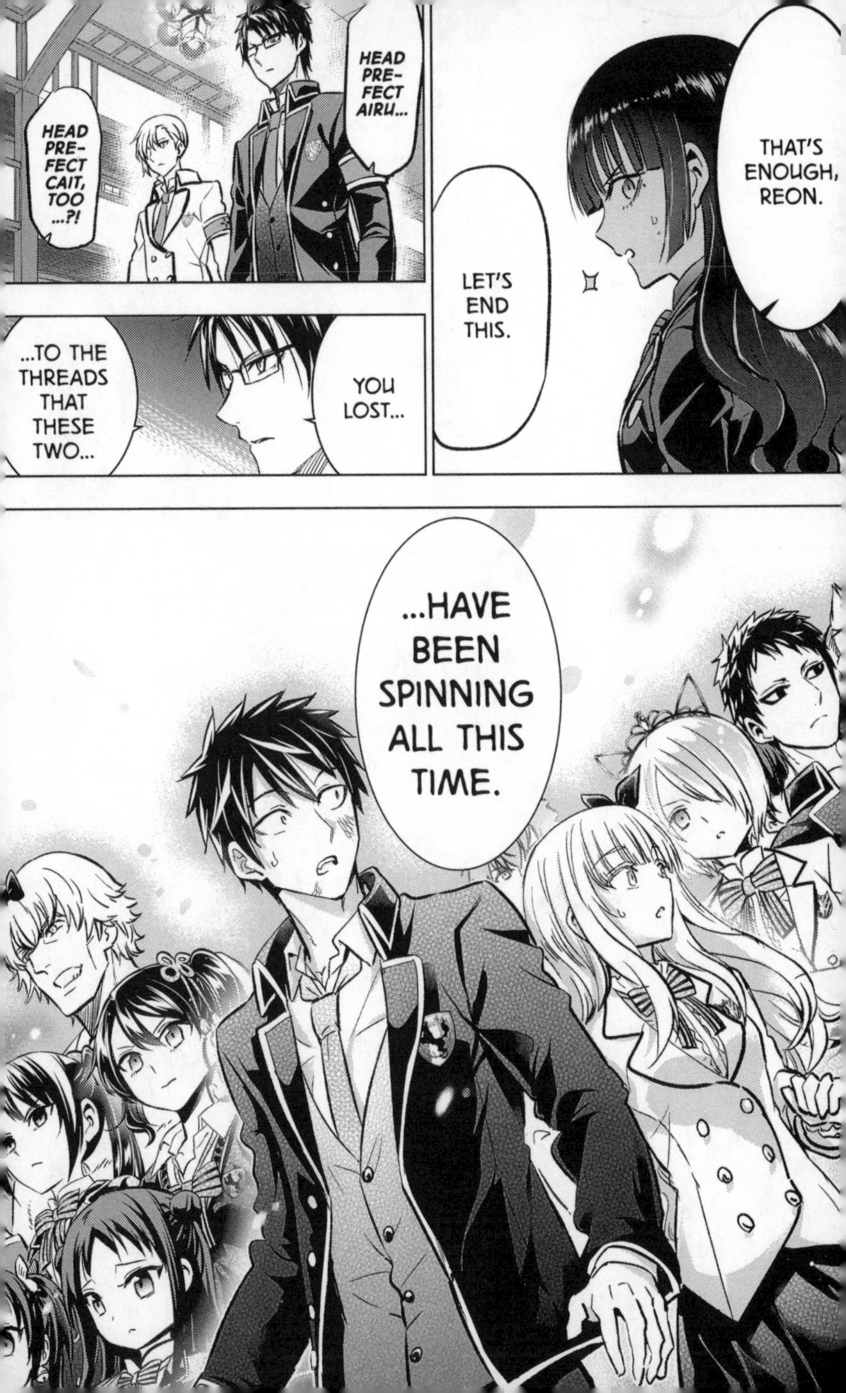
THAT'S ENOUGH, REON.
LET'S END THIS.
HEAD PRE-FECT AIRU...
HEAD PRE-FECT CAIT, TOO ...?!
YOU LOST...
...TO THE THREADS THAT THESE TWO...
...HAVE BEEN SPINNING ALL THIS TIME.

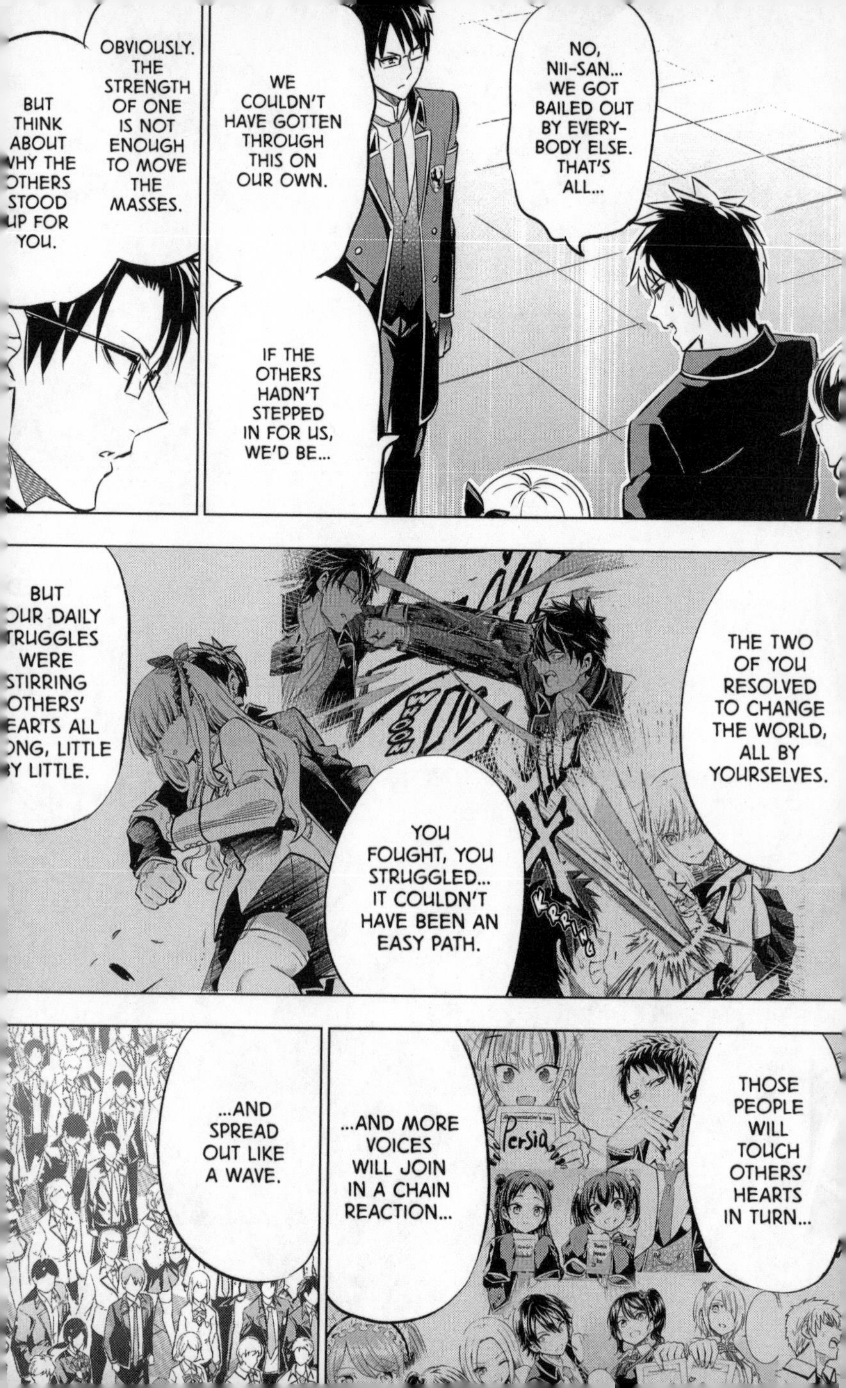
NO, NII-SAN... WE GOT BAILED OUT BY EVERYBODY ELSE. THAT'S ALL...
WE COULDN'T HAVE GOTTEN THROUGH THIS ON OUR OWN.
IF THE OTHERS HADN'T STEPPED IN FOR US, WE'D BE...
OBVIOUSLY. THE STRENGTH OF ONE IS NOT ENOUGH TO MOVE THE MASSES.
BUT THINK ABOUT VHY THE OTHERS STOOD UP FOR YOU.
THE TWO OF YOU RESOLVED TO CHANGE THE WORLD, ALL BY YOURSELVES.
YOU FOUGHT, YOU STRUGGLED... IT COULDN'T HAVE BEEN AN EASY PATH.
WHOOF
KRRING
BUT OUR DAILY TRUGGLES WERE STIRRING OTHERS' EARTS ALL ONG, LITTLE Y LITTLE.
THOSE PEOPLE WILL TOUCH OTHERS' HEARTS IN TURN...
Persia
...AND MORE VOICES WILL JOIN IN A CHAIN REACTION...
...AND SPREAD OUT LIKE A WAVE.

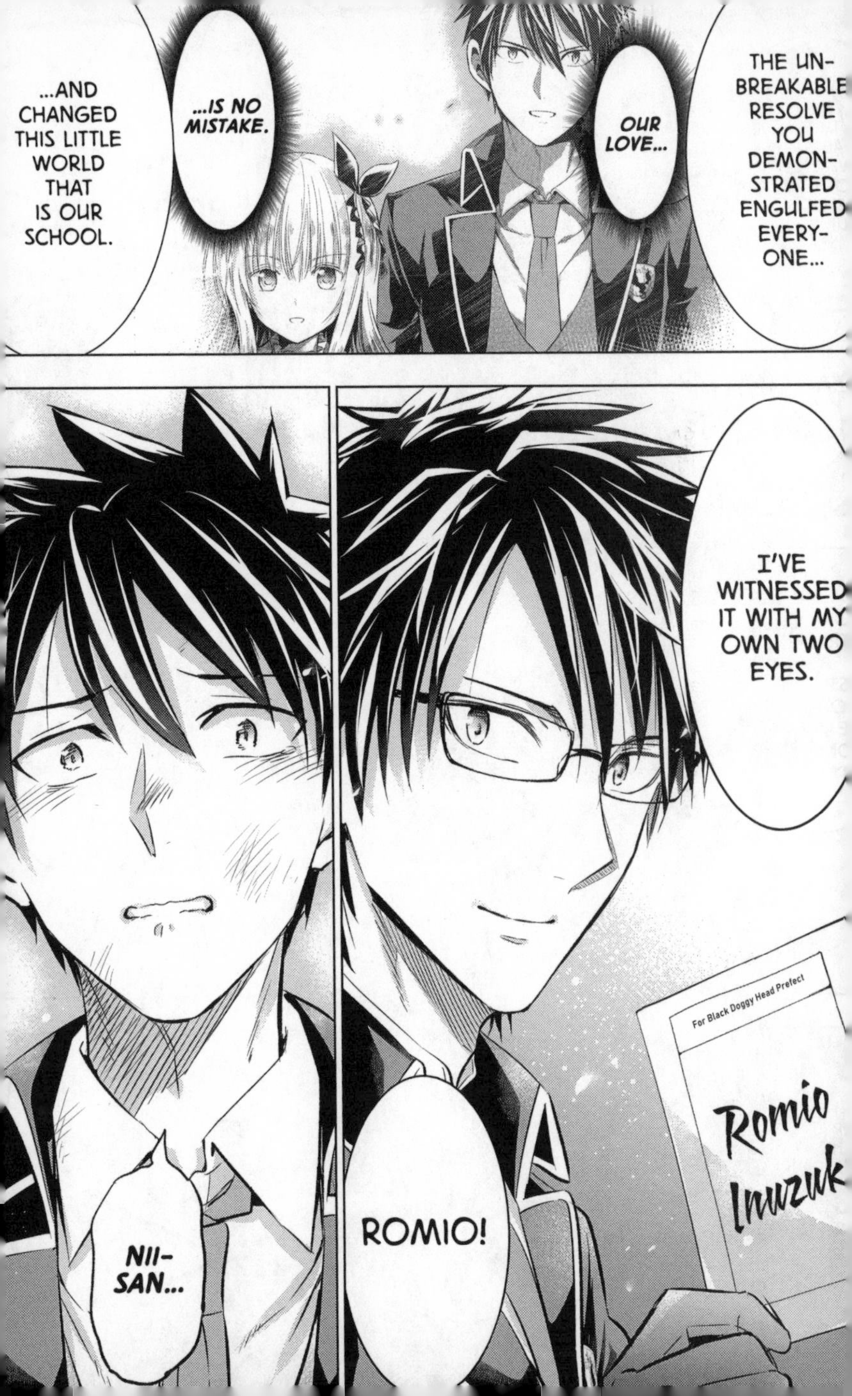
THE UN-BREAKABLE RESOLVE YOU DEMONSTRATED ENGULFED EVERYONE...
OUR LOVE...
...IS NO MISTAKE.
...AND CHANGED THIS LITTLE WORLD THAT IS OUR SCHOOL.
I'VE WITNESSED IT WITH MY OWN TWO EYES.
For Black Doggy Head Prefect
Romio Inuzuk
ROMIO!
NII-SAN...

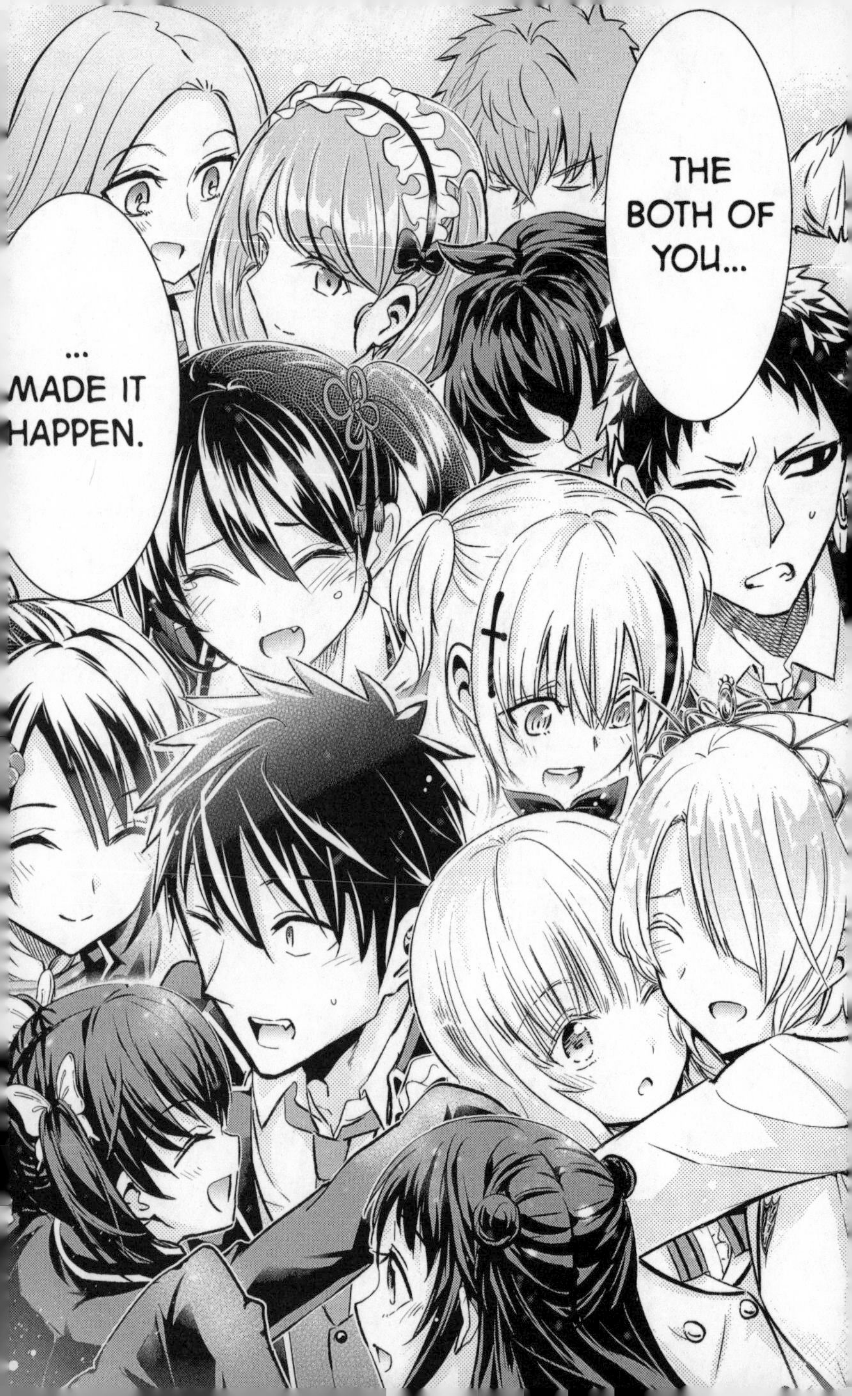
THE BOTH OF YOU...
...MADE IT HAPPEN.

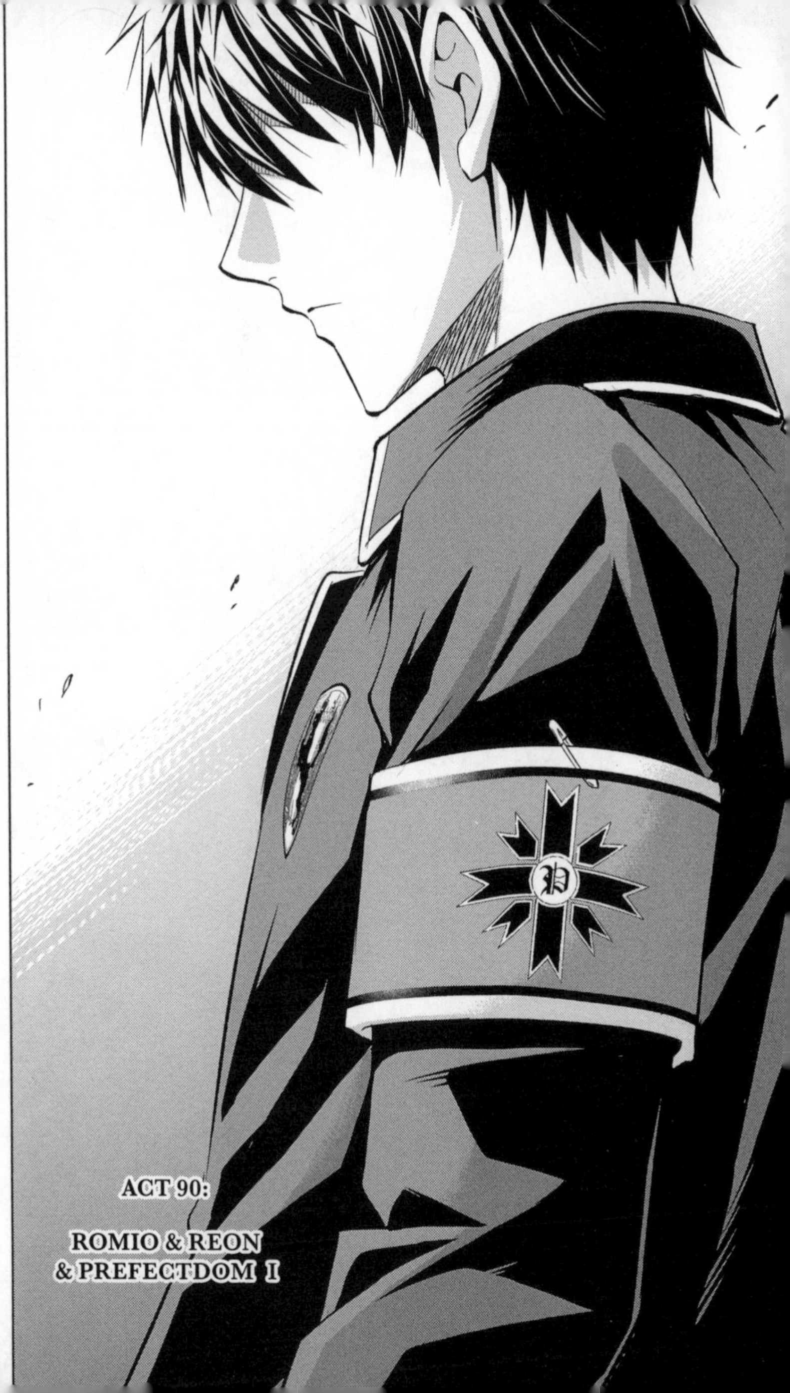
ACT 90:
ROMIO & REON
& PREFECTDOM I

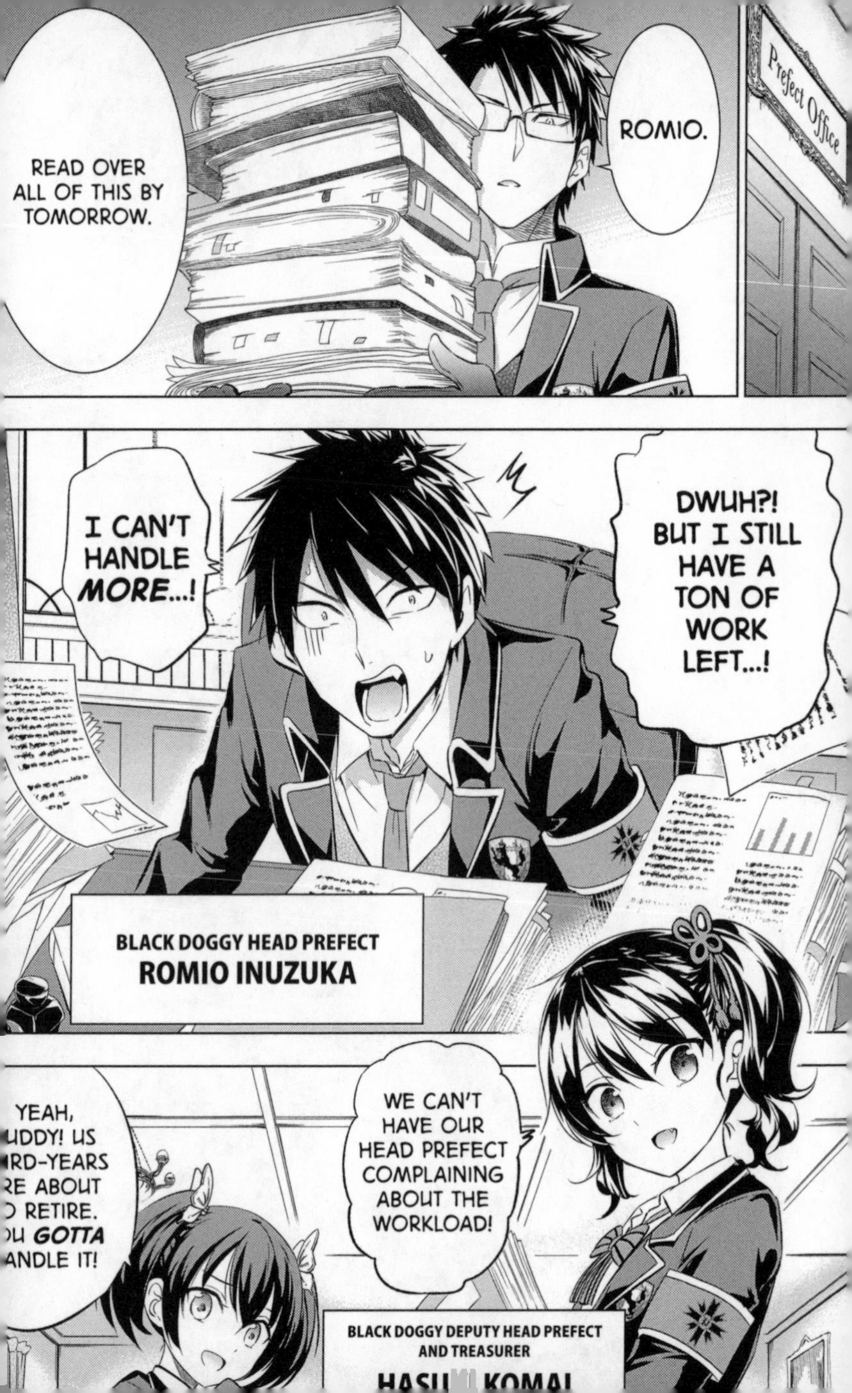
Prefect Office
ROMIO.
READ OVER ALL OF THIS BY TOMORROW.
DWUH?! BUT I STILL HAVE A TON OF WORK LEFT...!
I CAN'T HANDLE MORE...!
BLACK DOGGY HEAD PREFECT
ROMIO INUZUKA
WE CAN'T HAVE OUR HEAD PREFECT COMPLAINING ABOUT THE WORKLOAD!
YEAH, UDDY! US RD-YEARS RE ABOUT RETIRE. U GOTTA ANDLE IT!
BLACK DOGGY DEPUTY HEAD PREFECT AND TREASURER
HASU KOMAI

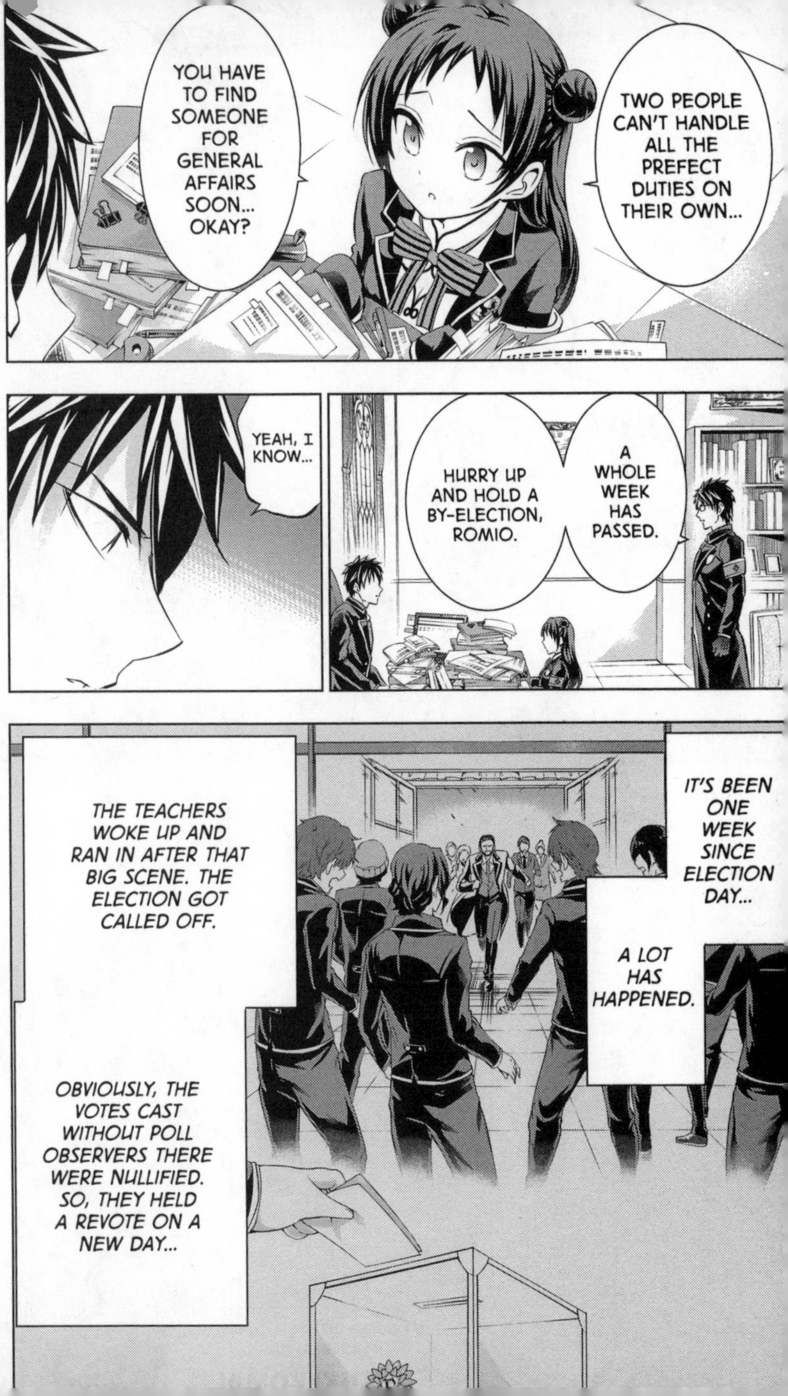
TWO PEOPLE CAN'T HANDLE ALL THE PREFECT DUTIES ON THEIR OWN...
YOU HAVE TO FIND SOMEONE FOR GENERAL AFFAIRS SOON... OKAY?
A WHOLE WEEK HAS PASSED.
HURRY UP AND HOLD A BY-ELECTION, ROMIO.
YEAH, I KNOW...
IT'S BEEN ONE WEEK SINCE ELECTION DAY...
A LOT HAS HAPPENED.
THE TEACHERS WOKE UP AND RAN IN AFTER THAT BIG SCENE. THE ELECTION GOT CALLED OFF.
OBVIOUSLY, THE VOTES CAST WITHOUT POLL OBSERVERS THERE WERE NULLIFIED. SO, THEY HELD A REVOTE ON A NEW DAY...

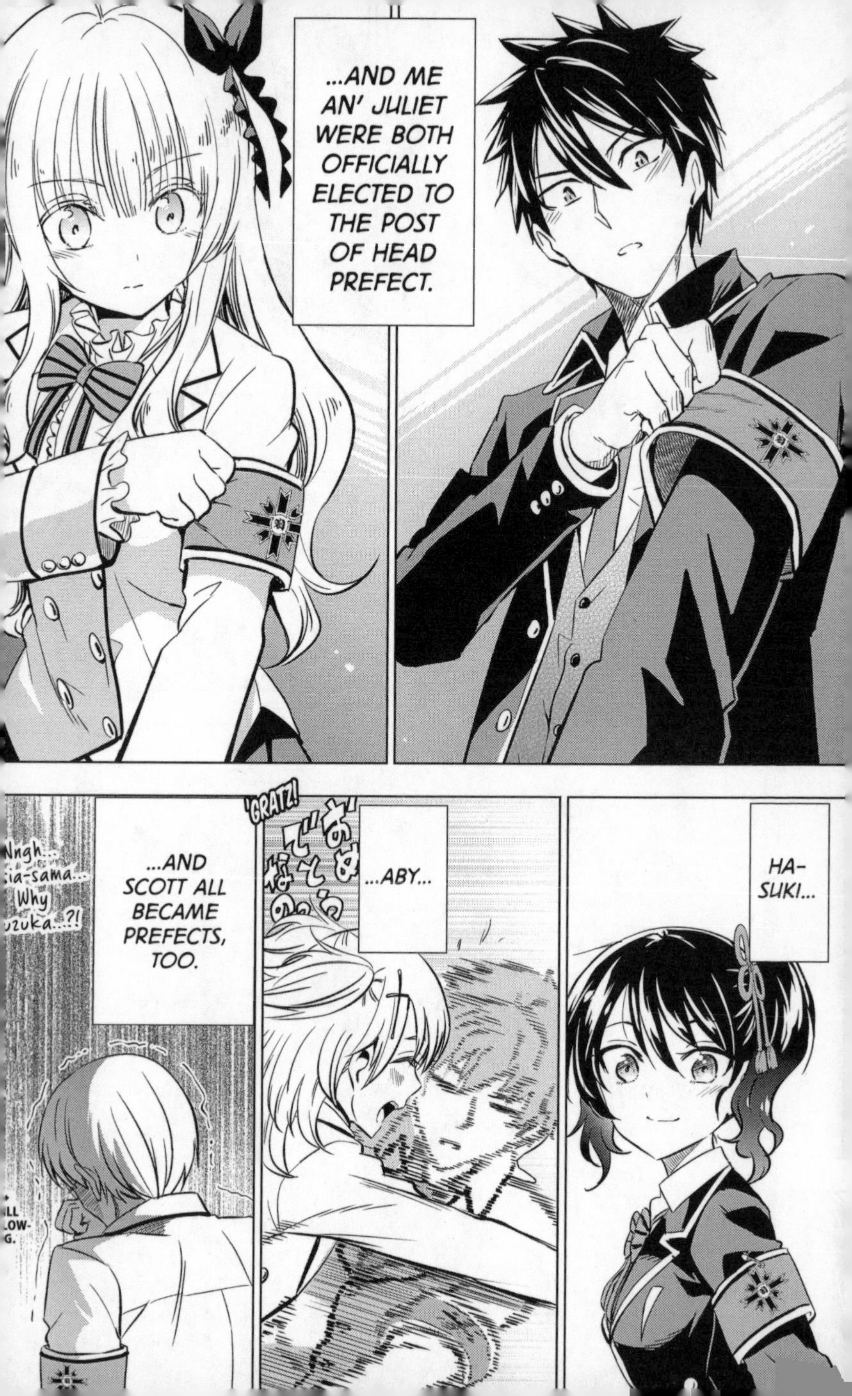
...AND ME AN' JULIET WERE BOTH OFFICIALLY ELECTED TO THE POST OF HEAD PREFECT.
HA-SUKI...
'GRATZ!
...ABY...
...AND SCOTT ALL BECAME PREFECTS, TOO.
Nngh...
Why

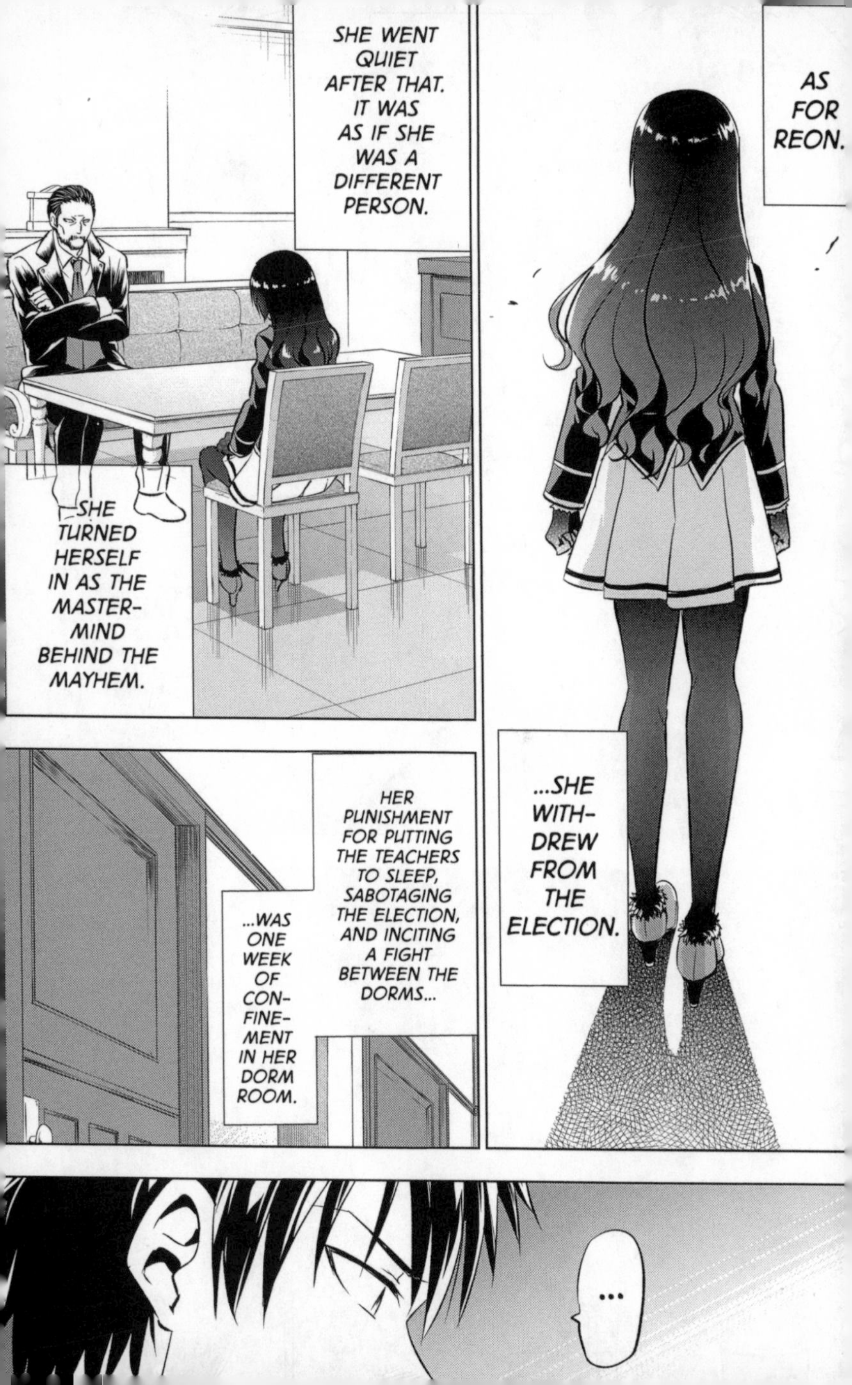
AS FOR REON.
...SHE WITHDREW FROM THE ELECTION.
SHE WENT QUIET AFTER THAT. IT WAS AS IF SHE WAS A DIFFERENT PERSON.
SHE TURNED HERSELF IN AS THE MASTERMIND BEHIND THE MAYHEM.
HER PUNISHMENT FOR PUTTING THE TEACHERS TO SLEEP, SABOTAGING THE ELECTION, AND INCITING A FIGHT BETWEEN THE DORMS...
...WAS ONE WEEK OF CONFINEMENT IN HER DORM ROOM.
...

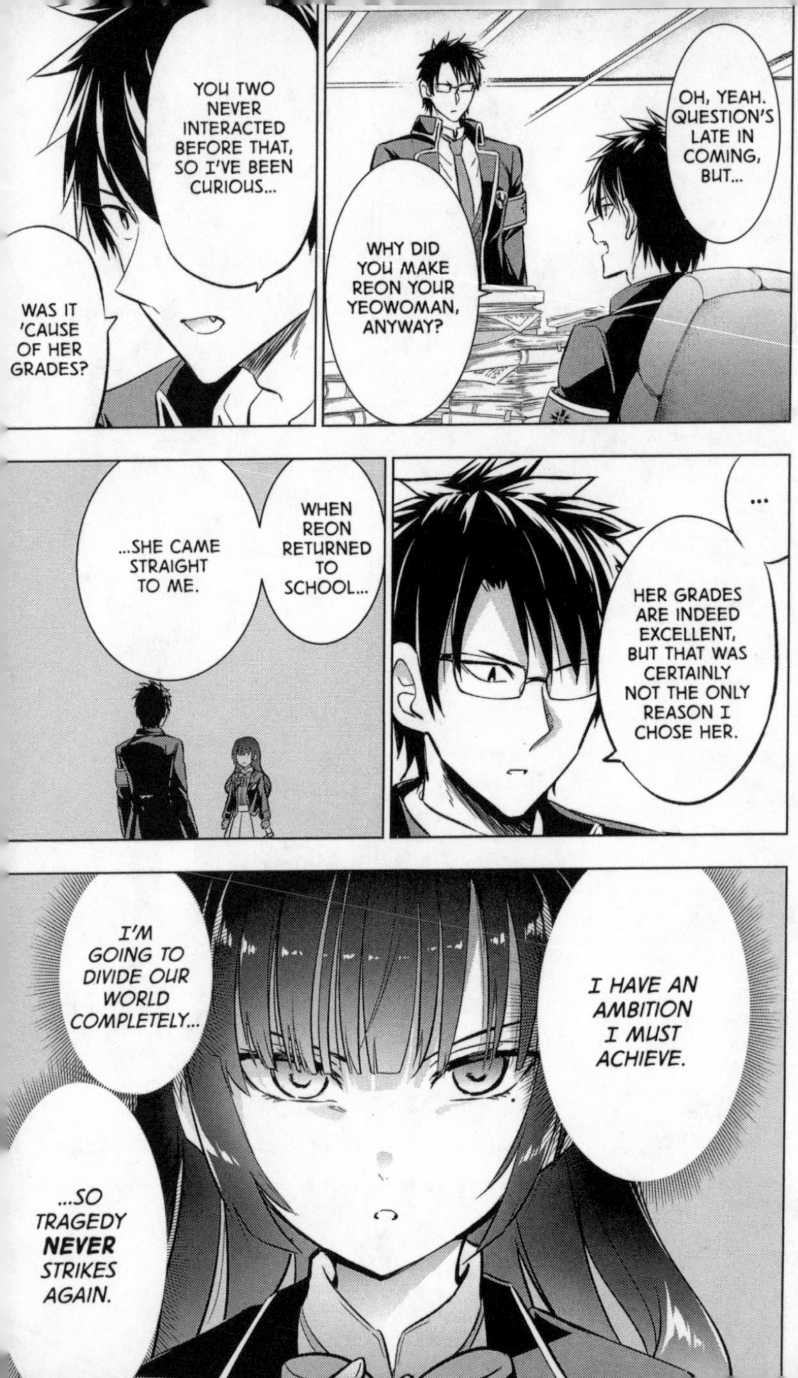
OH, YEAH. QUESTION'S LATE IN COMING, BUT...
WHY DID YOU MAKE REON YOUR YEOWOMAN, ANYWAY?
YOU TWO NEVER INTERACTED BEFORE THAT, SO I'VE BEEN CURIOUS...
WAS IT 'CAUSE OF HER GRADES?
...
HER GRADES ARE INDEED EXCELLENT, BUT THAT WAS CERTAINLY NOT THE ONLY REASON I CHOSE HER.
WHEN REON RETURNED TO SCHOOL...
...SHE CAME STRAIGHT TO ME.
*I HAVE AN AMBITION I MUST ACHIEVE.*
*I'M GOING TO DIVIDE OUR WORLD COMPLETELY...*
*...SO TRAGEDY **NEVER** STRIKES AGAIN.*

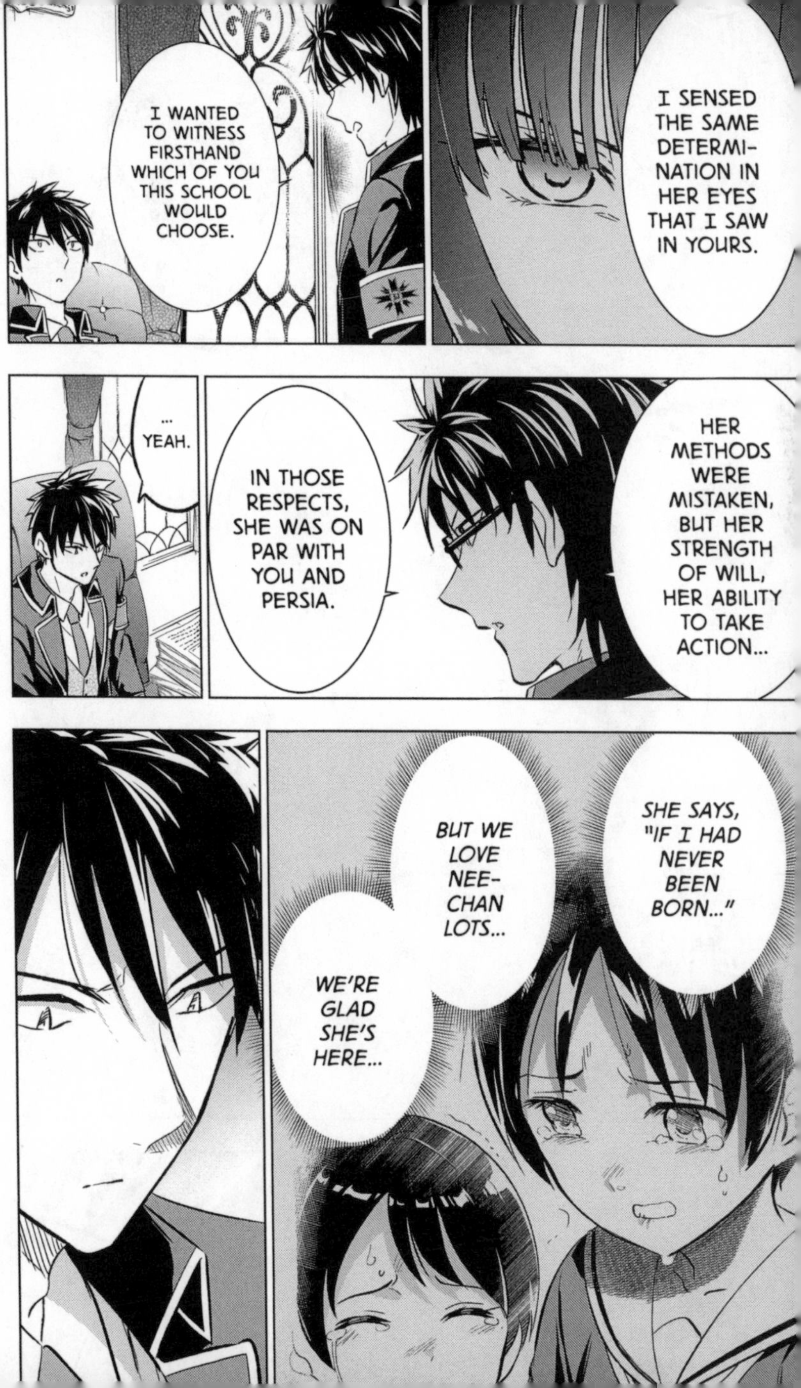
I SENSED THE SAME DETERMINATION IN HER EYES THAT I SAW IN YOURS.
I WANTED TO WITNESS FIRSTHAND WHICH OF YOU THIS SCHOOL WOULD CHOOSE.
HER METHODS WERE MISTAKEN, BUT HER STRENGTH OF WILL, HER ABILITY TO TAKE ACTION...
IN THOSE RESPECTS, SHE WAS ON PAR WITH YOU AND PERSIA.
... YEAH.
SHE SAYS, "IF I HAD NEVER BEEN BORN..."
BUT WE LOVE NEE-CHAN LOTS...
WE'RE GLAD SHE'S HERE...

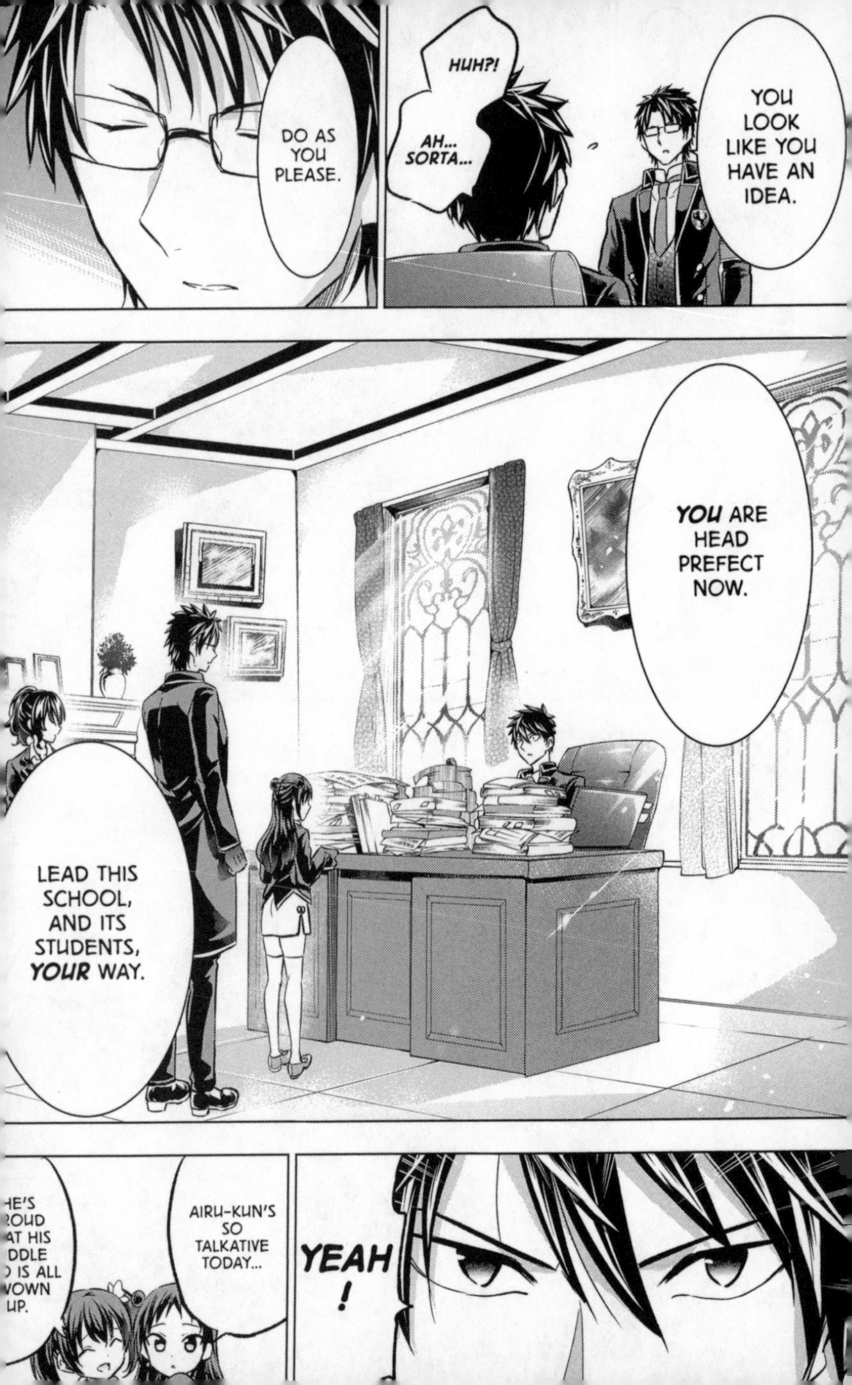
YOU LOOK LIKE YOU HAVE AN IDEA.
HUH?!
AH... SORTA...
DO AS YOU PLEASE.
YOU ARE HEAD PREFECT NOW.
LEAD THIS SCHOOL, AND ITS STUDENTS, YOUR WAY.
YEAH!
AIRU-KUN'S SO TALKATIVE TODAY...

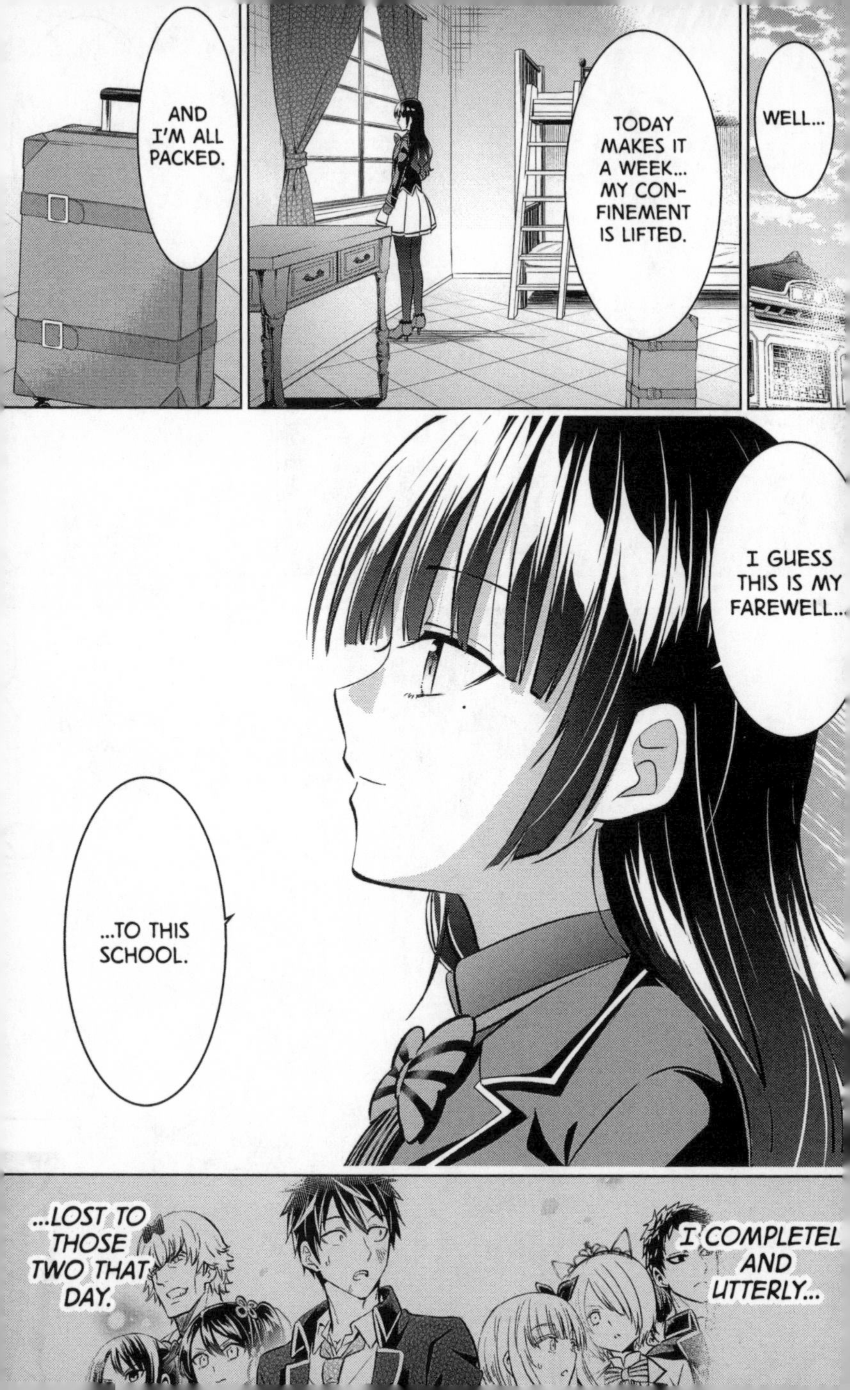
WELL...
TODAY MAKES IT A WEEK... MY CONFINEMENT IS LIFTED.
AND I'M ALL PACKED.
I GUESS THIS IS MY FAREWELL...
...TO THIS SCHOOL.
I COMPLETEL AND UTTERLY...
...LOST TO THOSE TWO THAT DAY.

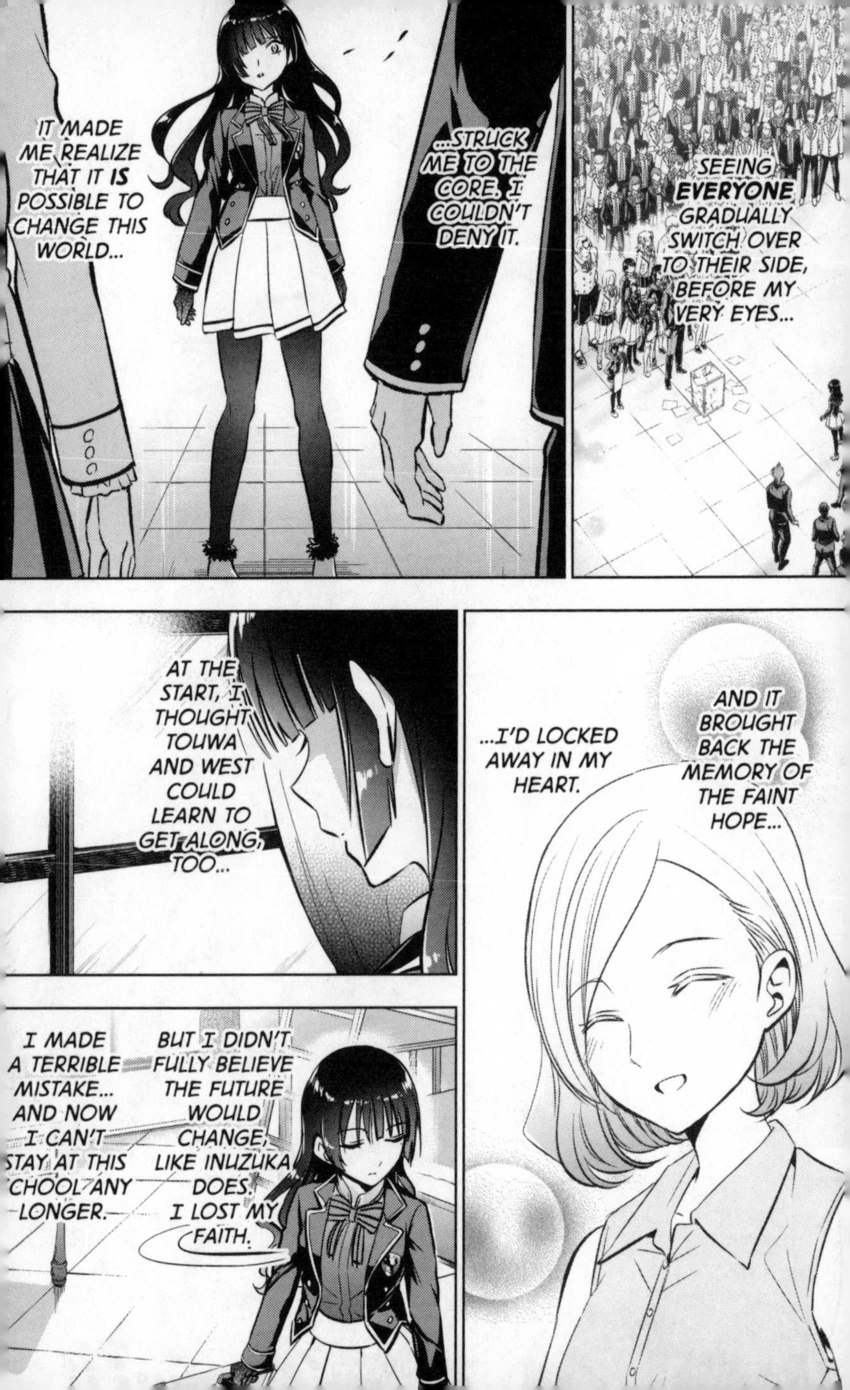
SEEING **EVERYONE** GRADUALLY SWITCH OVER TO THEIR SIDE, BEFORE MY VERY EYES...
...STRUCK ME TO THE CORE. I COULDN'T DENY IT.
IT MADE ME REALIZE THAT IT **IS** POSSIBLE TO CHANGE THIS WORLD...
AND IT BROUGHT BACK THE MEMORY OF THE FAINT HOPE...
...I'D LOCKED AWAY IN MY HEART.
AT THE START, I THOUGHT TOUWA AND WEST COULD LEARN TO GET ALONG, TOO...
BUT I DIDN'T FULLY BELIEVE THE FUTURE WOULD CHANGE, LIKE INUZUKA DOES. I LOST MY FAITH.
I MADE A TERRIBLE MISTAKE... AND NOW I CAN'T TAY AT THIS CHOOL ANY LONGER.

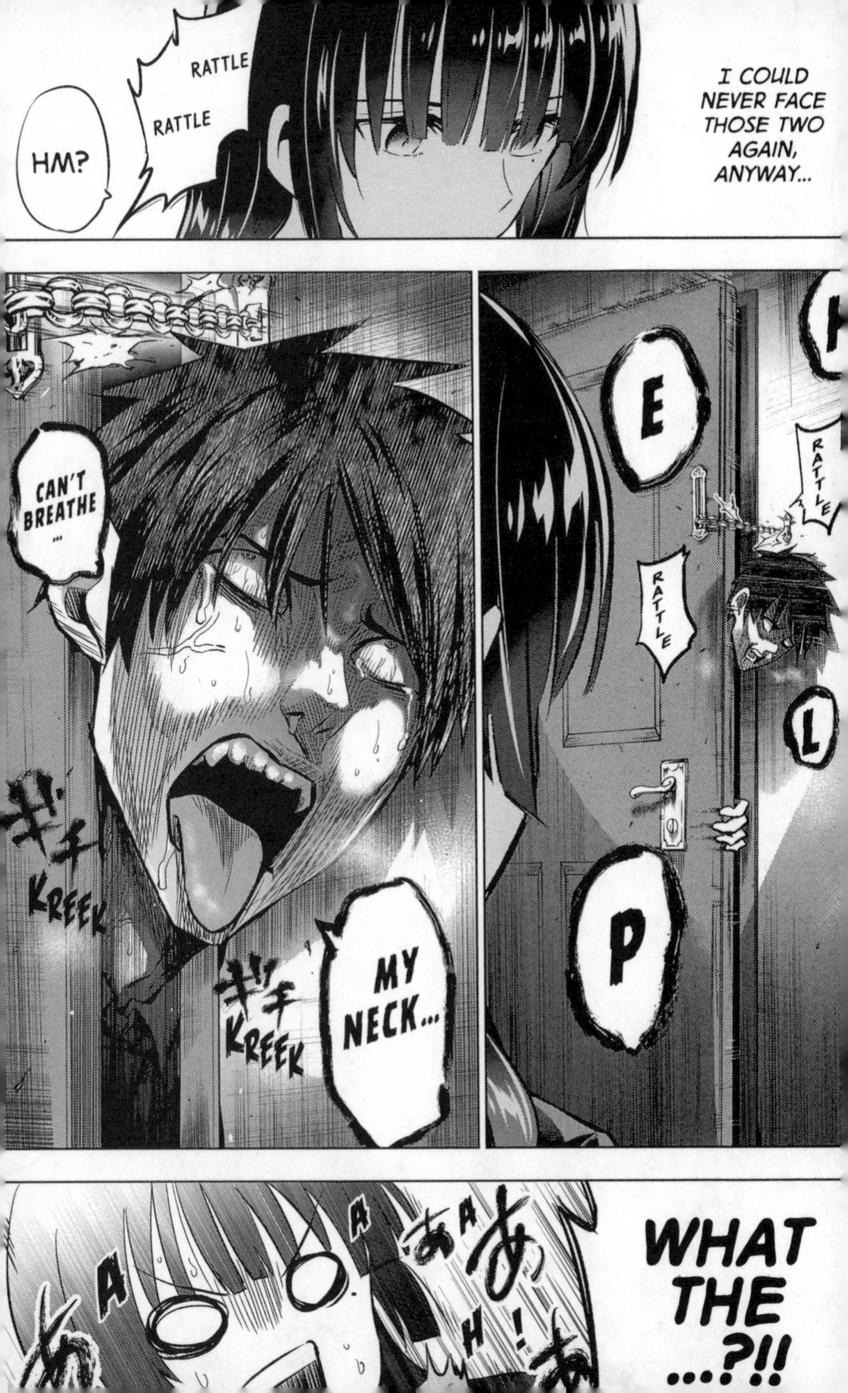
I COULD NEVER FACE THOSE TWO AGAIN, ANYWAY...
RATTLE
RATTLE
HM?
H
E
RATTLE
RATTLE
L
P
CAN'T BREATHE ...
ギチ KREEK
MY NECK...
ギチ KREEK
WHAT THE ...?!!
あ A
あ A H !
A
あ

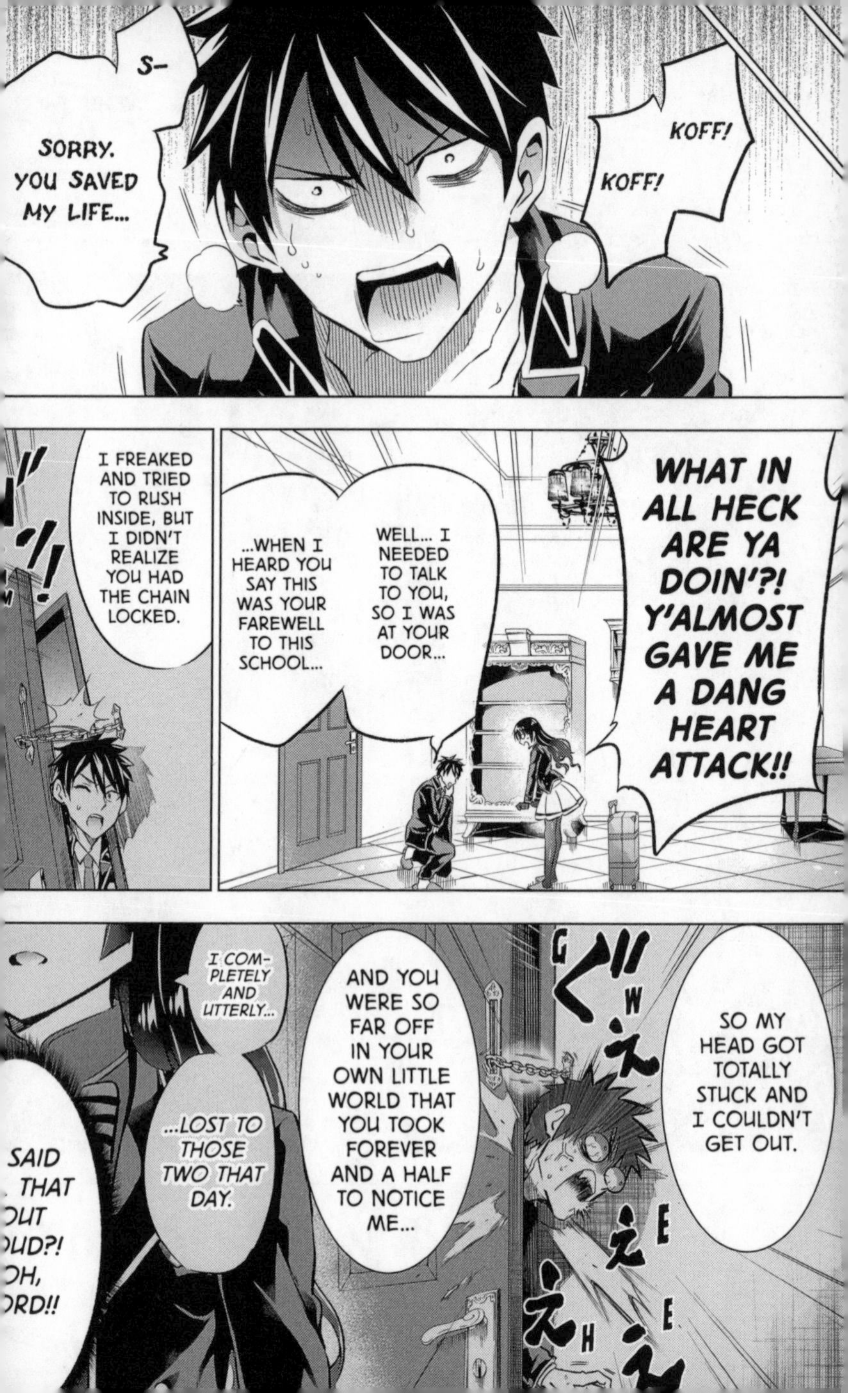
KOFF!
KOFF!
S-
SORRY. YOU SAVED MY LIFE...
WHAT IN ALL HECK ARE YA DOIN'?! Y'ALMOST GAVE ME A DANG HEART ATTACK!!
WELL... I NEEDED TO TALK TO YOU, SO I WAS AT YOUR DOOR...
...WHEN I HEARD YOU SAY THIS WAS YOUR FAREWELL TO THIS SCHOOL...
I FREAKED AND TRIED TO RUSH INSIDE, BUT I DIDN'T REALIZE YOU HAD THE CHAIN LOCKED.
SO MY HEAD GOT TOTALLY STUCK AND I COULDN'T GET OUT.
GWEEEH
AND YOU WERE SO FAR OFF IN YOUR OWN LITTLE WORLD THAT YOU TOOK FOREVER AND A HALF TO NOTICE ME...
I COMPLETELY AND UTTERLY...
...LOST TO THOSE TWO THAT DAY.
SAID THAT

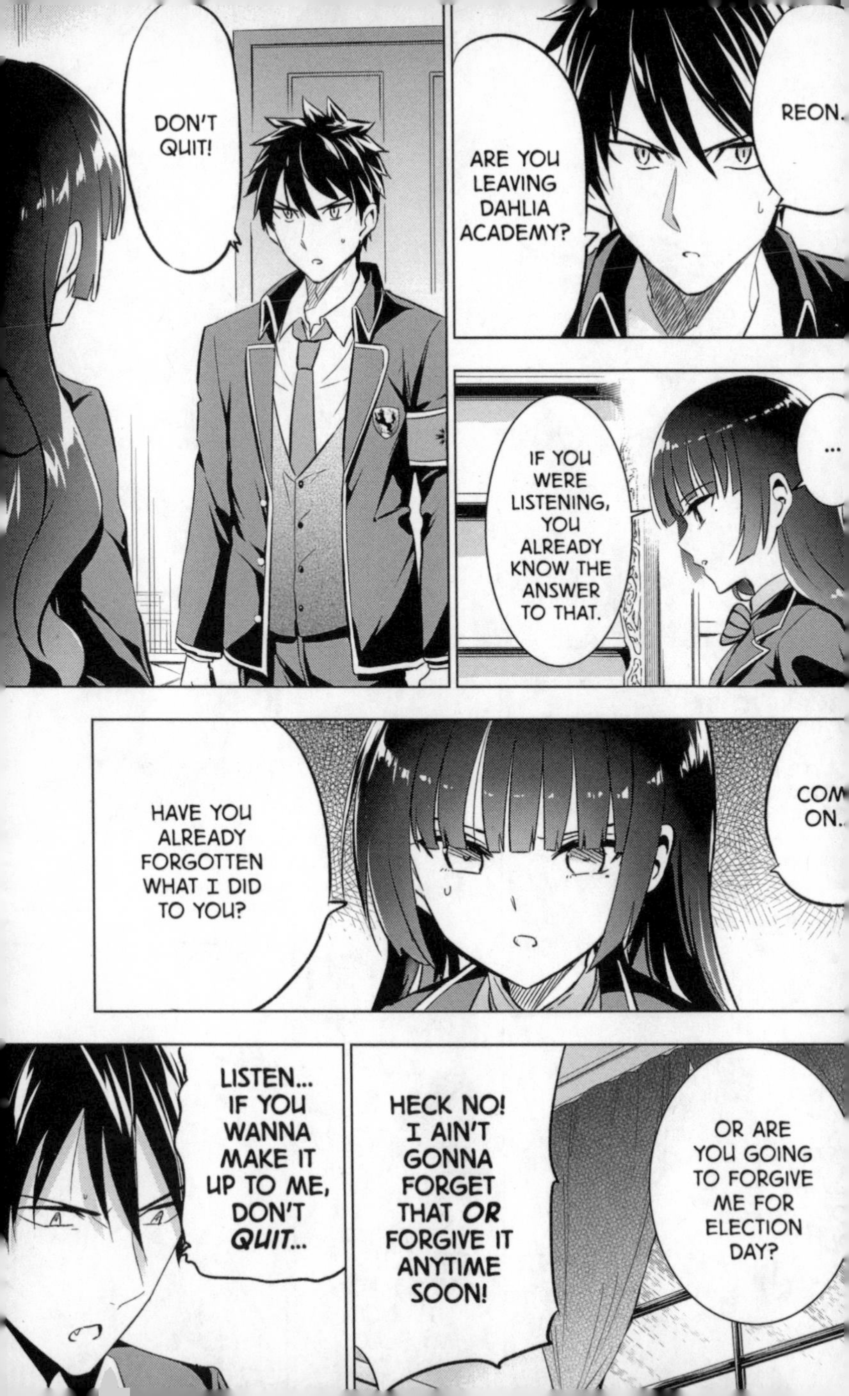
REON.
ARE YOU LEAVING DAHLIA ACADEMY?
...
IF YOU WERE LISTENING, YOU ALREADY KNOW THE ANSWER TO THAT.
DON'T QUIT!
COM ON..
HAVE YOU ALREADY FORGOTTEN WHAT I DID TO YOU?
OR ARE YOU GOING TO FORGIVE ME FOR ELECTION DAY?
HECK NO! I AIN'T GONNA FORGET THAT *OR* FORGIVE IT ANYTIME SOON!
LISTEN... IF YOU WANNA MAKE IT UP TO ME, DON'T *QUIT*...

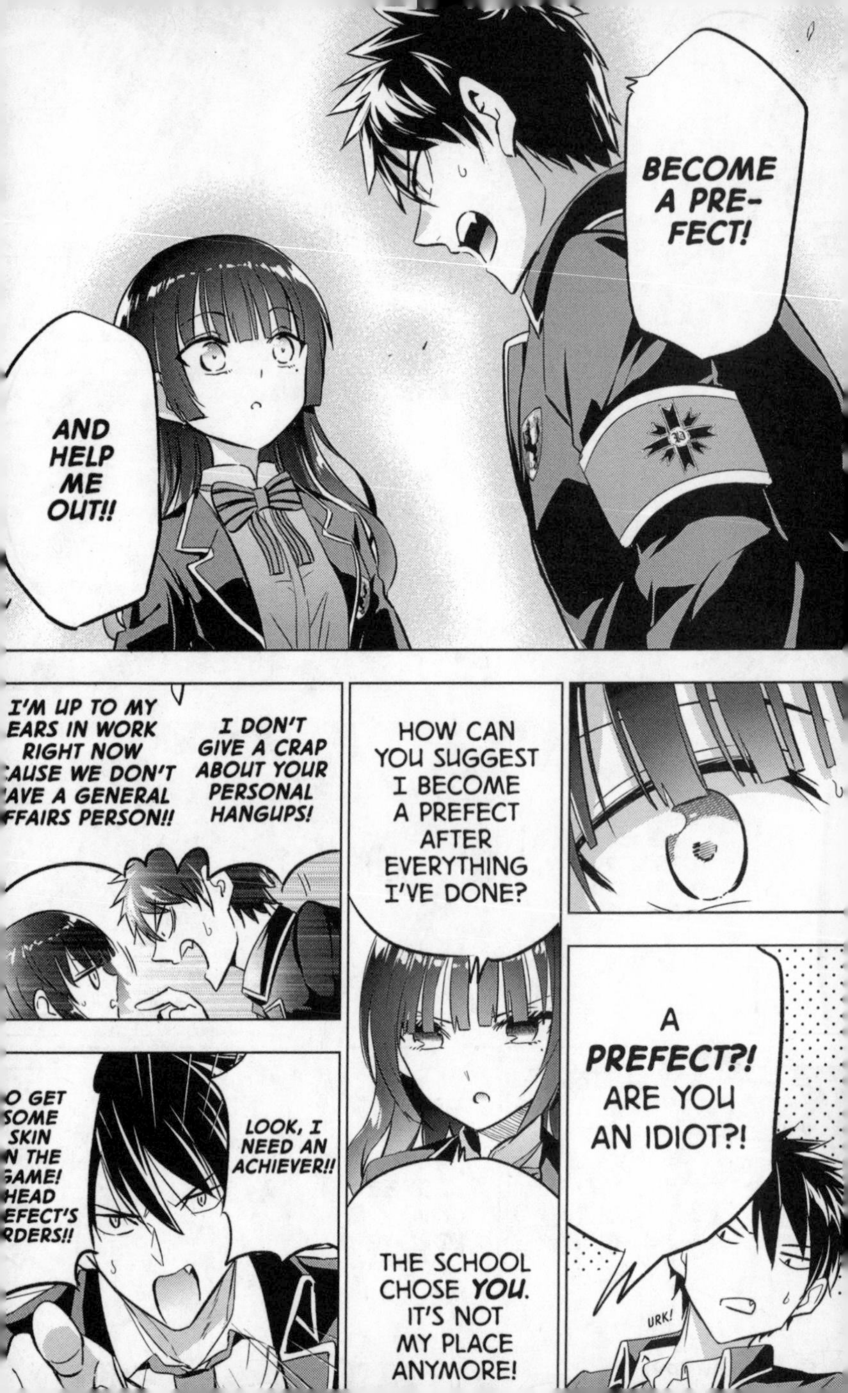
BECOME A PRE-FECT!
AND HELP ME OUT!!
A PREFECT?! ARE YOU AN IDIOT?!
URK!
HOW CAN YOU SUGGEST I BECOME A PREFECT AFTER EVERYTHING I'VE DONE?
THE SCHOOL CHOSE YOU. IT'S NOT MY PLACE ANYMORE!
I DON'T GIVE A CRAP ABOUT YOUR PERSONAL HANGUPS!
I'M UP TO MY EARS IN WORK RIGHT NOW AUSE WE DON'T AVE A GENERAL FFAIRS PERSON!!
LOOK, I NEED AN ACHIEVER!!
O GET SOME SKIN N THE GAME! HEAD EFECT'S RDERS!!

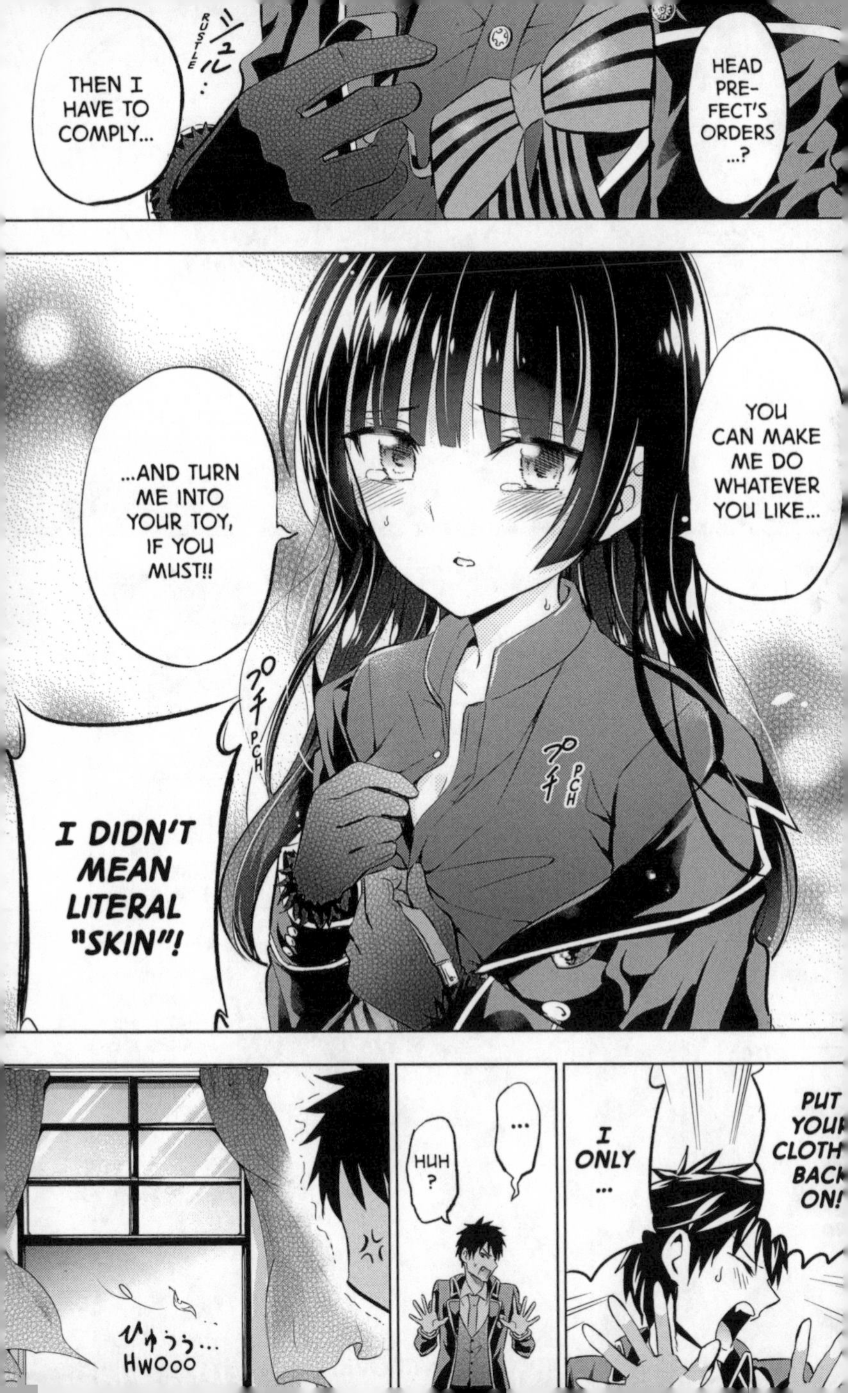
HEAD PRE-FECT'S ORDERS ...?
シュル… RUSTLE
THEN I HAVE TO COMPLY...
YOU CAN MAKE ME DO WHATEVER YOU LIKE...
...AND TURN ME INTO YOUR TOY, IF YOU MUST!!
プチ PCH
プチ PCH
I DIDN'T MEAN LITERAL "SKIN"!
PUT YOUR CLOTH BACK ON!
I ONLY ...
...
HUH ?
ひゅうう… HWOOO

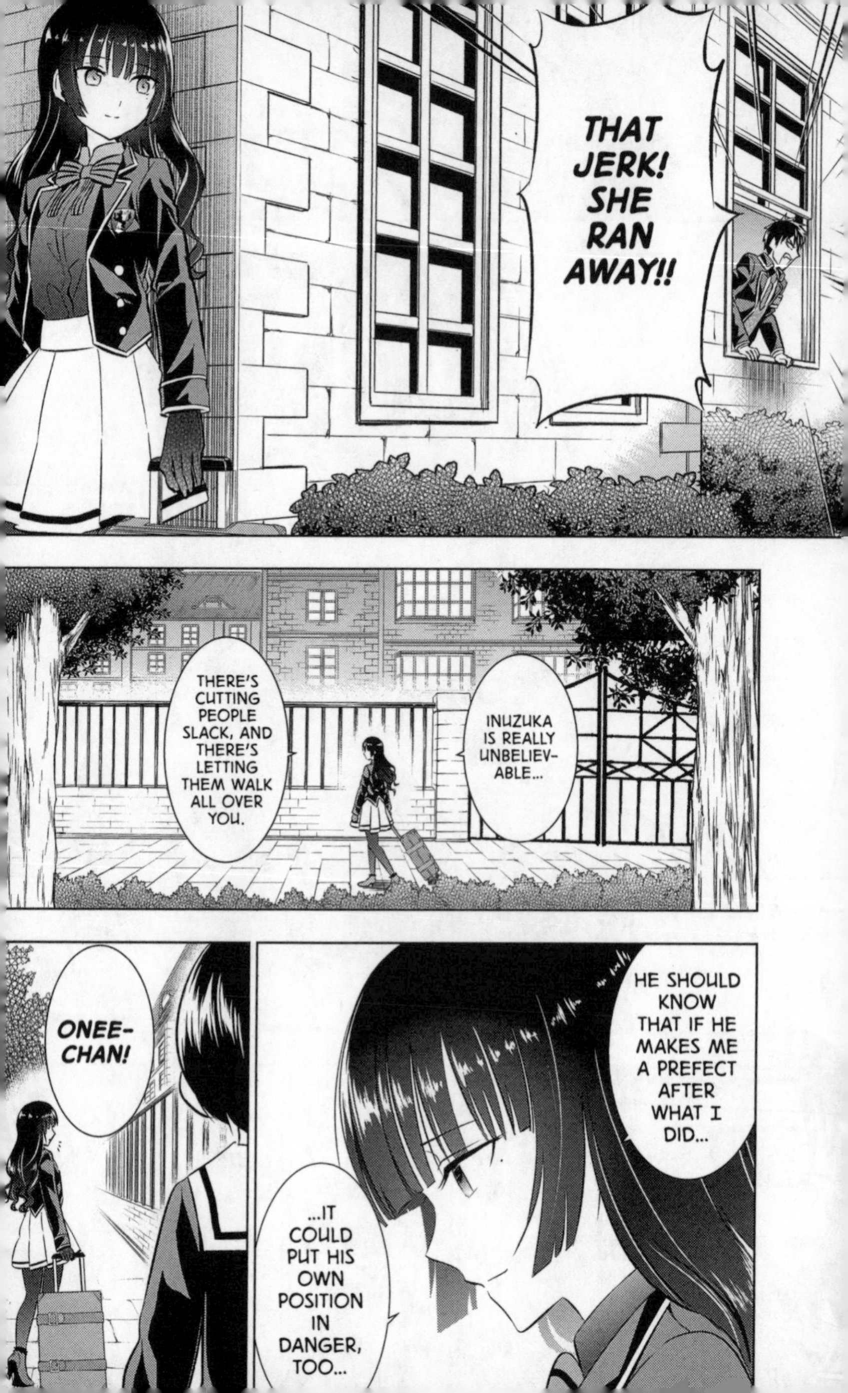
THAT JERK! SHE RAN AWAY!!
INUZUKA IS REALLY UNBELIEVABLE...
THERE'S CUTTING PEOPLE SLACK, AND THERE'S LETTING THEM WALK ALL OVER YOU.
HE SHOULD KNOW THAT IF HE MAKES ME A PREFECT AFTER WHAT I DID...
...IT COULD PUT HIS OWN POSITION IN DANGER, TOO...
ONEE-CHAN!

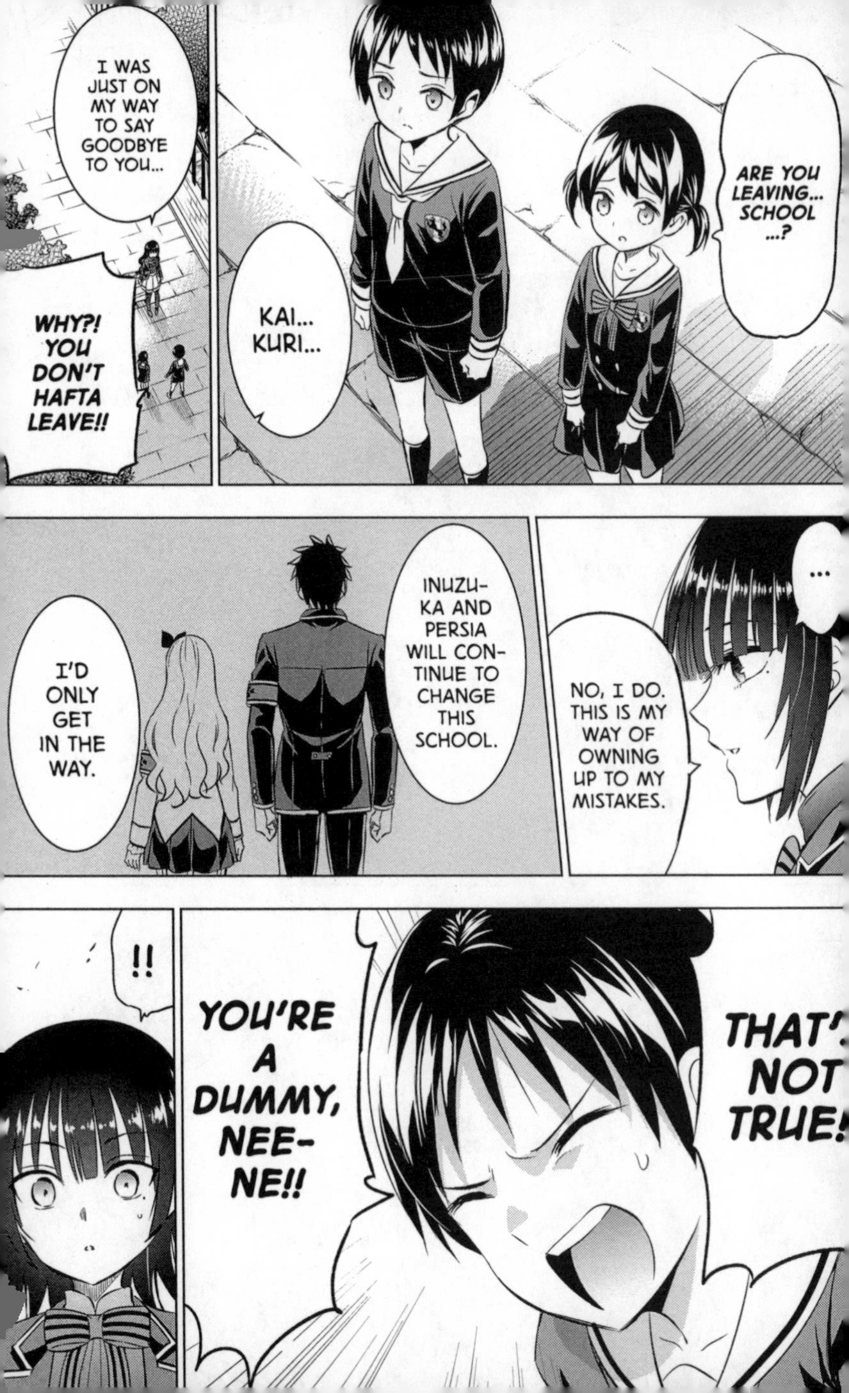
ARE YOU LEAVING... SCHOOL ...?
KAI... KURI...
I WAS JUST ON MY WAY TO SAY GOODBYE TO YOU...
WHY?! YOU DON'T HAFTA LEAVE!!
...
NO, I DO. THIS IS MY WAY OF OWNING UP TO MY MISTAKES.
INUZU-KA AND PERSIA WILL CON-TINUE TO CHANGE THIS SCHOOL.
I'D ONLY GET IN THE WAY.
THAT'S NOT TRUE!
YOU'RE A DUMMY, NEE-NE!!
!!

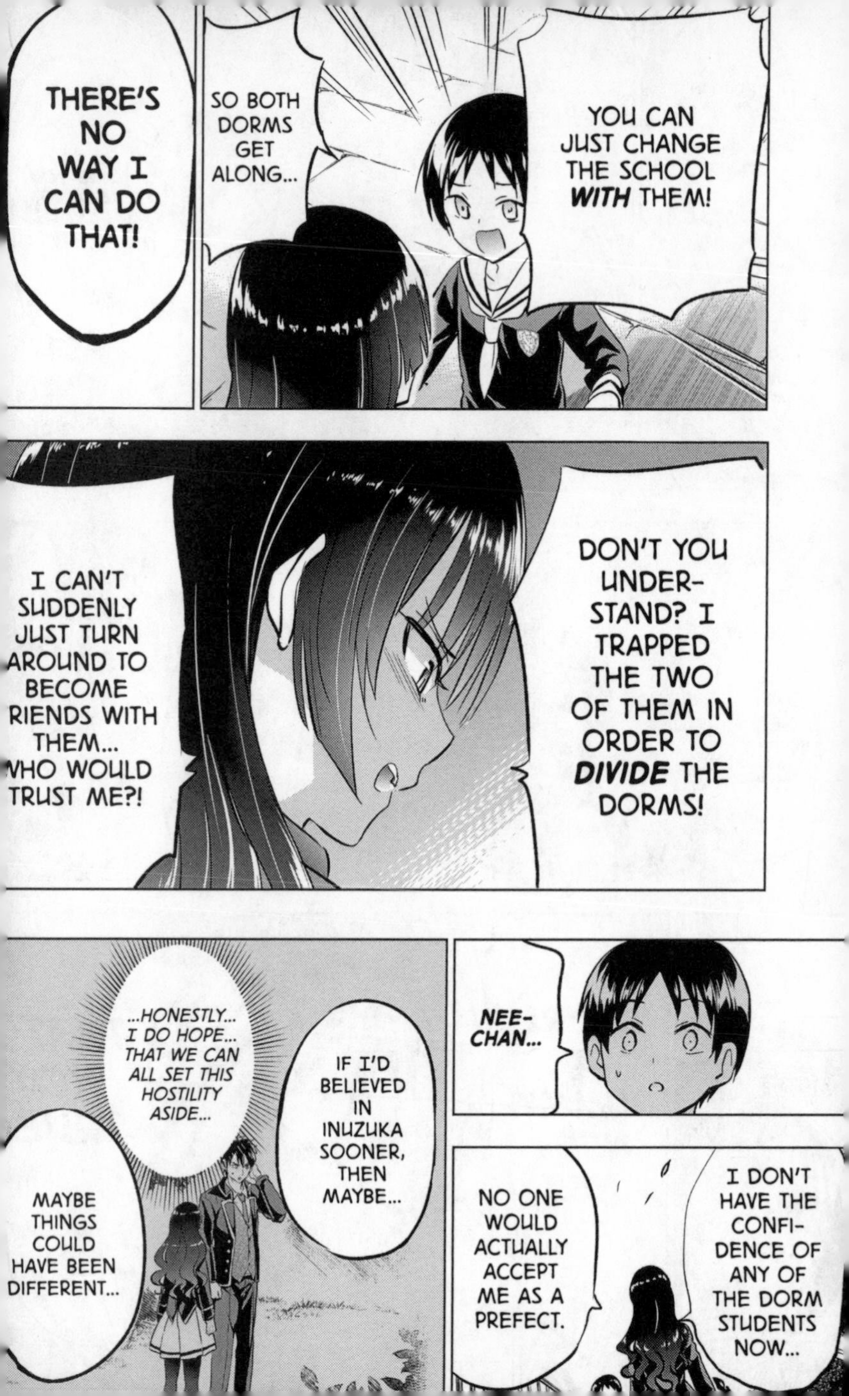
YOU CAN JUST CHANGE THE SCHOOL *WITH* THEM!
SO BOTH DORMS GET ALONG...
THERE'S NO WAY I CAN DO THAT!
DON'T YOU UNDER-STAND? I TRAPPED THE TWO OF THEM IN ORDER TO *DIVIDE* THE DORMS!
I CAN'T SUDDENLY JUST TURN AROUND TO BECOME RIENDS WITH THEM... VHO WOULD TRUST ME?!
*NEE-CHAN...*
I DON'T HAVE THE CONFI-DENCE OF ANY OF THE DORM STUDENTS NOW...
NO ONE WOULD ACTUALLY ACCEPT ME AS A PREFECT.
IF I'D BELIEVED IN INUZUKA SOONER, THEN MAYBE...
*...HONESTLY... I DO HOPE... THAT WE CAN ALL SET THIS HOSTILITY ASIDE...*
MAYBE THINGS COULD HAVE BEEN DIFFERENT...

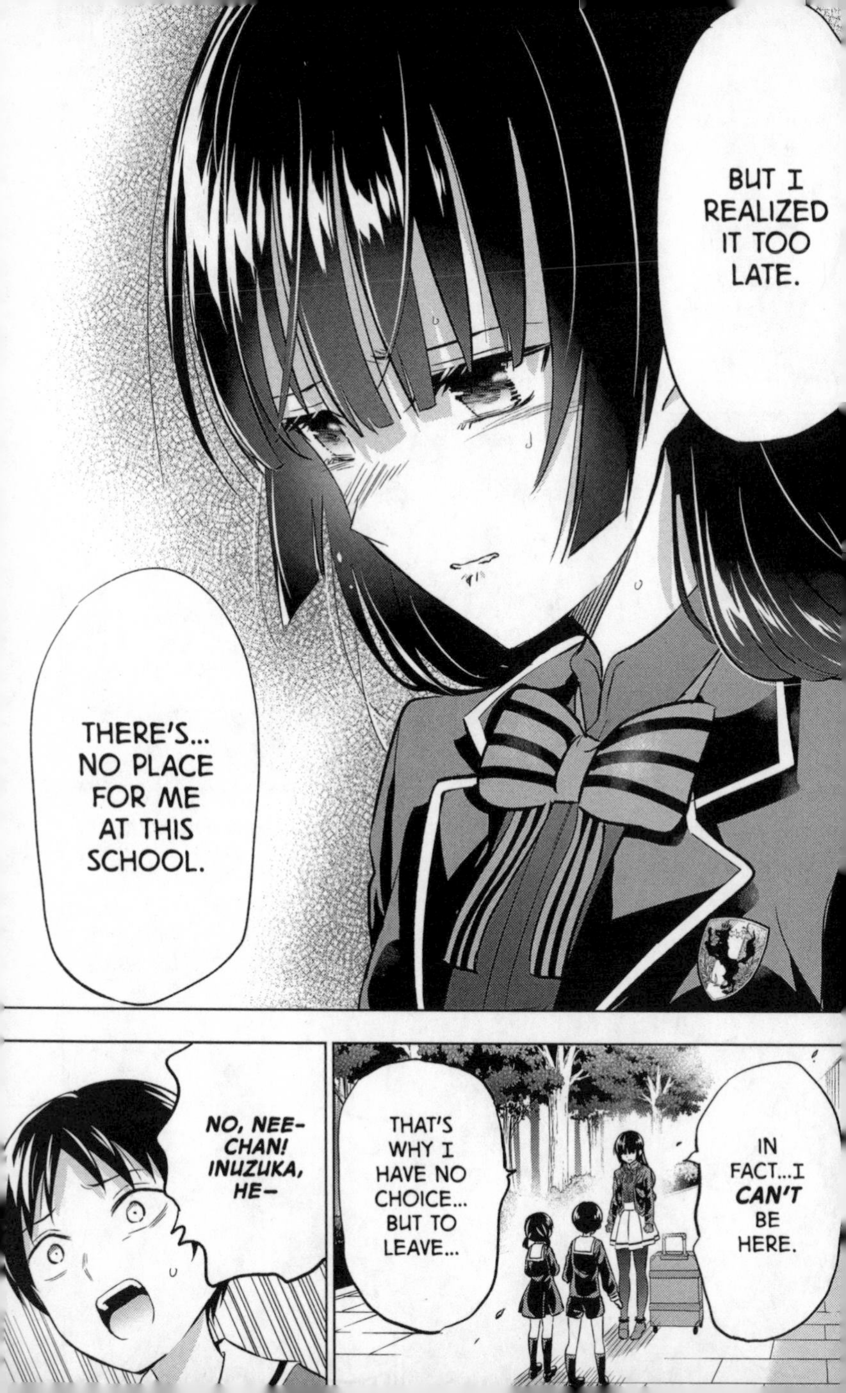
BUT I REALIZED IT TOO LATE.
THERE'S... NO PLACE FOR ME AT THIS SCHOOL.
IN FACT...I *CAN'T* BE HERE.
THAT'S WHY I HAVE NO CHOICE... BUT TO LEAVE...
*NO, NEE-CHAN! INUZUKA, HE–*

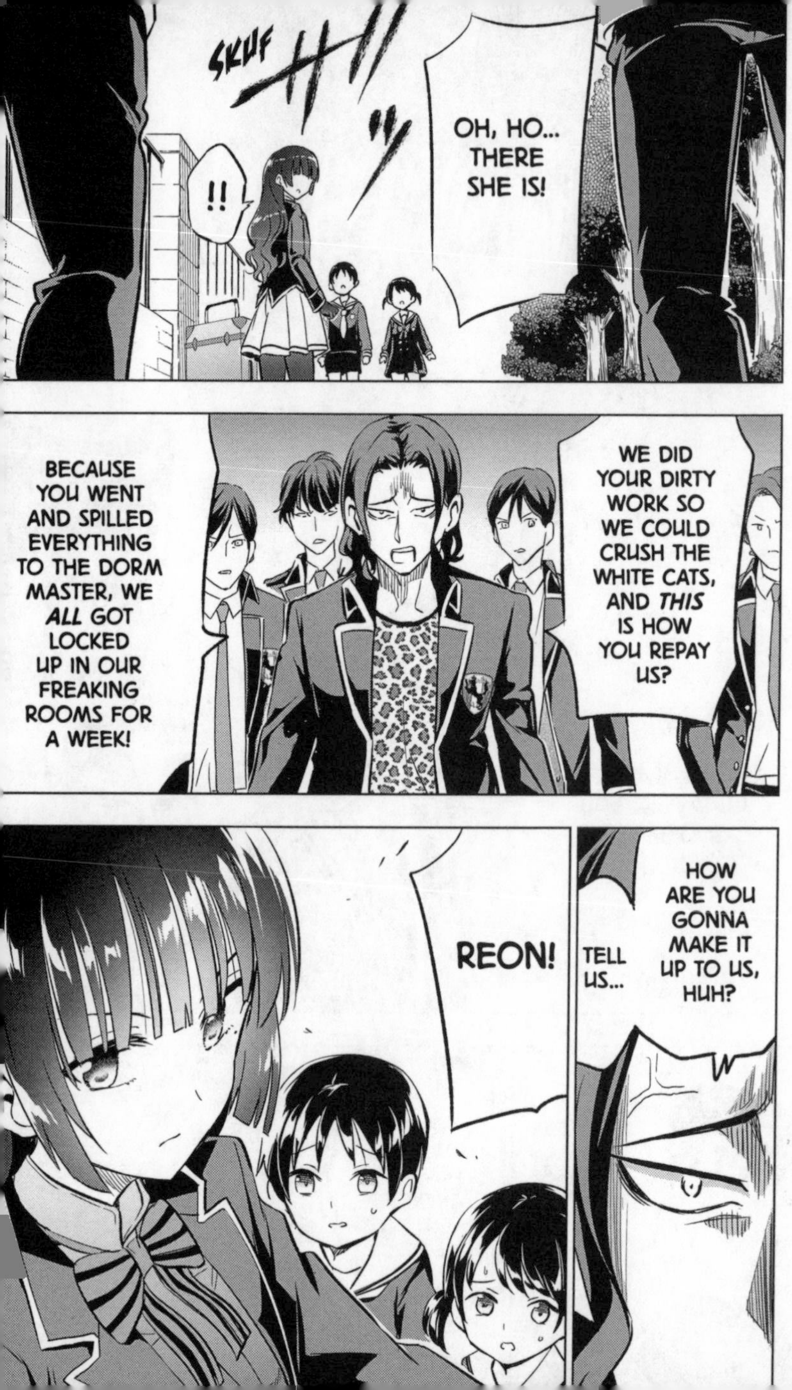
OH, HO... THERE SHE IS!
SKUF
!!
WE DID YOUR DIRTY WORK SO WE COULD CRUSH THE WHITE CATS, AND *THIS* IS HOW YOU REPAY US?
BECAUSE YOU WENT AND SPILLED EVERYTHING TO THE DORM MASTER, WE *ALL* GOT LOCKED UP IN OUR FREAKING ROOMS FOR A WEEK!
HOW ARE YOU GONNA MAKE IT UP TO US, HUH?
TELL US...
REON!

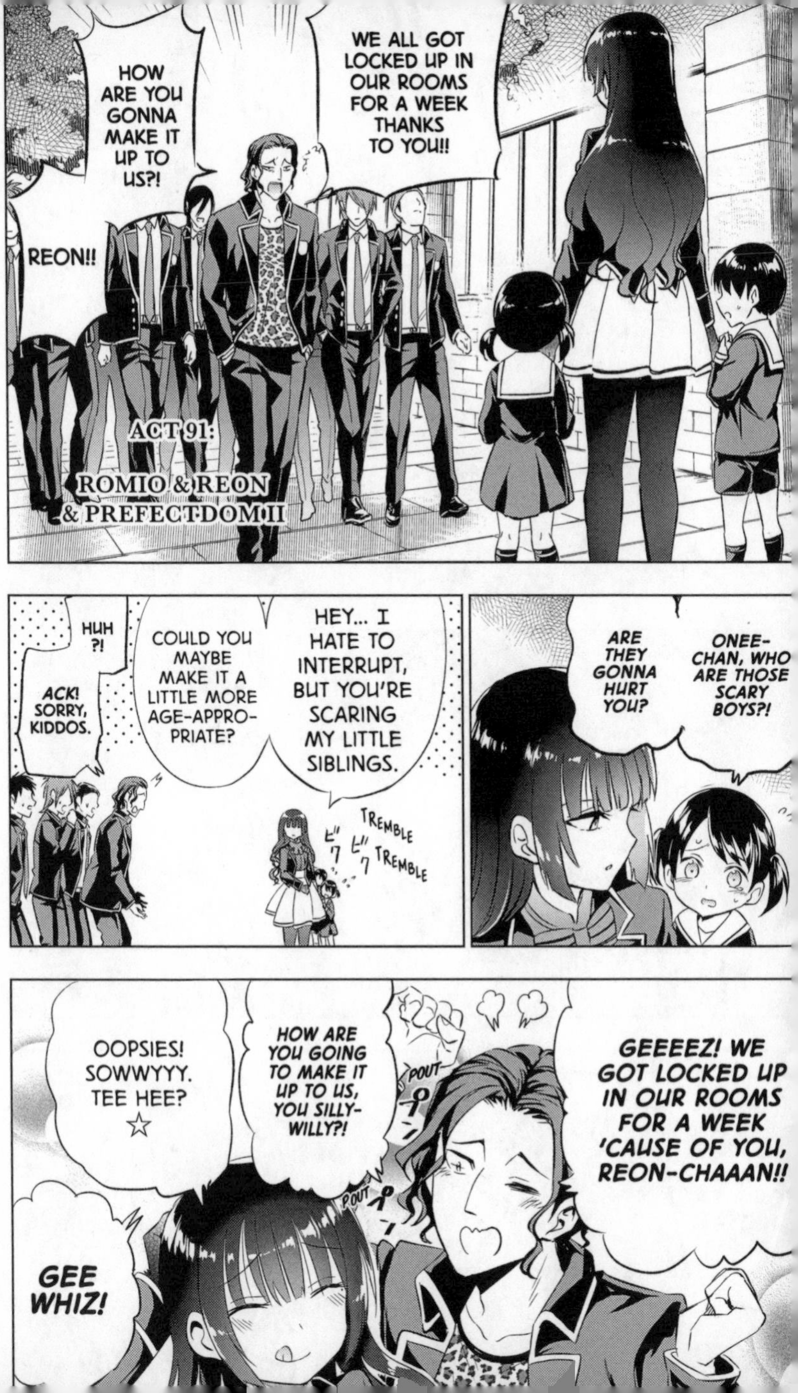
WE ALL GOT LOCKED UP IN OUR ROOMS FOR A WEEK THANKS TO YOU!!
HOW ARE YOU GONNA MAKE IT UP TO US?!
REON!!
ACT 91: ROMIO & REON & PREFECTDOM II
ONEE-CHAN, WHO ARE THOSE SCARY BOYS?!
ARE THEY GONNA HURT YOU?
HEY... I HATE TO INTERRUPT, BUT YOU'RE SCARING MY LITTLE SIBLINGS.
COULD YOU MAYBE MAKE IT A LITTLE MORE AGE-APPROPRIATE?
HUH ?!
ACK! SORRY, KIDDOS.
TREMBLE TREMBLE
GEEEEZ! WE GOT LOCKED UP IN OUR ROOMS FOR A WEEK 'CAUSE OF YOU, REON-CHAAAN!!
POUT
HOW ARE YOU GOING TO MAKE IT UP TO US, YOU SILLY-WILLY?!
OOPSIES! SOWWYYY. TEE HEE? ☆
POUT
GEE WHIZ!

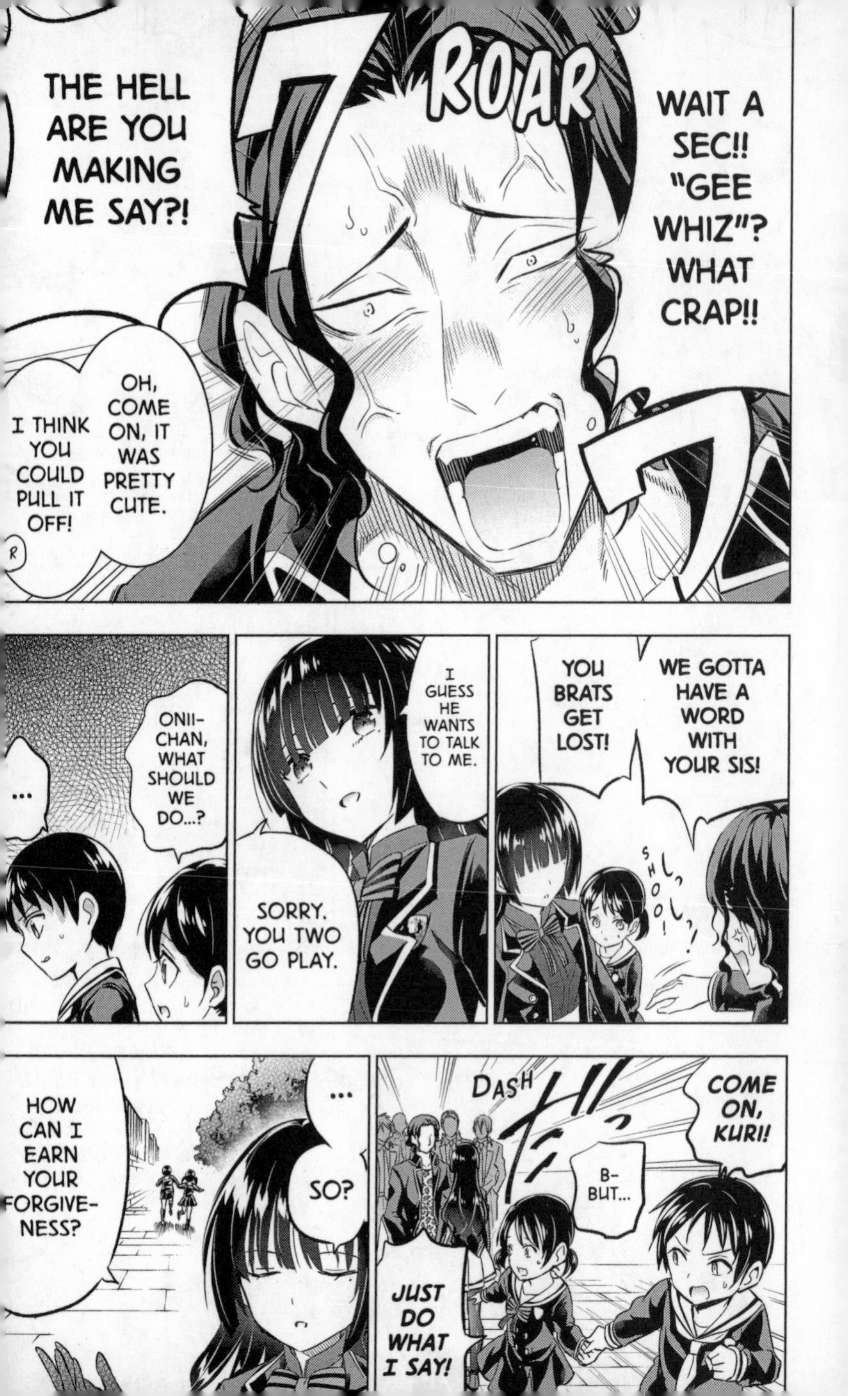
ROAR
WAIT A SEC!! "GEE WHIZ"? WHAT CRAP!!
THE HELL ARE YOU MAKING ME SAY?!
OH, COME ON, IT WAS PRETTY CUTE.
I THINK YOU COULD PULL IT OFF!
WE GOTTA HAVE A WORD WITH YOUR SIS!
YOU BRATS GET LOST!
SHOO!
I GUESS HE WANTS TO TALK TO ME.
SORRY. YOU TWO GO PLAY.
ONII-CHAN, WHAT SHOULD WE DO...?
...
COME ON, KURI!
DASH
B-BUT...
JUST DO WHAT I SAY!
...
SO?
HOW CAN I EARN YOUR FORGIVE-NESS?

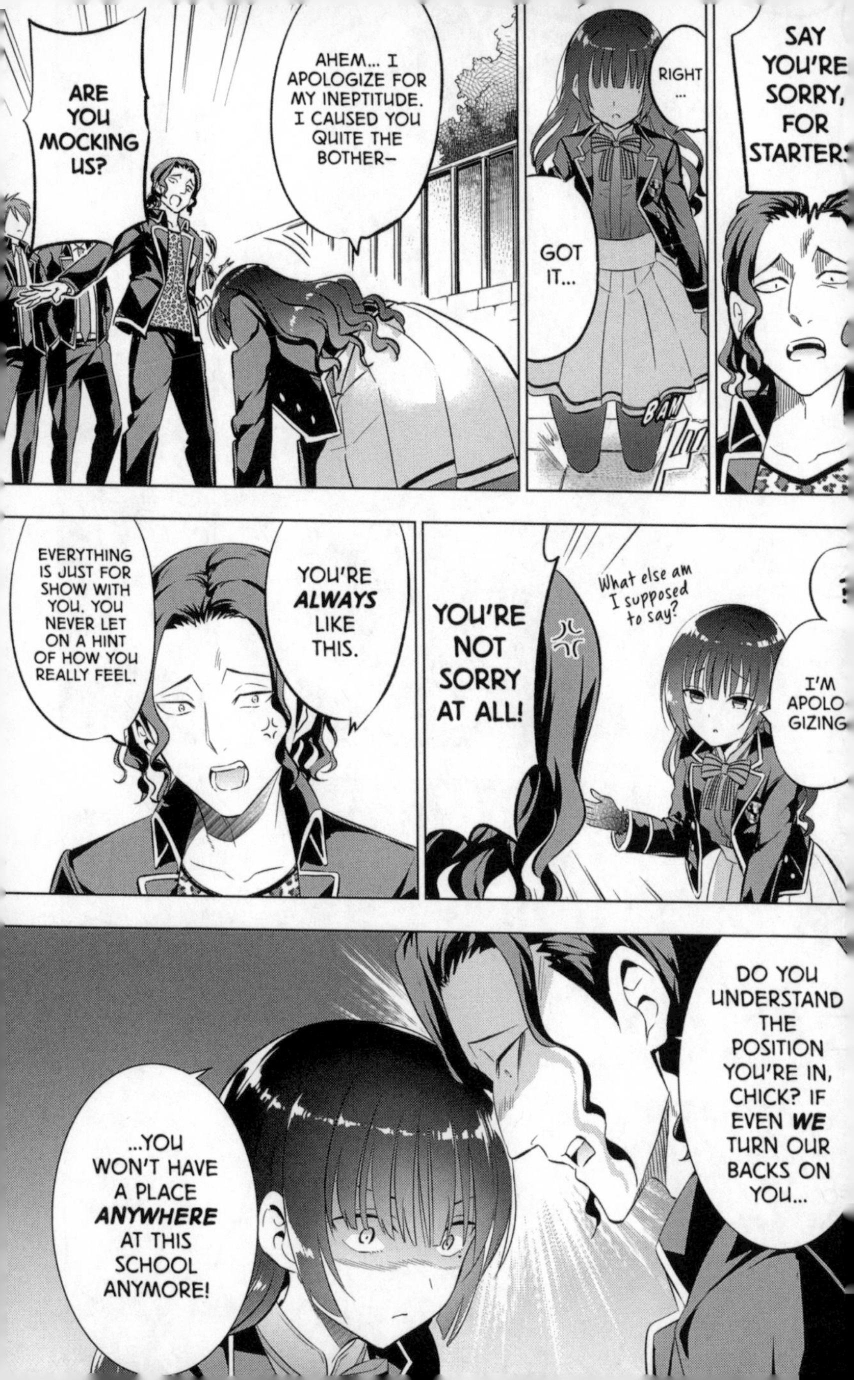
SAY YOU'RE SORRY, FOR STARTERS
RIGHT...
GOT IT...
BAM
AHEM... I APOLOGIZE FOR MY INEPTITUDE. I CAUSED YOU QUITE THE BOTHER—
ARE YOU MOCKING US?
I'M APOLOGIZING
What else am I supposed to say?
YOU'RE NOT SORRY AT ALL!
YOU'RE *ALWAYS* LIKE THIS.
EVERYTHING IS JUST FOR SHOW WITH YOU. YOU NEVER LET ON A HINT OF HOW YOU REALLY FEEL.
DO YOU UNDERSTAND THE POSITION YOU'RE IN, CHICK? IF EVEN *WE* TURN OUR BACKS ON YOU...
...YOU WON'T HAVE A PLACE *ANYWHERE* AT THIS SCHOOL ANYMORE!

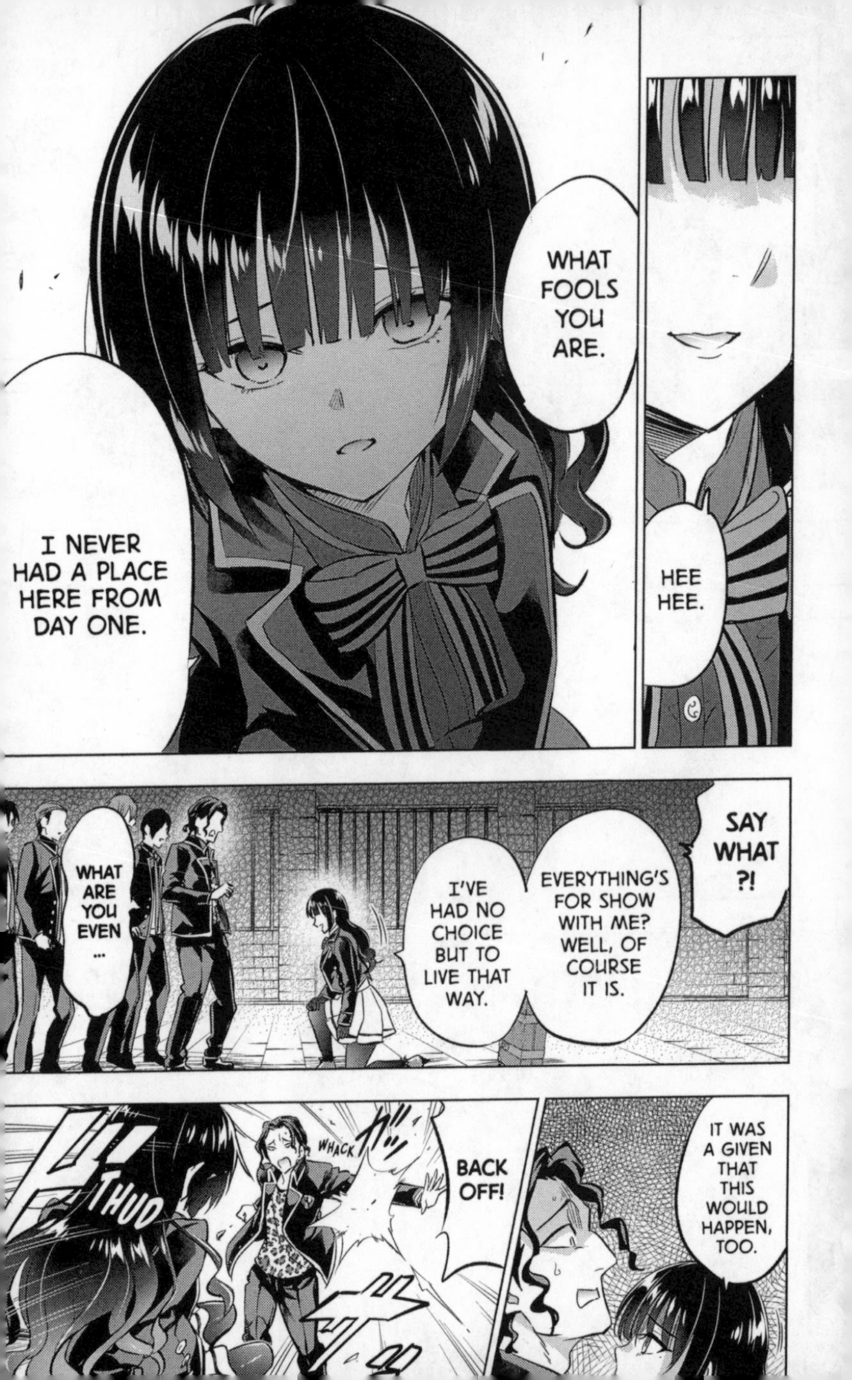
HEE HEE.
WHAT FOOLS YOU ARE.
I NEVER HAD A PLACE HERE FROM DAY ONE.
SAY WHAT?!
EVERYTHING'S FOR SHOW WITH ME? WELL, OF COURSE IT IS.
I'VE HAD NO CHOICE BUT TO LIVE THAT WAY.
WHAT ARE YOU EVEN ...
IT WAS A GIVEN THAT THIS WOULD HAPPEN, TOO.
BACK OFF!
WHACK
THUD

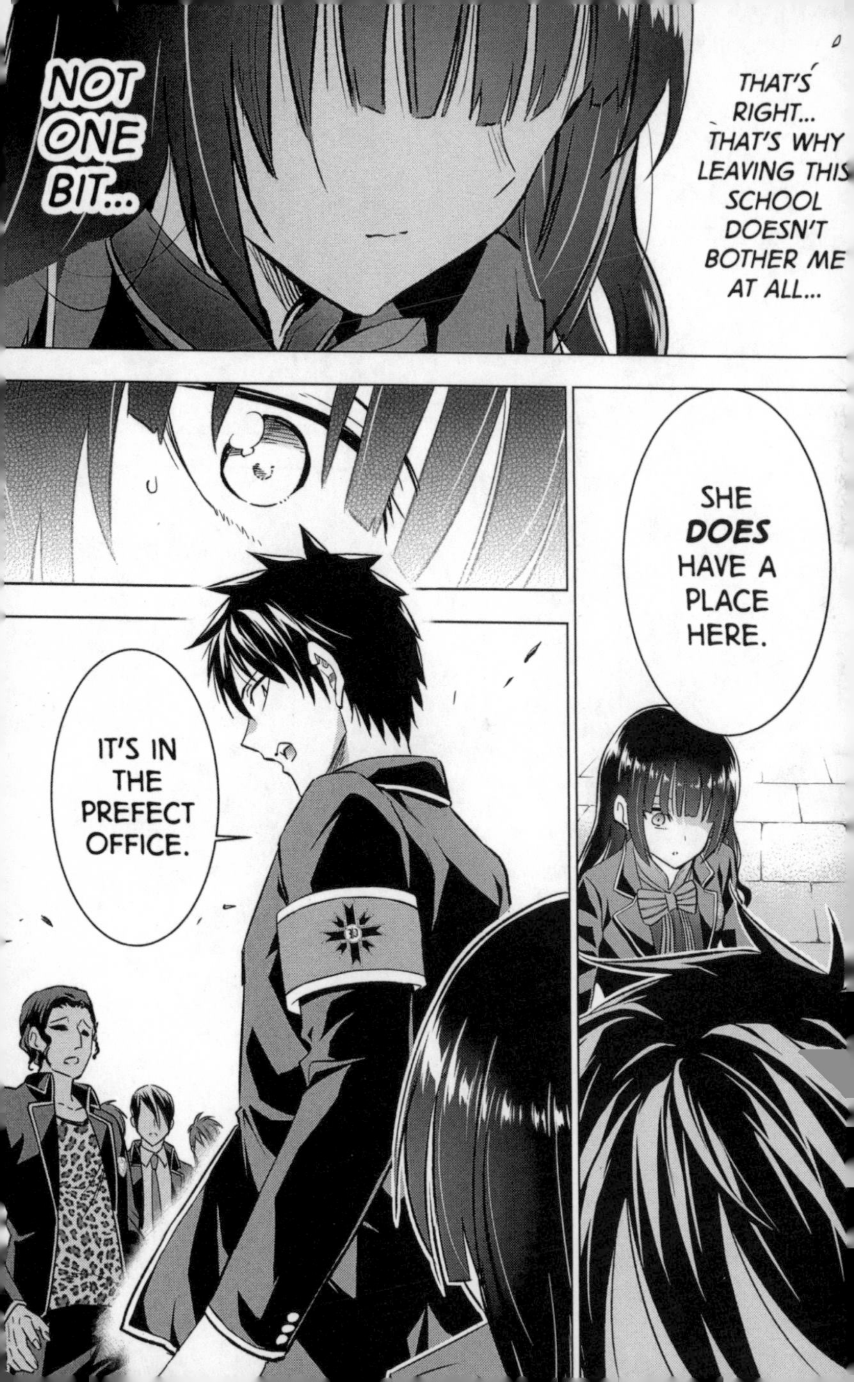
THAT'S RIGHT... THAT'S WHY LEAVING THIS SCHOOL DOESN'T BOTHER ME AT ALL...
NOT ONE BIT...
SHE **DOES** HAVE A PLACE HERE.
IT'S IN THE PREFECT OFFICE.

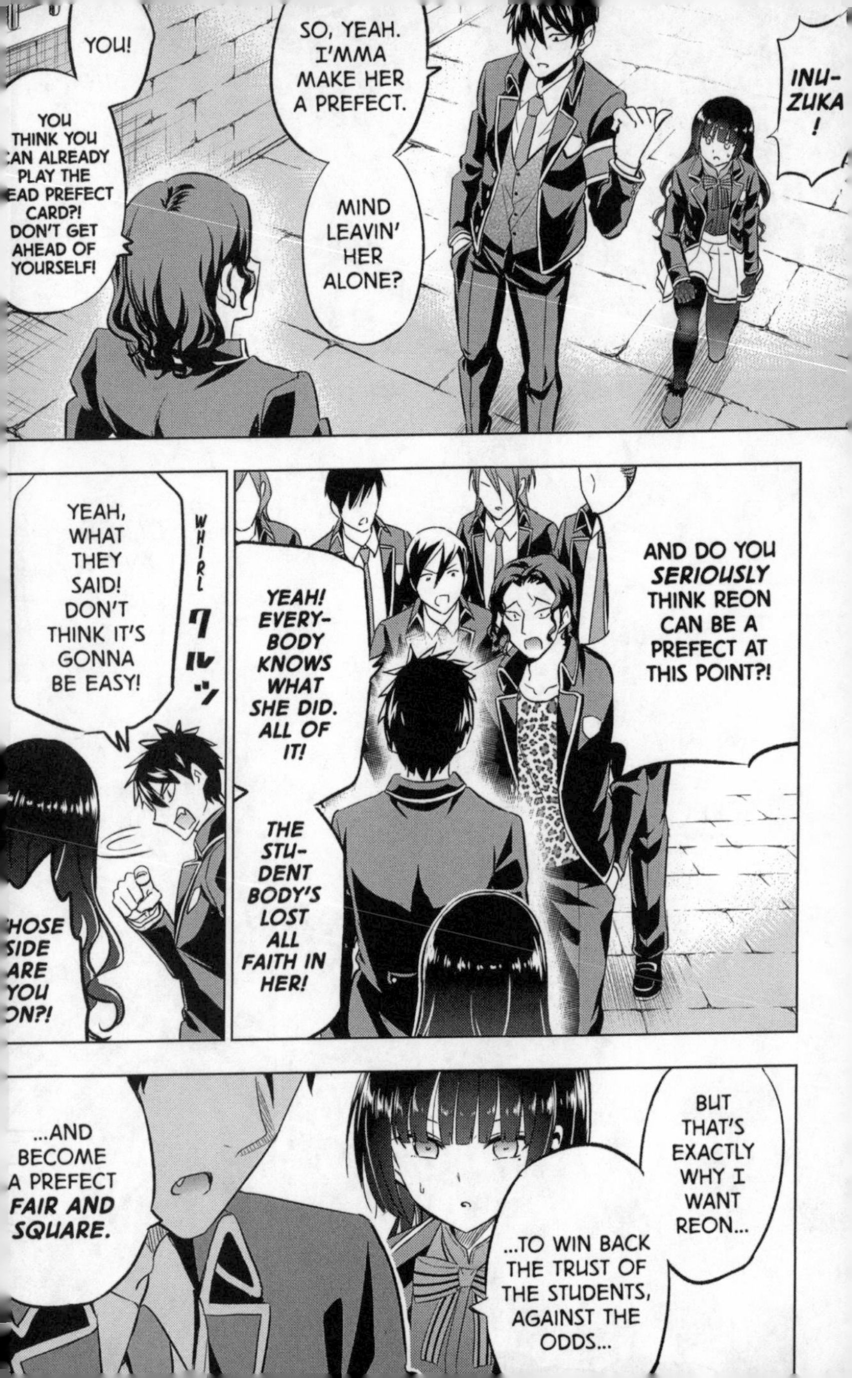
INU-ZUKA!
SO, YEAH. I'MMA MAKE HER A PREFECT.
MIND LEAVIN' HER ALONE?
YOU!
YOU THINK YOU AN ALREADY PLAY THE EAD PREFECT CARD?! DON'T GET AHEAD OF YOURSELF!
AND DO YOU SERIOUSLY THINK REON CAN BE A PREFECT AT THIS POINT?!
YEAH! EVERY-BODY KNOWS WHAT SHE DID. ALL OF IT!
THE STU-DENT BODY'S LOST ALL FAITH IN HER!
YEAH, WHAT THEY SAID! DON'T THINK IT'S GONNA BE EASY!
WHIRL
HOSE SIDE ARE YOU ON?!
BUT THAT'S EXACTLY WHY I WANT REON...
...TO WIN BACK THE TRUST OF THE STUDENTS, AGAINST THE ODDS...
...AND BECOME A PREFECT FAIR AND SQUARE.

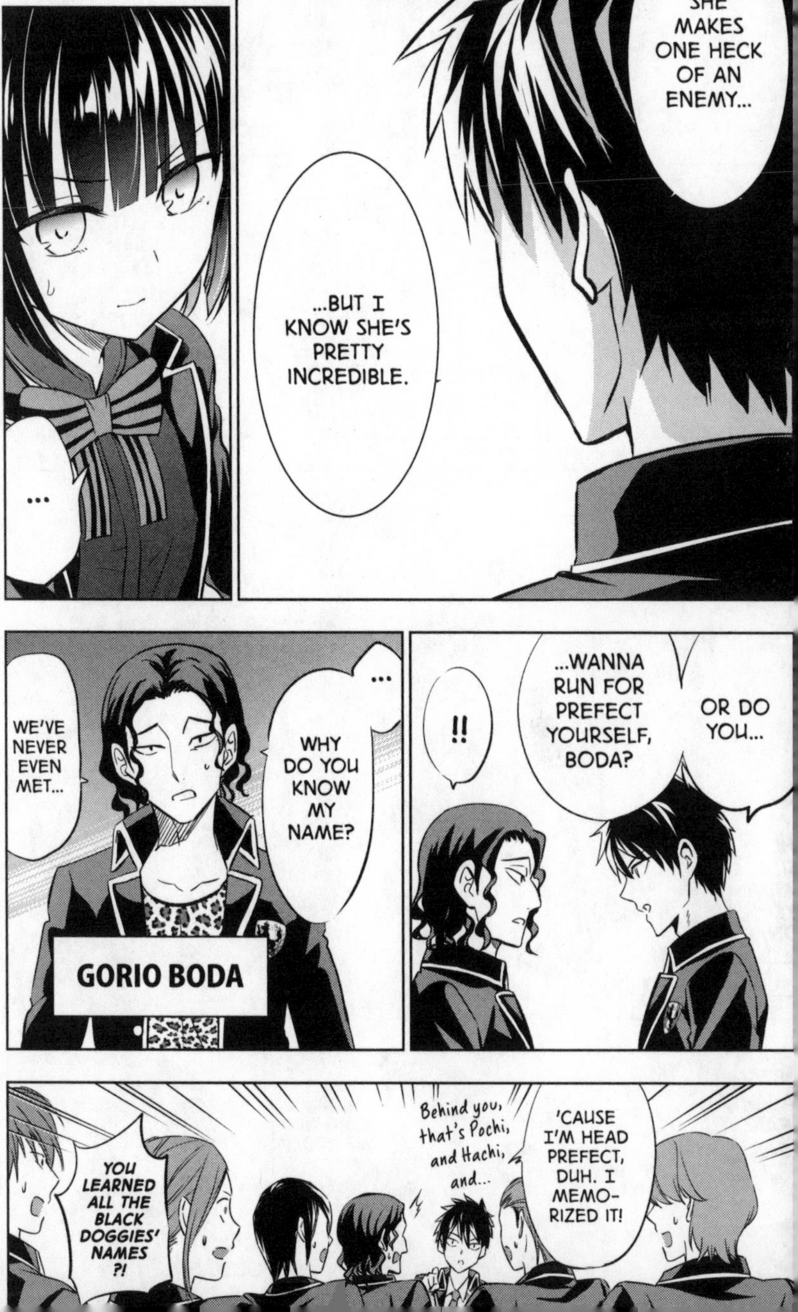
SHE MAKES ONE HECK OF AN ENEMY...
...BUT I KNOW SHE'S PRETTY INCREDIBLE.
...
OR DO YOU...
...WANNA RUN FOR PREFECT YOURSELF, BODA?
!!
...
WHY DO YOU KNOW MY NAME?
WE'VE NEVER EVEN MET...
GORIO BODA
'CAUSE I'M HEAD PREFECT, DUH. I MEMORIZED IT!
Behind you, that's Pochi, and Hachi, and...
YOU LEARNED ALL THE BLACK DOGGIES' NAMES ?!

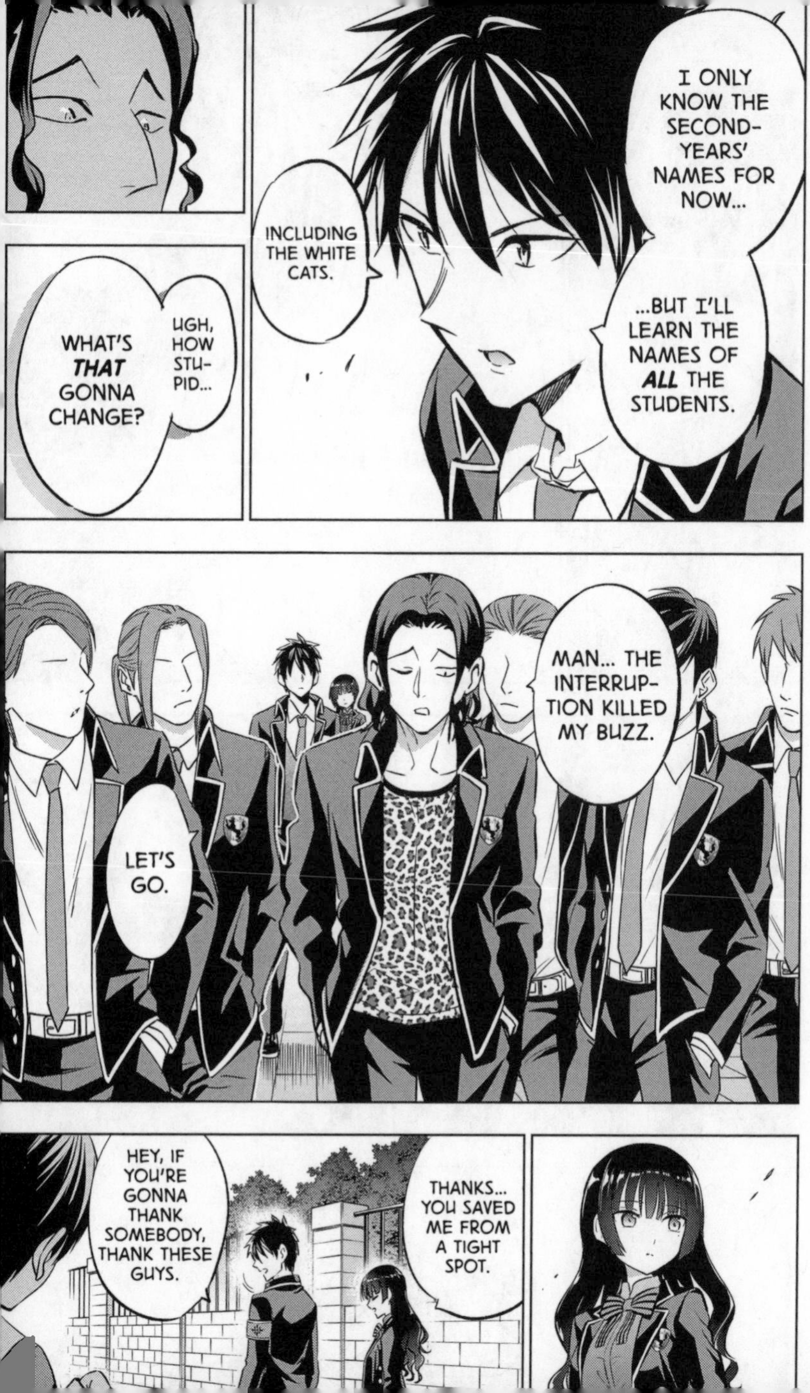
I ONLY KNOW THE SECOND-YEARS' NAMES FOR NOW...
...BUT I'LL LEARN THE NAMES OF *ALL* THE STUDENTS.
INCLUDING THE WHITE CATS.
UGH, HOW STUPID...
WHAT'S *THAT* GONNA CHANGE?
MAN... THE INTERRUPTION KILLED MY BUZZ.
LET'S GO.
THANKS... YOU SAVED ME FROM A TIGHT SPOT.
HEY, IF YOU'RE GONNA THANK SOMEBODY, THANK THESE GUYS.

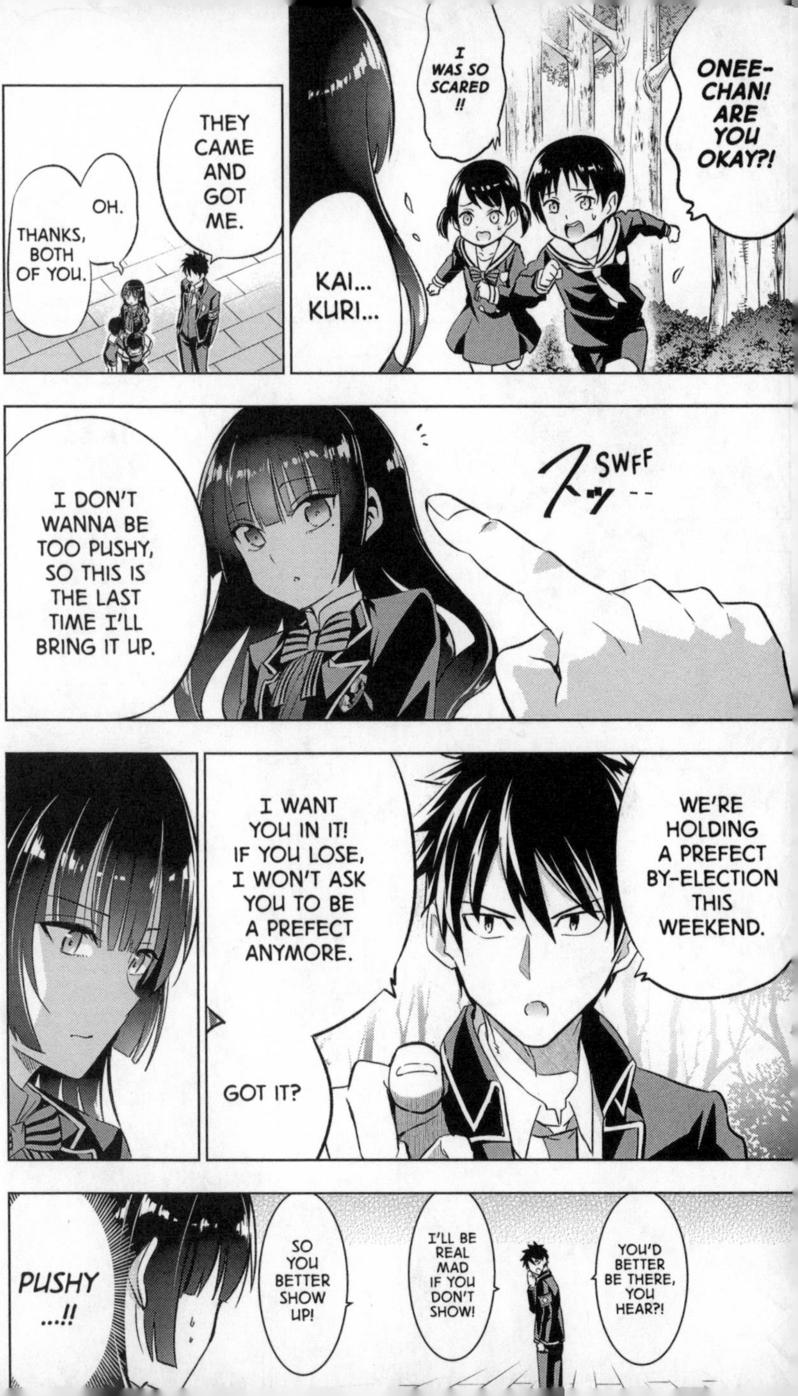

ONEE-CHAN! ARE YOU OKAY?!
I WAS SO SCARED!!
KAI... KURI...
THEY CAME AND GOT ME.
OH. THANKS, BOTH OF YOU.
SWFF
I DON'T WANNA BE TOO PUSHY, SO THIS IS THE LAST TIME I'LL BRING IT UP.
WE'RE HOLDING A PREFECT BY-ELECTION THIS WEEKEND.
I WANT YOU IN IT! IF YOU LOSE, I WON'T ASK YOU TO BE A PREFECT ANYMORE.
GOT IT?
YOU'D BETTER BE THERE, YOU HEAR?!
I'LL BE REAL MAD IF YOU DON'T SHOW!
SO YOU BETTER SHOW UP!
PUSHY...!!

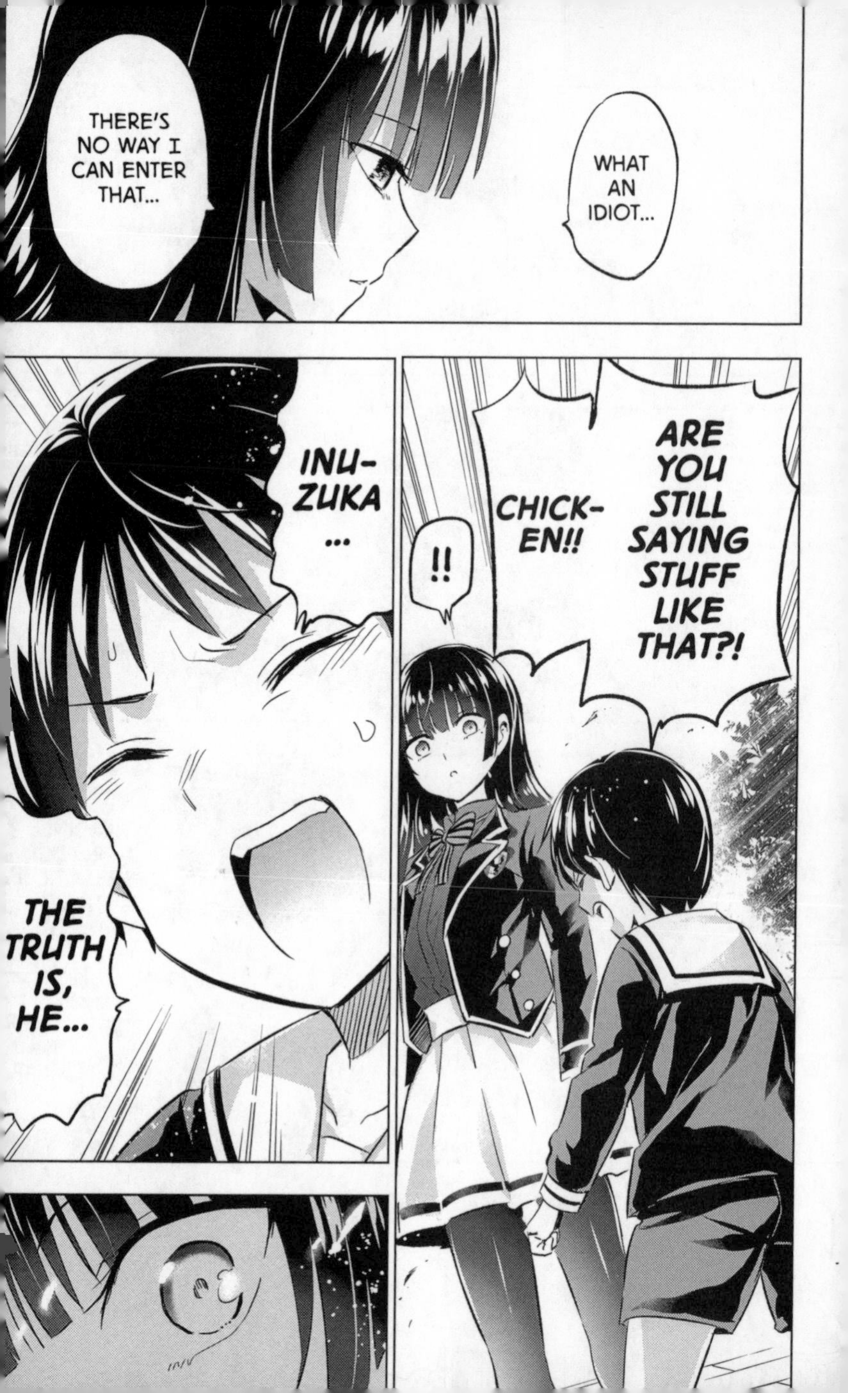
WHAT AN IDIOT...
THERE'S NO WAY I CAN ENTER THAT...
ARE YOU STILL SAYING STUFF LIKE THAT?!
CHICK-EN!!
!!
INU-ZUKA ...
THE TRUTH IS, HE...

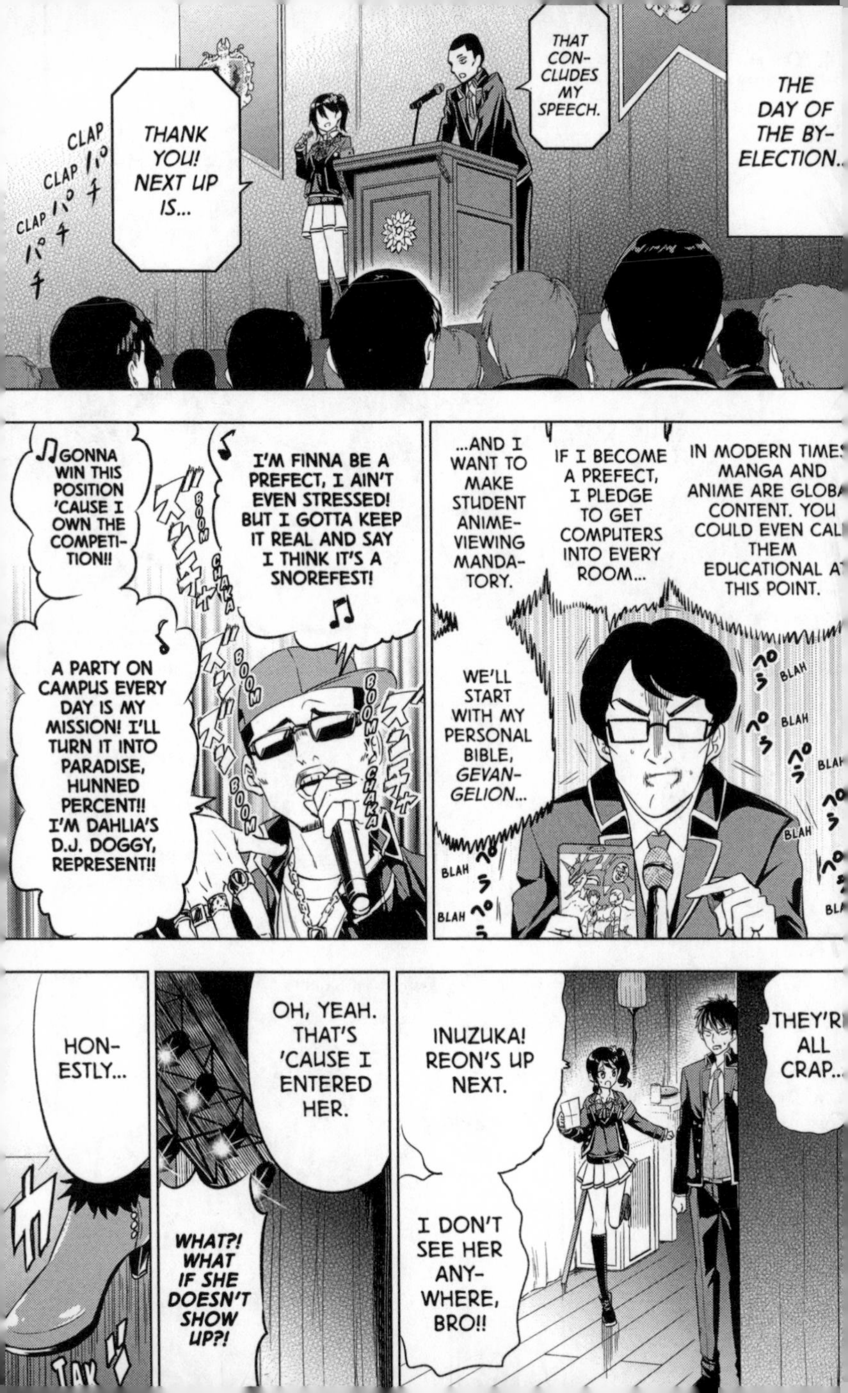
THE DAY OF THE BY-ELECTION...
THAT CONCLUDES MY SPEECH.
THANK YOU! NEXT UP IS...
CLAP CLAP CLAP
IN MODERN TIMES MANGA AND ANIME ARE GLOBA CONTENT. YOU COULD EVEN CAL THEM EDUCATIONAL AT THIS POINT.
IF I BECOME A PREFECT, I PLEDGE TO GET COMPUTERS INTO EVERY ROOM...
...AND I WANT TO MAKE STUDENT ANIME-VIEWING MANDATORY.
WE'LL START WITH MY PERSONAL BIBLE, GEVANGELION...
BLAH BLAH BLAH BLAH BLAH BLAH
I'M FINNA BE A PREFECT, I AIN'T EVEN STRESSED! BUT I GOTTA KEEP IT REAL AND SAY I THINK IT'S A SNOREFEST!
GONNA WIN THIS POSITION 'CAUSE I OWN THE COMPETITION!!
A PARTY ON CAMPUS EVERY DAY IS MY MISSION! I'LL TURN IT INTO PARADISE, HUNNED PERCENT!! I'M DAHLIA'S D.J. DOGGY, REPRESENT!!
BOOM CHAKA BOOM BOOM BOOM CHAKA BOOM
THEY'RE ALL CRAP...
INUZUKA! REON'S UP NEXT.
I DON'T SEE HER ANYWHERE, BRO!!
OH, YEAH. THAT'S 'CAUSE I ENTERED HER.
WHAT?! WHAT IF SHE DOESN'T SHOW UP?!
HONESTLY...
TAK

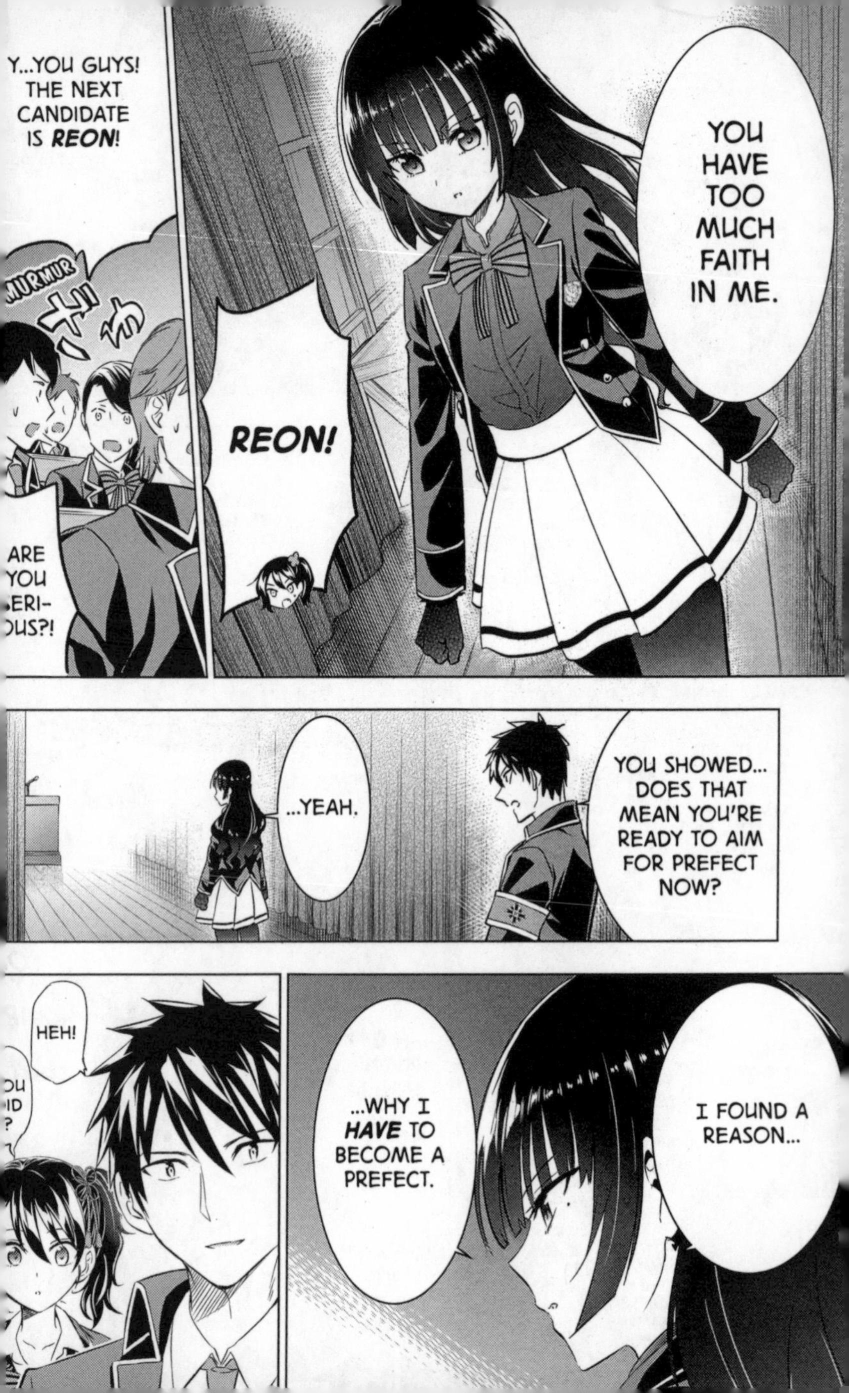
YOU HAVE TOO MUCH FAITH IN ME.
REON!
Y...YOU GUYS! THE NEXT CANDIDATE IS REON!
MURMUR
ARE YOU SERI-OUS?!
YOU SHOWED... DOES THAT MEAN YOU'RE READY TO AIM FOR PREFECT NOW?
...YEAH.
I FOUND A REASON...
...WHY I HAVE TO BECOME A PREFECT.
HEH!

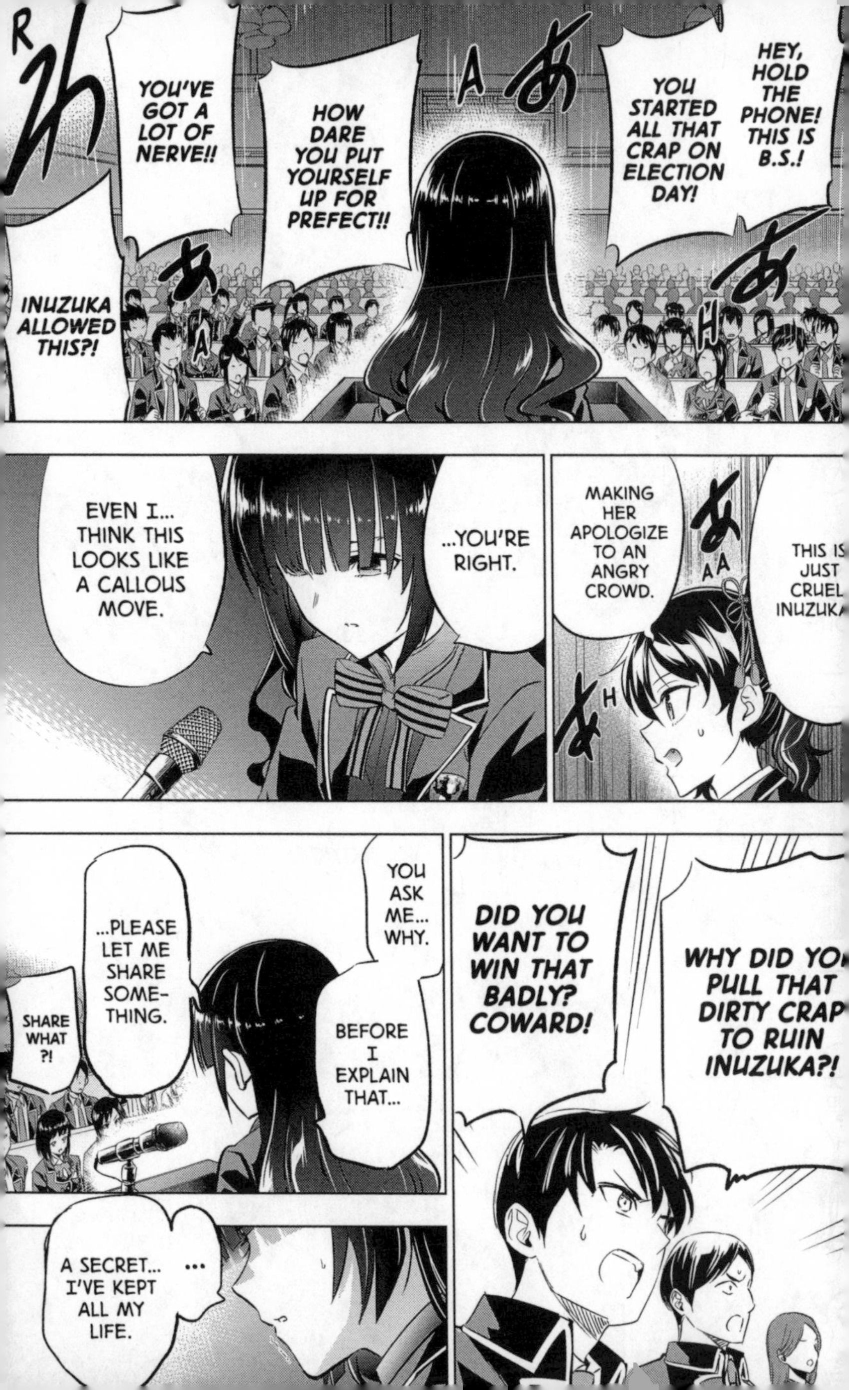
HEY, HOLD THE PHONE! THIS IS B.S.!
YOU STARTED ALL THAT CRAP ON ELECTION DAY!
あ H
あ A
HOW DARE YOU PUT YOURSELF UP FOR PREFECT!!
YOU'VE GOT A LOT OF NERVE!!
わ R
あ A
INUZUKA ALLOWED THIS?!
THIS IS JUST CRUEL INUZUKA
あ A
MAKING HER APOLOGIZE TO AN ANGRY CROWD.
あ H
...YOU'RE RIGHT.
EVEN I... THINK THIS LOOKS LIKE A CALLOUS MOVE.
WHY DID YO PULL THAT DIRTY CRAP TO RUIN INUZUKA?!
DID YOU WANT TO WIN THAT BADLY? COWARD!
YOU ASK ME... WHY.
BEFORE I EXPLAIN THAT...
...PLEASE LET ME SHARE SOMETHING.
SHARE WHAT ?!
...
A SECRET... I'VE KEPT ALL MY LIFE.

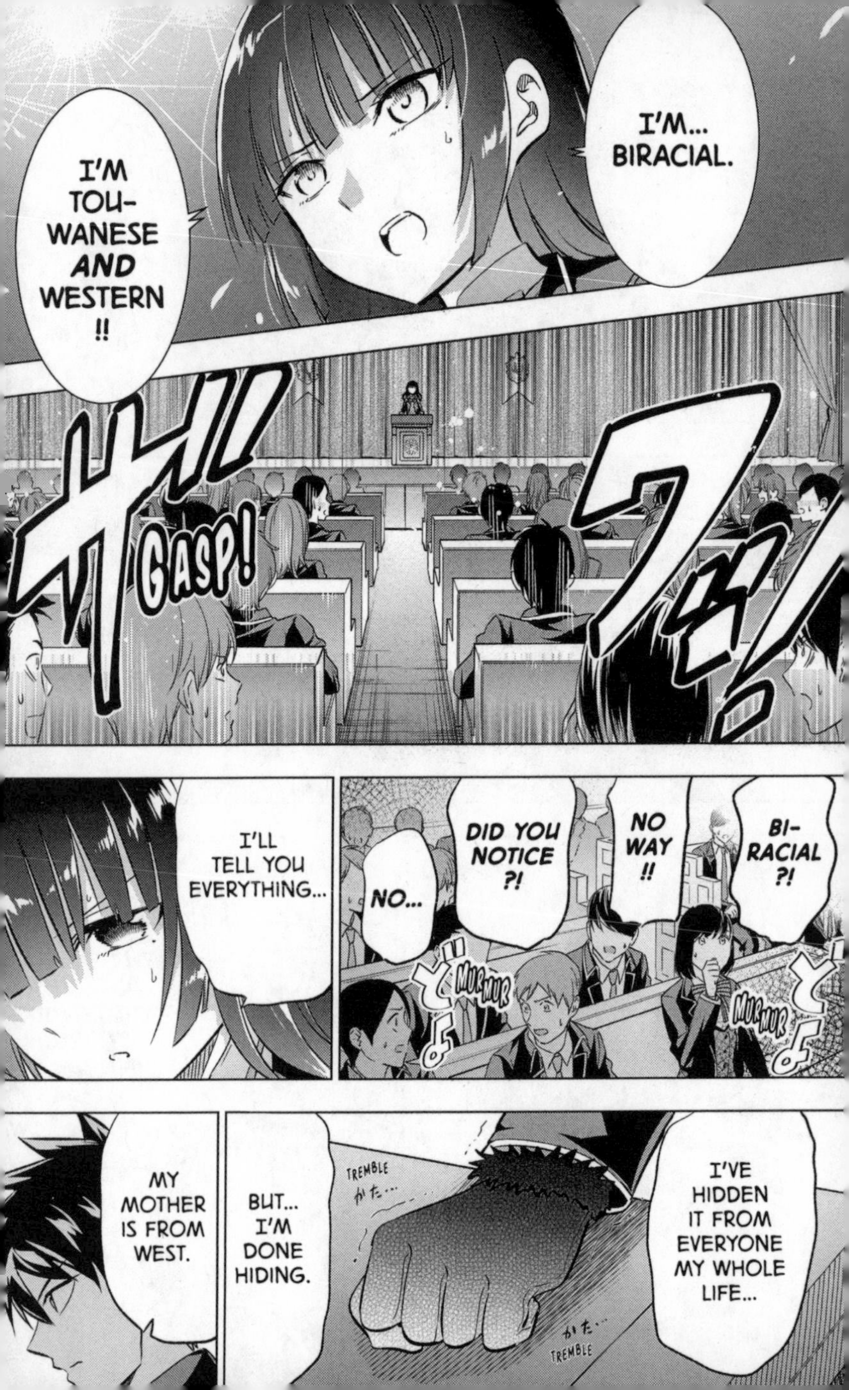
I'M... BIRACIAL.
I'M TOU-WANESE AND WESTERN!!
GASP!
BI-RACIAL?!
NO WAY!!
DID YOU NOTICE?!
NO...
MURMUR
MURMUR
I'LL TELL YOU EVERYTHING...
I'VE HIDDEN IT FROM EVERYONE MY WHOLE LIFE...
TREMBLE
かた…
かた…
TREMBLE
BUT... I'M DONE HIDING.
MY MOTHER IS FROM WEST.

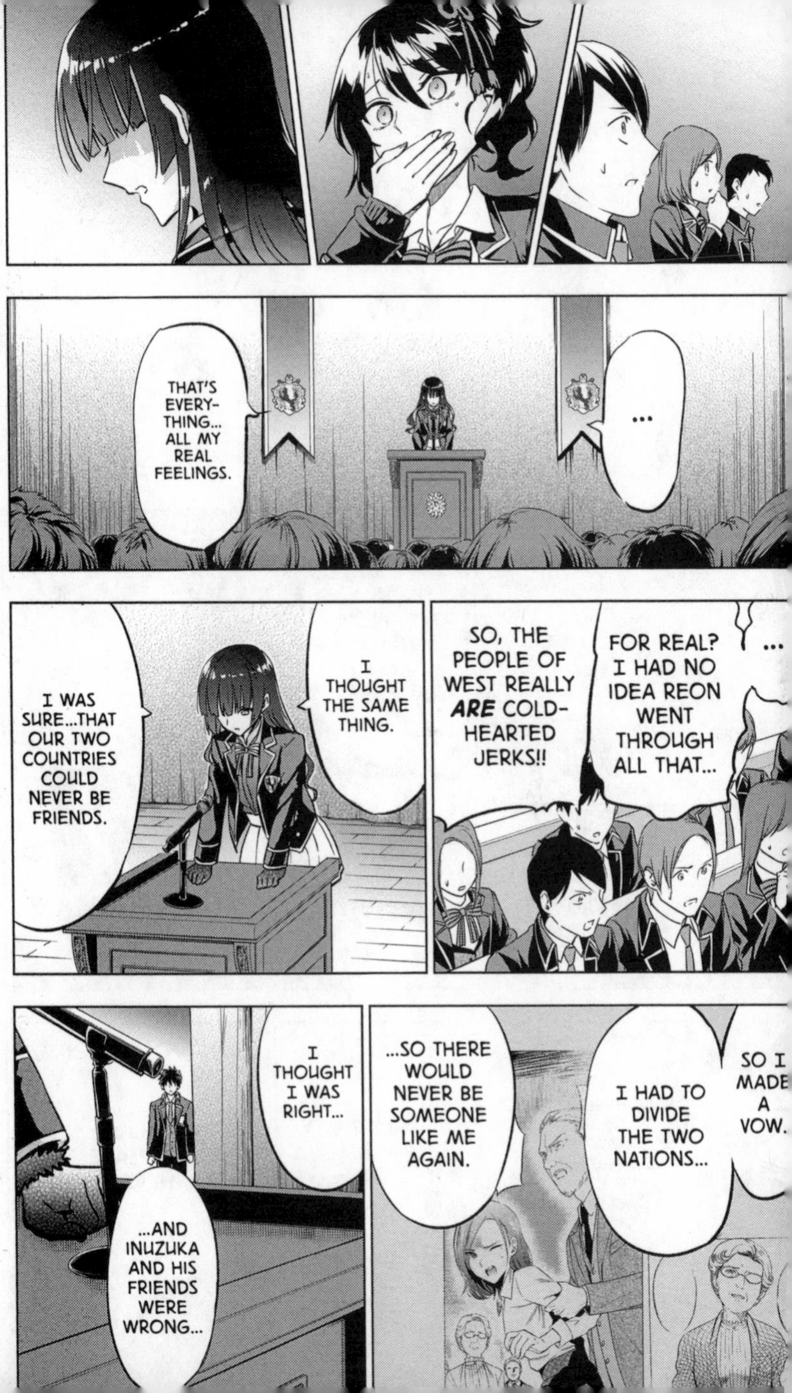
...
THAT'S EVERYTHING... ALL MY REAL FEELINGS.
...
FOR REAL? I HAD NO IDEA REON WENT THROUGH ALL THAT...
SO, THE PEOPLE OF WEST REALLY *ARE* COLD-HEARTED JERKS!!
I THOUGHT THE SAME THING.
I WAS SURE...THAT OUR TWO COUNTRIES COULD NEVER BE FRIENDS.
SO I MADE A VOW.
I HAD TO DIVIDE THE TWO NATIONS...
...SO THERE WOULD NEVER BE SOMEONE LIKE ME AGAIN.
I THOUGHT I WAS RIGHT...
...AND INUZUKA AND HIS FRIENDS WERE WRONG...

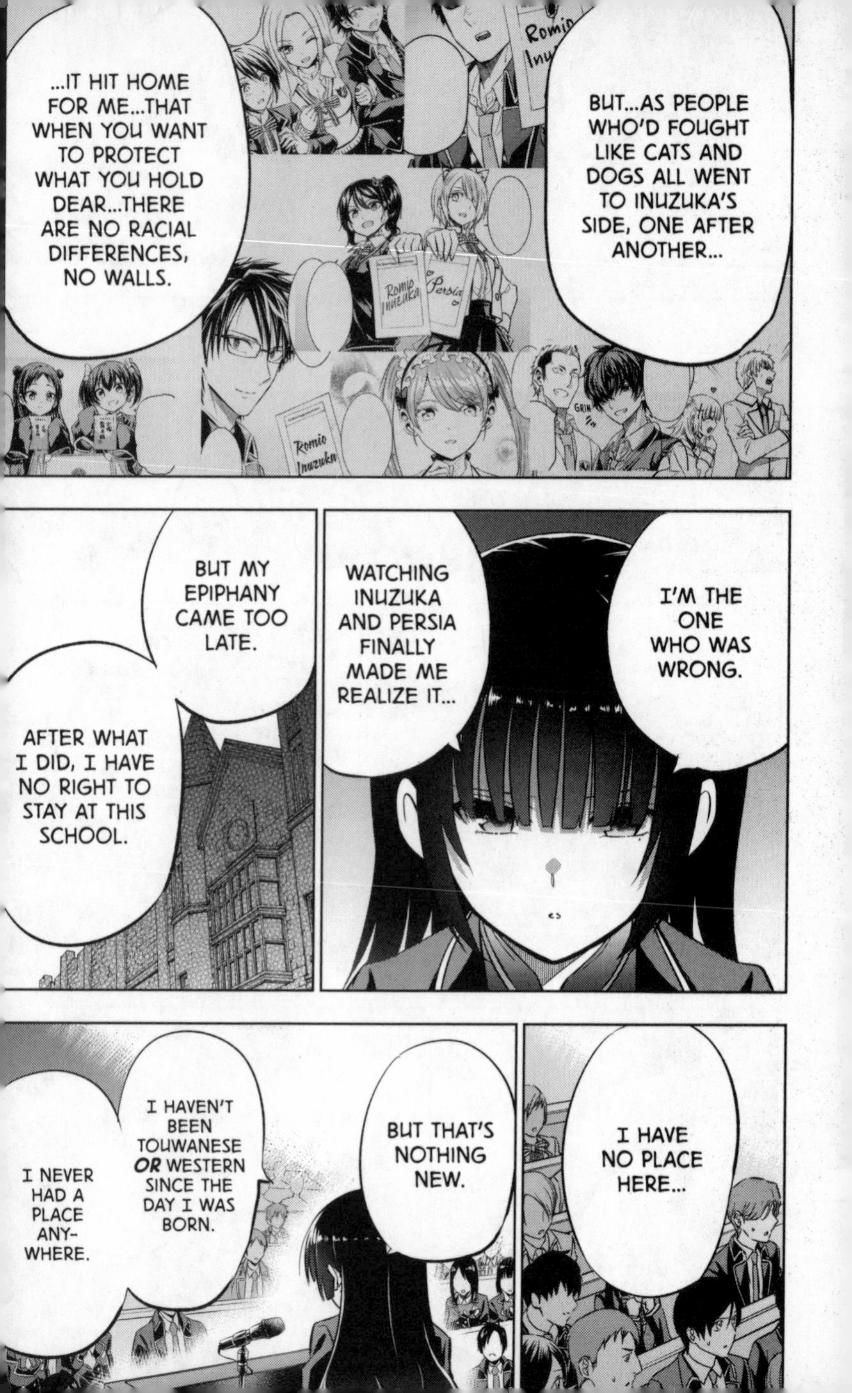
BUT...AS PEOPLE WHO'D FOUGHT LIKE CATS AND DOGS ALL WENT TO INUZUKA'S SIDE, ONE AFTER ANOTHER...
...IT HIT HOME FOR ME...THAT WHEN YOU WANT TO PROTECT WHAT YOU HOLD DEAR...THERE ARE NO RACIAL DIFFERENCES, NO WALLS.
Romio Inuzuka
Romio Inuzuka
Persia
GRIN
Romio Inuzuka
I'M THE ONE WHO WAS WRONG.
WATCHING INUZUKA AND PERSIA FINALLY MADE ME REALIZE IT...
BUT MY EPIPHANY CAME TOO LATE.
AFTER WHAT I DID, I HAVE NO RIGHT TO STAY AT THIS SCHOOL.
I HAVE NO PLACE HERE...
BUT THAT'S NOTHING NEW.
I HAVEN'T BEEN TOUWANESE **OR** WESTERN SINCE THE DAY I WAS BORN.
I NEVER HAD A PLACE ANY-WHERE.

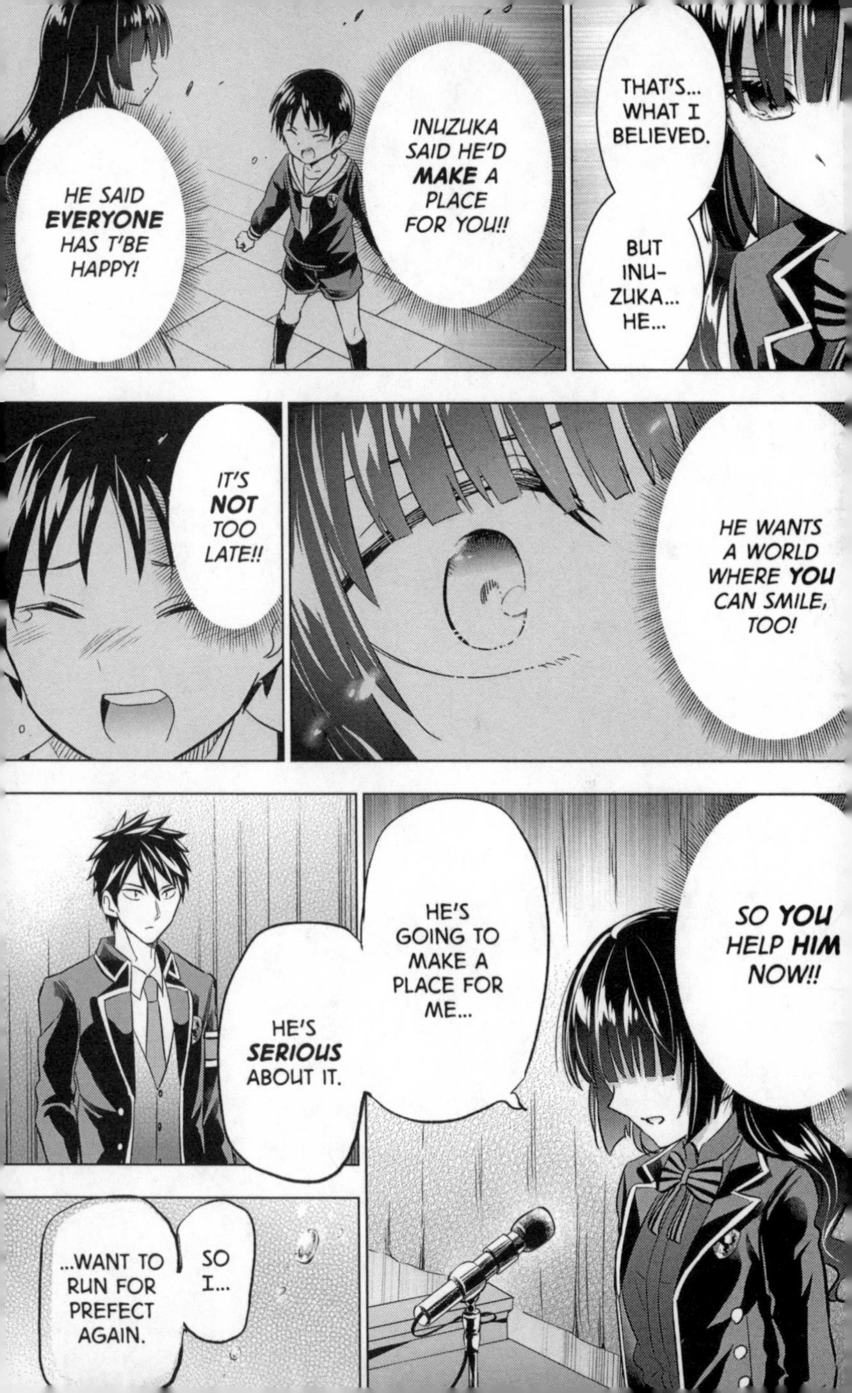

THAT'S... WHAT I BELIEVED.
BUT INUZUKA... HE...
INUZUKA SAID HE'D MAKE A PLACE FOR YOU!!
HE SAID EVERYONE HAS T'BE HAPPY!
HE WANTS A WORLD WHERE YOU CAN SMILE, TOO!
IT'S NOT TOO LATE!!
SO YOU HELP HIM NOW!!
HE'S GOING TO MAKE A PLACE FOR ME...
HE'S SERIOUS ABOUT IT.
SO I...
...WANT TO RUN FOR PREFECT AGAIN.

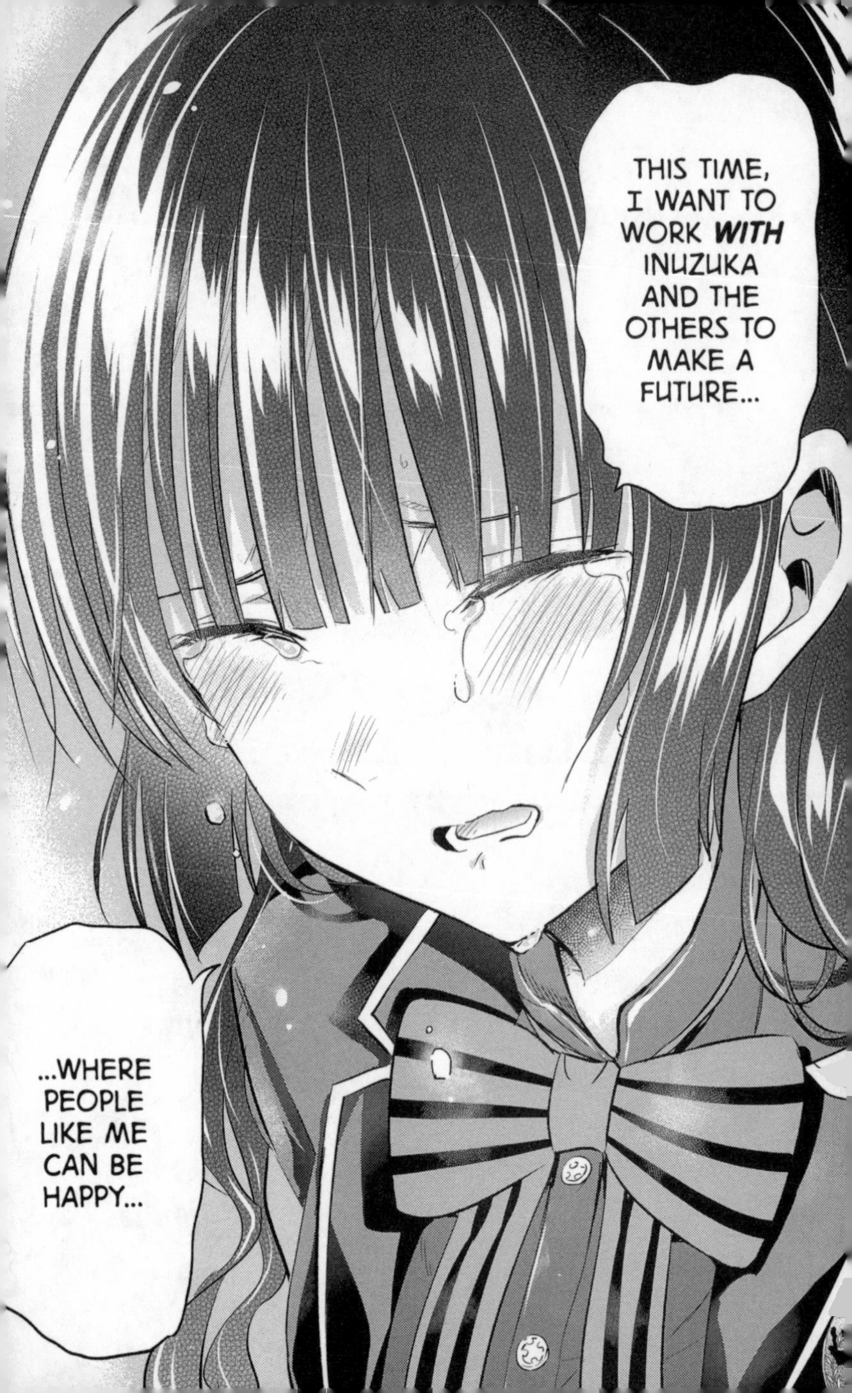
THIS TIME, I WANT TO WORK **WITH** INUZUKA AND THE OTHERS TO MAKE A FUTURE...
...WHERE PEOPLE LIKE ME CAN BE HAPPY...

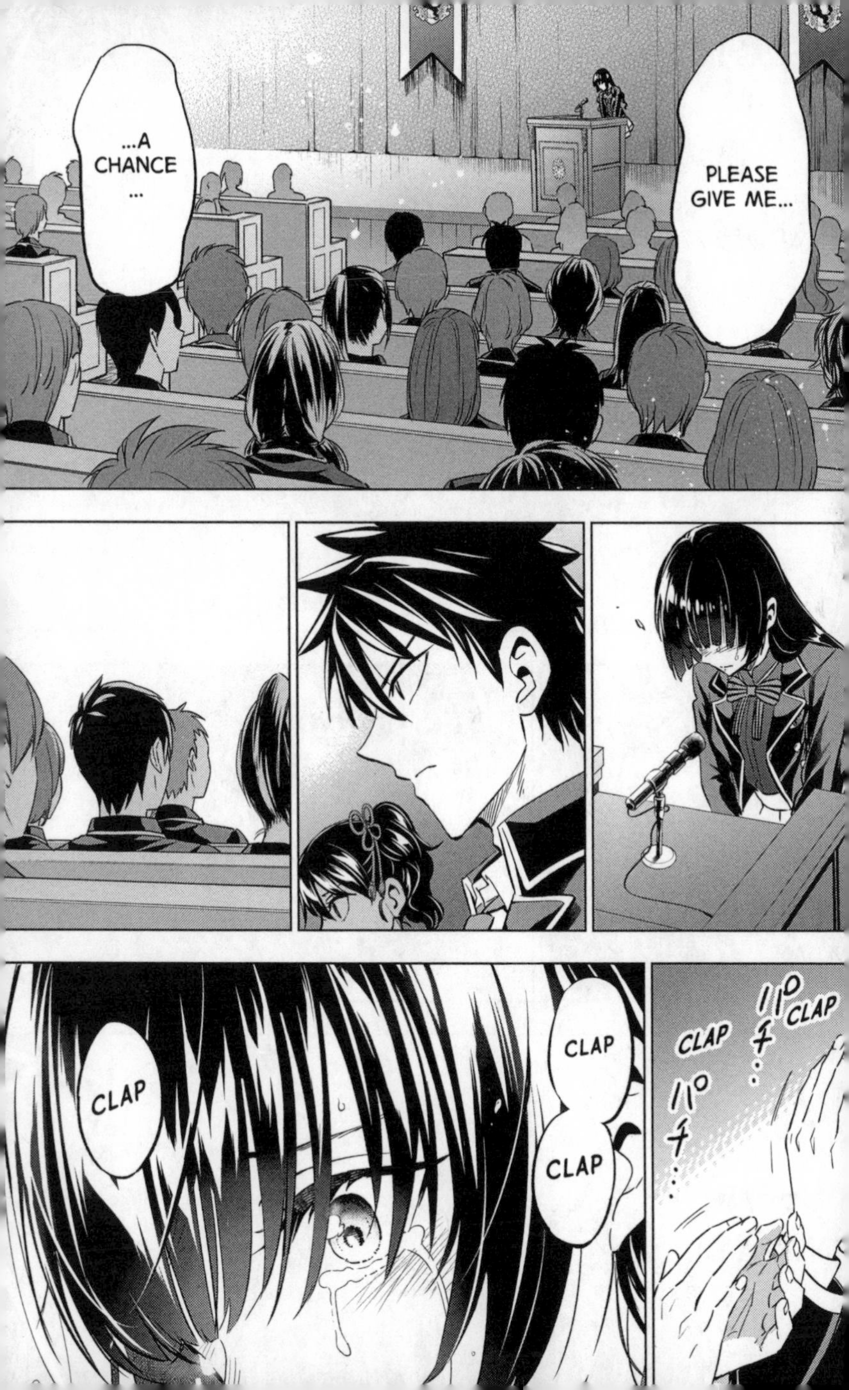
PLEASE GIVE ME...
...A CHANCE ...
パチ…
CLAP
CLAP
パチ…
CLAP
CLAP
CLAP

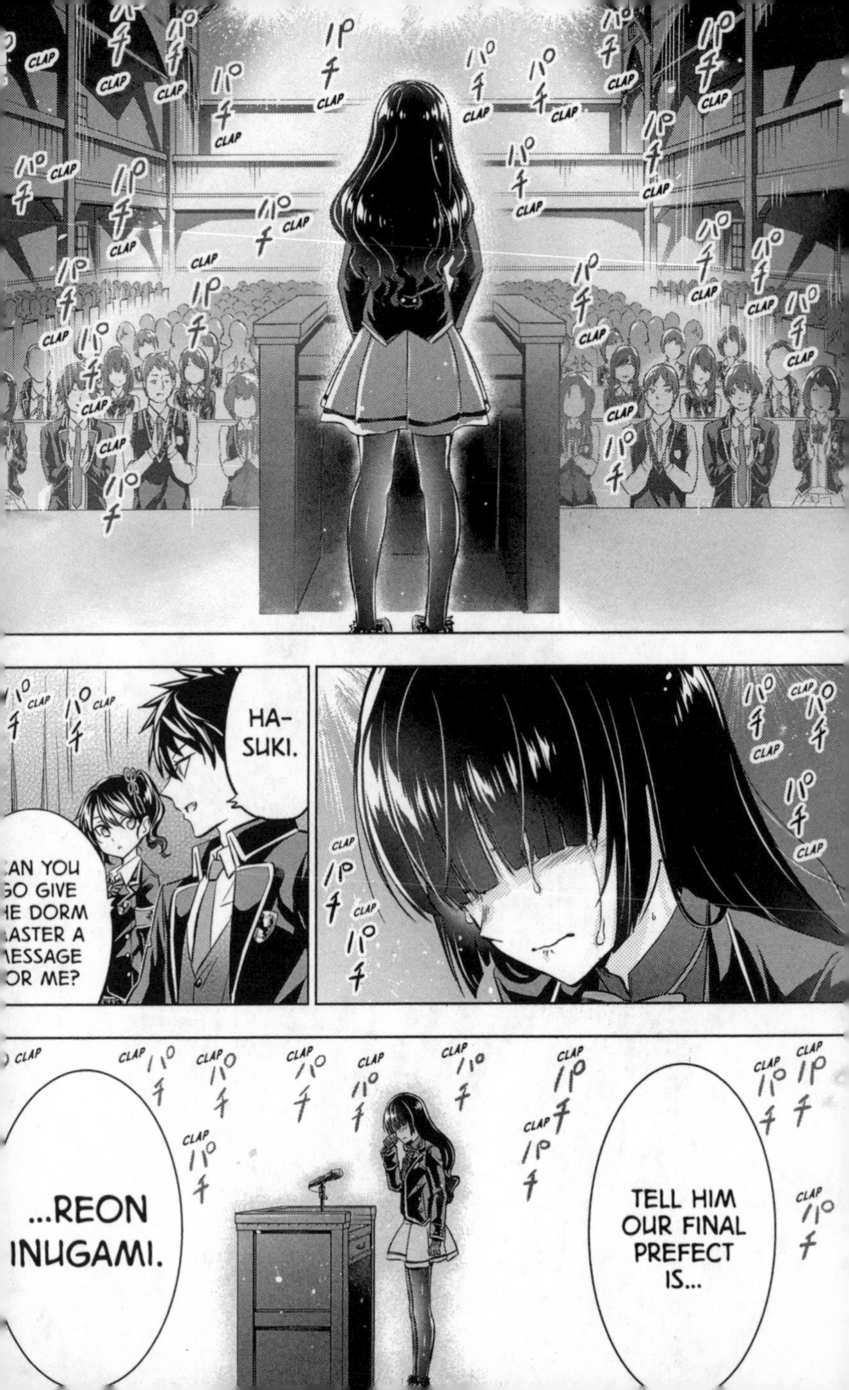
パチ CLAP パチ CLAP パチ CLAP
パチ CLAP パチ CLAP
パチ CLAP
HA-SUKI.
AN YOU GO GIVE HE DORM ASTER A ESSAGE OR ME?
CLAP パチ CLAP パチ
TELL HIM OUR FINAL PREFECT IS...
...REON INUGAMI.

Boarding
School *Juliet*

To LOVE, or not to LOVE

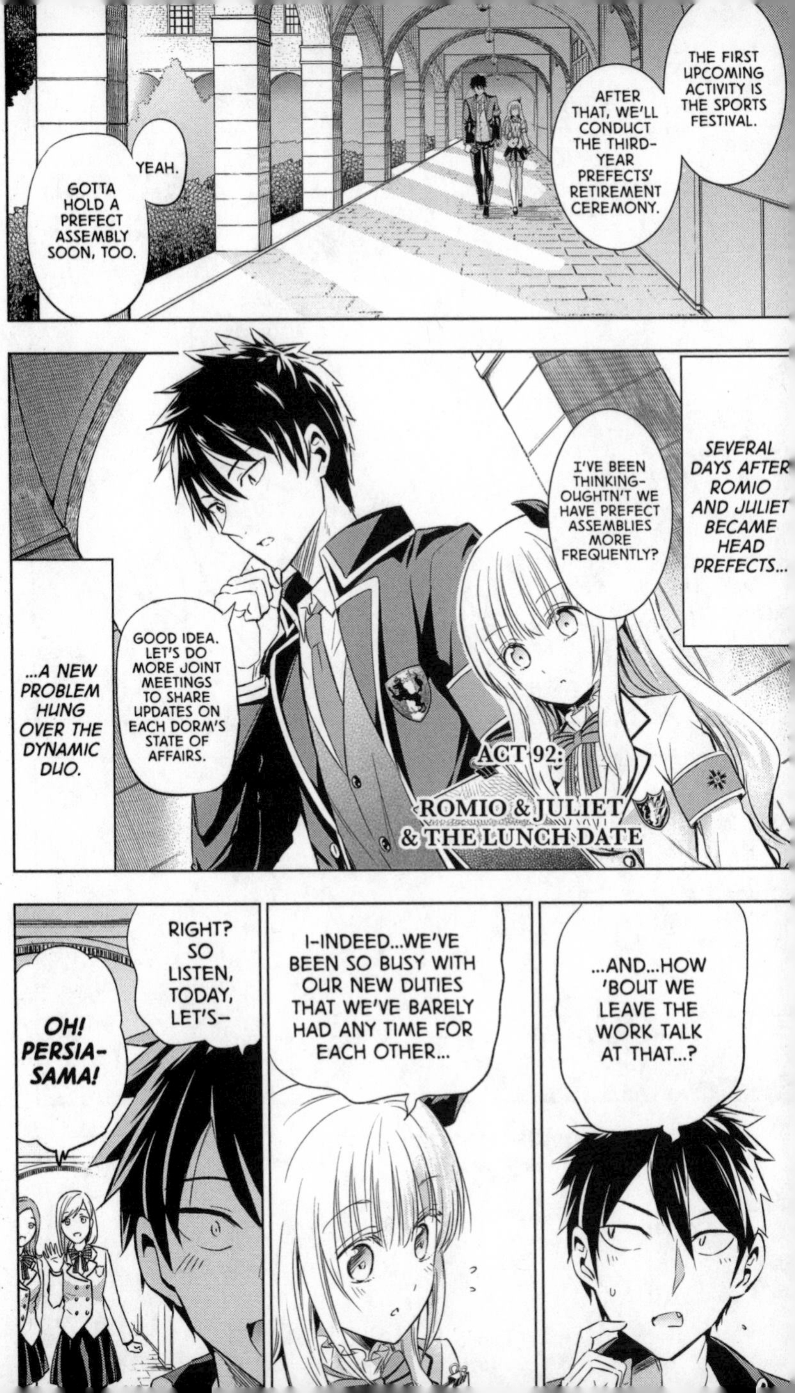
THE FIRST UPCOMING ACTIVITY IS THE SPORTS FESTIVAL.
AFTER THAT, WE'LL CONDUCT THE THIRD-YEAR PREFECTS' RETIREMENT CEREMONY.
YEAH.
GOTTA HOLD A PREFECT ASSEMBLY SOON, TOO.
SEVERAL DAYS AFTER ROMIO AND JULIET BECAME HEAD PREFECTS...
I'VE BEEN THINKING- OUGHTN'T WE HAVE PREFECT ASSEMBLIES MORE FREQUENTLY?
GOOD IDEA. LET'S DO MORE JOINT MEETINGS TO SHARE UPDATES ON EACH DORM'S STATE OF AFFAIRS.
...A NEW PROBLEM HUNG OVER THE DYNAMIC DUO.
ACT 92:
ROMIO & JULIET & THE LUNCH DATE
...AND...HOW 'BOUT WE LEAVE THE WORK TALK AT THAT...?
I-INDEED...WE'VE BEEN SO BUSY WITH OUR NEW DUTIES THAT WE'VE BARELY HAD ANY TIME FOR EACH OTHER...
RIGHT? SO LISTEN, TODAY, LET'S—
OH! PERSIA-SAMA!

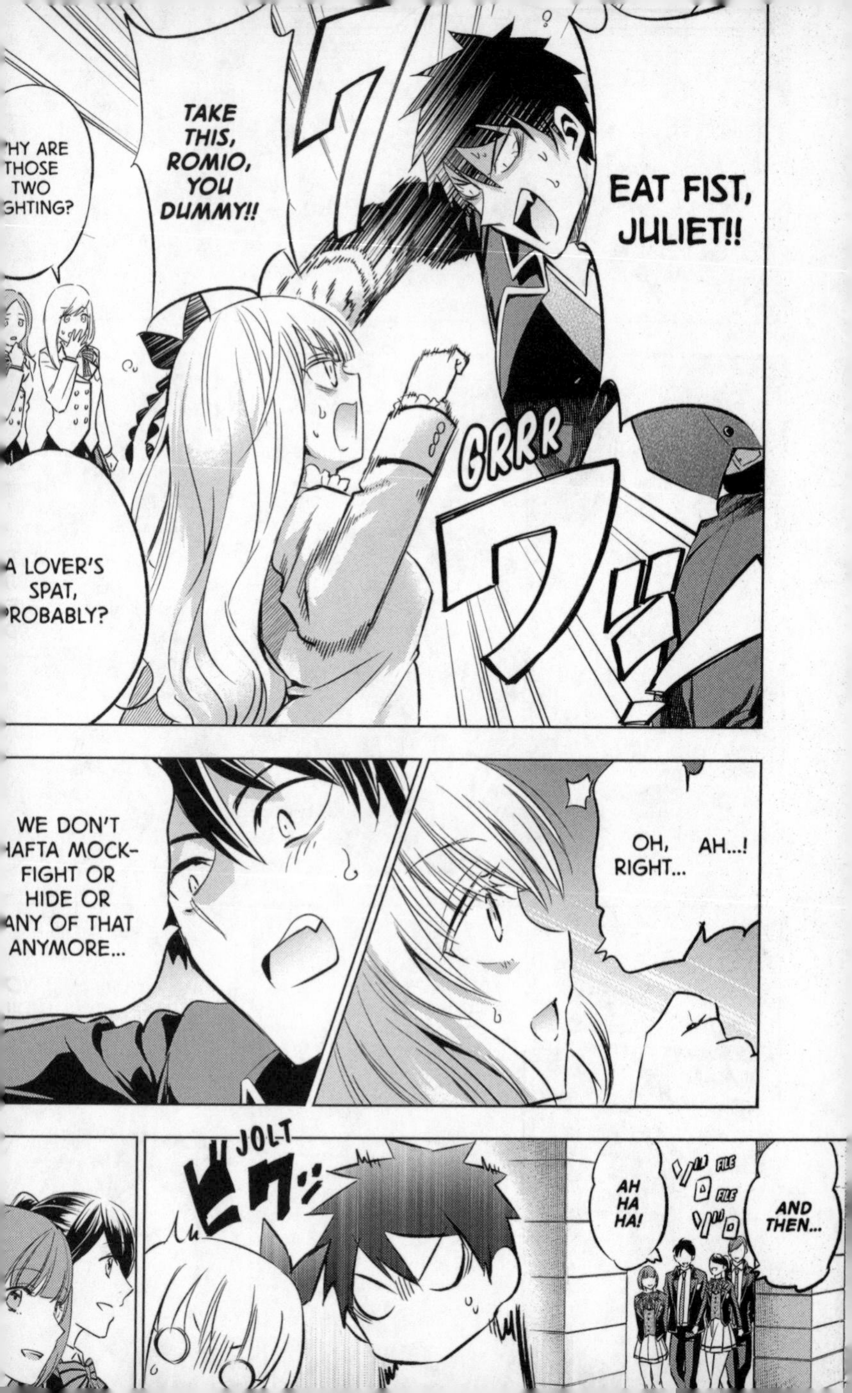
EAT FIST, JULIET!!
TAKE THIS, ROMIO, YOU DUMMY!!
GRRR
HY ARE THOSE TWO GHTING?
A LOVER'S SPAT, ROBABLY?
AH...!
OH, RIGHT...
WE DON'T IAFTA MOCK-FIGHT OR HIDE OR NY OF THAT ANYMORE...
AND THEN...
FILE
FILE
AH HA HA!
JOLT

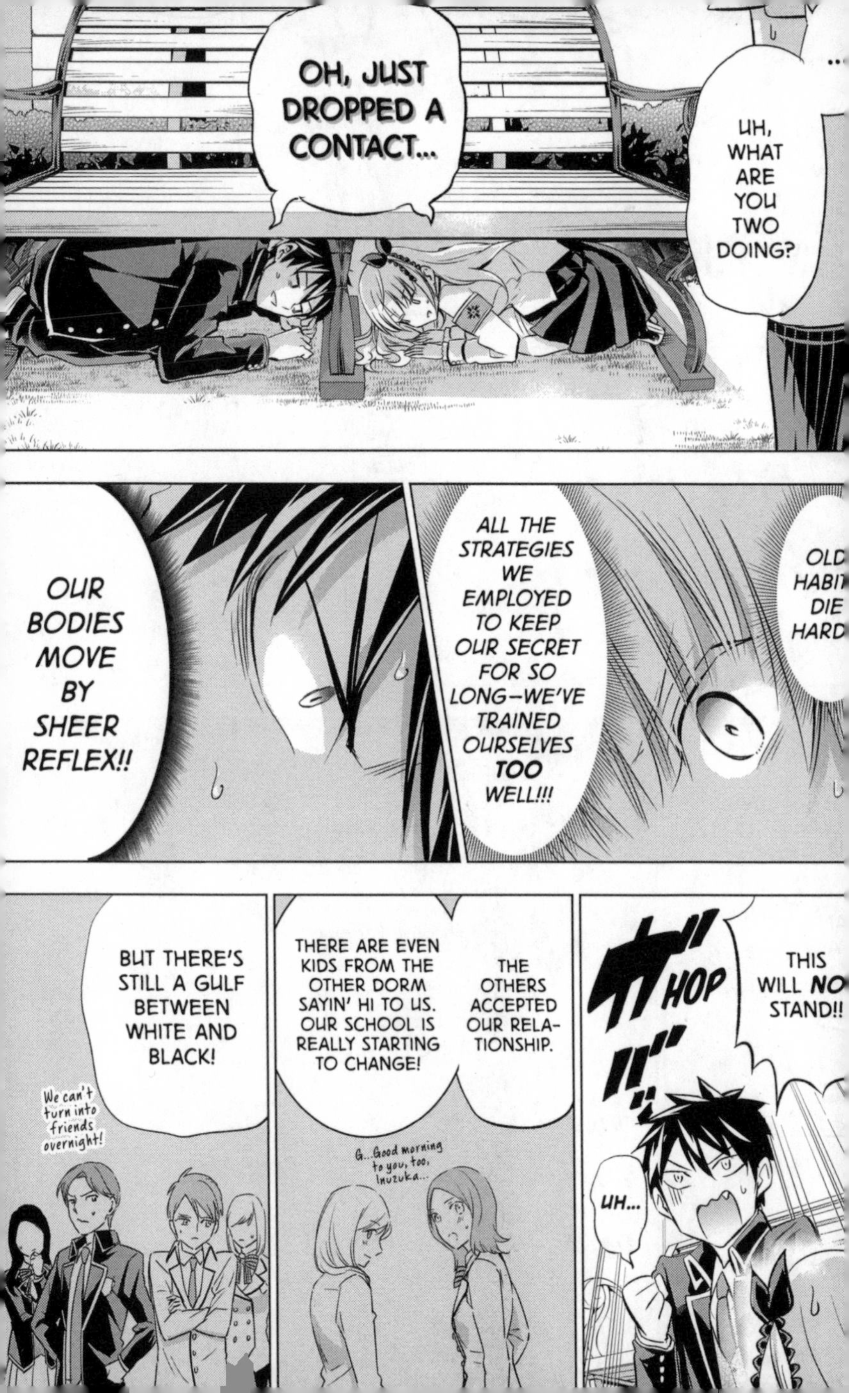
...
UH, WHAT ARE YOU TWO DOING?
OH, JUST DROPPED A CONTACT...
OLD HABIT DIE HARD
ALL THE STRATEGIES WE EMPLOYED TO KEEP OUR SECRET FOR SO LONG—WE'VE TRAINED OURSELVES TOO WELL!!!
OUR BODIES MOVE BY SHEER REFLEX!!
THIS WILL NO STAND!!
HOP
UH...
THE OTHERS ACCEPTED OUR RELA-TIONSHIP.
THERE ARE EVEN KIDS FROM THE OTHER DORM SAYIN' HI TO US. OUR SCHOOL IS REALLY STARTING TO CHANGE!
G...Good morning to you, too, Inuzuka...
BUT THERE'S STILL A GULF BETWEEN WHITE AND BLACK!
We can't turn into friends overnight!

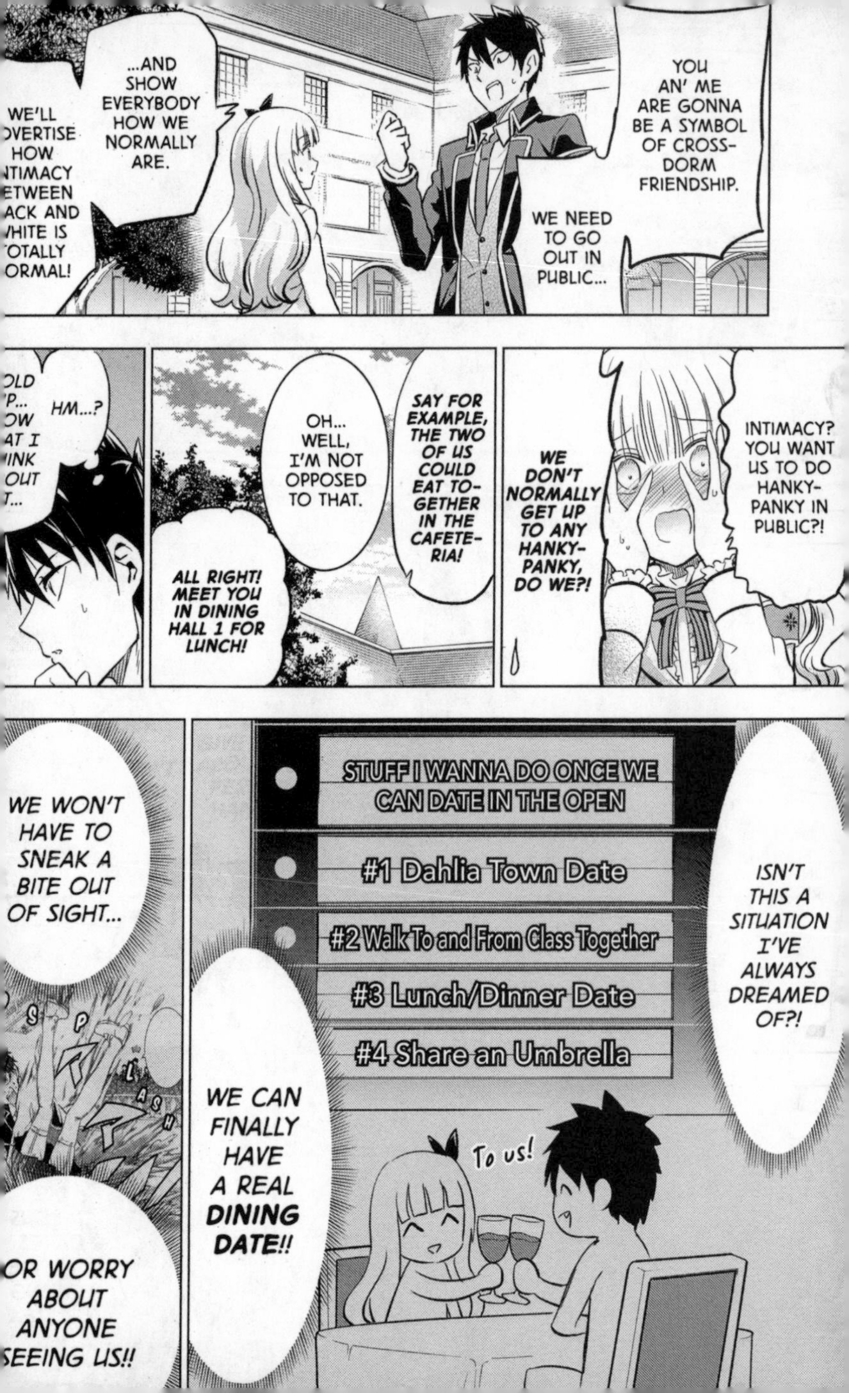
YOU AN' ME ARE GONNA BE A SYMBOL OF CROSS-DORM FRIENDSHIP.
WE NEED TO GO OUT IN PUBLIC...
...AND SHOW EVERYBODY HOW WE NORMALLY ARE.
WE'LL VERTISE HOW NTIMACY ETWEEN ACK AND HITE IS OTALLY ORMAL!
INTIMACY? YOU WANT US TO DO HANKY-PANKY IN PUBLIC?!
WE DON'T NORMALLY GET UP TO ANY HANKY-PANKY, DO WE?!
SAY FOR EXAMPLE, THE TWO OF US COULD EAT TO-GETHER IN THE CAFETE-RIA!
OH... WELL, I'M NOT OPPOSED TO THAT.
ALL RIGHT! MEET YOU IN DINING HALL 1 FOR LUNCH!
HM...?
OLD P... OW AT I INK OUT T...
ISN'T THIS A SITUATION I'VE ALWAYS DREAMED OF?!
STUFF I WANNA DO ONCE WE CAN DATE IN THE OPEN
#1 Dahlia Town Date
#2 Walk To and From Class Together
#3 Lunch/Dinner Date
#4 Share an Umbrella
WE CAN FINALLY HAVE A REAL DINING DATE!!
To us!
WE WON'T HAVE TO SNEAK A BITE OUT OF SIGHT...
SPLASH
OR WORRY ABOUT ANYONE SEEING US!!

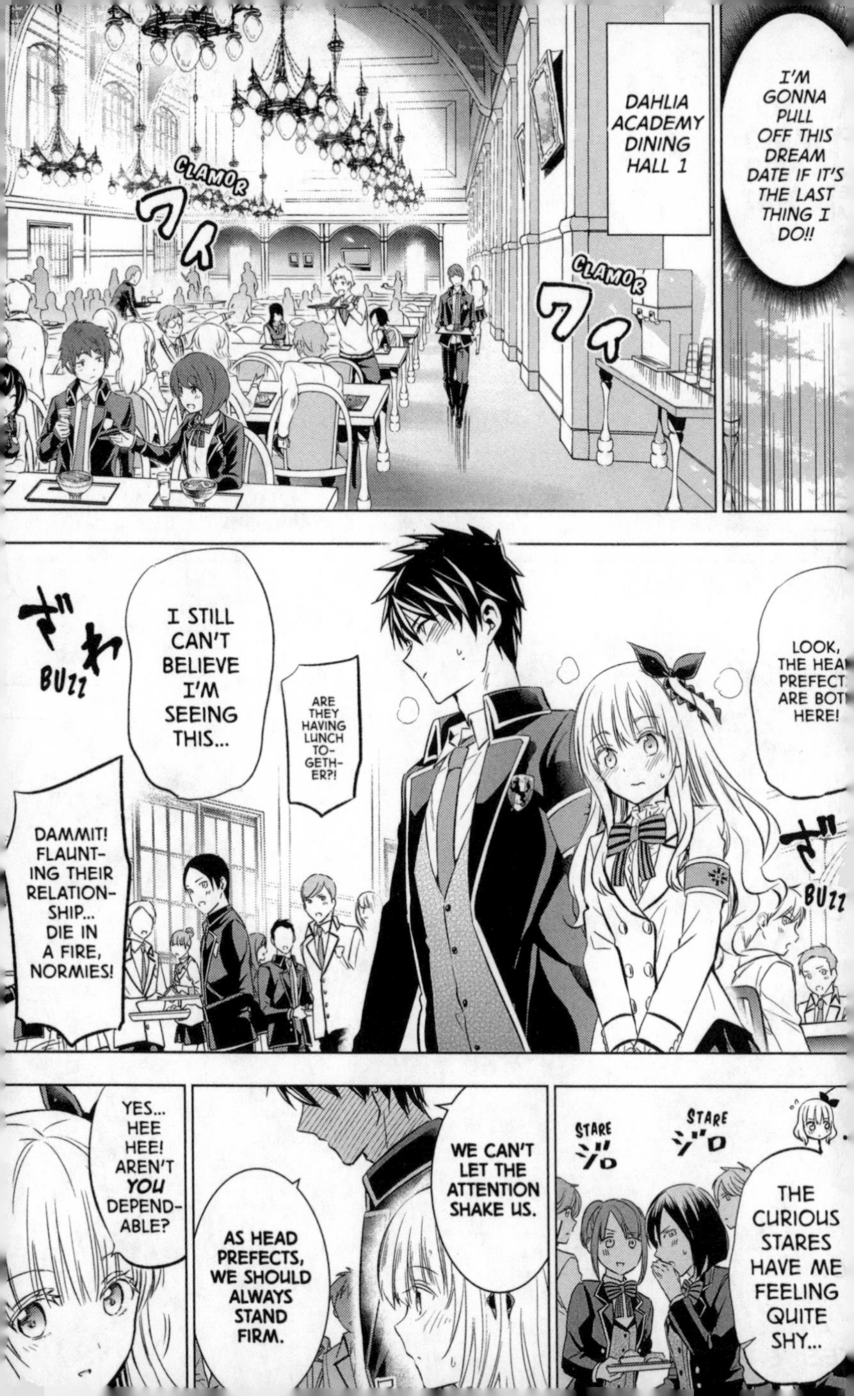
I'M GONNA PULL OFF THIS DREAM DATE IF IT'S THE LAST THING I DO!!
DAHLIA ACADEMY DINING HALL 1
CLAMOR ワイ
CLAMOR ワイ
LOOK, THE HEA PREFECT ARE BOT HERE!
ざ BUZZ
I STILL CAN'T BELIEVE I'M SEEING THIS...
ARE THEY HAVING LUNCH TO-GETH-ER?!
ざわ BUZZ
DAMMIT! FLAUNT-ING THEIR RELATION-SHIP... DIE IN A FIRE, NORMIES!
STARE ジロ
STARE ジロ
THE CURIOUS STARES HAVE ME FEELING QUITE SHY...
WE CAN'T LET THE ATTENTION SHAKE US.
AS HEAD PREFECTS, WE SHOULD ALWAYS STAND FIRM.
YES... HEE HEE! AREN'T *YOU* DEPENDABLE?

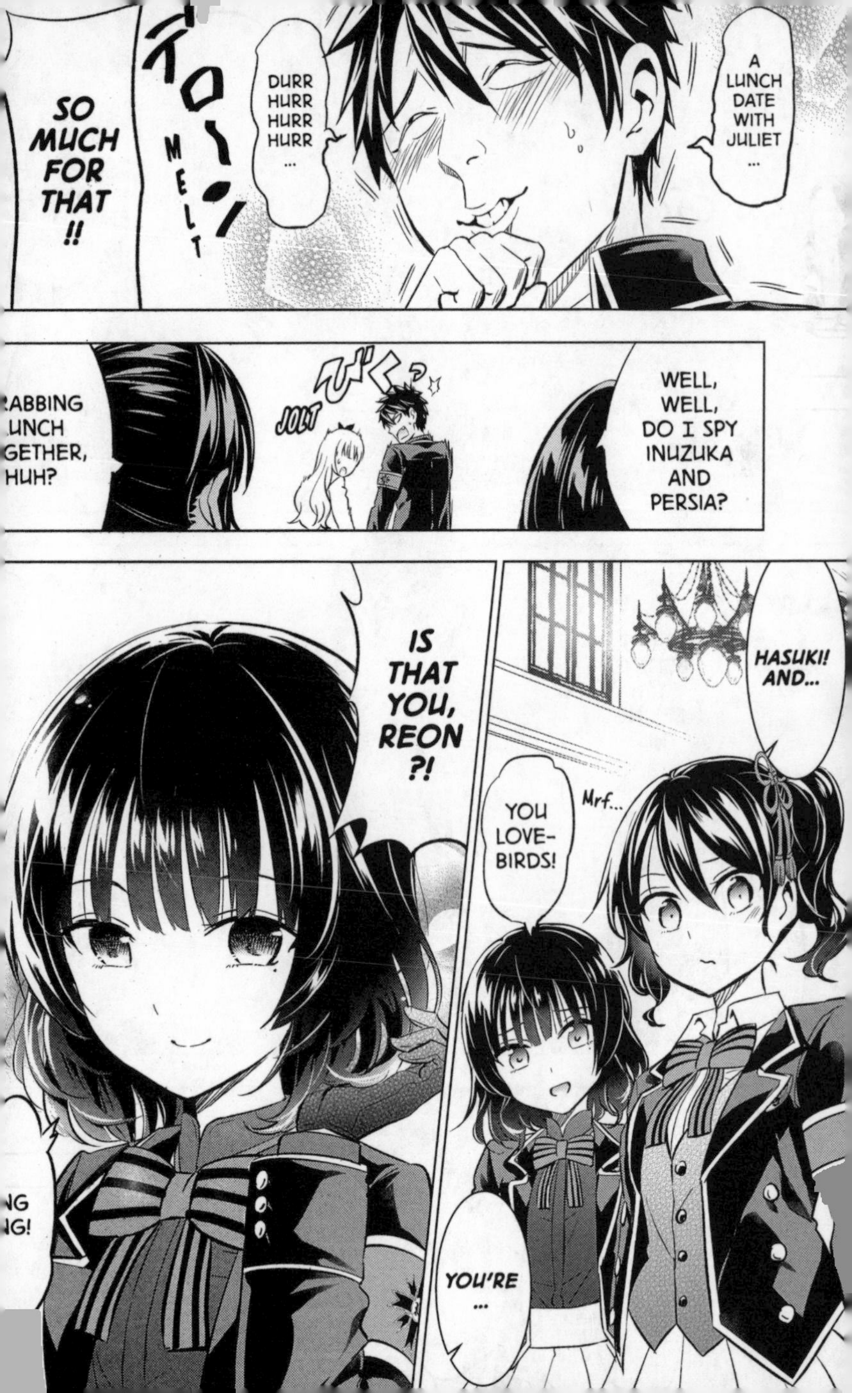
A LUNCH DATE WITH JULIET ...
DURR HURR HURR HURR ...
MELT
SO MUCH FOR THAT !!
WELL, WELL, DO I SPY INUZUKA AND PERSIA?
JOLT
ABBING UNCH GETHER, HUH?
HASUKI! AND...
Mrf...
YOU LOVE-BIRDS!
YOU'RE ...
IS THAT YOU, REON ?!
NG NG!

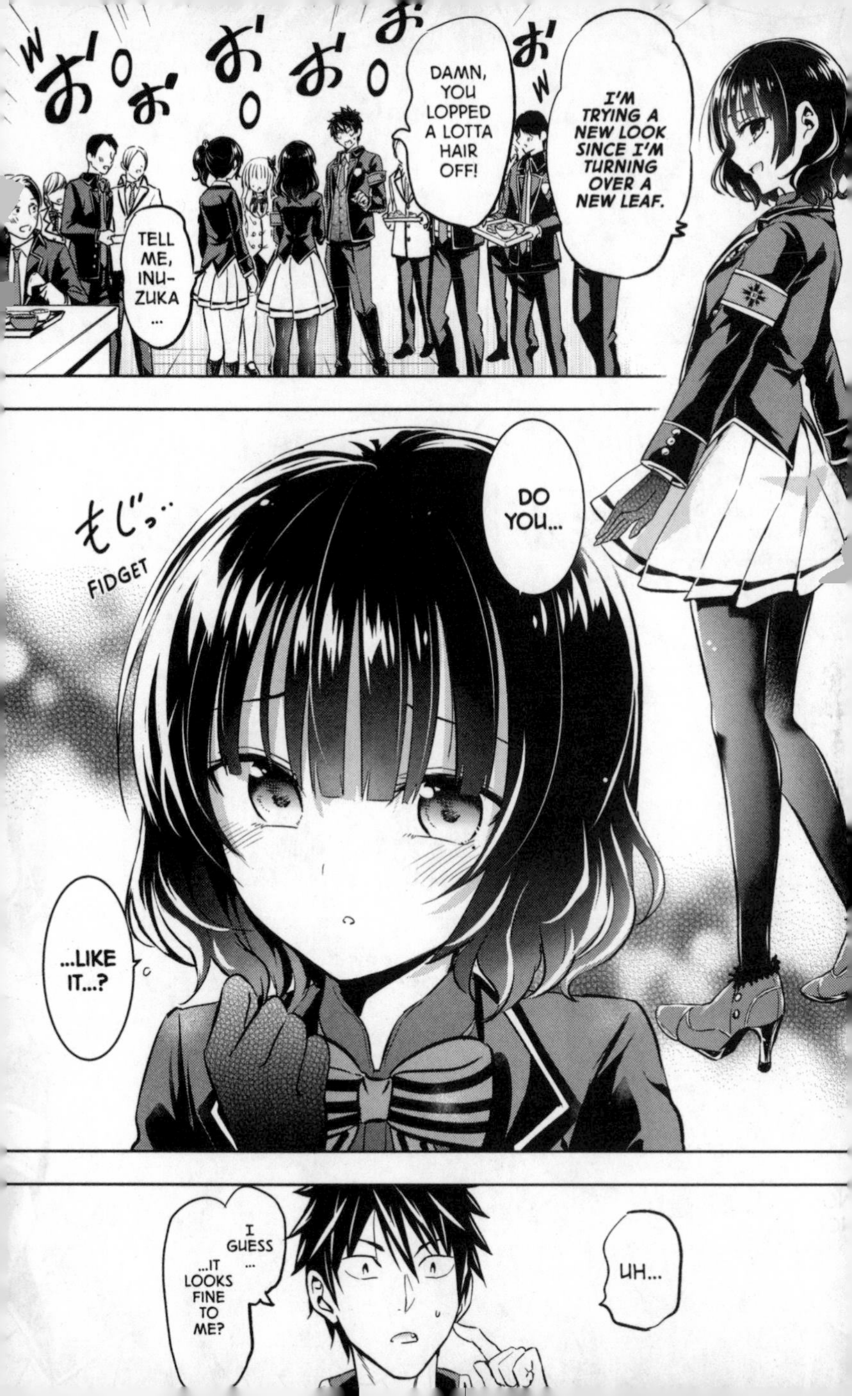
I'M TRYING A NEW LOOK SINCE I'M TURNING OVER A NEW LEAF.
DAMN, YOU LOPPED A LOTTA HAIR OFF!
TELL ME, INU-ZUKA ...
DO YOU...
もじっ…
FIDGET
...LIKE IT...?
UH...
I GUESS ...
...IT LOOKS FINE TO ME?

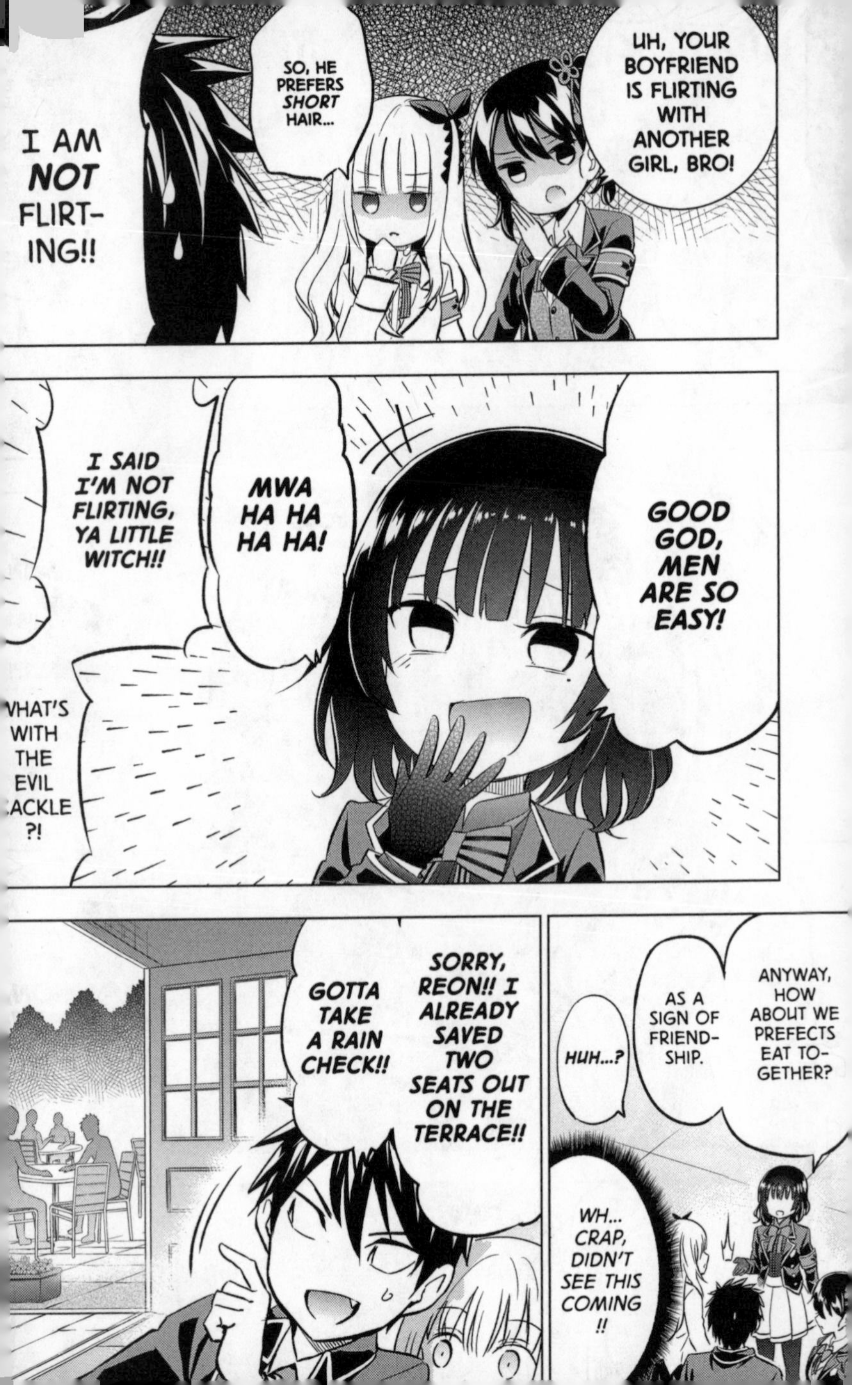
UH, YOUR BOYFRIEND IS FLIRTING WITH ANOTHER GIRL, BRO!
SO, HE PREFERS *SHORT* HAIR...
I AM *NOT* FLIRT-ING!!
GOOD GOD, MEN ARE SO EASY!
MWA HA HA HA HA!
I SAID I'M NOT FLIRTING, YA LITTLE WITCH!!
WHAT'S WITH THE EVIL CACKLE?!
ANYWAY, HOW ABOUT WE PREFECTS EAT TO-GETHER?
AS A SIGN OF FRIEND-SHIP.
HUH...?
WH... CRAP, DIDN'T SEE THIS COMING!!
SORRY, REON!! I ALREADY SAVED TWO SEATS OUT ON THE TERRACE!!
GOTTA TAKE A RAIN CHECK!!

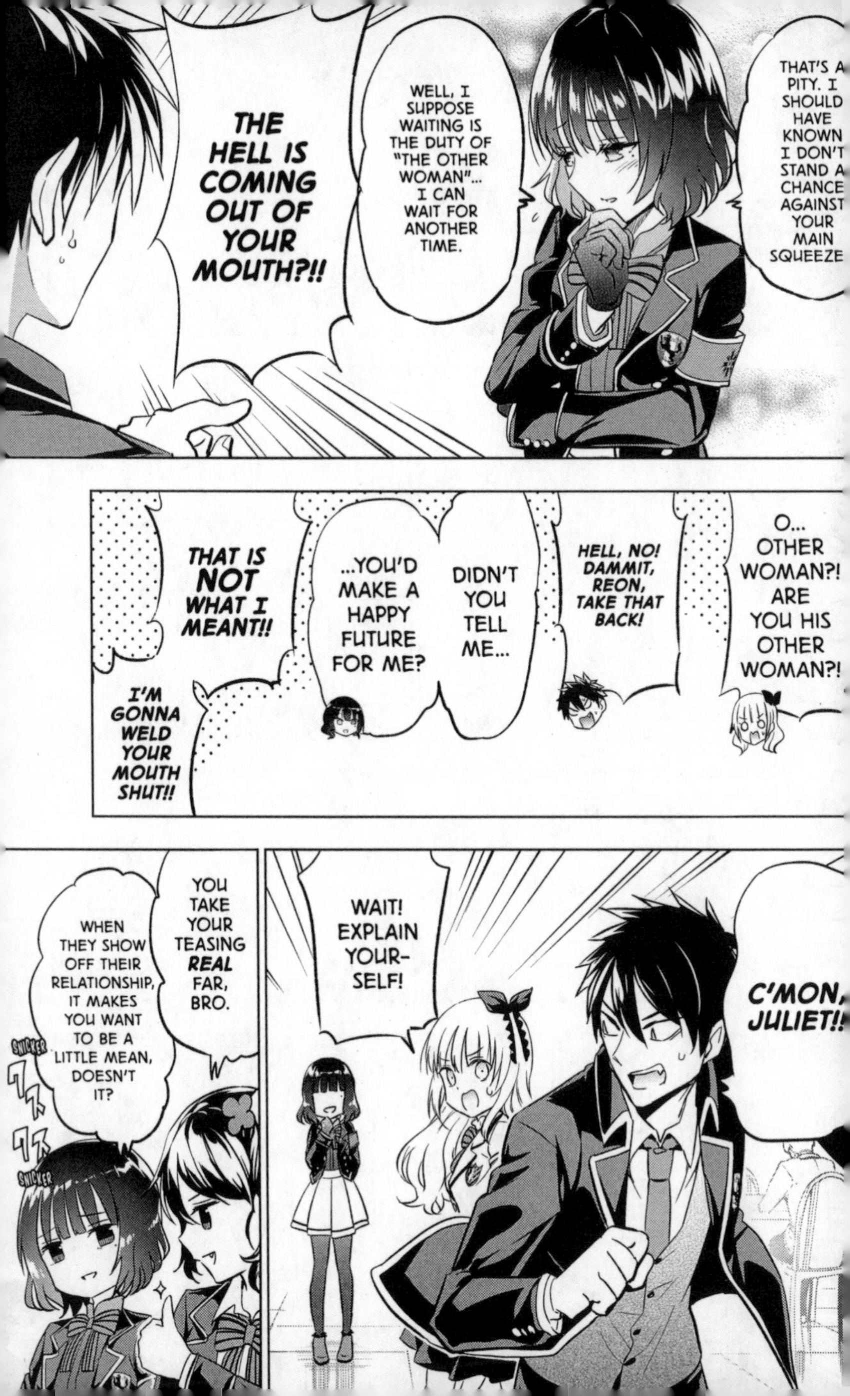
THAT'S A PITY. I SHOULD HAVE KNOWN I DON'T STAND A CHANCE AGAINST YOUR MAIN SQUEEZE
WELL, I SUPPOSE WAITING IS THE DUTY OF "THE OTHER WOMAN"... I CAN WAIT FOR ANOTHER TIME.
THE HELL IS COMING OUT OF YOUR MOUTH?!!
O... OTHER WOMAN?! ARE YOU HIS OTHER WOMAN?!
HELL, NO! DAMMIT, REON, TAKE THAT BACK!
DIDN'T YOU TELL ME...
...YOU'D MAKE A HAPPY FUTURE FOR ME?
THAT IS NOT WHAT I MEANT!!
I'M GONNA WELD YOUR MOUTH SHUT!!
C'MON, JULIET!!
WAIT! EXPLAIN YOUR-SELF!
YOU TAKE YOUR TEASING REAL FAR, BRO.
WHEN THEY SHOW OFF THEIR RELATIONSHIP, IT MAKES YOU WANT TO BE A LITTLE MEAN, DOESN'T IT?
SNICKER
SNICKER

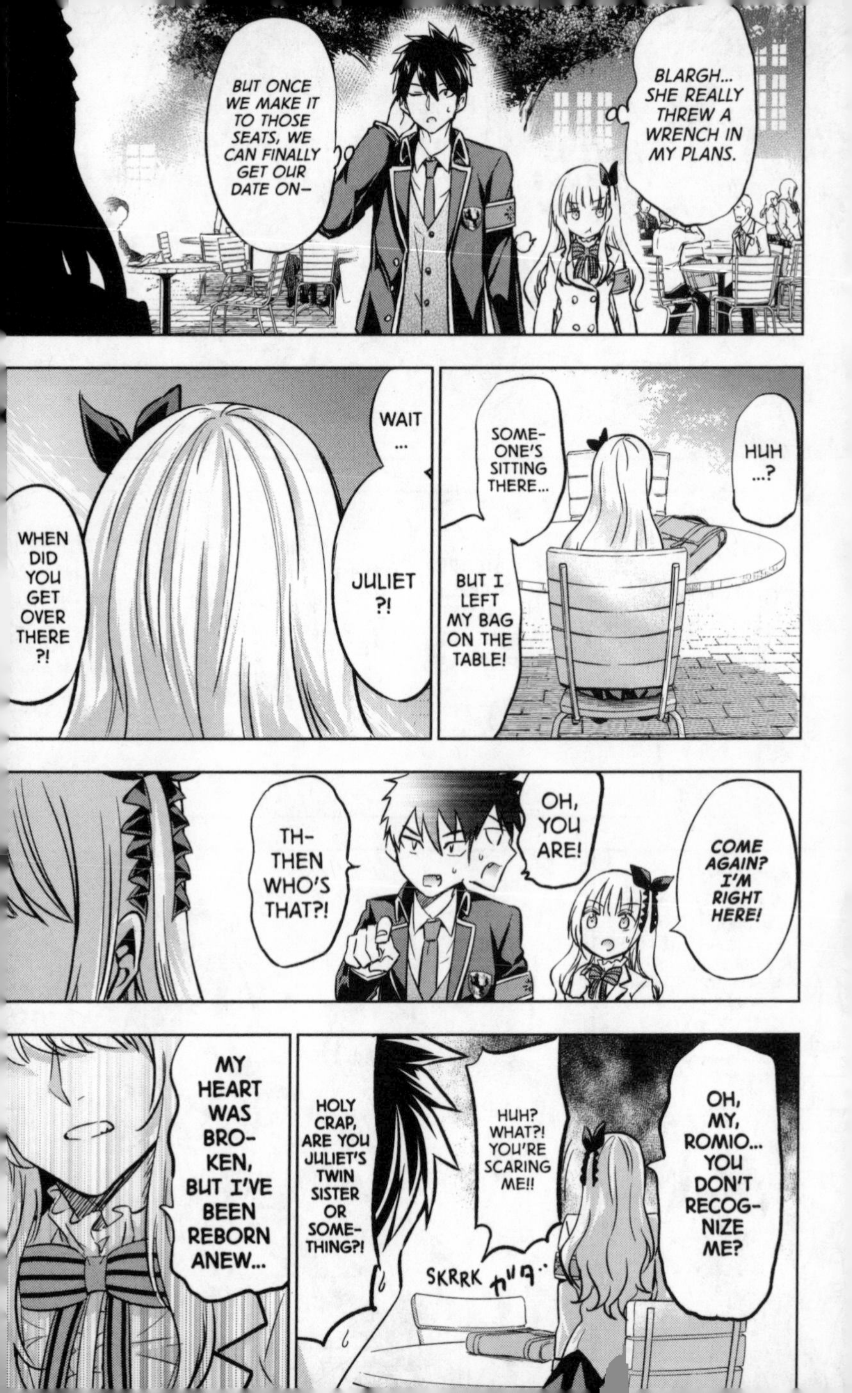
BLARGH... SHE REALLY THREW A WRENCH IN MY PLANS.
BUT ONCE WE MAKE IT TO THOSE SEATS, WE CAN FINALLY GET OUR DATE ON–
HUH ...?
SOME-ONE'S SITTING THERE...
BUT I LEFT MY BAG ON THE TABLE!
WAIT ...
JULIET ?!
WHEN DID YOU GET OVER THERE ?!
COME AGAIN? I'M RIGHT HERE!
OH, YOU ARE!
TH-THEN WHO'S THAT?!
OH, MY, ROMIO... YOU DON'T RECOG-NIZE ME?
HUH? WHAT?! YOU'RE SCARING ME!!
HOLY CRAP, ARE YOU JULIET'S TWIN SISTER OR SOME-THING?!
SKRRK ガタ‥
MY HEART WAS BRO-KEN, BUT I'VE BEEN REBORN ANEW...

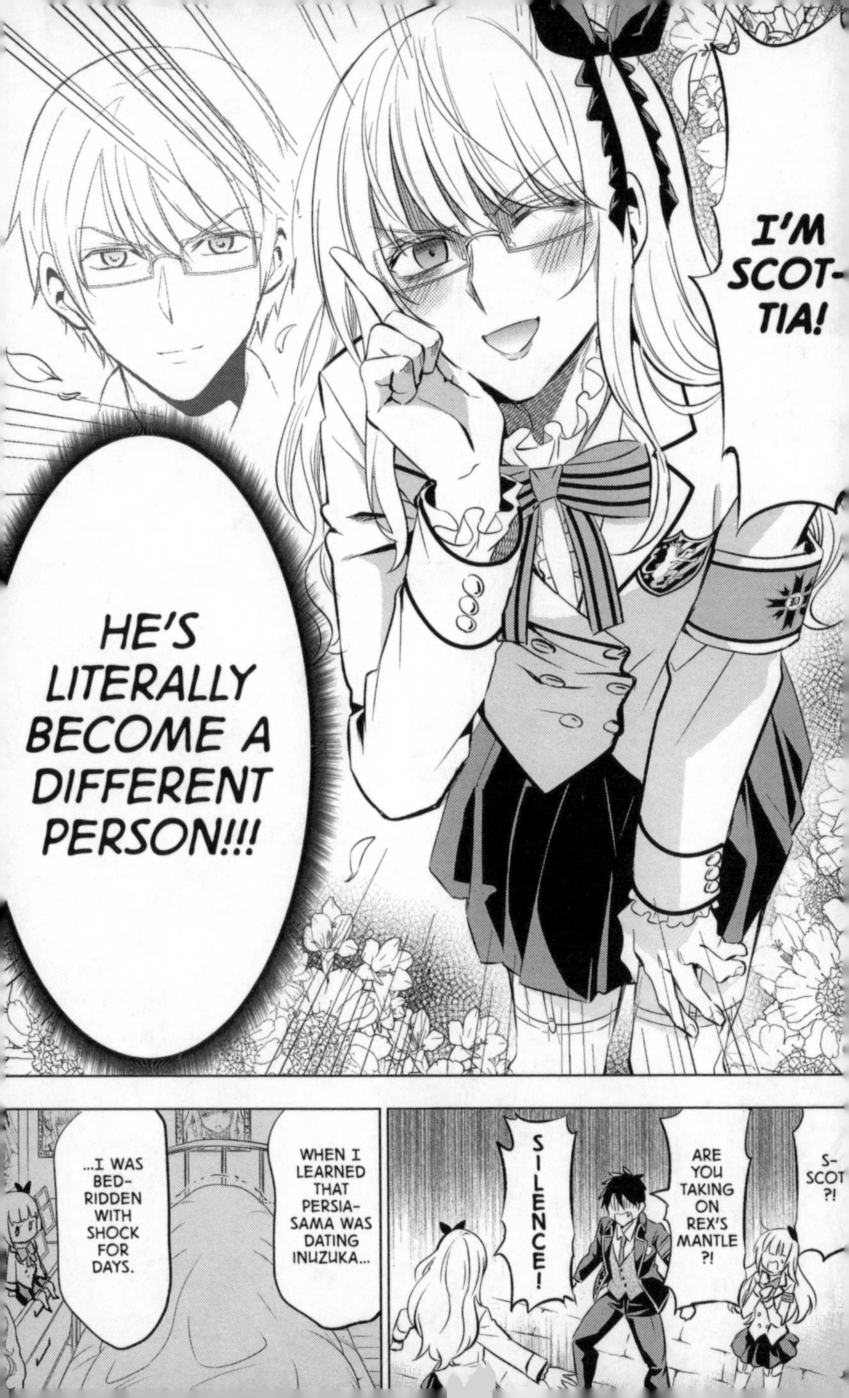
I'M SCOT-TIA!
HE'S LITERALLY BECOME A DIFFERENT PERSON!!!
S-SCOT?!
ARE YOU TAKING ON REX'S MANTLE?!
SILENCE!
WHEN I LEARNED THAT PERSIA-SAMA WAS DATING INUZUKA...
...I WAS BED-RIDDEN WITH SHOCK FOR DAYS.

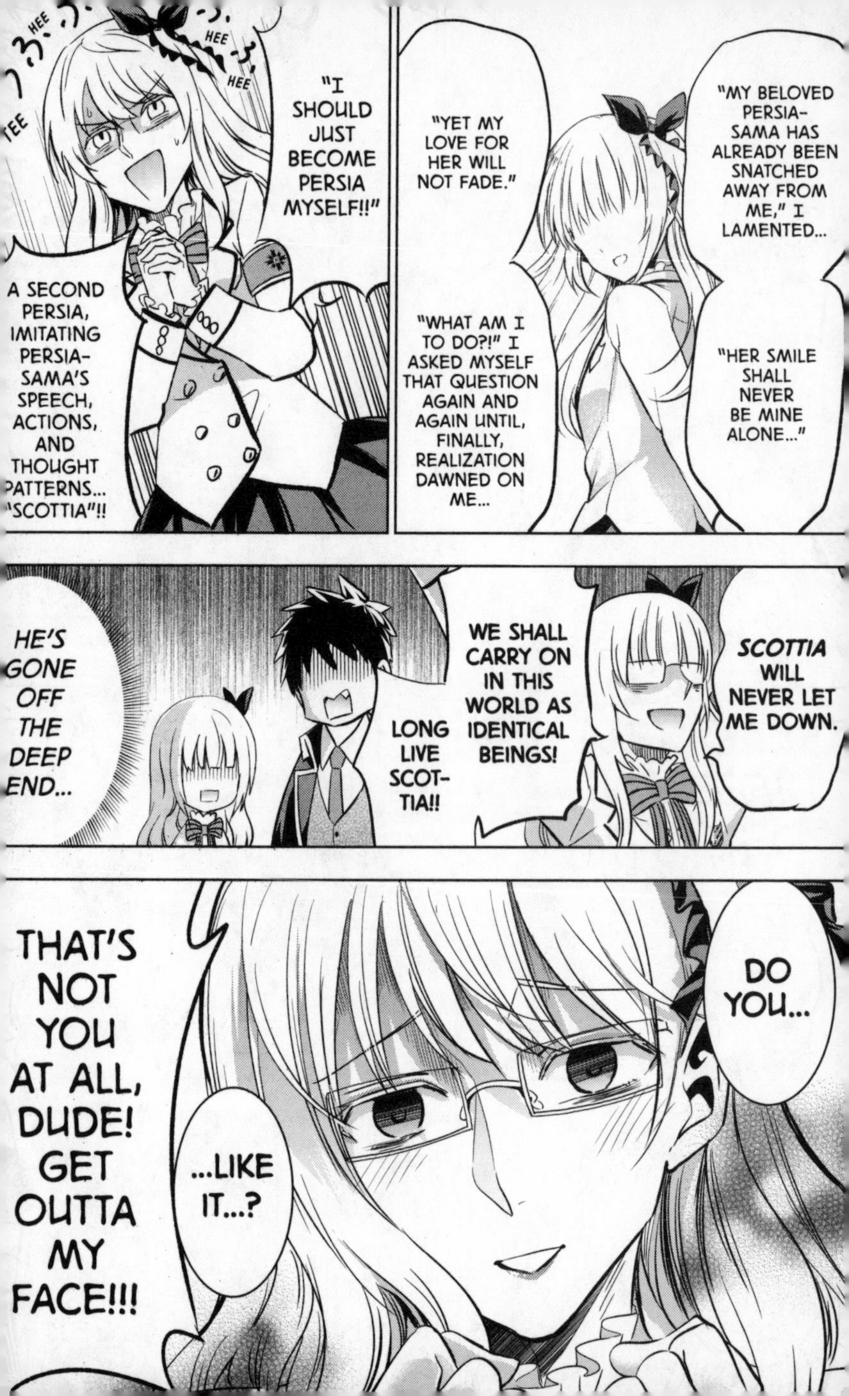
"MY BELOVED PERSIA-SAMA HAS ALREADY BEEN SNATCHED AWAY FROM ME," I LAMENTED...
"YET MY LOVE FOR HER WILL NOT FADE."
"HER SMILE SHALL NEVER BE MINE ALONE..."
"WHAT AM I TO DO?!" I ASKED MYSELF THAT QUESTION AGAIN AND AGAIN UNTIL, FINALLY, REALIZATION DAWNED ON ME...
HEE HEE HEE TEE
"I SHOULD JUST BECOME PERSIA MYSELF!!"
A SECOND PERSIA, IMITATING PERSIA-SAMA'S SPEECH, ACTIONS, AND THOUGHT PATTERNS... "SCOTTIA"!!
*SCOTTIA* WILL NEVER LET ME DOWN.
WE SHALL CARRY ON IN THIS WORLD AS IDENTICAL BEINGS!
LONG LIVE SCOT-TIA!!
*HE'S GONE OFF THE DEEP END...*
DO YOU...
...LIKE IT...?
THAT'S NOT YOU AT ALL, DUDE! GET OUTTA MY FACE!!!

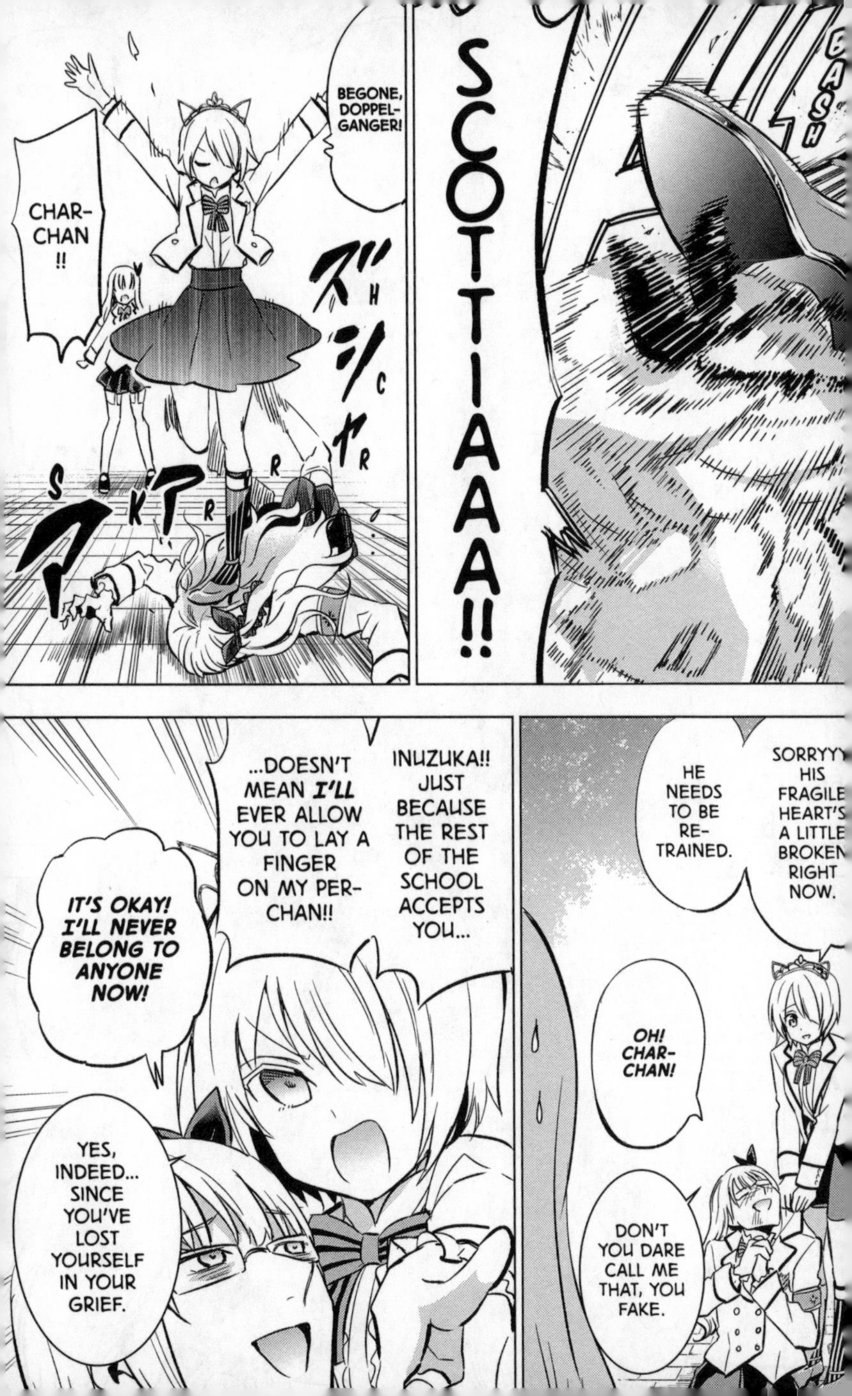
BASH
SCOTTIAAA!!
BEGONE, DOPPEL-GANGER!
CHAR-CHAN!!
SORRYYY HIS FRAGILE HEART'S A LITTLE BROKEN RIGHT NOW.
HE NEEDS TO BE RE-TRAINED.
OH! CHAR-CHAN!
DON'T YOU DARE CALL ME THAT, YOU FAKE.
INUZUKA!! JUST BECAUSE THE REST OF THE SCHOOL ACCEPTS YOU...
...DOESN'T MEAN I'LL EVER ALLOW YOU TO LAY A FINGER ON MY PER-CHAN!!
IT'S OKAY! I'LL NEVER BELONG TO ANYONE NOW!
YES, INDEED... SINCE YOU'VE LOST YOURSELF IN YOUR GRIEF.

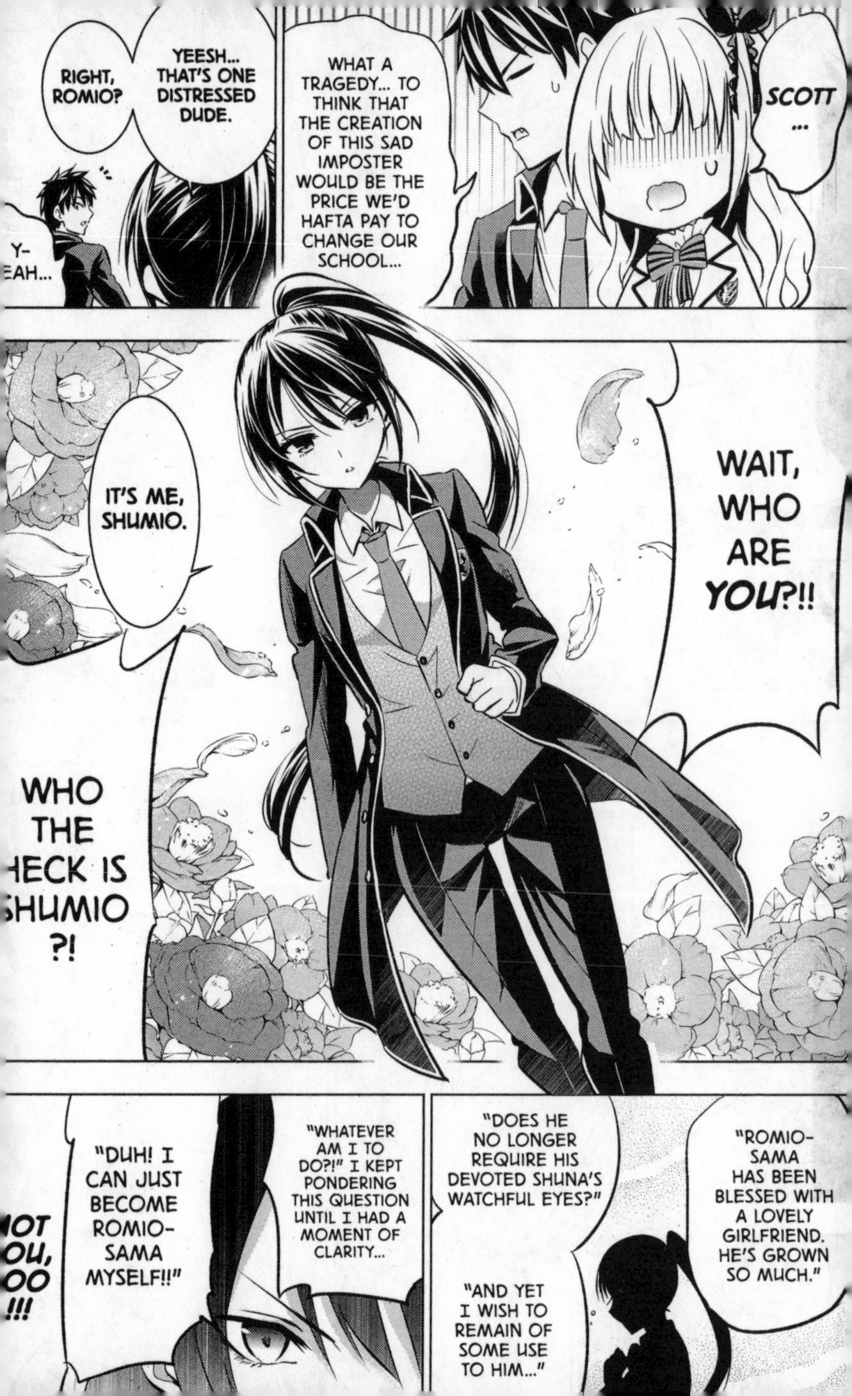
SCOTT ...
WHAT A TRAGEDY... TO THINK THAT THE CREATION OF THIS SAD IMPOSTER WOULD BE THE PRICE WE'D HAFTA PAY TO CHANGE OUR SCHOOL...
YEESH... THAT'S ONE DISTRESSED DUDE.
RIGHT, ROMIO?
Y- EAH...
WAIT, WHO ARE YOU?!!
IT'S ME, SHUMIO.
WHO THE ECK IS HUMIO ?!
"ROMIO-SAMA HAS BEEN BLESSED WITH A LOVELY GIRLFRIEND. HE'S GROWN SO MUCH."
"DOES HE NO LONGER REQUIRE HIS DEVOTED SHUNA'S WATCHFUL EYES?"
"AND YET I WISH TO REMAIN OF SOME USE TO HIM..."
"WHATEVER AM I TO DO?!" I KEPT PONDERING THIS QUESTION UNTIL I HAD A MOMENT OF CLARITY...
"DUH! I CAN JUST BECOME ROMIO-SAMA MYSELF!!"
OT OU, OO !!!

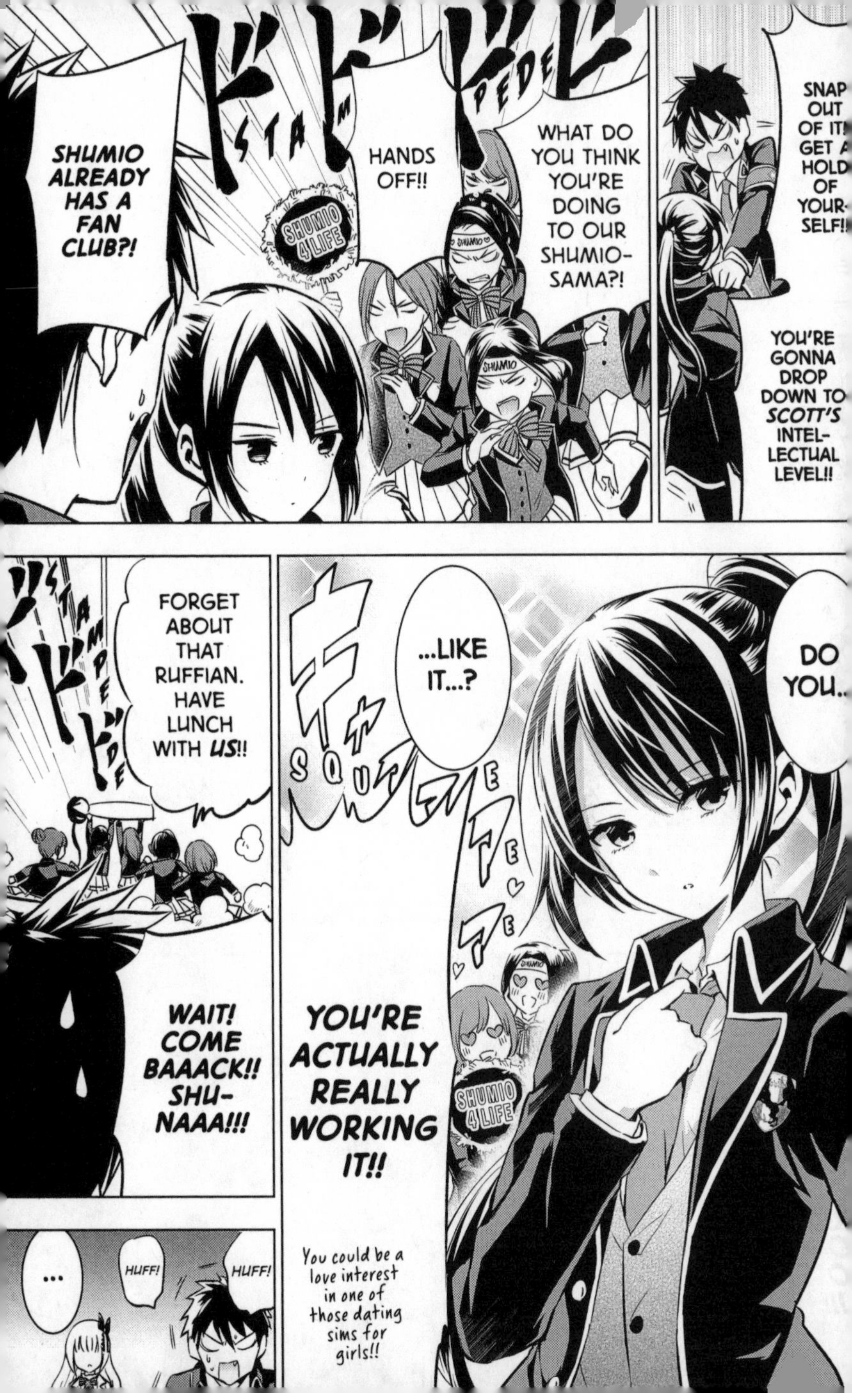
SNAP OUT OF IT! GET A HOLD OF YOUR-SELF!!
YOU'RE GONNA DROP DOWN TO SCOTT'S INTEL-LECTUAL LEVEL!!
STAMPEDE
WHAT DO YOU THINK YOU'RE DOING TO OUR SHUMIO-SAMA?!
SHUMIO
HANDS OFF!!
SHUMIO
SHUMIO 4 LIFE
SHUMIO ALREADY HAS A FAN CLUB?!
DO YOU...
...LIKE IT...?
SQUEEEEE
YOU'RE ACTUALLY REALLY WORKING IT!!
SHUMIO 4 LIFE
You could be a love interest in one of those dating sims for girls!!
STAMPEDE
FORGET ABOUT THAT RUFFIAN. HAVE LUNCH WITH US!!
WAIT! COME BAAACK!! SHU-NAAAA!!!
HUFF!
HUFF!
...

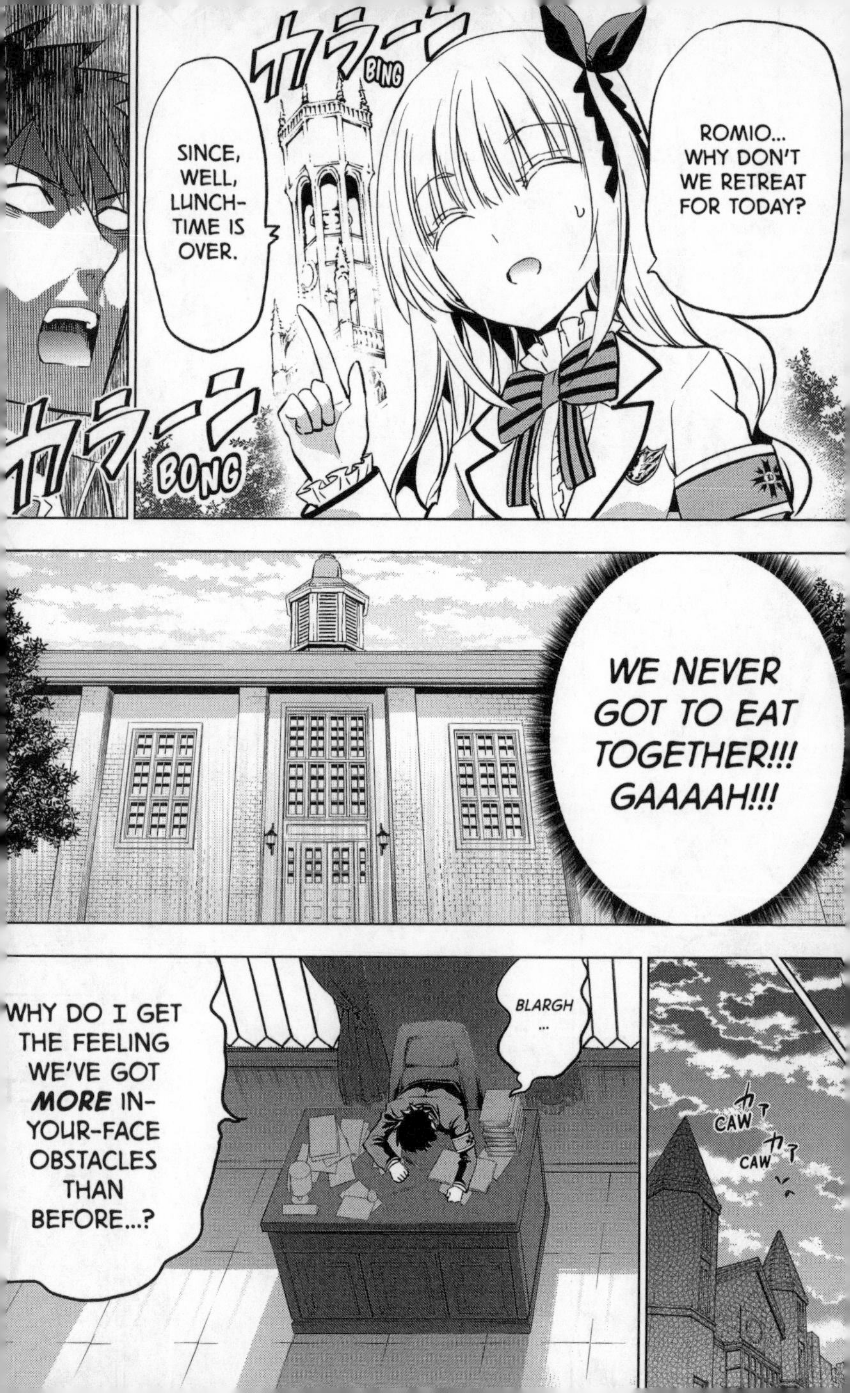
ROMIO... WHY DON'T WE RETREAT FOR TODAY?
ウラ〜ン
BING
SINCE, WELL, LUNCH-TIME IS OVER.
ウラ〜ン
BONG
WE NEVER GOT TO EAT TOGETHER!!! GAAAAH!!!
カァ
CAW
カァ
CAW
BLARGH ...
WHY DO I GET THE FEELING WE'VE GOT *MORE* IN-YOUR-FACE OBSTACLES THAN BEFORE...?

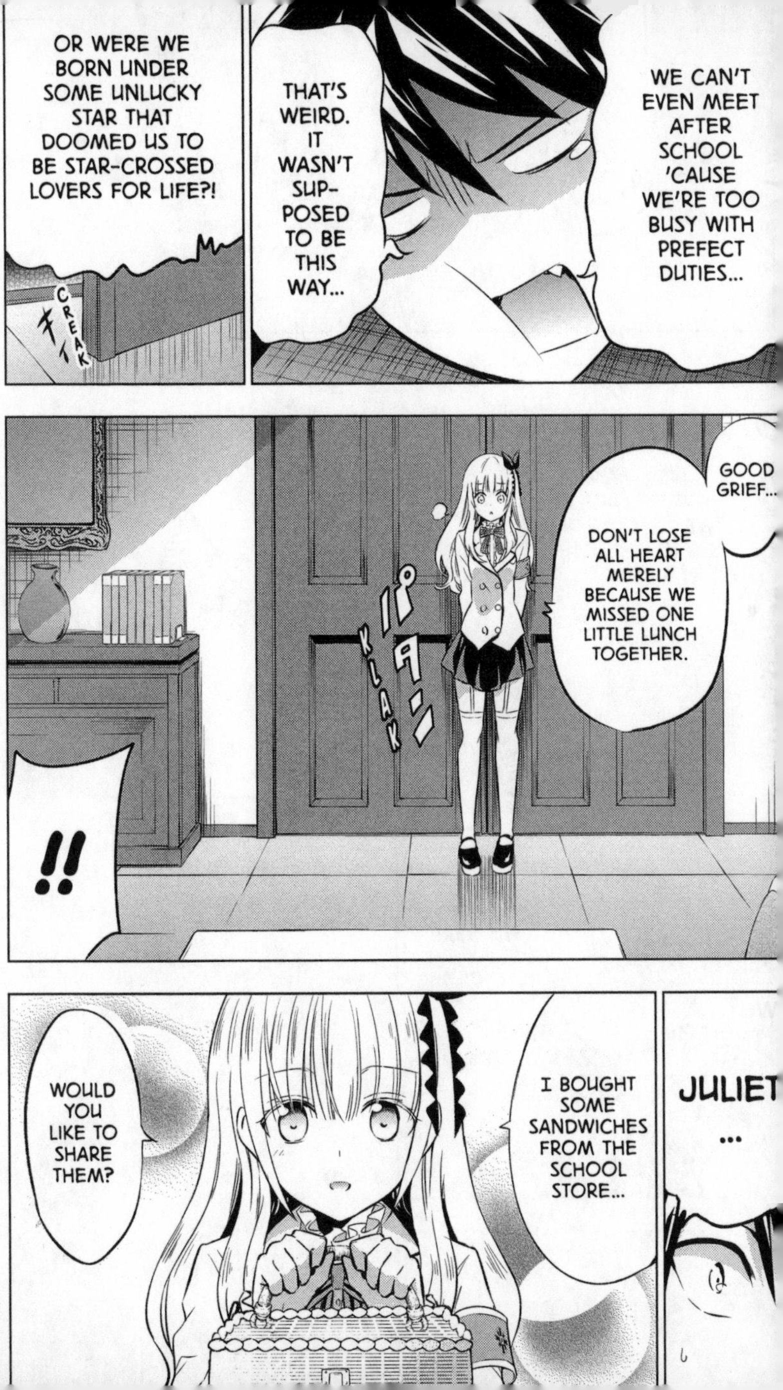
WE CAN'T EVEN MEET AFTER SCHOOL 'CAUSE WE'RE TOO BUSY WITH PREFECT DUTIES...
THAT'S WEIRD. IT WASN'T SUP-POSED TO BE THIS WAY...
OR WERE WE BORN UNDER SOME UNLUCKY STAR THAT DOOMED US TO BE STAR-CROSSED LOVERS FOR LIFE?!
CREAK
GOOD GRIEF...
DON'T LOSE ALL HEART MERELY BECAUSE WE MISSED ONE LITTLE LUNCH TOGETHER.
KLAK
!!
JULIET...
I BOUGHT SOME SANDWICHES FROM THE SCHOOL STORE...
WOULD YOU LIKE TO SHARE THEM?

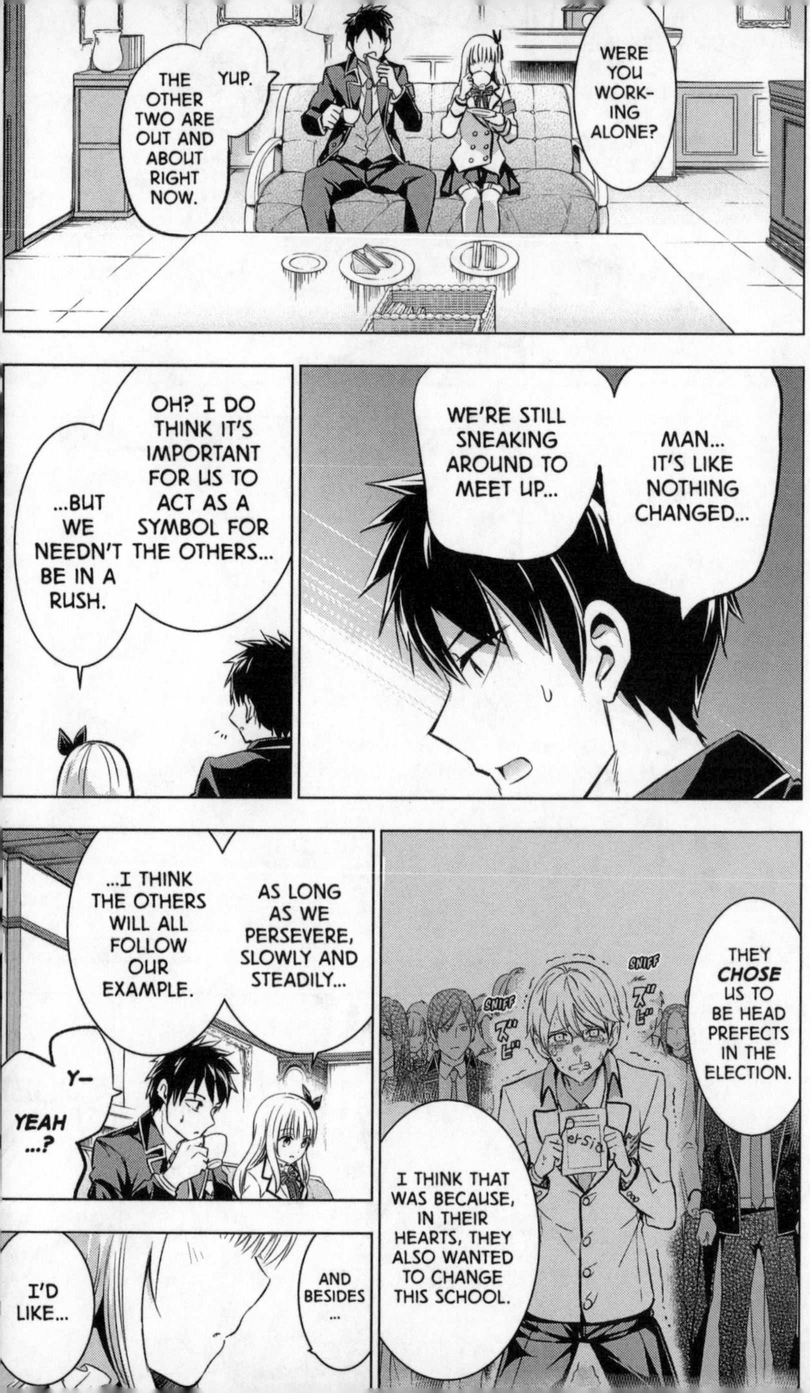
WERE YOU WORKING-ING ALONE?
YUP. THE OTHER TWO ARE OUT AND ABOUT RIGHT NOW.
MAN... IT'S LIKE NOTHING CHANGED...
WE'RE STILL SNEAKING AROUND TO MEET UP...
OH? I DO THINK IT'S IMPORTANT FOR US TO ACT AS A SYMBOL FOR THE OTHERS...
...BUT WE NEEDN'T BE IN A RUSH.
THEY CHOSE US TO BE HEAD PREFECTS IN THE ELECTION.
SNIFF
SNIFF
I THINK THAT WAS BECAUSE, IN THEIR HEARTS, THEY ALSO WANTED TO CHANGE THIS SCHOOL.
AS LONG AS WE PERSEVERE, SLOWLY AND STEADILY...
...I THINK THE OTHERS WILL ALL FOLLOW OUR EXAMPLE.
Y— YEAH ...?
AND BESIDES ...
I'D LIKE...

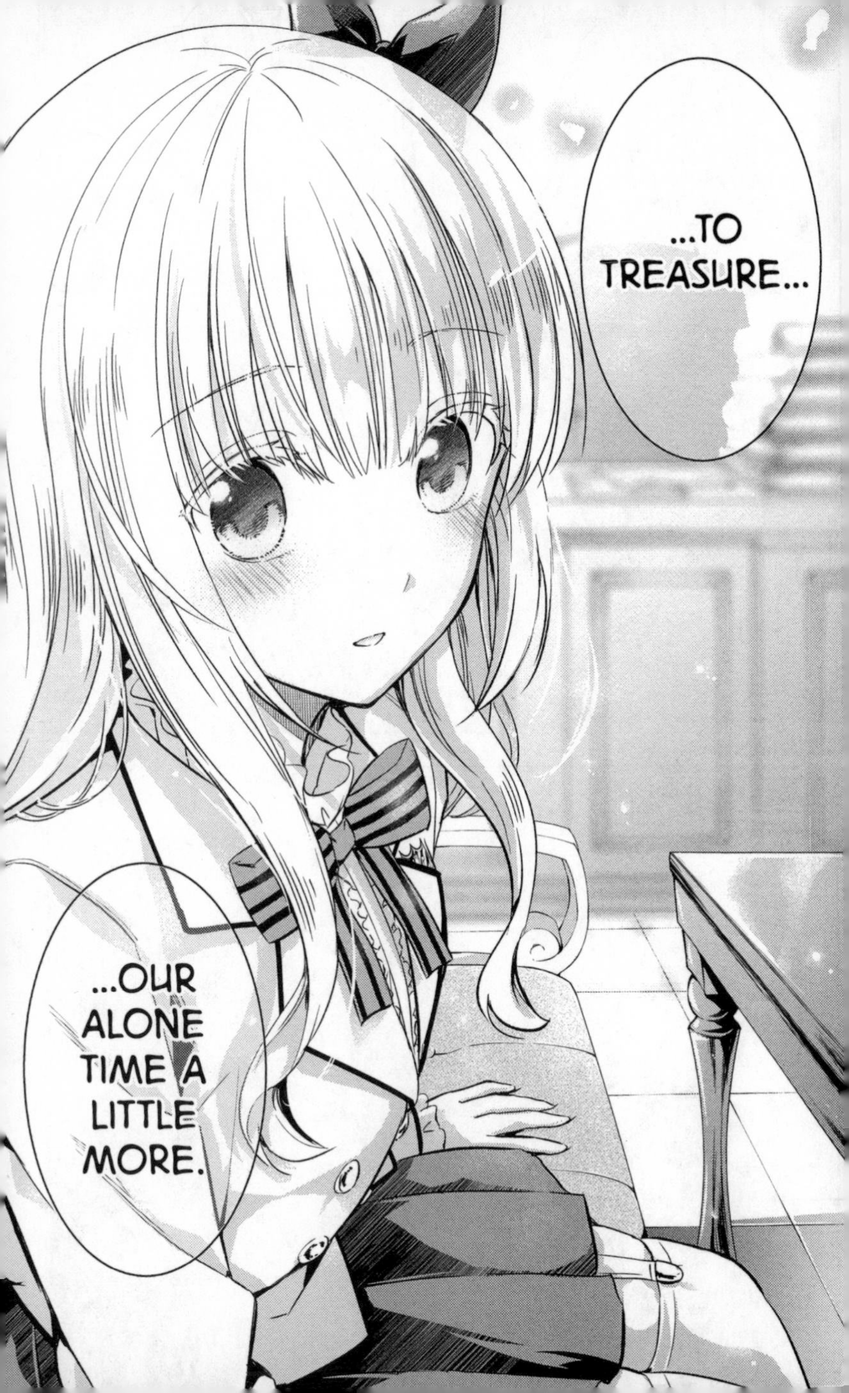
...TO TREASURE...
...OUR ALONE TIME A LITTLE MORE.

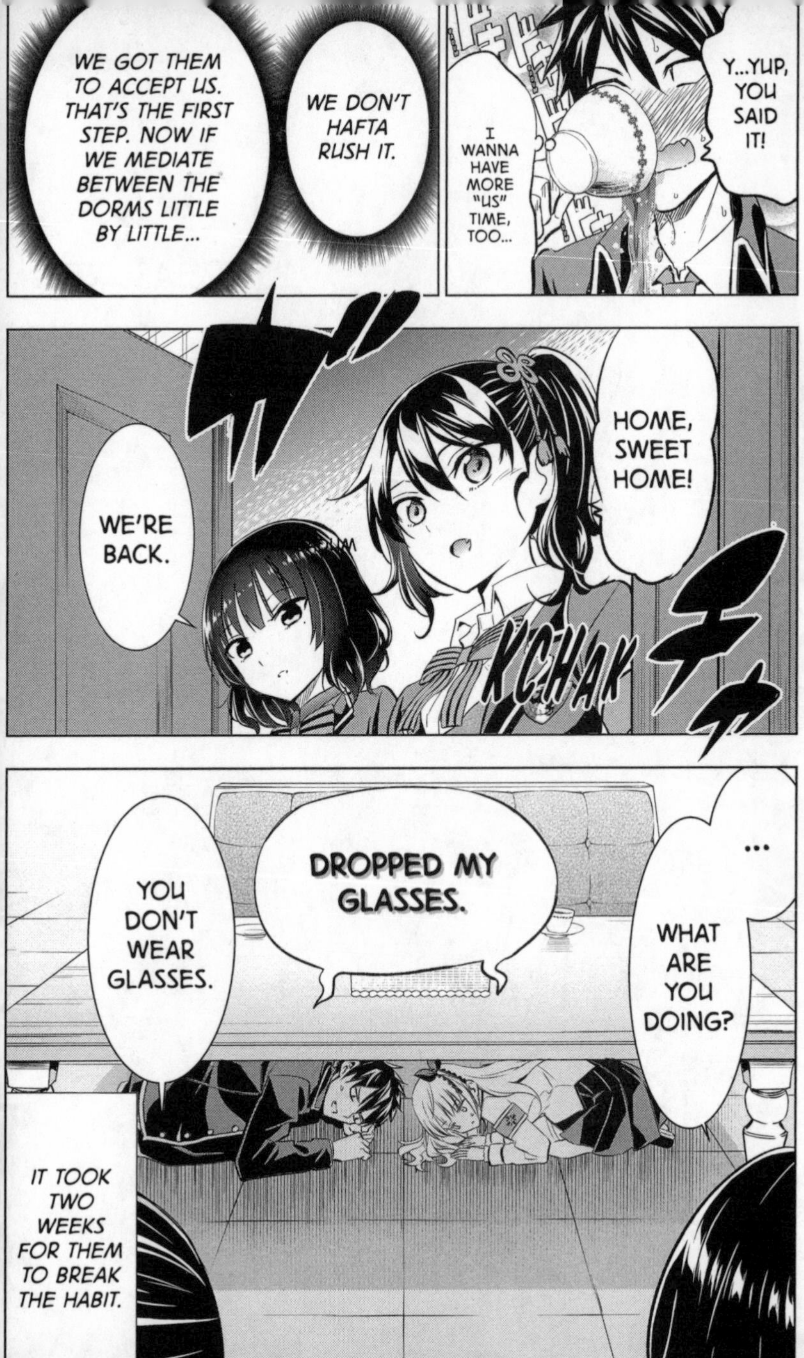
Y...YUP, YOU SAID IT!
I WANNA HAVE MORE "US" TIME, TOO...
WE DON'T HAFTA RUSH IT.
WE GOT THEM TO ACCEPT US. THAT'S THE FIRST STEP. NOW IF WE MEDIATE BETWEEN THE DORMS LITTLE BY LITTLE...
HOME, SWEET HOME!
KCHAK
WE'RE BACK.
...
WHAT ARE YOU DOING?
DROPPED MY GLASSES.
YOU DON'T WEAR GLASSES.
IT TOOK TWO WEEKS FOR THEM TO BREAK THE HABIT.

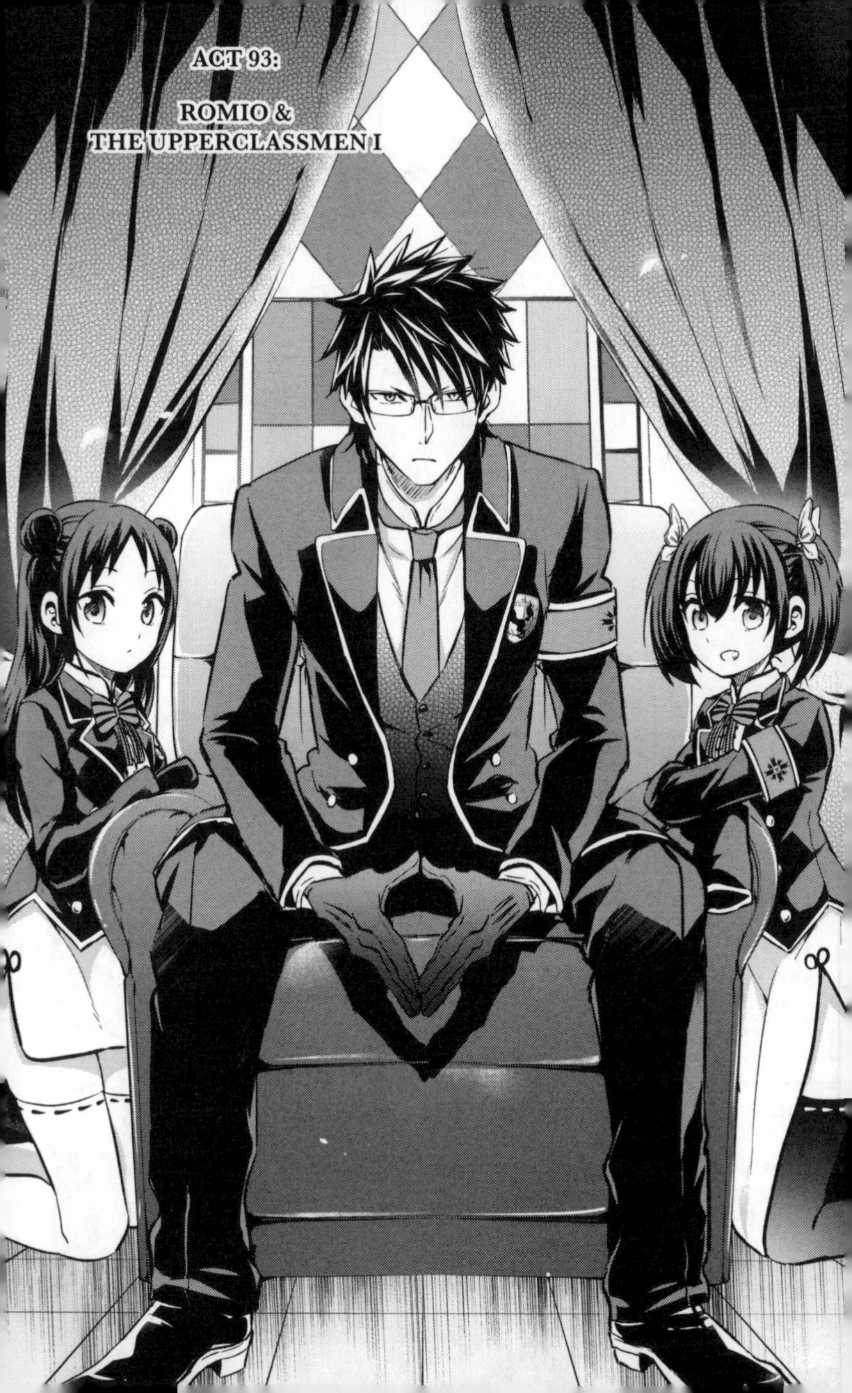
ACT 93:
ROMIO &
THE UPPERCLASSMEN I

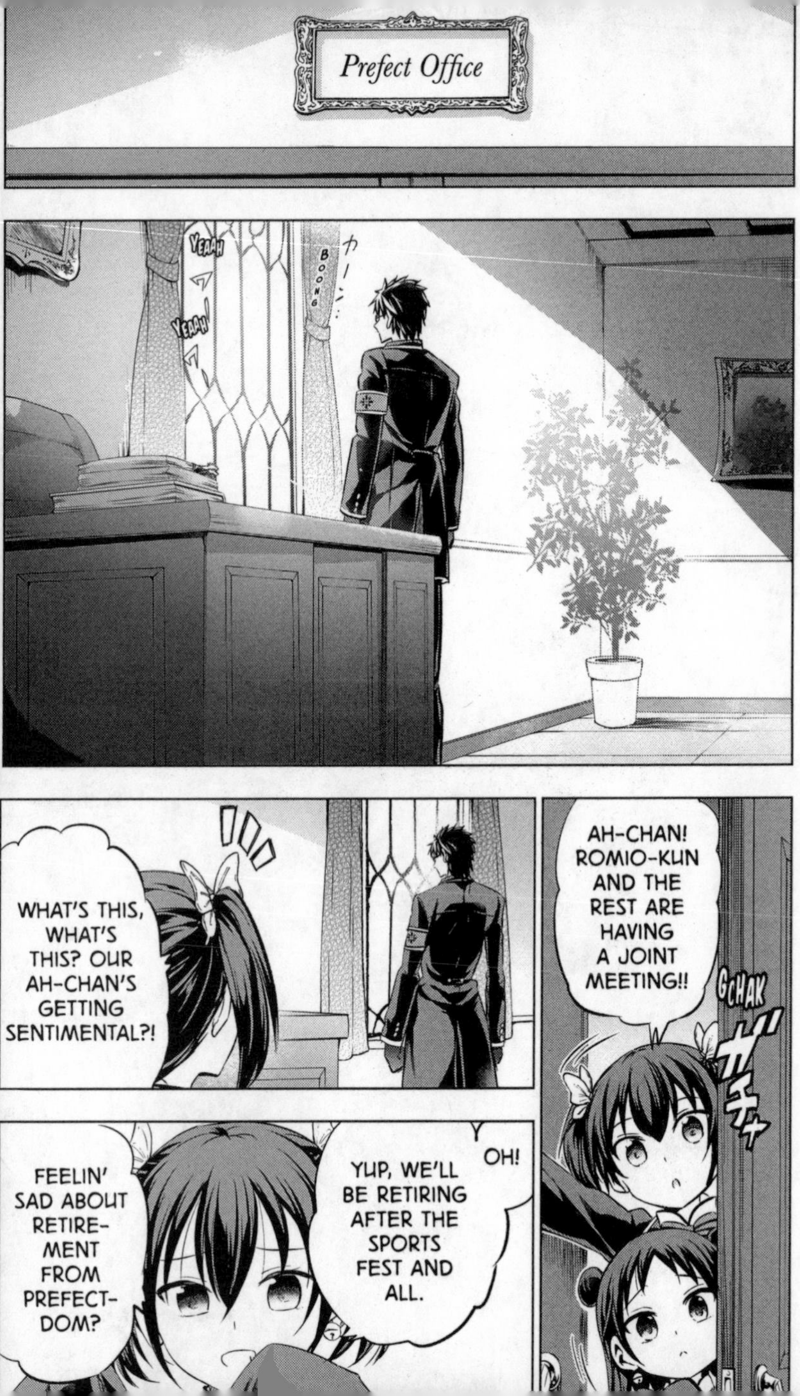
Prefect Office
YEAAH
BOOONG
YEAAH!
AH-CHAN! ROMIO-KUN AND THE REST ARE HAVING A JOINT MEETING!!
GCHAK
WHAT'S THIS, WHAT'S THIS? OUR AH-CHAN'S GETTING SENTIMENTAL?!
OH!
YUP, WE'LL BE RETIRING AFTER THE SPORTS FEST AND ALL.
FEELIN' SAD ABOUT RETIRE-MENT FROM PREFECT-DOM?

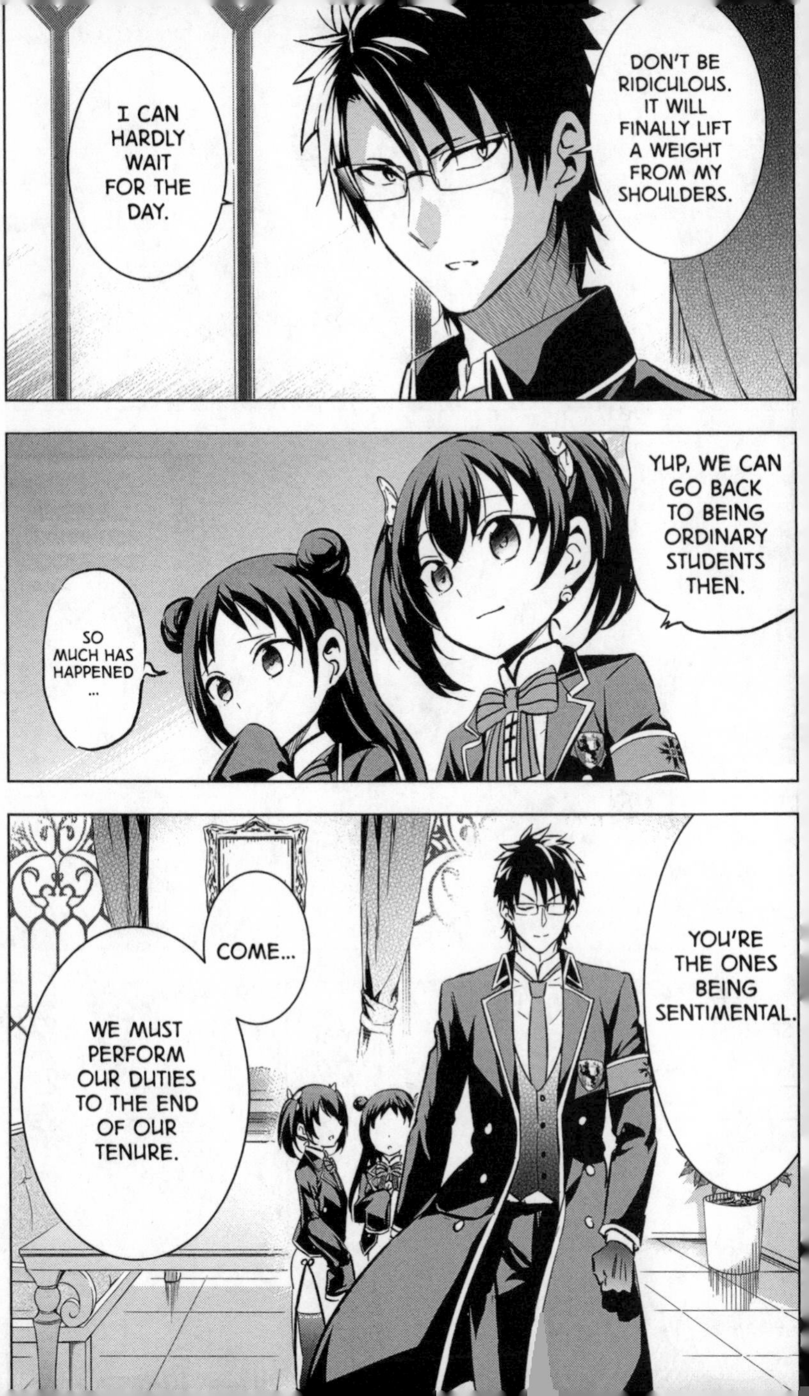
DON'T BE RIDICULOUS. IT WILL FINALLY LIFT A WEIGHT FROM MY SHOULDERS.
I CAN HARDLY WAIT FOR THE DAY.
YUP, WE CAN GO BACK TO BEING ORDINARY STUDENTS THEN.
SO MUCH HAS HAPPENED ...
YOU'RE THE ONES BEING SENTIMENTAL.
COME...
WE MUST PERFORM OUR DUTIES TO THE END OF OUR TENURE.

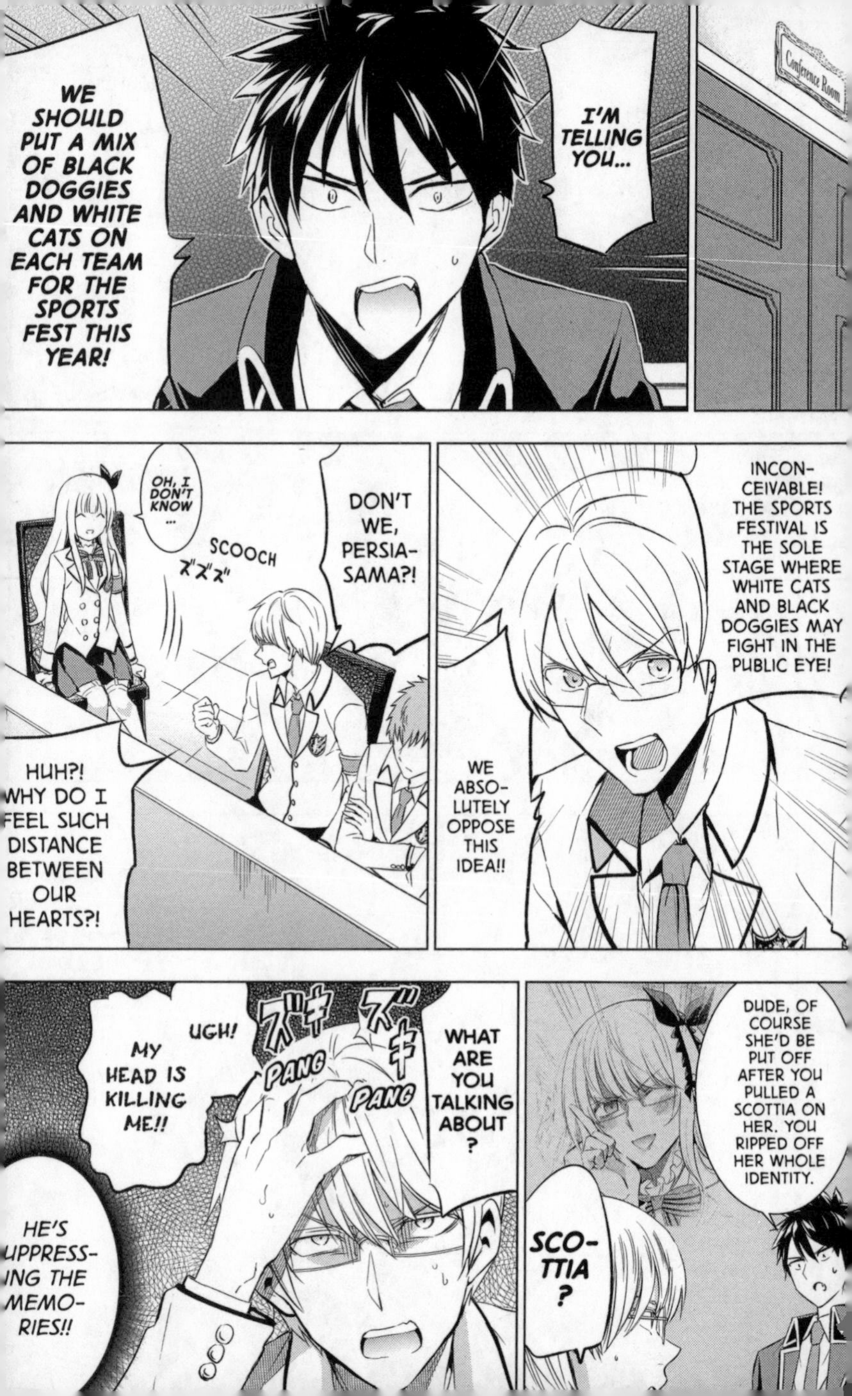
Conference Room
I'M TELLING YOU...
WE SHOULD PUT A MIX OF BLACK DOGGIES AND WHITE CATS ON EACH TEAM FOR THE SPORTS FEST THIS YEAR!
INCON-CEIVABLE! THE SPORTS FESTIVAL IS THE SOLE STAGE WHERE WHITE CATS AND BLACK DOGGIES MAY FIGHT IN THE PUBLIC EYE!
WE ABSO-LUTELY OPPOSE THIS IDEA!!
DON'T WE, PERSIA-SAMA?!
OH, I DON'T KNOW ...
SCOOCH
ズズズ
HUH?! WHY DO I FEEL SUCH DISTANCE BETWEEN OUR HEARTS?!
DUDE, OF COURSE SHE'D BE PUT OFF AFTER YOU PULLED A SCOTTIA ON HER. YOU RIPPED OFF HER WHOLE IDENTITY.
SCO-TTIA ?
WHAT ARE YOU TALKING ABOUT ?
ズキ ズキ
PANG PANG
UGH!
MY HEAD IS KILLING ME!!
HE'S UPPRESS-ING THE MEMO-RIES!!

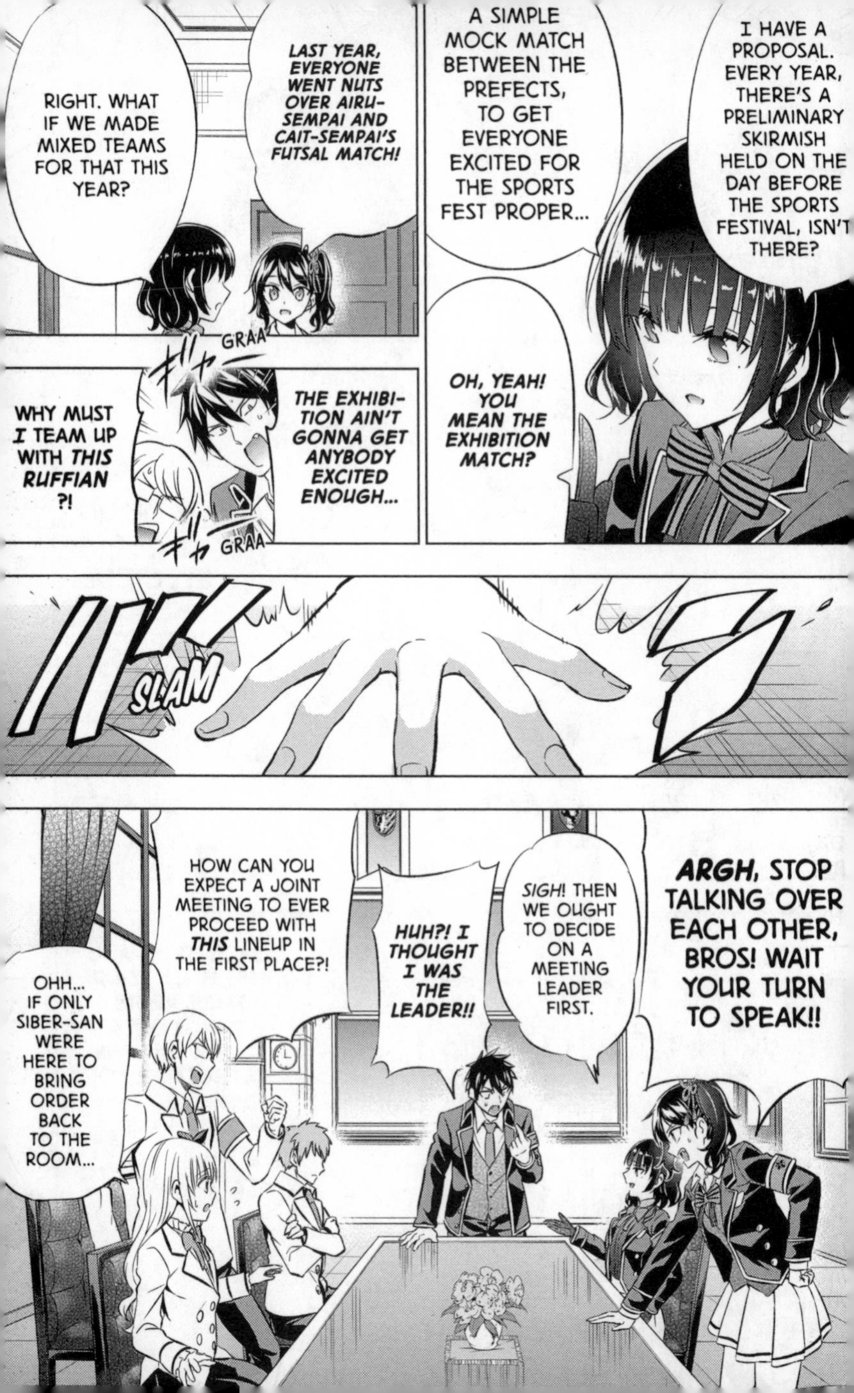
I HAVE A PROPOSAL. EVERY YEAR, THERE'S A PRELIMINARY SKIRMISH HELD ON THE DAY BEFORE THE SPORTS FESTIVAL, ISN'T THERE?
A SIMPLE MOCK MATCH BETWEEN THE PREFECTS, TO GET EVERYONE EXCITED FOR THE SPORTS FEST PROPER...
OH, YEAH! YOU MEAN THE EXHIBITION MATCH?
LAST YEAR, EVERYONE WENT NUTS OVER AIRU-SEMPAI AND CAIT-SEMPAI'S FUTSAL MATCH!
RIGHT. WHAT IF WE MADE MIXED TEAMS FOR THAT THIS YEAR?
GRAA
THE EXHIBITION AIN'T GONNA GET ANYBODY EXCITED ENOUGH...
WHY MUST I TEAM UP WITH THIS RUFFIAN ?!
GRAA
SLAM
ARGH, STOP TALKING OVER EACH OTHER, BROS! WAIT YOUR TURN TO SPEAK!!
SIGH! THEN WE OUGHT TO DECIDE ON A MEETING LEADER FIRST.
HUH?! I THOUGHT I WAS THE LEADER!!
HOW CAN YOU EXPECT A JOINT MEETING TO EVER PROCEED WITH THIS LINEUP IN THE FIRST PLACE?!
OHH... IF ONLY SIBER-SAN WERE HERE TO BRING ORDER BACK TO THE ROOM...

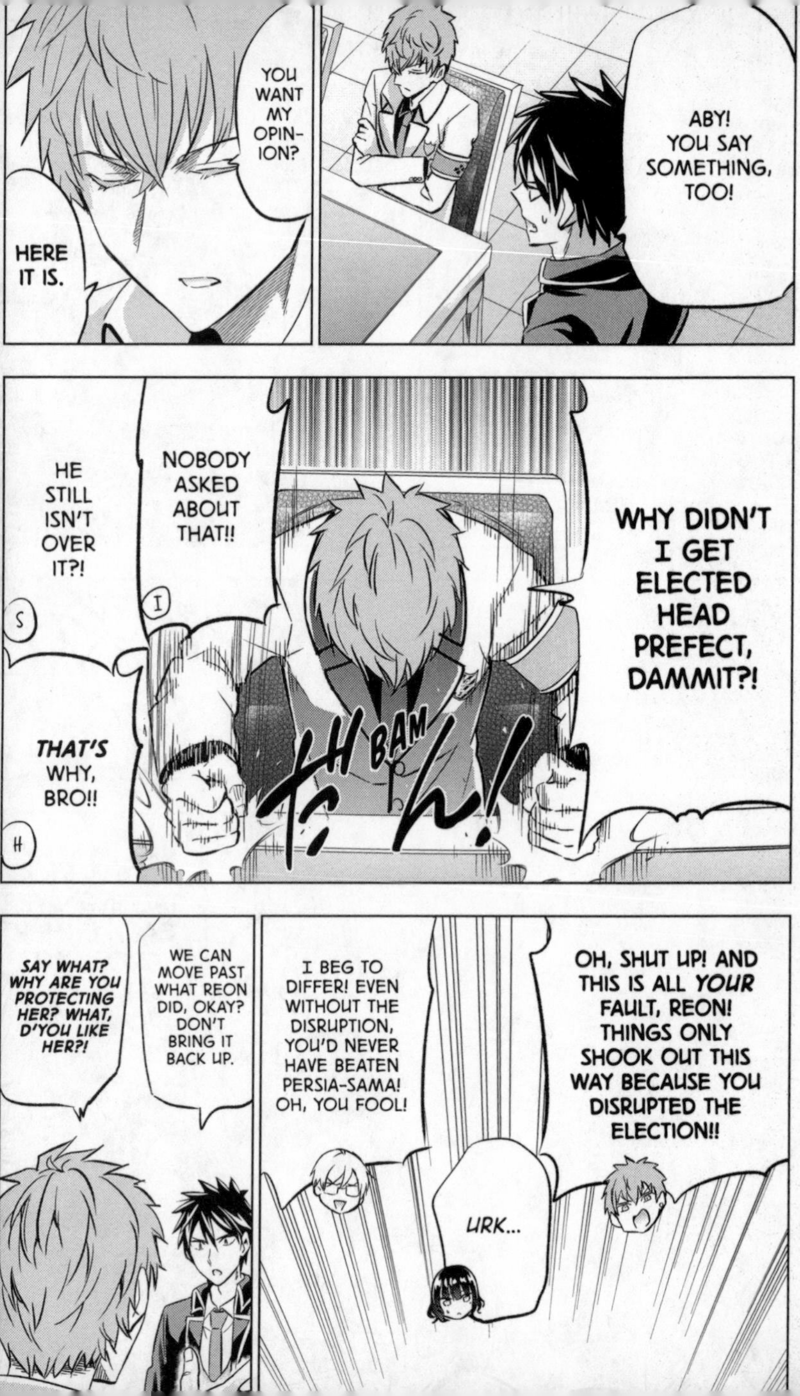

ABY! YOU SAY SOMETHING, TOO!
YOU WANT MY OPIN-ION?
HERE IT IS.
WHY DIDN'T I GET ELECTED HEAD PREFECT, DAMMIT?!
BAM
I
NOBODY ASKED ABOUT THAT!!
S
HE STILL ISN'T OVER IT?!
H
*THAT'S* WHY, BRO!!
OH, SHUT UP! AND THIS IS ALL *YOUR* FAULT, REON! THINGS ONLY SHOOK OUT THIS WAY BECAUSE YOU DISRUPTED THE ELECTION!!
I BEG TO DIFFER! EVEN WITHOUT THE DISRUPTION, YOU'D NEVER HAVE BEATEN PERSIA-SAMA! OH, YOU FOOL!
URK...
WE CAN MOVE PAST WHAT REON DID, OKAY? DON'T BRING IT BACK UP.
SAY WHAT? WHY ARE YOU PROTECTING HER? WHAT, D'YOU LIKE HER?!

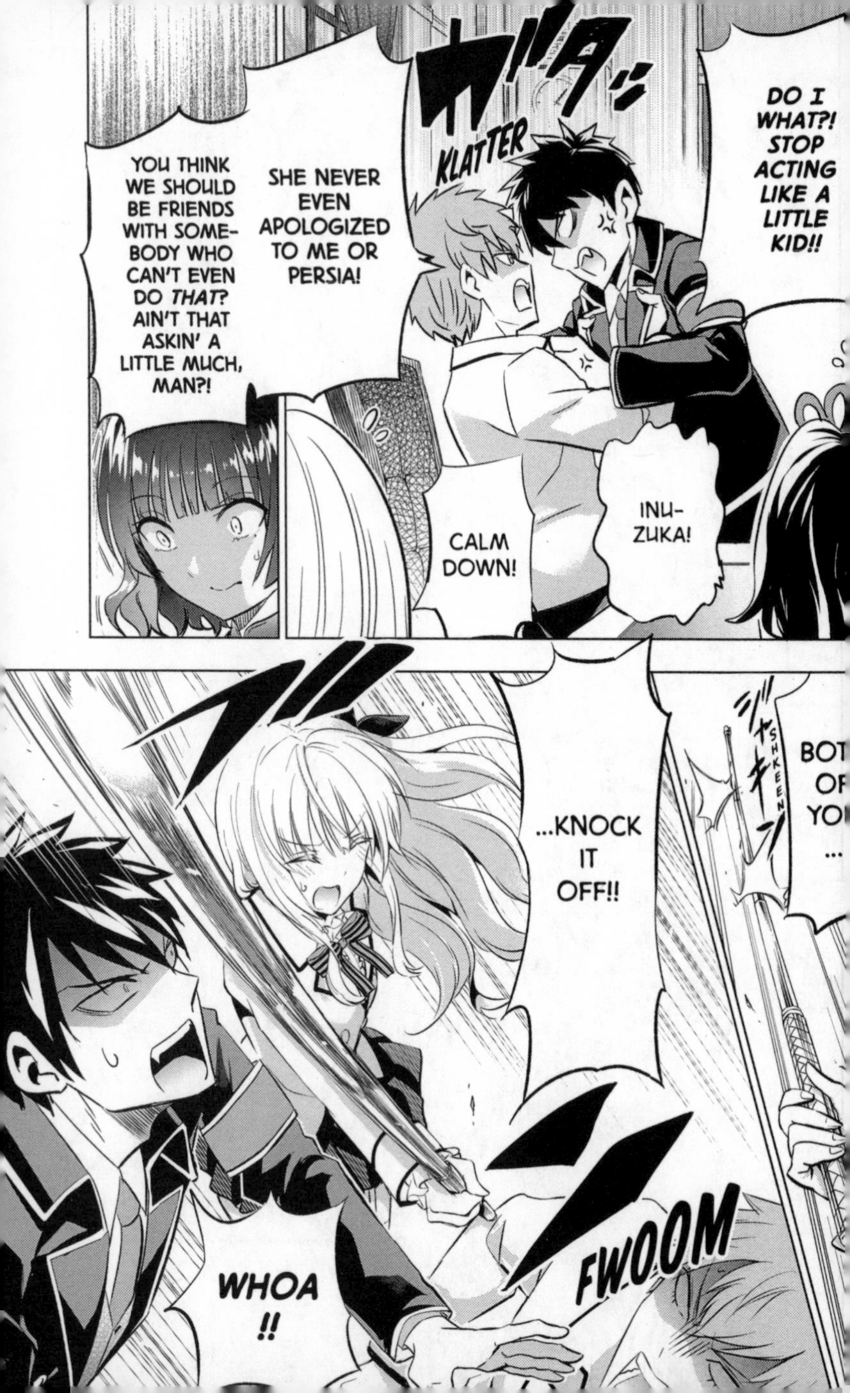
DO I WHAT?! STOP ACTING LIKE A LITTLE KID!!
KLATTER
SHE NEVER EVEN APOLOGIZED TO ME OR PERSIA!
YOU THINK WE SHOULD BE FRIENDS WITH SOME-BODY WHO CAN'T EVEN DO *THAT*? AIN'T THAT ASKIN' A LITTLE MUCH, MAN?!
INU-ZUKA!
CALM DOWN!
BOT OF YO ...
SHKEEN
...KNOCK IT OFF!!
FWOOM
WHOA !!

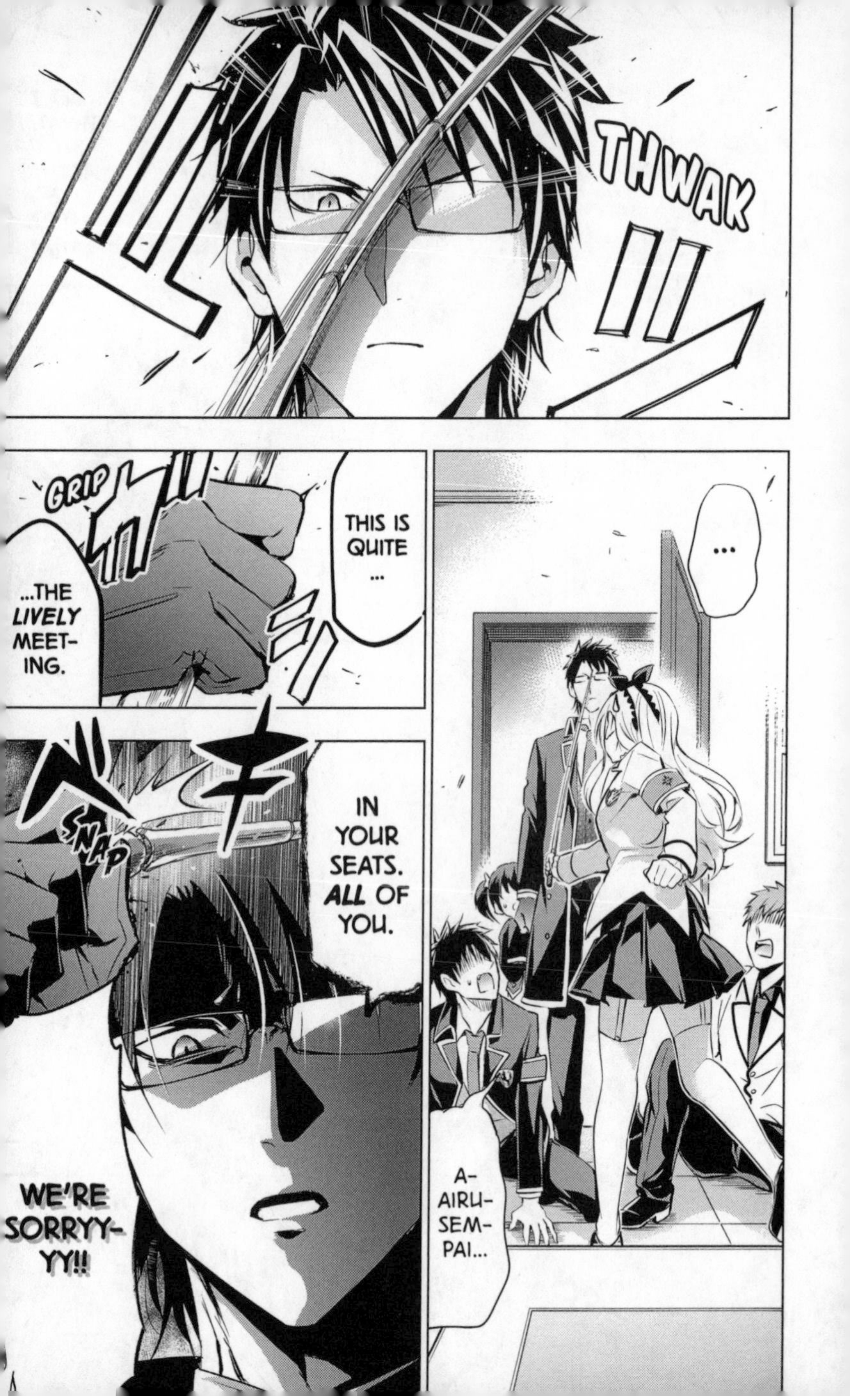
THWAK
...
A-AIRU-SEMPAI...
GRIP
THIS IS QUITE ...
...THE LIVELY MEETING.
SNAP
IN YOUR SEATS. ALL OF YOU.
WE'RE SORRYYY-YY!!

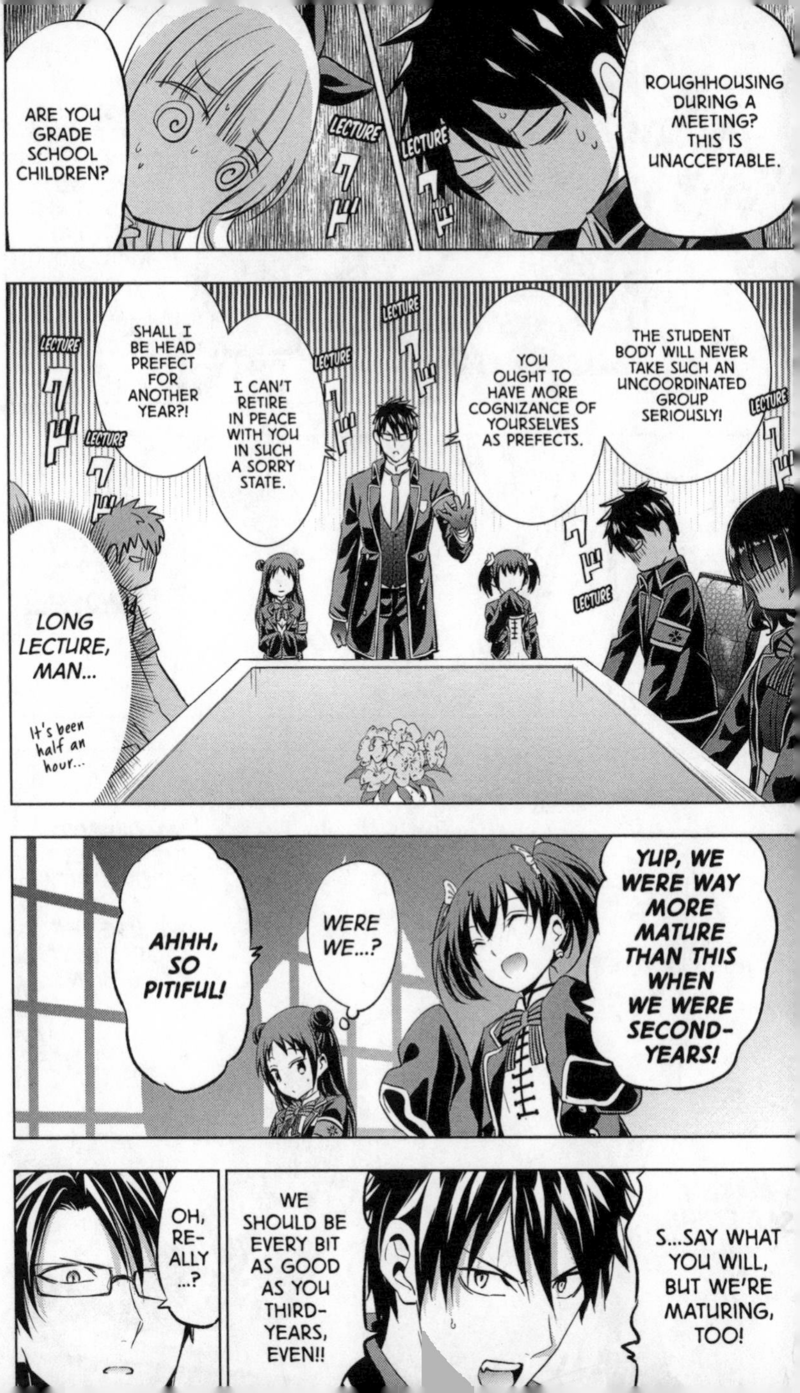
ROUGHHOUSING DURING A MEETING? THIS IS UNACCEPTABLE.
LECTURE
LECTURE
ARE YOU GRADE SCHOOL CHILDREN?
LECTURE
THE STUDENT BODY WILL NEVER TAKE SUCH AN UNCOORDINATED GROUP SERIOUSLY!
LECTURE
YOU OUGHT TO HAVE MORE COGNIZANCE OF YOURSELVES AS PREFECTS.
LECTURE
LECTURE
I CAN'T RETIRE IN PEACE WITH YOU IN SUCH A SORRY STATE.
SHALL I BE HEAD PREFECT FOR ANOTHER YEAR?!
LECTURE
LECTURE
LONG LECTURE, MAN...
It's been half an hour...
YUP, WE WERE WAY MORE MATURE THAN THIS WHEN WE WERE SECOND-YEARS!
WERE WE...?
AHHH, SO PITIFUL!
S...SAY WHAT YOU WILL, BUT WE'RE MATURING, TOO!
WE SHOULD BE EVERY BIT AS GOOD AS YOU THIRD-YEARS, EVEN!!
OH, REALLY...?

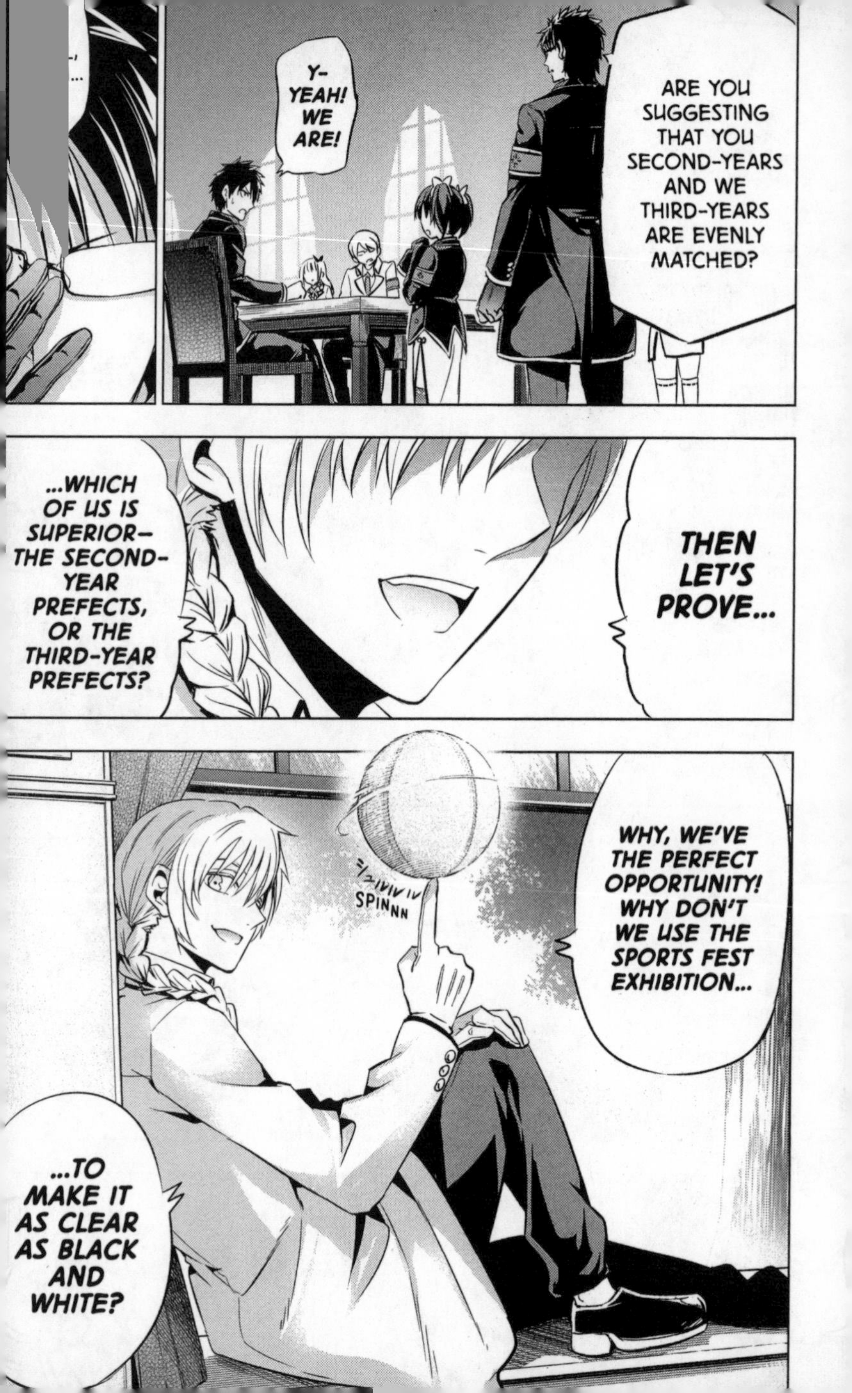
ARE YOU SUGGESTING THAT YOU SECOND-YEARS AND WE THIRD-YEARS ARE EVENLY MATCHED?
Y-YEAH! WE ARE!
THEN LET'S PROVE...
...WHICH OF US IS SUPERIOR—THE SECOND-YEAR PREFECTS, OR THE THIRD-YEAR PREFECTS?
WHY, WE'VE THE PERFECT OPPORTUNITY! WHY DON'T WE USE THE SPORTS FEST EXHIBITION...
SPINNN
...TO MAKE IT AS CLEAR AS BLACK AND WHITE?

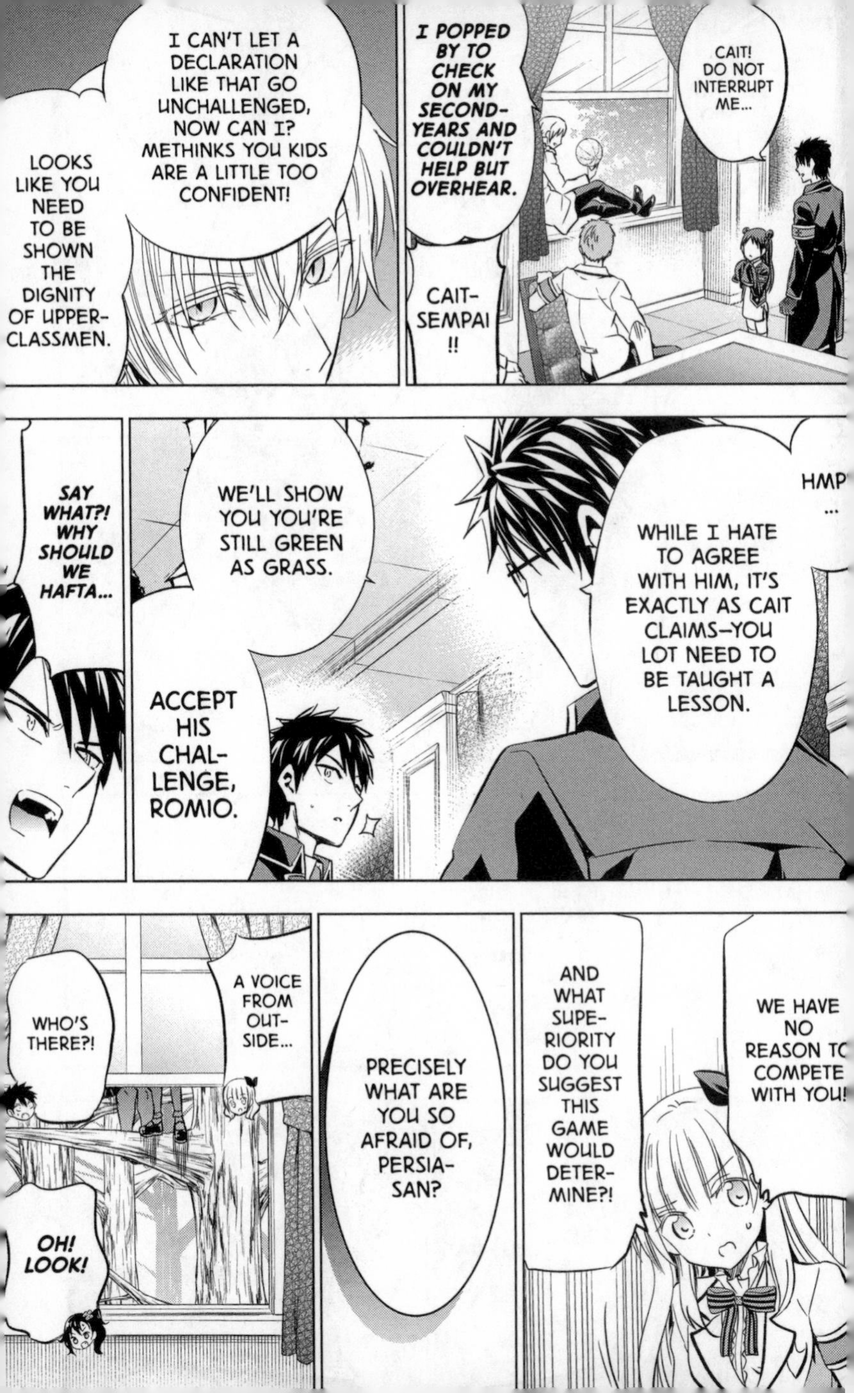
CAIT! DO NOT INTERRUPT ME...
I POPPED BY TO CHECK ON MY SECOND-YEARS AND COULDN'T HELP BUT OVERHEAR.
CAIT-SEMPAI !!
I CAN'T LET A DECLARATION LIKE THAT GO UNCHALLENGED, NOW CAN I? METHINKS YOU KIDS ARE A LITTLE TOO CONFIDENT!
LOOKS LIKE YOU NEED TO BE SHOWN THE DIGNITY OF UPPER-CLASSMEN.
HMP ...
WHILE I HATE TO AGREE WITH HIM, IT'S EXACTLY AS CAIT CLAIMS—YOU LOT NEED TO BE TAUGHT A LESSON.
WE'LL SHOW YOU YOU'RE STILL GREEN AS GRASS.
ACCEPT HIS CHAL-LENGE, ROMIO.
SAY WHAT?! WHY SHOULD WE HAFTA...
WE HAVE NO REASON TO COMPETE WITH YOU!
AND WHAT SUPE-RIORITY DO YOU SUGGEST THIS GAME WOULD DETER-MINE?!
PRECISELY WHAT ARE YOU SO AFRAID OF, PERSIA-SAN?
A VOICE FROM OUT-SIDE...
WHO'S THERE?!
OH! LOOK!

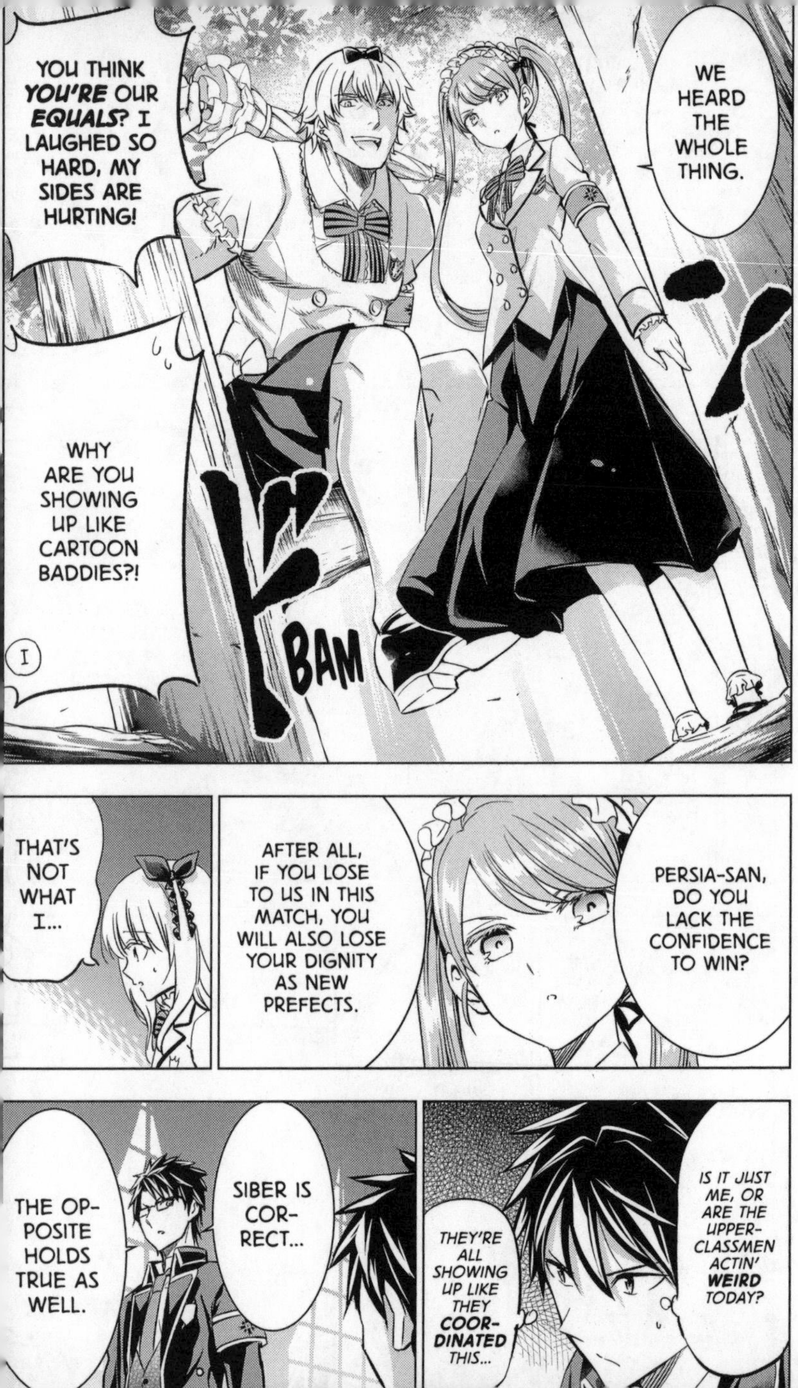
WE HEARD THE WHOLE THING.
YOU THINK *YOU'RE* OUR *EQUALS*? I LAUGHED SO HARD, MY SIDES ARE HURTING!
BAM
WHY ARE YOU SHOWING UP LIKE CARTOON BADDIES?!
I
PERSIA-SAN, DO YOU LACK THE CONFIDENCE TO WIN?
AFTER ALL, IF YOU LOSE TO US IN THIS MATCH, YOU WILL ALSO LOSE YOUR DIGNITY AS NEW PREFECTS.
THAT'S NOT WHAT I...
*IS IT JUST ME, OR ARE THE UPPER-CLASSMEN ACTIN'* ***WEIRD*** *TODAY?*
*THEY'RE ALL SHOWING UP LIKE THEY* ***COOR-DINATED*** *THIS...*
SIBER IS COR-RECT...
THE OP-POSITE HOLDS TRUE AS WELL.

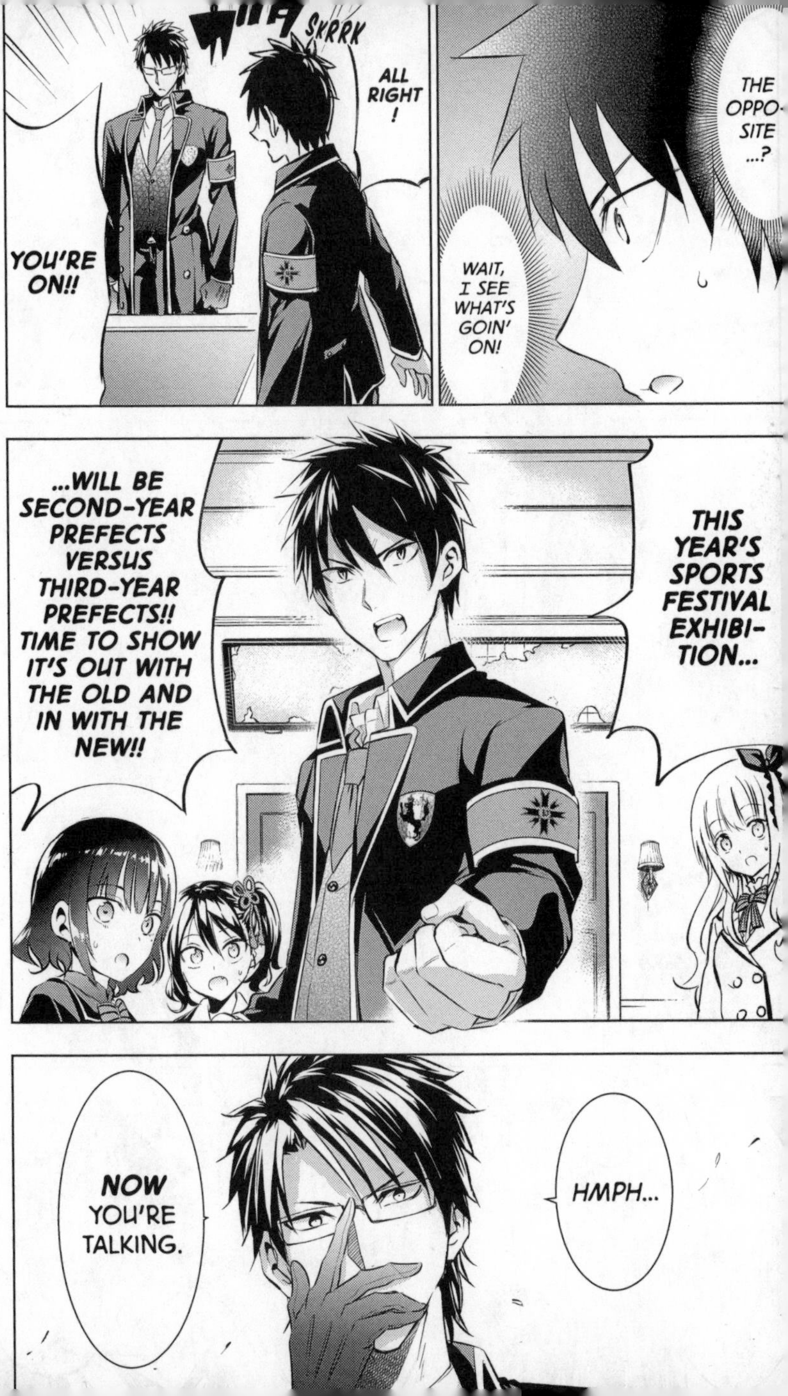
THE OPPO-SITE ...?
WAIT, I SEE WHAT'S GOIN' ON!
SKRRK
ALL RIGHT!
YOU'RE ON!!
THIS YEAR'S SPORTS FESTIVAL EXHIBI-TION...
...WILL BE SECOND-YEAR PREFECTS VERSUS THIRD-YEAR PREFECTS!! TIME TO SHOW IT'S OUT WITH THE OLD AND IN WITH THE NEW!!
HMPH...
NOW YOU'RE TALKING.

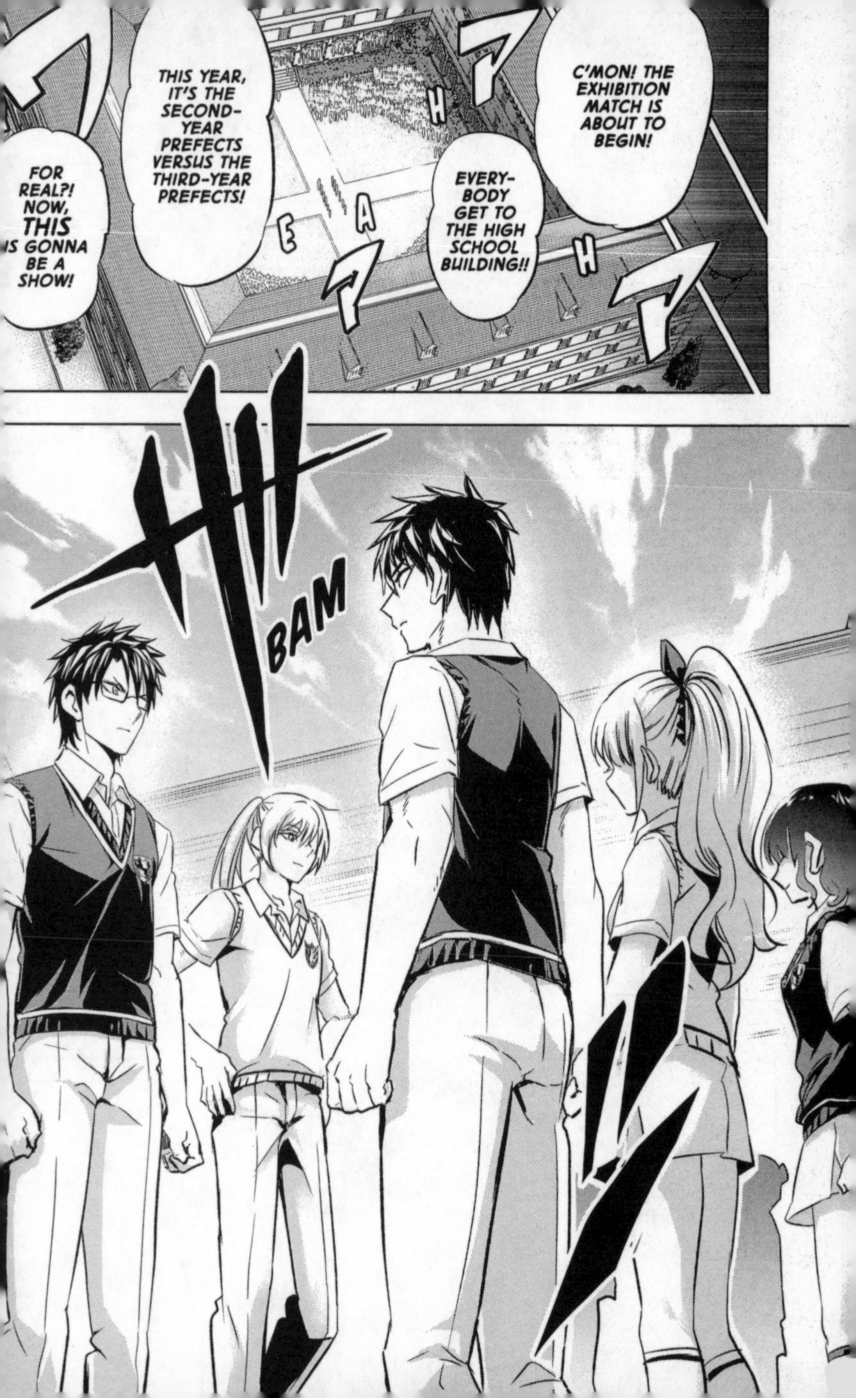
C'MON! THE EXHIBITION MATCH IS ABOUT TO BEGIN!
EVERYBODY GET TO THE HIGH SCHOOL BUILDING!!
THIS YEAR, IT'S THE SECOND-YEAR PREFECTS VERSUS THE THIRD-YEAR PREFECTS!
FOR REAL?! NOW, THIS IS GONNA BE A SHOW!
BAM

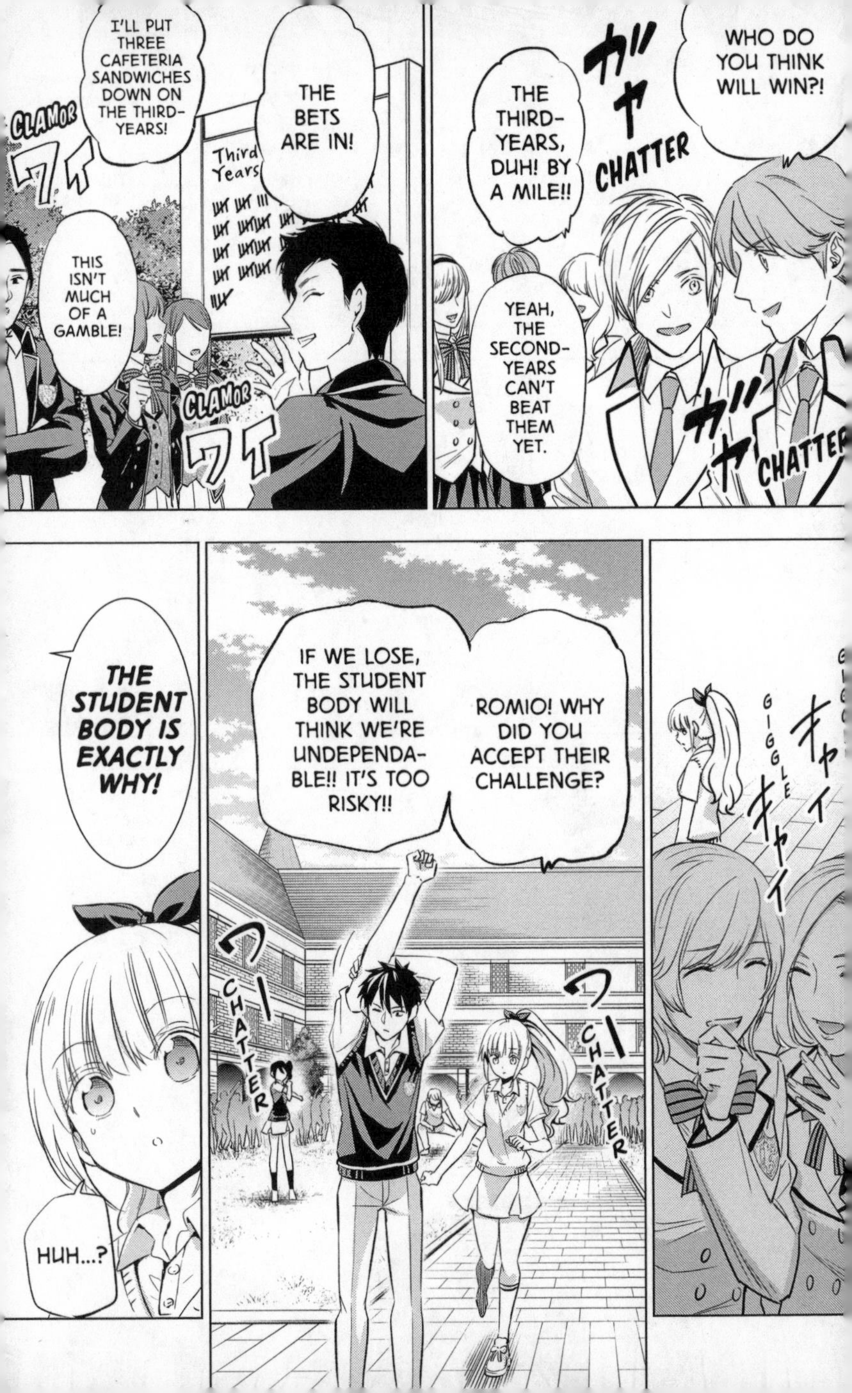
WHO DO YOU THINK WILL WIN?!
ガヤ
CHATTER
THE THIRD-YEARS, DUH! BY A MILE!!
YEAH, THE SECOND-YEARS CAN'T BEAT THEM YET.
ガヤ
CHATTER
THE BETS ARE IN!
I'LL PUT THREE CAFETERIA SANDWICHES DOWN ON THE THIRD-YEARS!
CLAMOR
ワイ
Third Years
THIS ISN'T MUCH OF A GAMBLE!
CLAMOR
ワイ
キャイ キャイ
GIGGLE
ROMIO! WHY DID YOU ACCEPT THEIR CHALLENGE?
IF WE LOSE, THE STUDENT BODY WILL THINK WE'RE UNDEPENDABLE!! IT'S TOO RISKY!!
ワー
CHATTER
ワー
CHATTER
THE STUDENT BODY IS EXACTLY WHY!
HUH...?

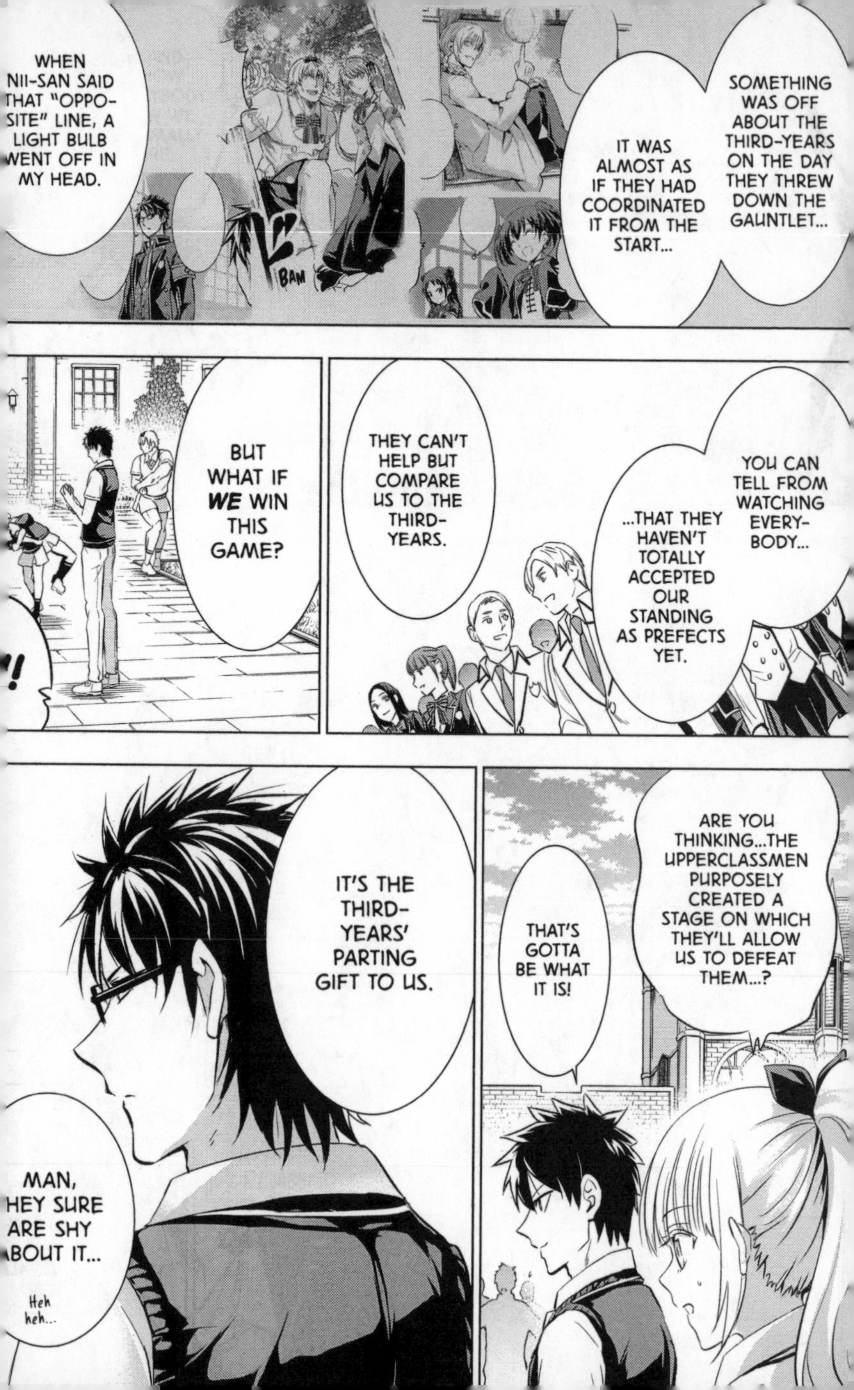
SOMETHING WAS OFF ABOUT THE THIRD-YEARS ON THE DAY THEY THREW DOWN THE GAUNTLET...
IT WAS ALMOST AS IF THEY HAD COORDINATED IT FROM THE START...
BAM
WHEN NII-SAN SAID THAT "OPPO-SITE" LINE, A LIGHT BULB WENT OFF IN MY HEAD.
YOU CAN TELL FROM WATCHING EVERY-BODY...
...THAT THEY HAVEN'T TOTALLY ACCEPTED OUR STANDING AS PREFECTS YET.
THEY CAN'T HELP BUT COMPARE US TO THE THIRD-YEARS.
BUT WHAT IF *WE* WIN THIS GAME?
!
ARE YOU THINKING...THE UPPERCLASSMEN PURPOSELY CREATED A STAGE ON WHICH THEY'LL ALLOW US TO DEFEAT THEM...?
THAT'S GOTTA BE WHAT IT IS!
IT'S THE THIRD-YEARS' PARTING GIFT TO US.
MAN, HEY SURE ARE SHY BOUT IT...
Heh heh...

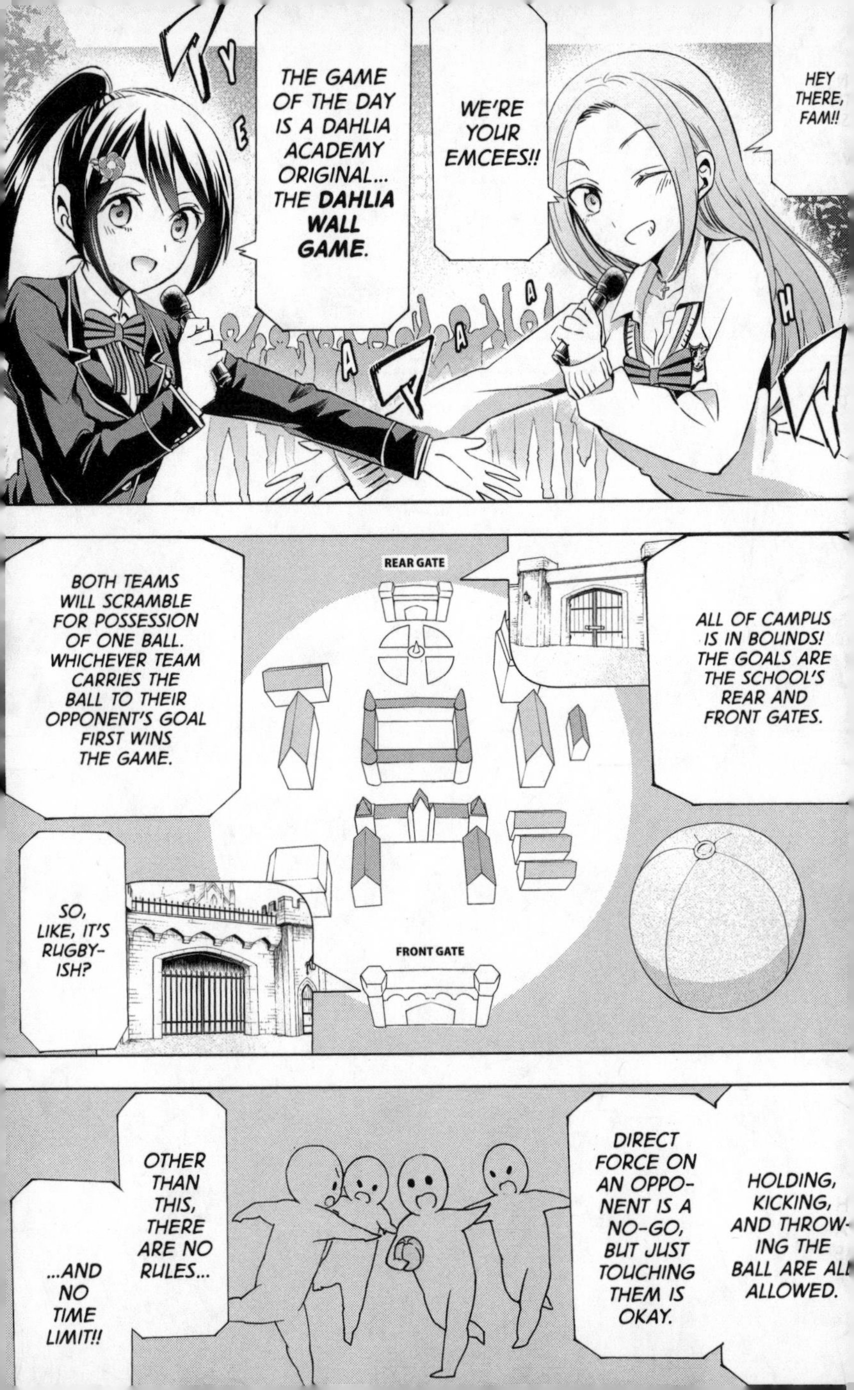
HEY THERE, FAM!!
WE'RE YOUR EMCEES!!
THE GAME OF THE DAY IS A DAHLIA ACADEMY ORIGINAL... THE **DAHLIA WALL GAME.**
YEAAAAH
ALL OF CAMPUS IS IN BOUNDS! THE GOALS ARE THE SCHOOL'S REAR AND FRONT GATES.
REAR GATE
FRONT GATE
BOTH TEAMS WILL SCRAMBLE FOR POSSESSION OF ONE BALL. WHICHEVER TEAM CARRIES THE BALL TO THEIR OPPONENT'S GOAL FIRST WINS THE GAME.
SO, LIKE, IT'S RUGBY-ISH?
HOLDING, KICKING, AND THROWING THE BALL ARE ALL ALLOWED.
DIRECT FORCE ON AN OPPONENT IS A NO-GO, BUT JUST TOUCHING THEM IS OKAY.
OTHER THAN THIS, THERE ARE NO RULES...
...AND NO TIME LIMIT!!

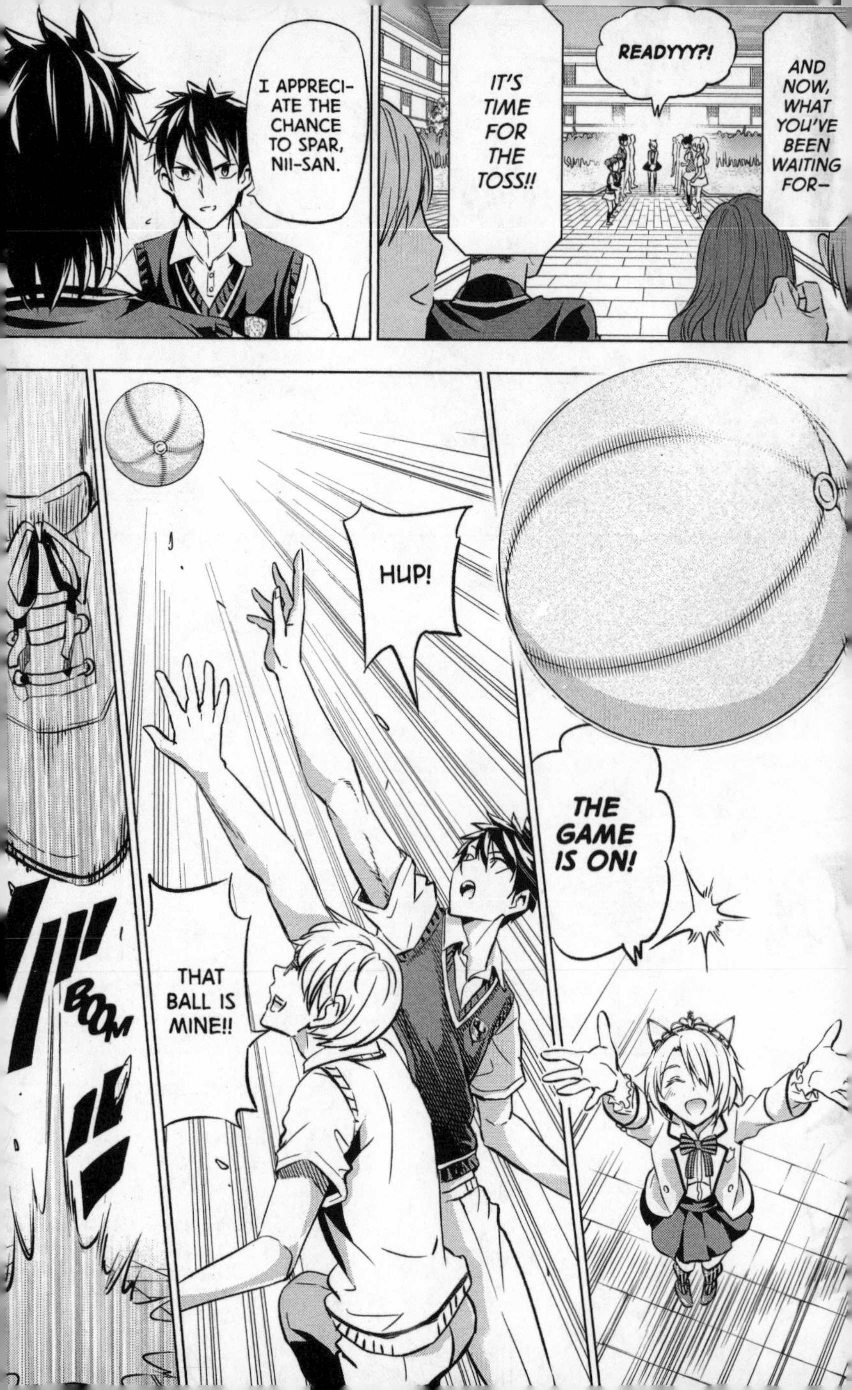
AND NOW, WHAT YOU'VE BEEN WAITING FOR—
READYYY?!
IT'S TIME FOR THE TOSS!!
I APPRECI-ATE THE CHANCE TO SPAR, NII-SAN.
THE GAME IS ON!
HUP!
THAT BALL IS MINE!!
BOOM

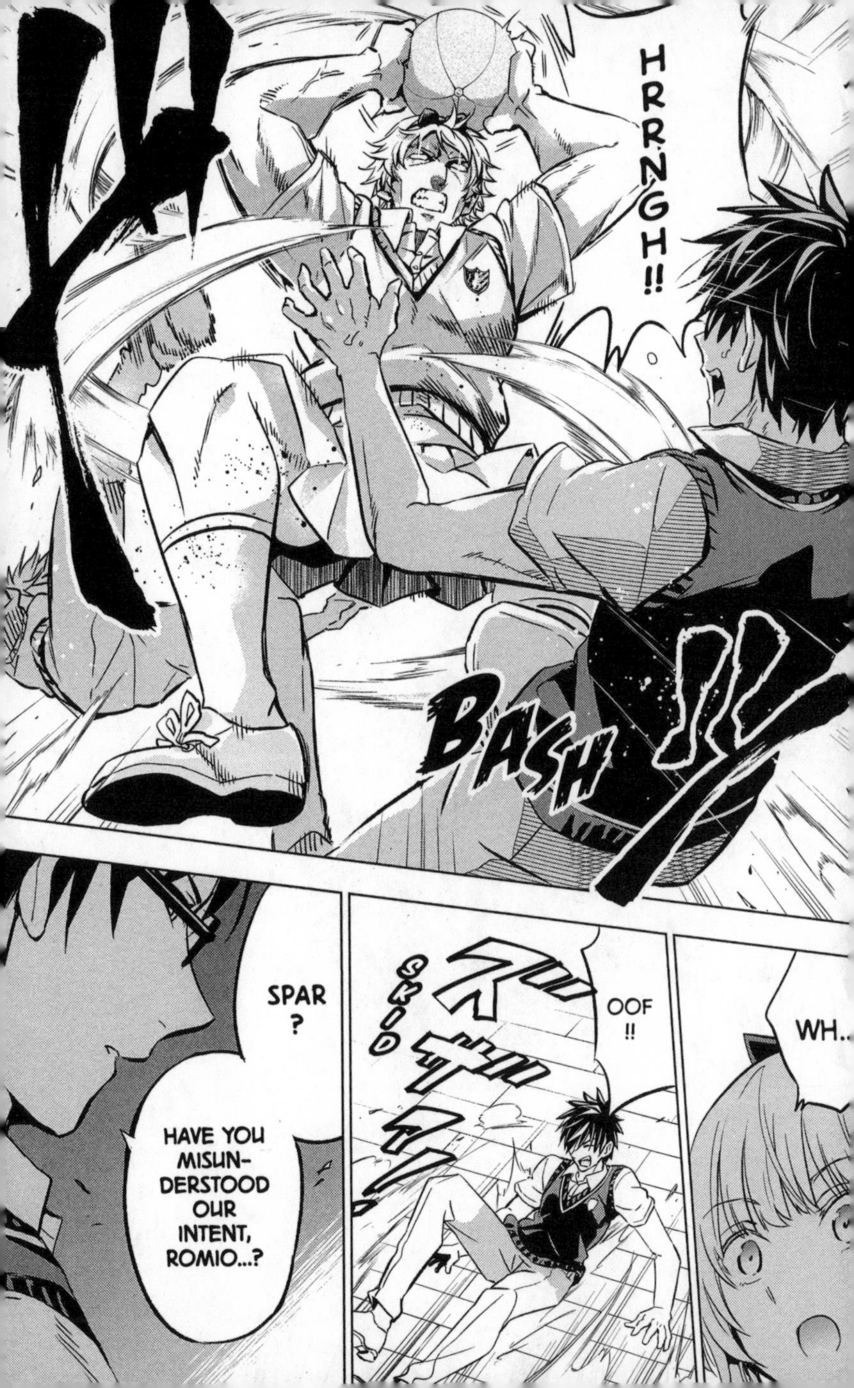
HRRNGH!!
BASH!!
WH...
OOF!!
SKID
SPAR?
HAVE YOU MISUNDERSTOOD OUR INTENT, ROMIO...?

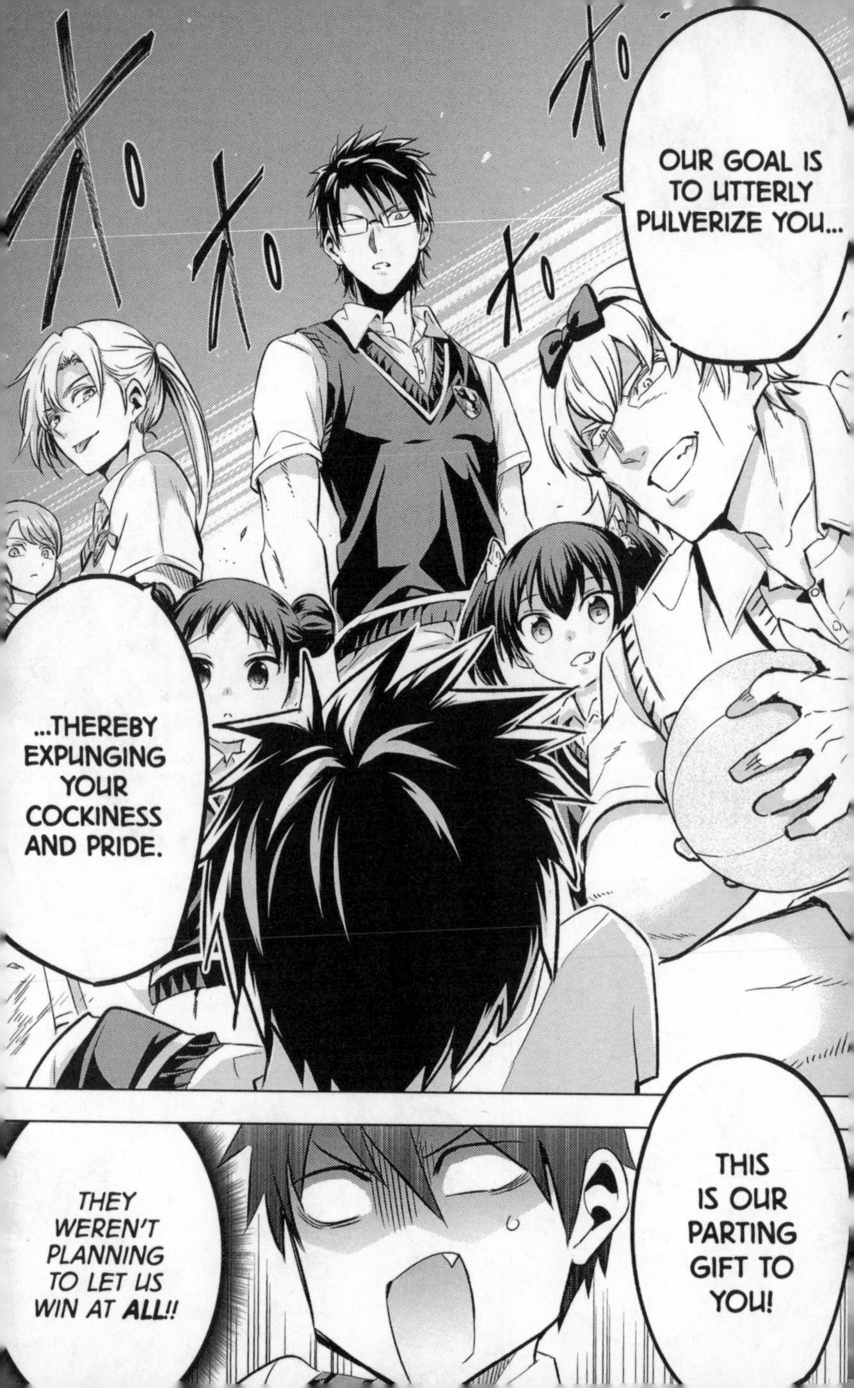
OUR GOAL IS TO UTTERLY PULVERIZE YOU...
...THEREBY EXPUNGING YOUR COCKINESS AND PRIDE.
THIS IS OUR PARTING GIFT TO YOU!
THEY WEREN'T PLANNING TO LET US WIN AT ALL!!

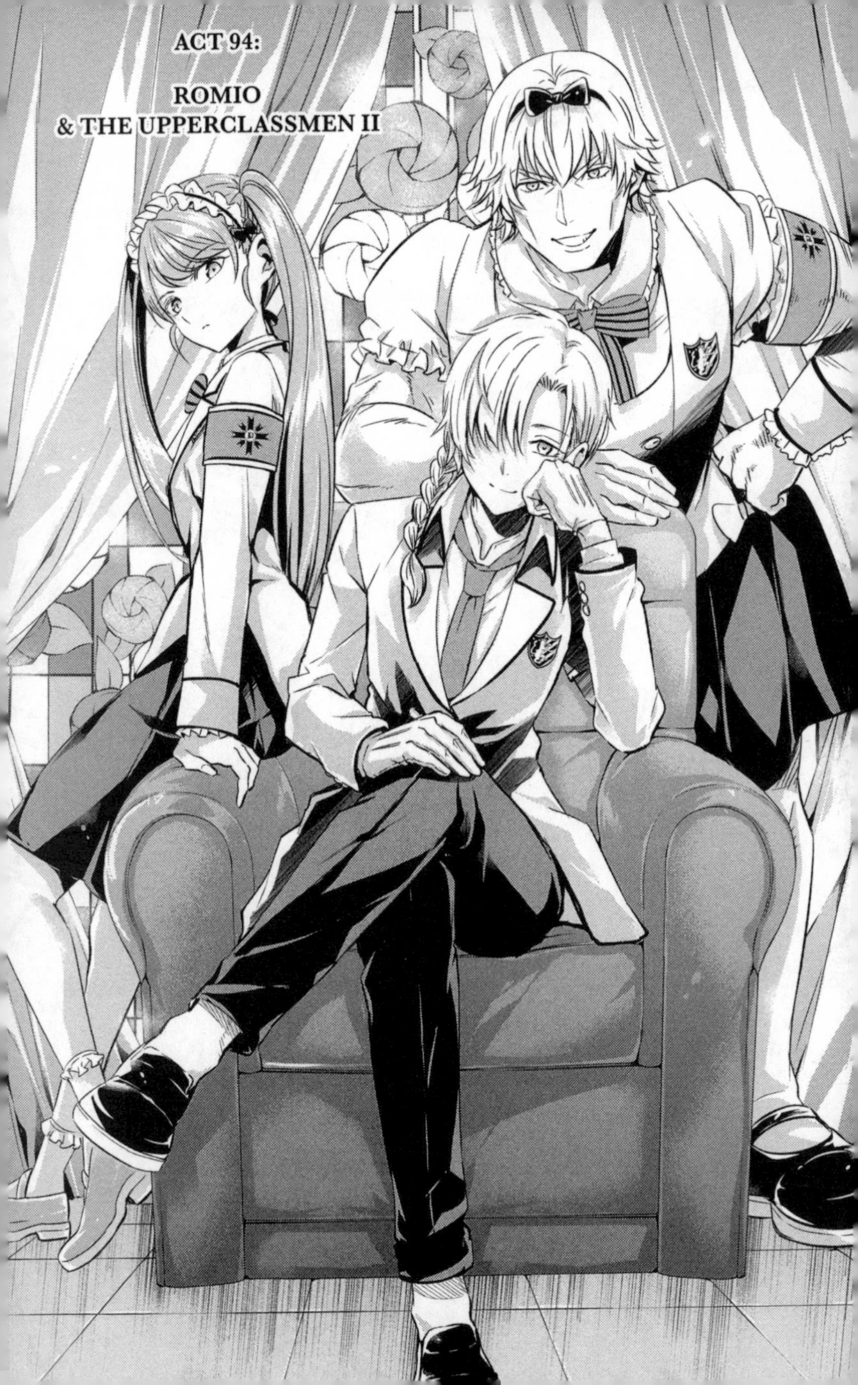
ACT 94:
ROMIO
& THE UPPERCLASSMEN II

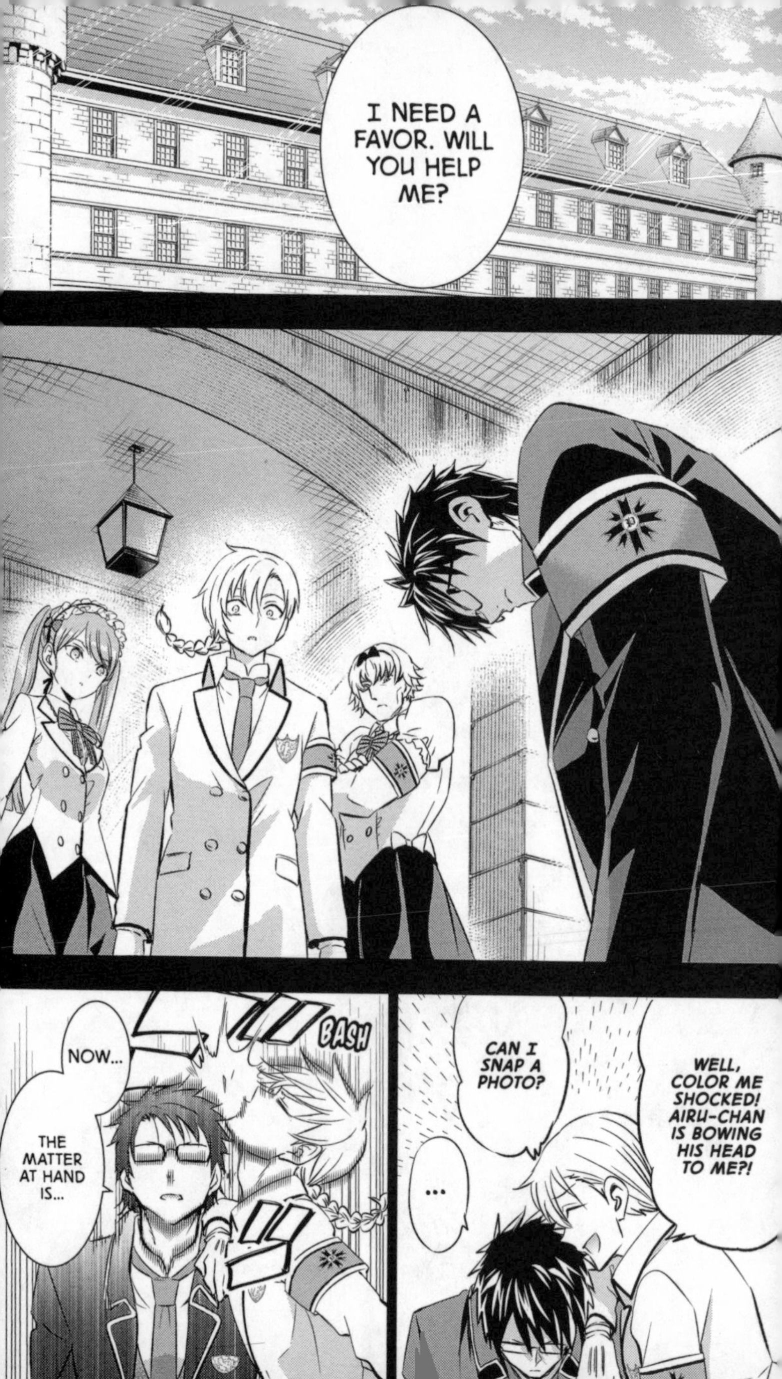

I NEED A FAVOR. WILL YOU HELP ME?
WELL, COLOR ME SHOCKED! AIRU-CHAN IS BOWING HIS HEAD TO ME?!
CAN I SNAP A PHOTO?
...
BASH
NOW...
THE MATTER AT HAND IS...

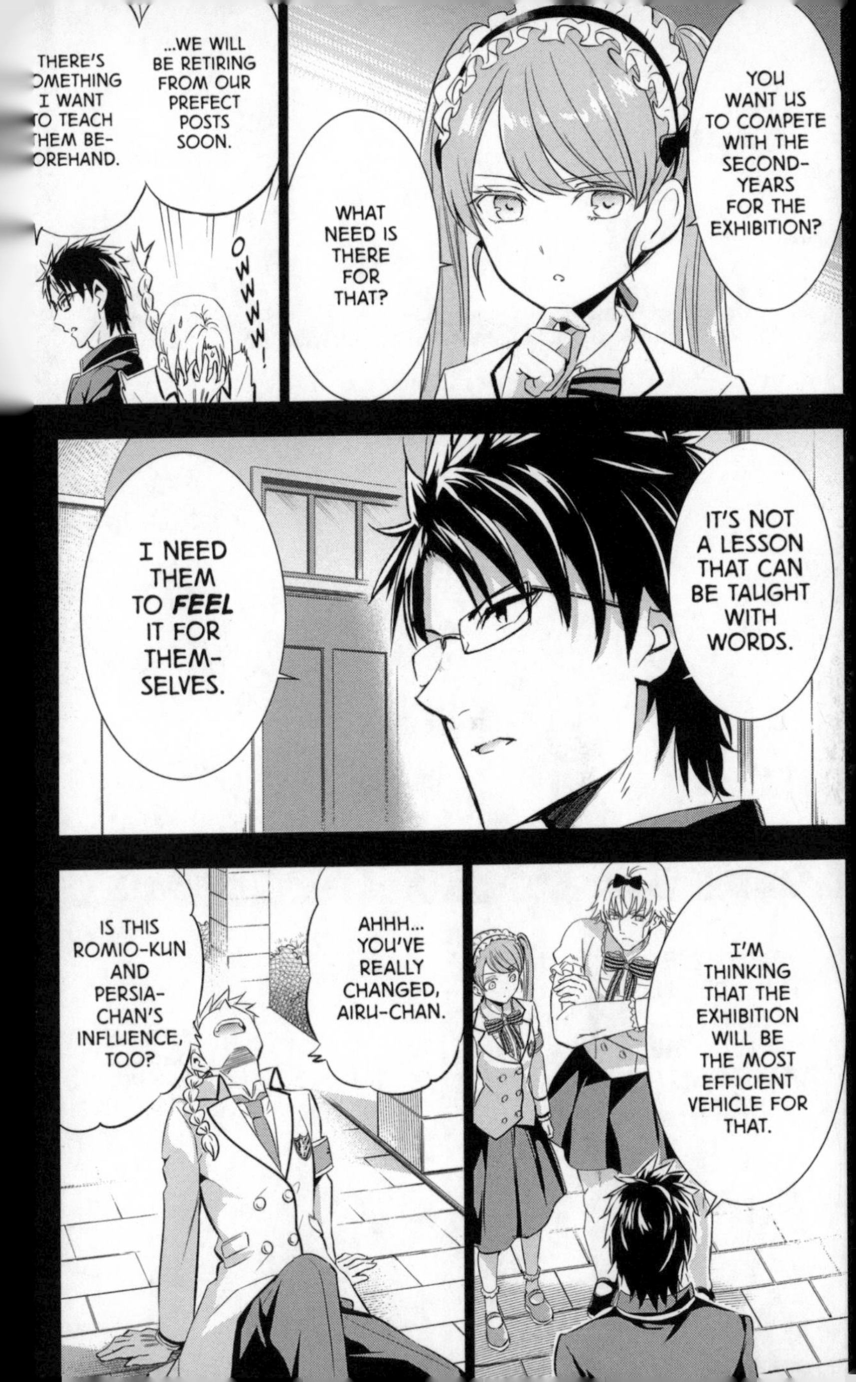
YOU WANT US TO COMPETE WITH THE SECOND-YEARS FOR THE EXHIBITION?
WHAT NEED IS THERE FOR THAT?
...WE WILL BE RETIRING FROM OUR PREFECT POSTS SOON.
THERE'S OMETHING I WANT TO TEACH THEM BE-OREHAND.
OWWWW!
IT'S NOT A LESSON THAT CAN BE TAUGHT WITH WORDS.
I NEED THEM TO ***FEEL*** IT FOR THEM-SELVES.
I'M THINKING THAT THE EXHIBITION WILL BE THE MOST EFFICIENT VEHICLE FOR THAT.
AHHH... YOU'VE REALLY CHANGED, AIRU-CHAN.
IS THIS ROMIO-KUN AND PERSIA-CHAN'S INFLUENCE, TOO?

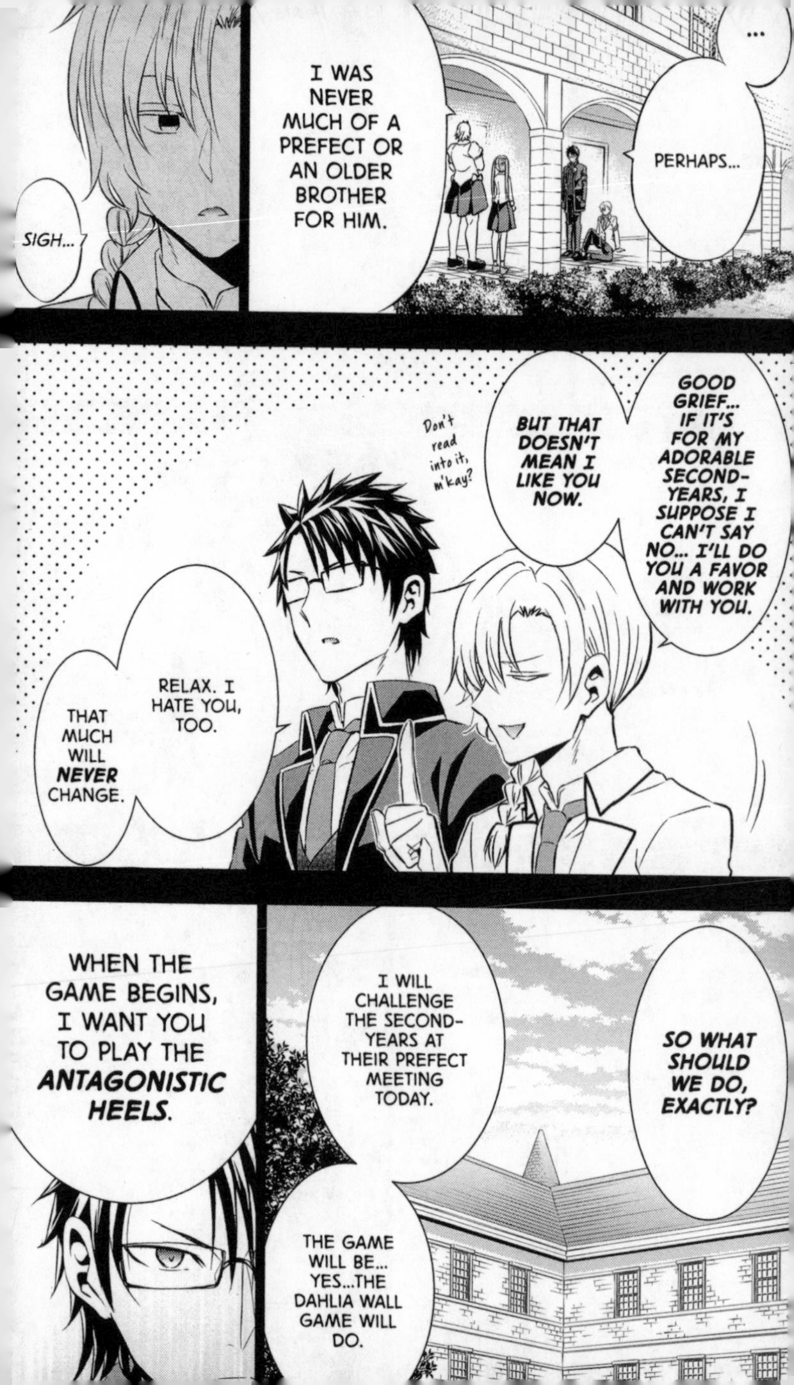
...
PERHAPS...
I WAS NEVER MUCH OF A PREFECT OR AN OLDER BROTHER FOR HIM.
SIGH...
GOOD GRIEF... IF IT'S FOR MY ADORABLE SECOND-YEARS, I SUPPOSE I CAN'T SAY NO... I'LL DO YOU A FAVOR AND WORK WITH YOU.
BUT THAT DOESN'T MEAN I LIKE YOU NOW.
Don't read into it, m'kay?
RELAX. I HATE YOU, TOO.
THAT MUCH WILL *NEVER* CHANGE.
SO WHAT SHOULD WE DO, EXACTLY?
I WILL CHALLENGE THE SECOND-YEARS AT THEIR PREFECT MEETING TODAY.
THE GAME WILL BE... YES...THE DAHLIA WALL GAME WILL DO.
WHEN THE GAME BEGINS, I WANT YOU TO PLAY THE *ANTAGONISTIC HEELS*.

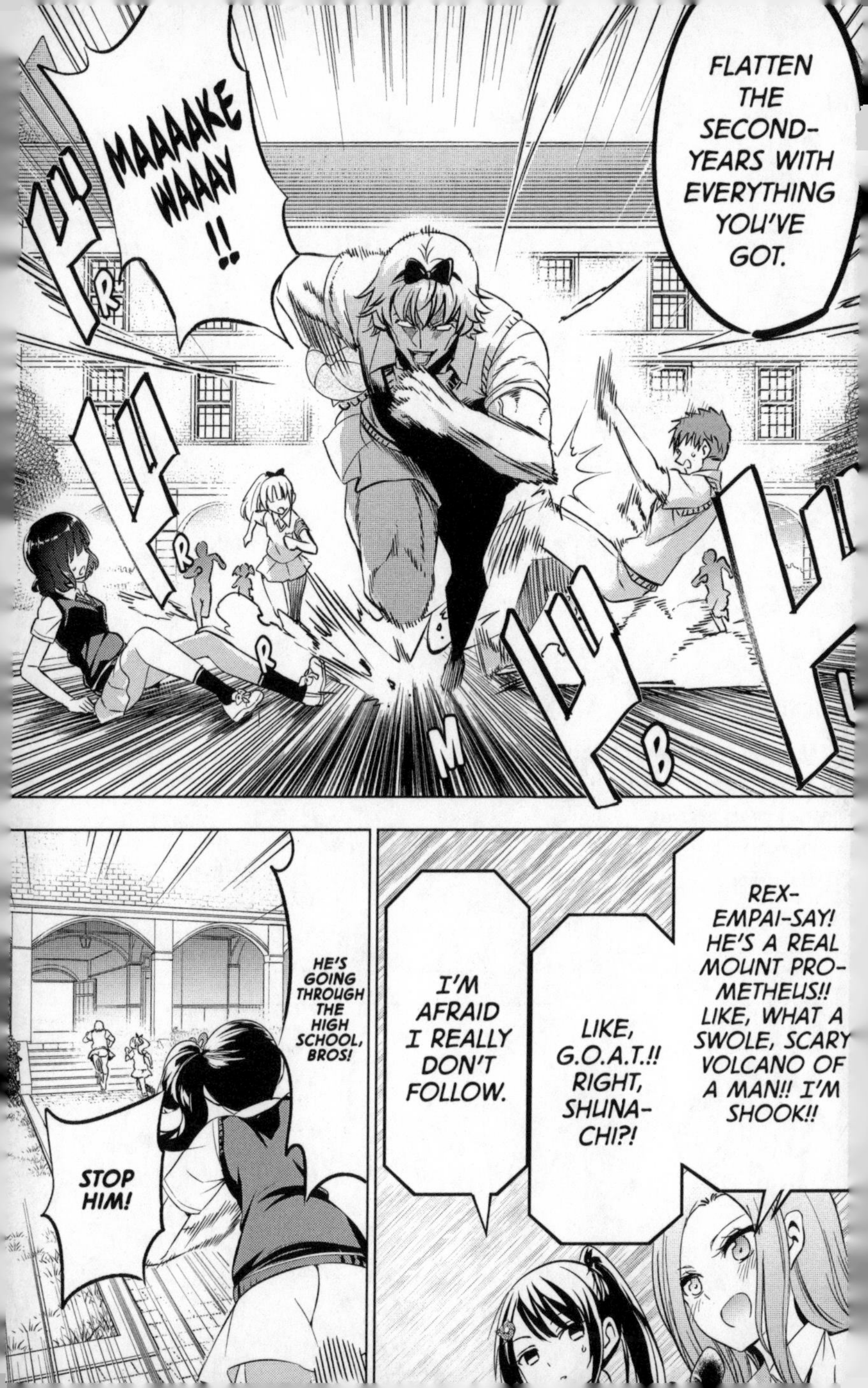
FLATTEN THE SECOND-YEARS WITH EVERYTHING YOU'VE GOT.
MAAAAKE WAAAY!!
REX-EMPAI-SAY! HE'S A REAL MOUNT PROMETHEUS!! LIKE, WHAT A SWOLE, SCARY VOLCANO OF A MAN!! I'M SHOOK!!
LIKE, G.O.A.T.!! RIGHT, SHUNA-CHI?!
I'M AFRAID I REALLY DON'T FOLLOW.
HE'S GOING THROUGH THE HIGH SCHOOL, BROS!
STOP HIM!

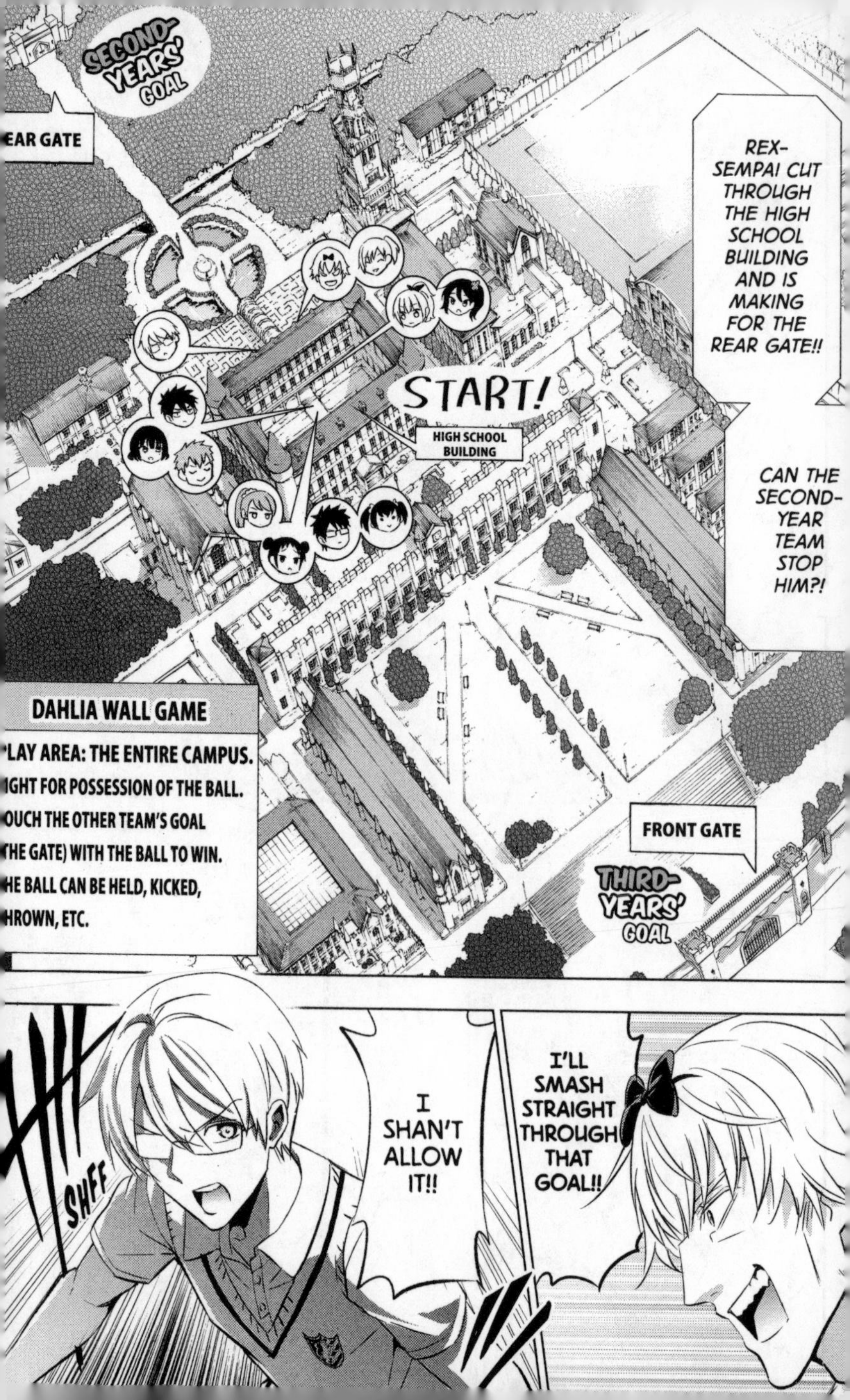

REX-SEMPAI CUT THROUGH THE HIGH SCHOOL BUILDING AND IS MAKING FOR THE REAR GATE!!
CAN THE SECOND-YEAR TEAM STOP HIM?!
SECOND-YEARS' GOAL
EAR GATE
START!
HIGH SCHOOL BUILDING
DAHLIA WALL GAME
'LAY AREA: THE ENTIRE CAMPUS.
IGHT FOR POSSESSION OF THE BALL.
OUCH THE OTHER TEAM'S GOAL
THE GATE) WITH THE BALL TO WIN.
HE BALL CAN BE HELD, KICKED,
HROWN, ETC.
FRONT GATE
THIRD-YEARS' GOAL
I'LL SMASH STRAIGHT THROUGH THAT GOAL!!
I SHAN'T ALLOW IT!!
SHFF

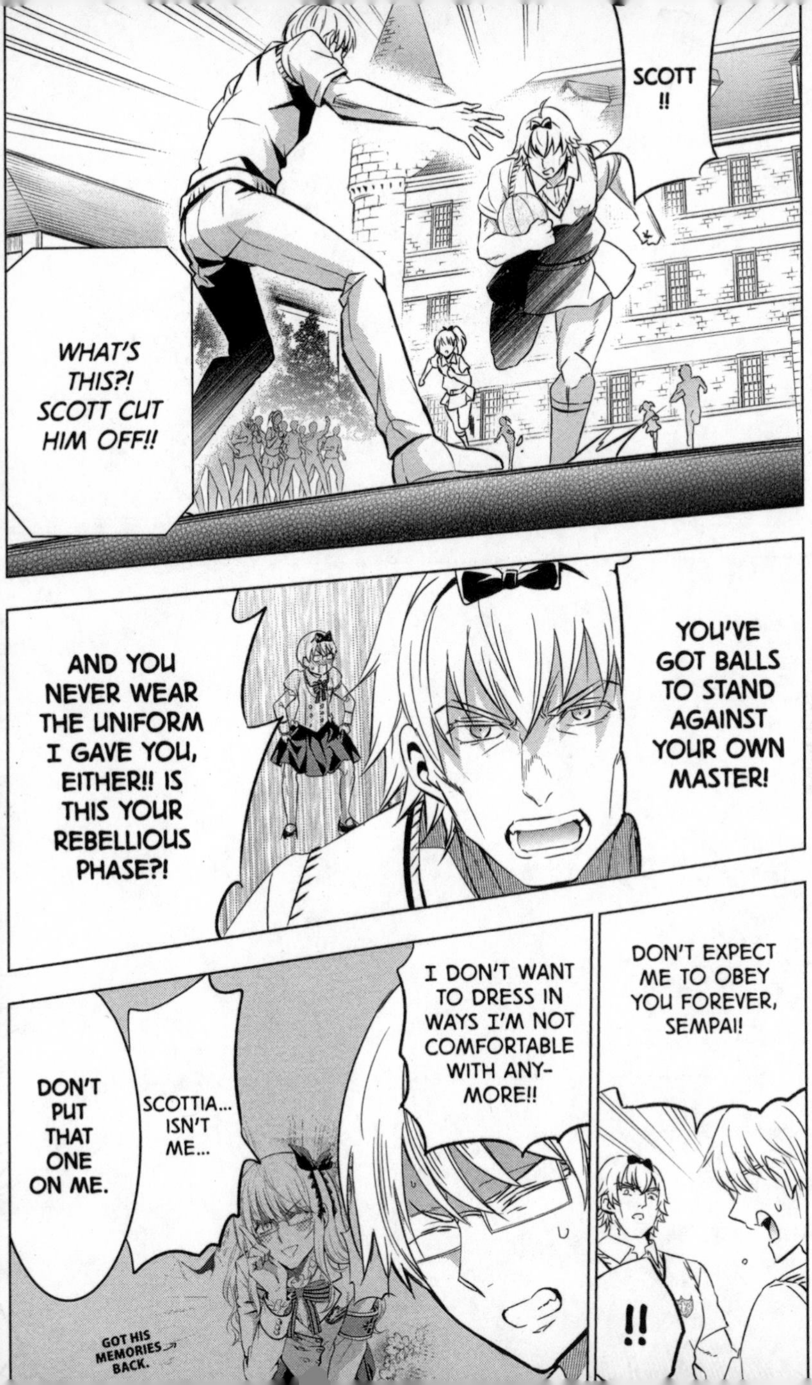
SCOTT !!
WHAT'S THIS?! SCOTT CUT HIM OFF!!
YOU'VE GOT BALLS TO STAND AGAINST YOUR OWN MASTER!
AND YOU NEVER WEAR THE UNIFORM I GAVE YOU, EITHER!! IS THIS YOUR REBELLIOUS PHASE?!
DON'T EXPECT ME TO OBEY YOU FOREVER, SEMPAI!
!!
I DON'T WANT TO DRESS IN WAYS I'M NOT COMFORTABLE WITH ANY-MORE!!
SCOTTIA... ISN'T ME...
DON'T PUT THAT ONE ON ME.
GOT HIS MEMORIES BACK.

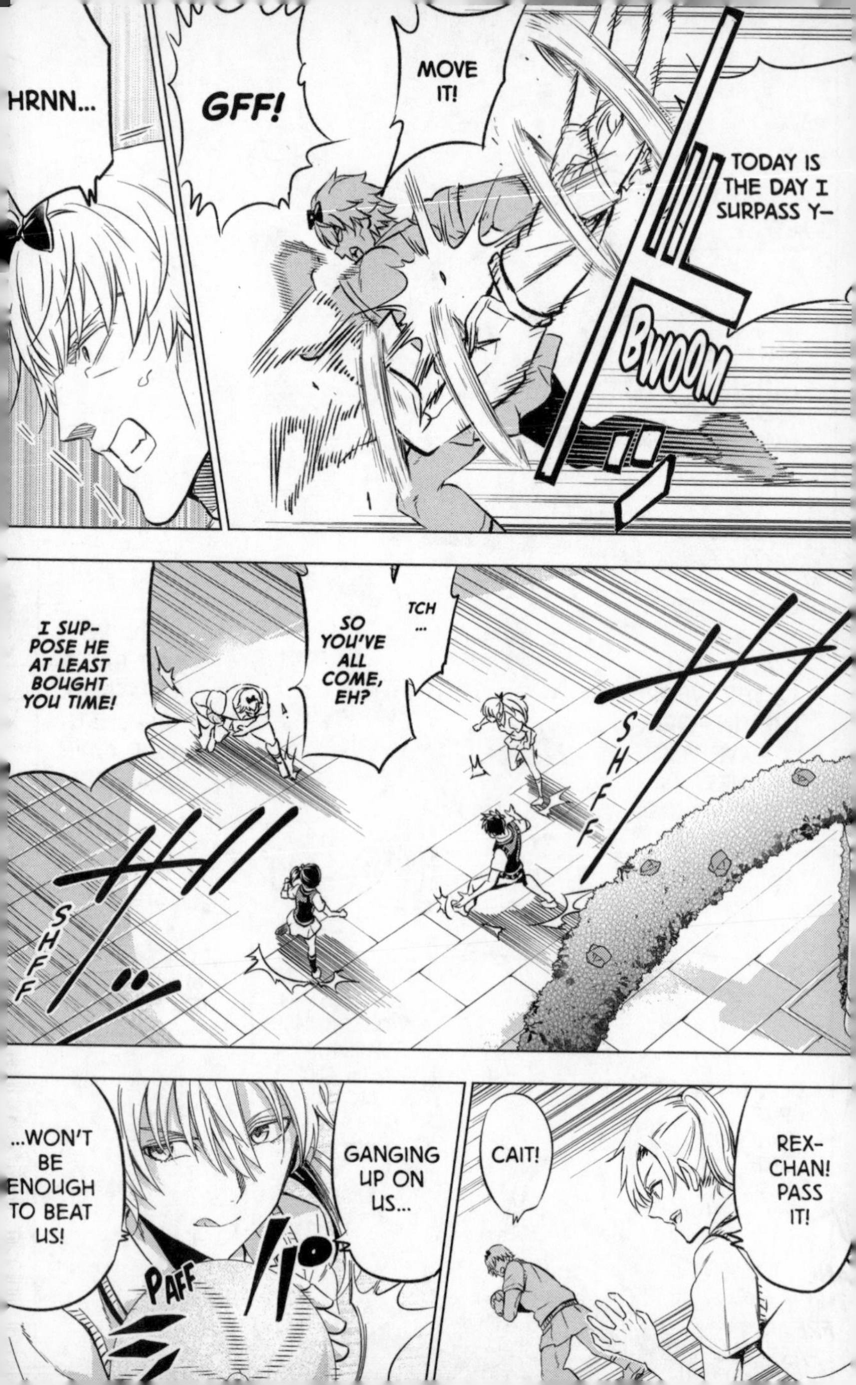
TODAY IS THE DAY I SURPASS Y—
MOVE IT!
GFF!
BWOOM
HRNN...
TCH ...
SO YOU'VE ALL COME, EH?
I SUP- POSE HE AT LEAST BOUGHT YOU TIME!
SHFF
SHFF
REX- CHAN! PASS IT!
CAIT!
GANGING UP ON US...
...WON'T BE ENOUGH TO BEAT US!
PAFF

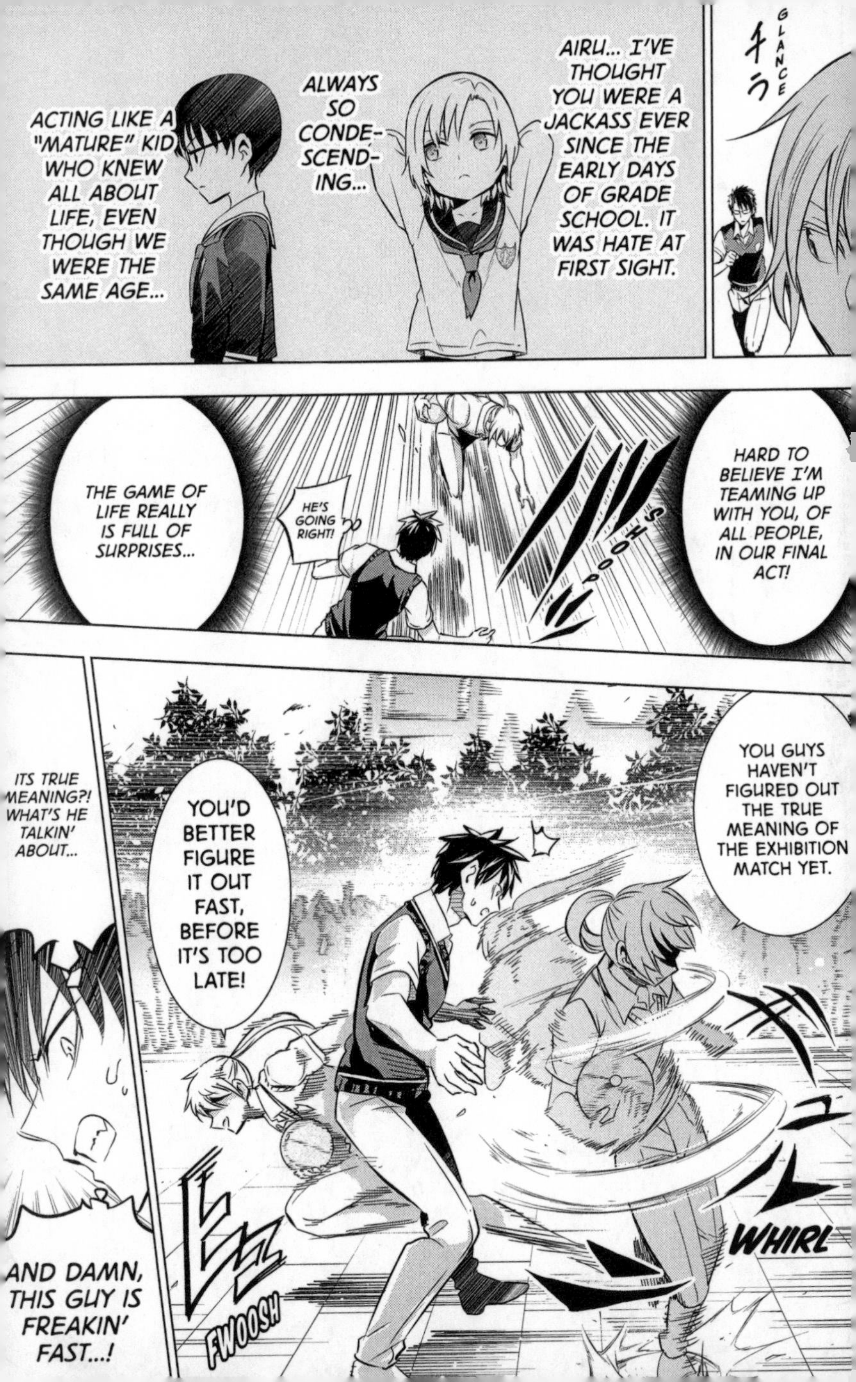
チラ
GLANCE
AIRU... I'VE THOUGHT YOU WERE A JACKASS EVER SINCE THE EARLY DAYS OF GRADE SCHOOL. IT WAS HATE AT FIRST SIGHT.
ALWAYS SO CONDE-SCEND-ING...
ACTING LIKE A "MATURE" KID WHO KNEW ALL ABOUT LIFE, EVEN THOUGH WE WERE THE SAME AGE...
HARD TO BELIEVE I'M TEAMING UP WITH YOU, OF ALL PEOPLE, IN OUR FINAL ACT!
SHOOP
HE'S GOING RIGHT!
THE GAME OF LIFE REALLY IS FULL OF SURPRISES...
YOU GUYS HAVEN'T FIGURED OUT THE TRUE MEANING OF THE EXHIBITION MATCH YET.
WHIRL
YOU'D BETTER FIGURE IT OUT FAST, BEFORE IT'S TOO LATE!
FWOOSH
ITS TRUE MEANING?! WHAT'S HE TALKIN' ABOUT...
AND DAMN, THIS GUY IS FREAKIN' FAST...!

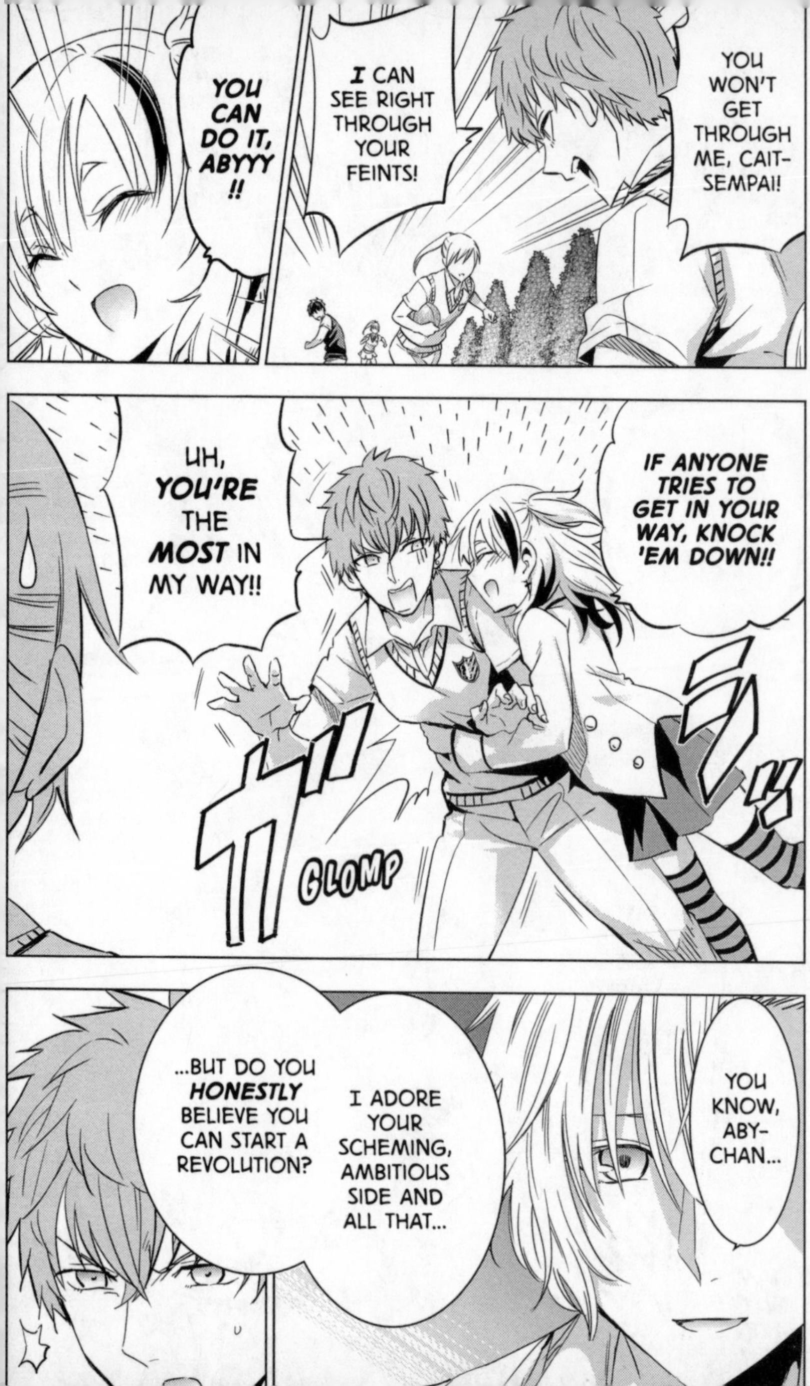
YOU WON'T GET THROUGH ME, CAIT-SEMPAI!
I CAN SEE RIGHT THROUGH YOUR FEINTS!
YOU CAN DO IT, ABYYY!!
IF ANYONE TRIES TO GET IN YOUR WAY, KNOCK 'EM DOWN!!
UH, YOU'RE THE MOST IN MY WAY!!
GLOMP
YOU KNOW, ABY-CHAN...
I ADORE YOUR SCHEMING, AMBITIOUS SIDE AND ALL THAT...
...BUT DO YOU HONESTLY BELIEVE YOU CAN START A REVOLUTION?

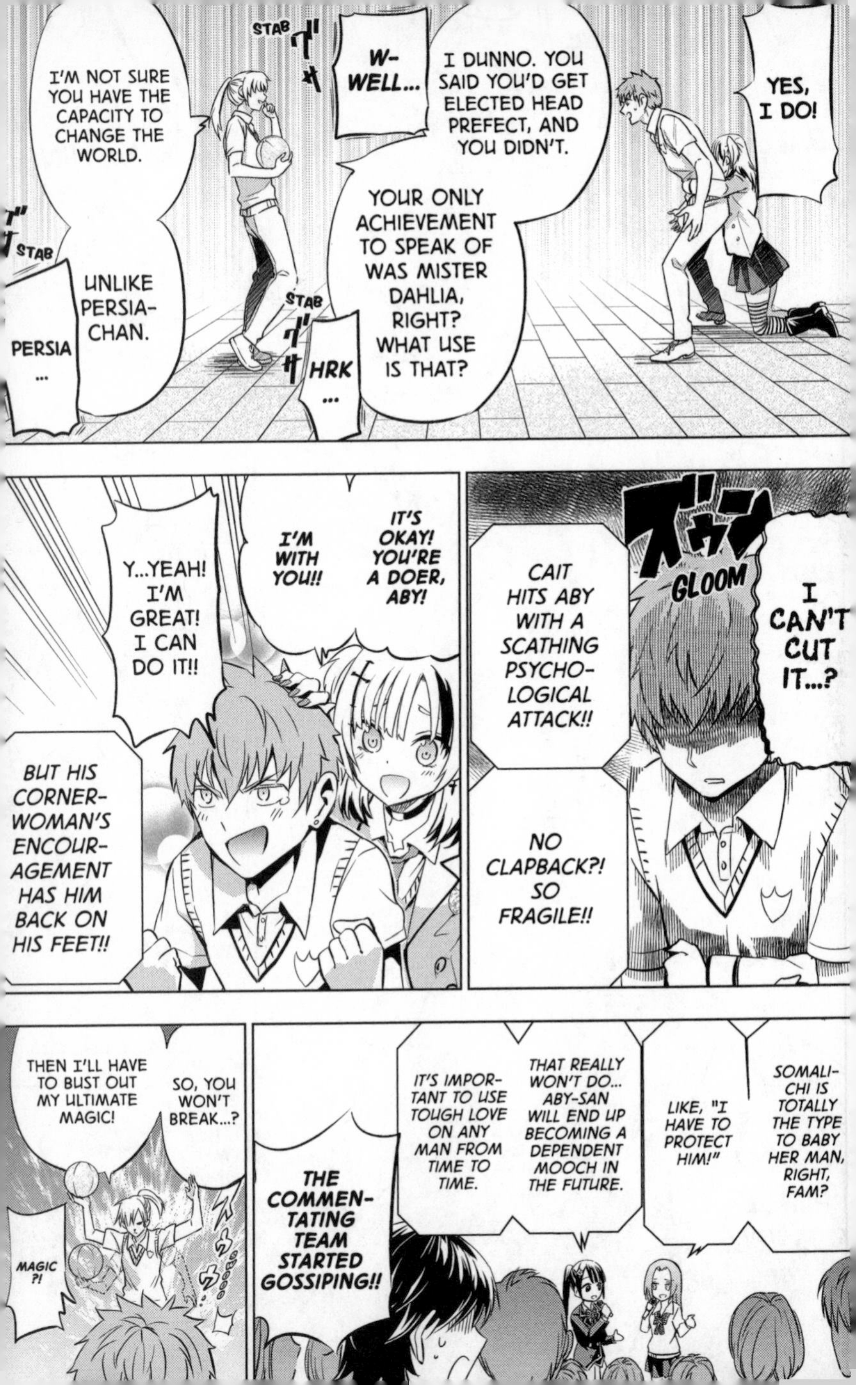
YES, I DO!
I DUNNO. YOU SAID YOU'D GET ELECTED HEAD PREFECT, AND YOU DIDN'T.
STAB
W-WELL...
YOUR ONLY ACHIEVEMENT TO SPEAK OF WAS MISTER DAHLIA, RIGHT? WHAT USE IS THAT?
STAB
HRK...
I'M NOT SURE YOU HAVE THE CAPACITY TO CHANGE THE WORLD.
UNLIKE PERSIA-CHAN.
STAB
PERSIA...
GLOOM
I CAN'T CUT IT...?
CAIT HITS ABY WITH A SCATHING PSYCHO-LOGICAL ATTACK!!
NO CLAPBACK?! SO FRAGILE!!
IT'S OKAY! YOU'RE A DOER, ABY!
I'M WITH YOU!!
Y...YEAH! I'M GREAT! I CAN DO IT!!
BUT HIS CORNER-WOMAN'S ENCOUR-AGEMENT HAS HIM BACK ON HIS FEET!!
SOMALI-CHI IS TOTALLY THE TYPE TO BABY HER MAN, RIGHT, FAM?
LIKE, "I HAVE TO PROTECT HIM!"
THAT REALLY WON'T DO... ABY-SAN WILL END UP BECOMING A DEPENDENT MOOCH IN THE FUTURE.
IT'S IMPOR-TANT TO USE TOUGH LOVE ON ANY MAN FROM TIME TO TIME.
THE COMMEN-TATING TEAM STARTED GOSSIPING!!
SO, YOU WON'T BREAK...?
THEN I'LL HAVE TO BUST OUT MY ULTIMATE MAGIC!
MAGIC?!

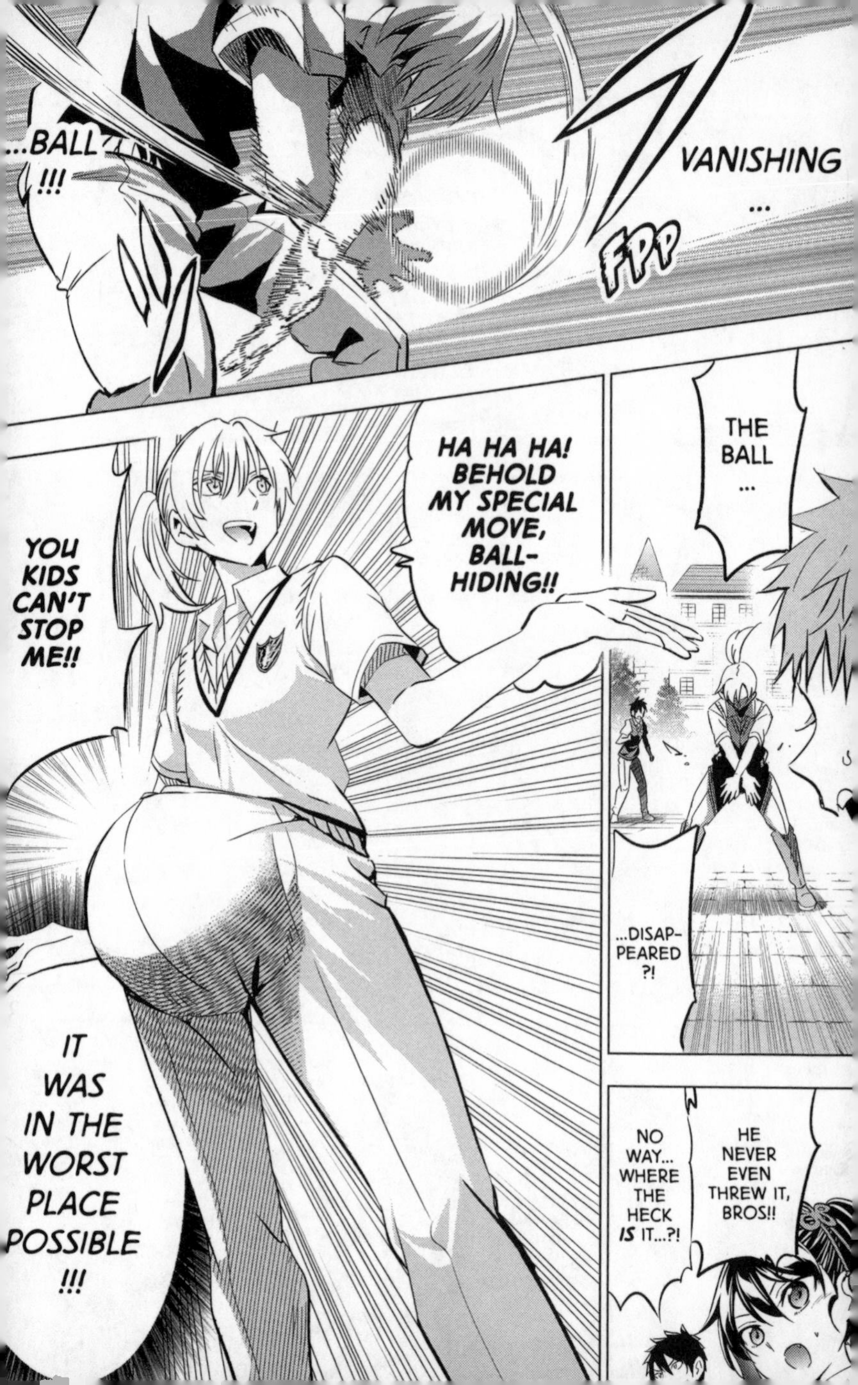
VANISHING ...
FPP
...BALL !!!
THE BALL ...
...DISAPPEARED ?!
HE NEVER EVEN THREW IT, BROS!!
NO WAY... WHERE THE HECK *IS* IT...?!
HA HA HA! BEHOLD MY SPECIAL MOVE, BALL-HIDING!!
YOU KIDS CAN'T STOP ME!!
IT WAS IN THE WORST PLACE POSSIBLE !!!

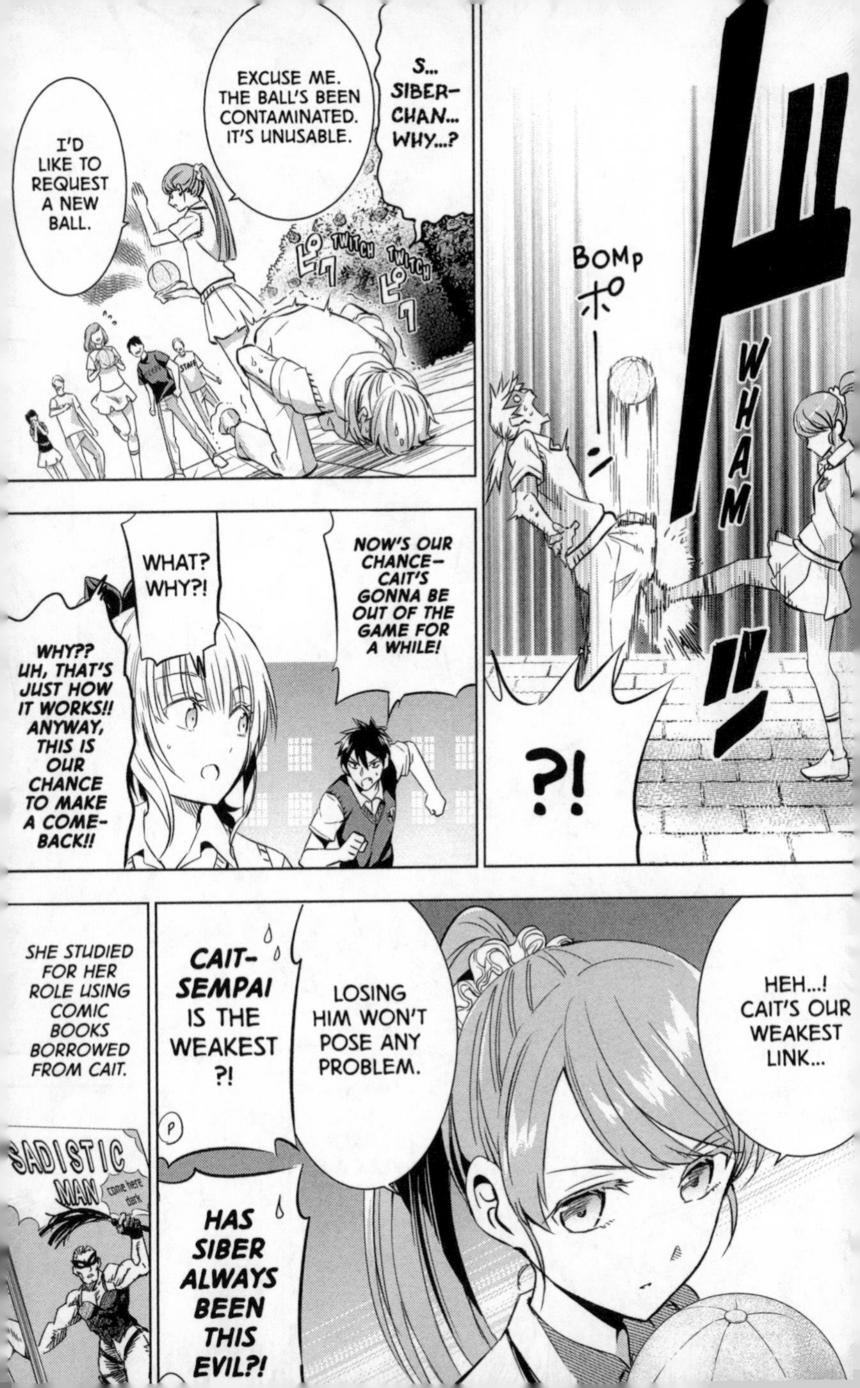
WHAM
BOMP
ポ
?!
S... SIBER-CHAN... WHY...?
ピク TWITCH
ピク TWITCH
EXCUSE ME. THE BALL'S BEEN CONTAMINATED. IT'S UNUSABLE.
I'D LIKE TO REQUEST A NEW BALL.
STAFF
NOW'S OUR CHANCE— CAIT'S GONNA BE OUT OF THE GAME FOR A WHILE!
WHAT? WHY?!
WHY?? UH, THAT'S JUST HOW IT WORKS!! ANYWAY, THIS IS OUR CHANCE TO MAKE A COME-BACK!!
HEH...! CAIT'S OUR WEAKEST LINK...
LOSING HIM WON'T POSE ANY PROBLEM.
CAIT-SEMPAI IS THE WEAKEST ?!
HAS SIBER ALWAYS BEEN THIS EVIL?!
SHE STUDIED FOR HER ROLE USING COMIC BOOKS BORROWED FROM CAIT.
SADISTIC MAN
come here dark

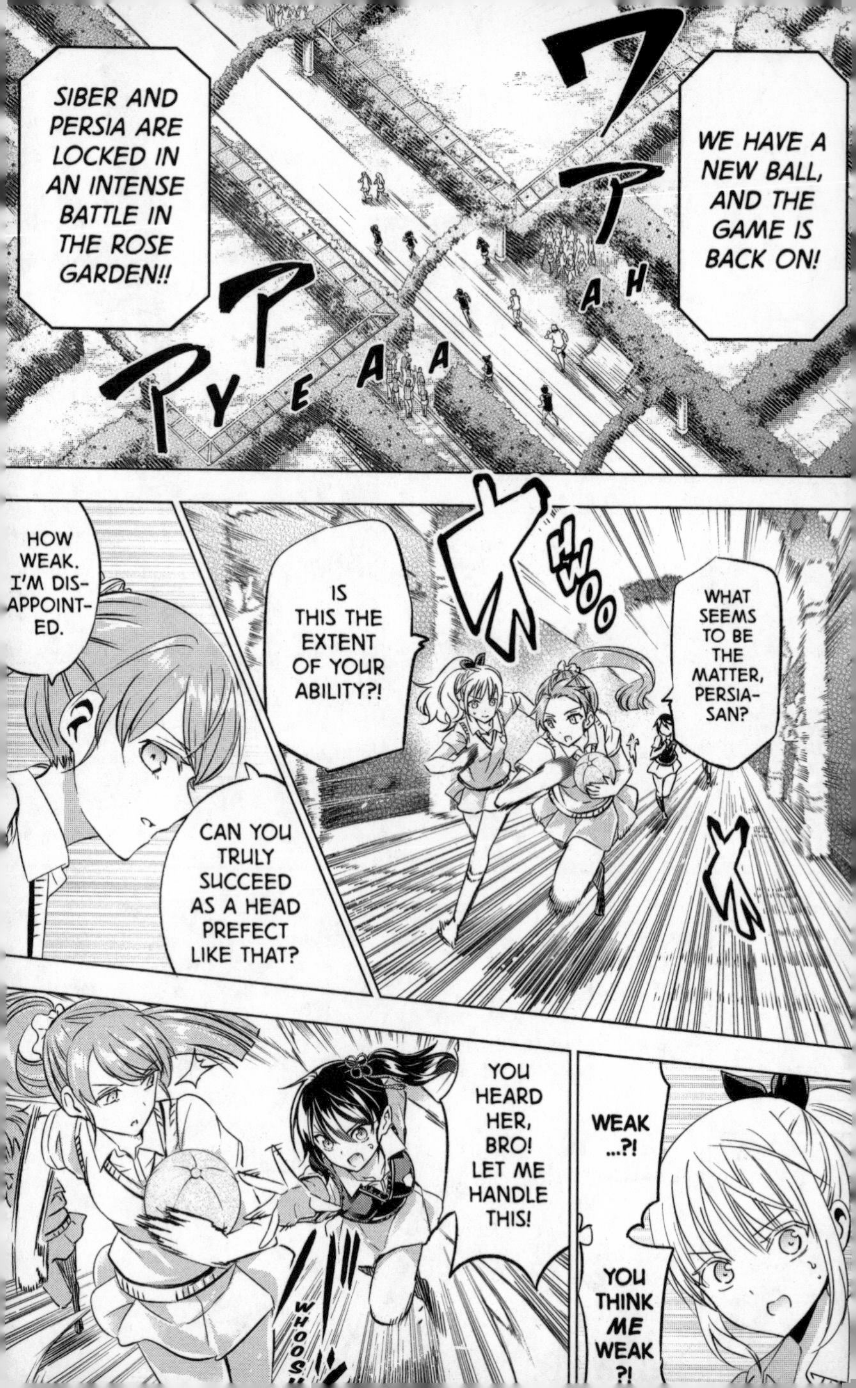
WE HAVE A NEW BALL, AND THE GAME IS BACK ON!
AH
SIBER AND PERSIA ARE LOCKED IN AN INTENSE BATTLE IN THE ROSE GARDEN!!
YEAAA
WHAT SEEMS TO BE THE MATTER, PERSIA-SAN?
HWOO
IS THIS THE EXTENT OF YOUR ABILITY?!
HOW WEAK. I'M DIS-APPOINT-ED.
CAN YOU TRULY SUCCEED AS A HEAD PREFECT LIKE THAT?
WEAK ...?!
YOU THINK *ME* WEAK?!
YOU HEARD HER, BRO! LET ME HANDLE THIS!
WHOOSH

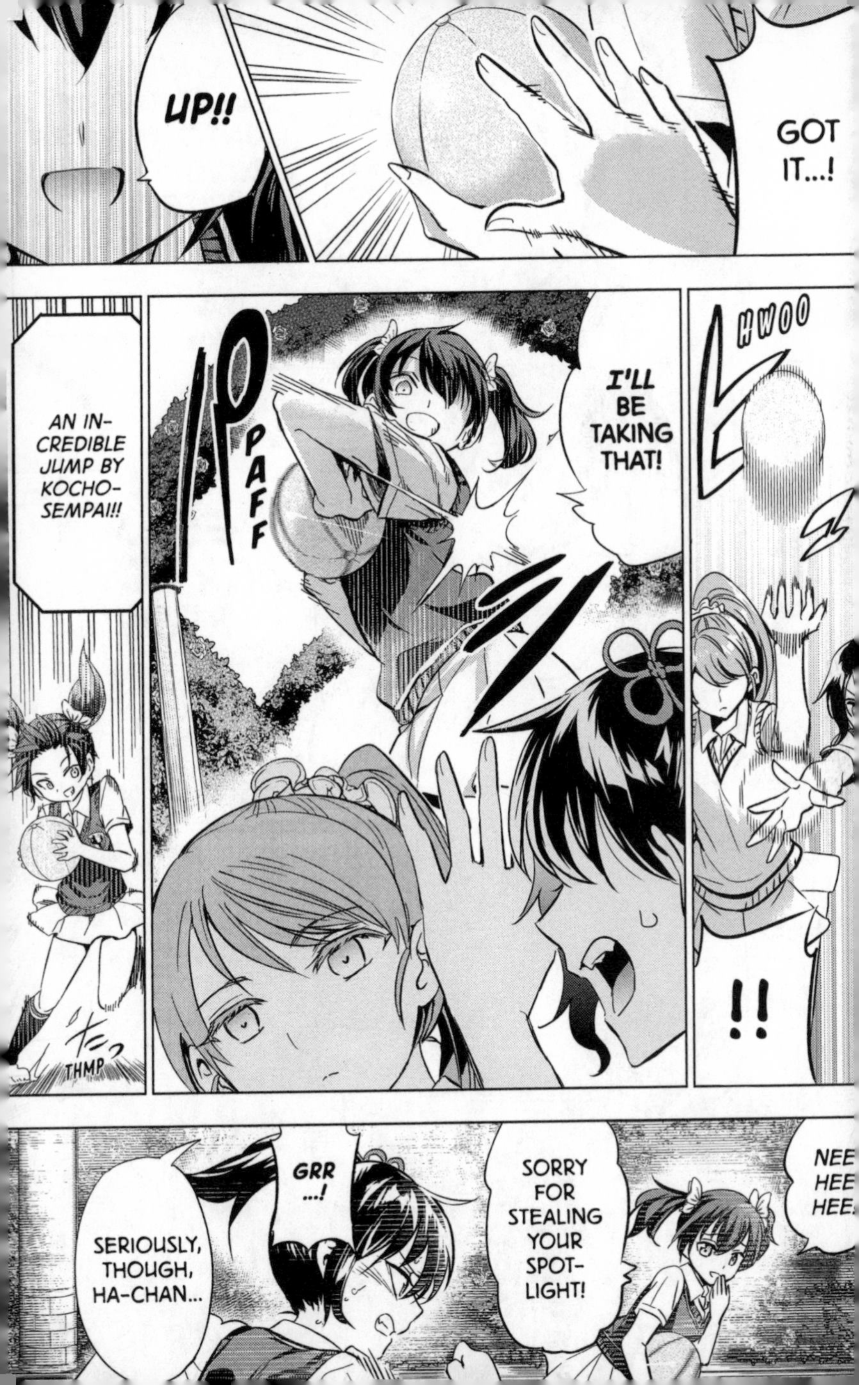
GOT IT...!
UP!!
HWOO
!!
I'LL BE TAKING THAT!
PAFF
AN IN-CREDIBLE JUMP BY KOCHO-SEMPAI!!
THMP
NEE HEE HEE.
SORRY FOR STEALING YOUR SPOT-LIGHT!
GRR ...!
SERIOUSLY, THOUGH, HA-CHAN...

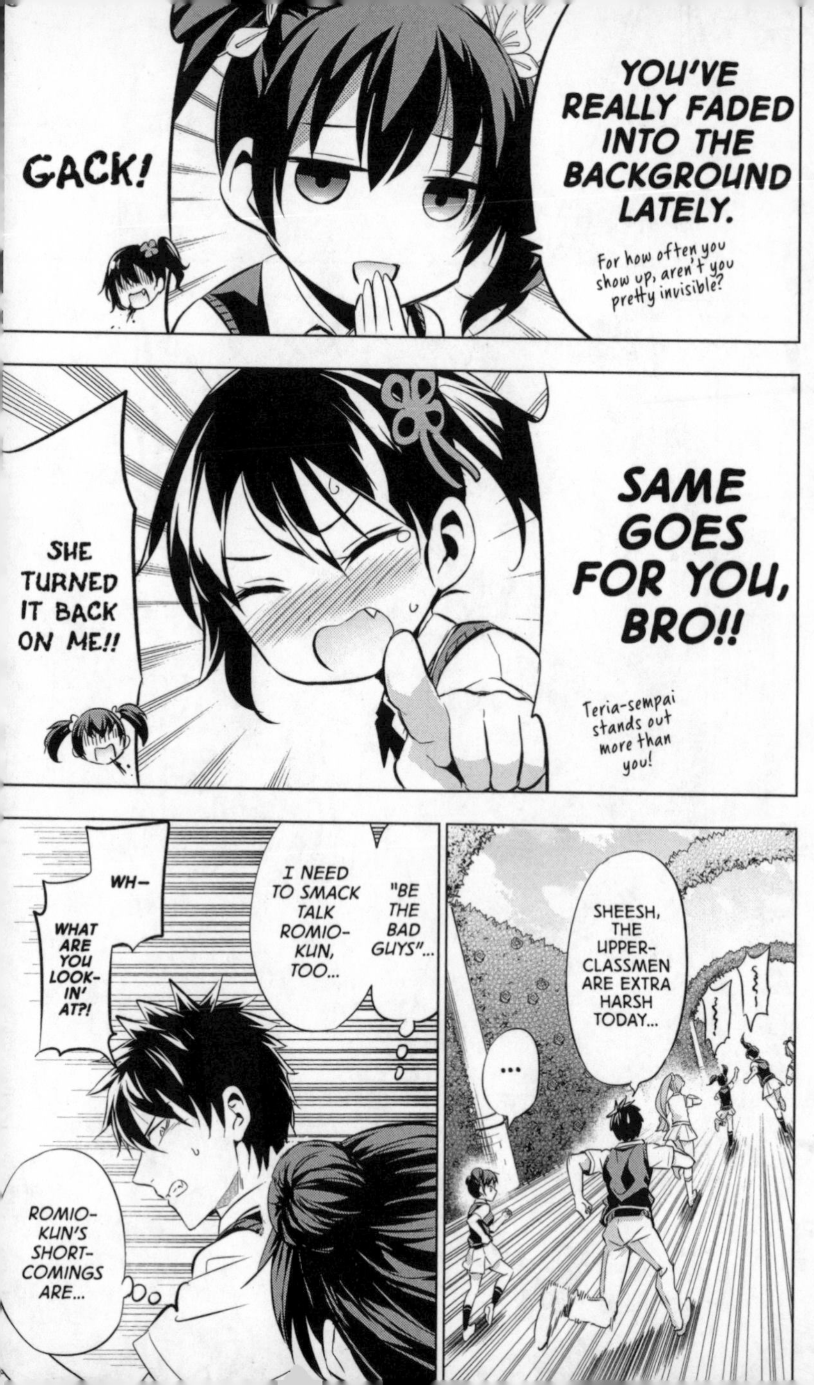
YOU'VE REALLY FADED INTO THE BACKGROUND LATELY.
For how often you show up, aren't you pretty invisible?
GACK!
SAME GOES FOR YOU, BRO!!
Teria-sempai stands out more than you!
SHE TURNED IT BACK ON ME!!
SHEESH, THE UPPER-CLASSMEN ARE EXTRA HARSH TODAY...
...
"BE THE BAD GUYS"...
I NEED TO SMACK TALK ROMIO-KUN, TOO...
WH—
WHAT ARE YOU LOOKIN' AT?!
ROMIO-KUN'S SHORT-COMINGS ARE...

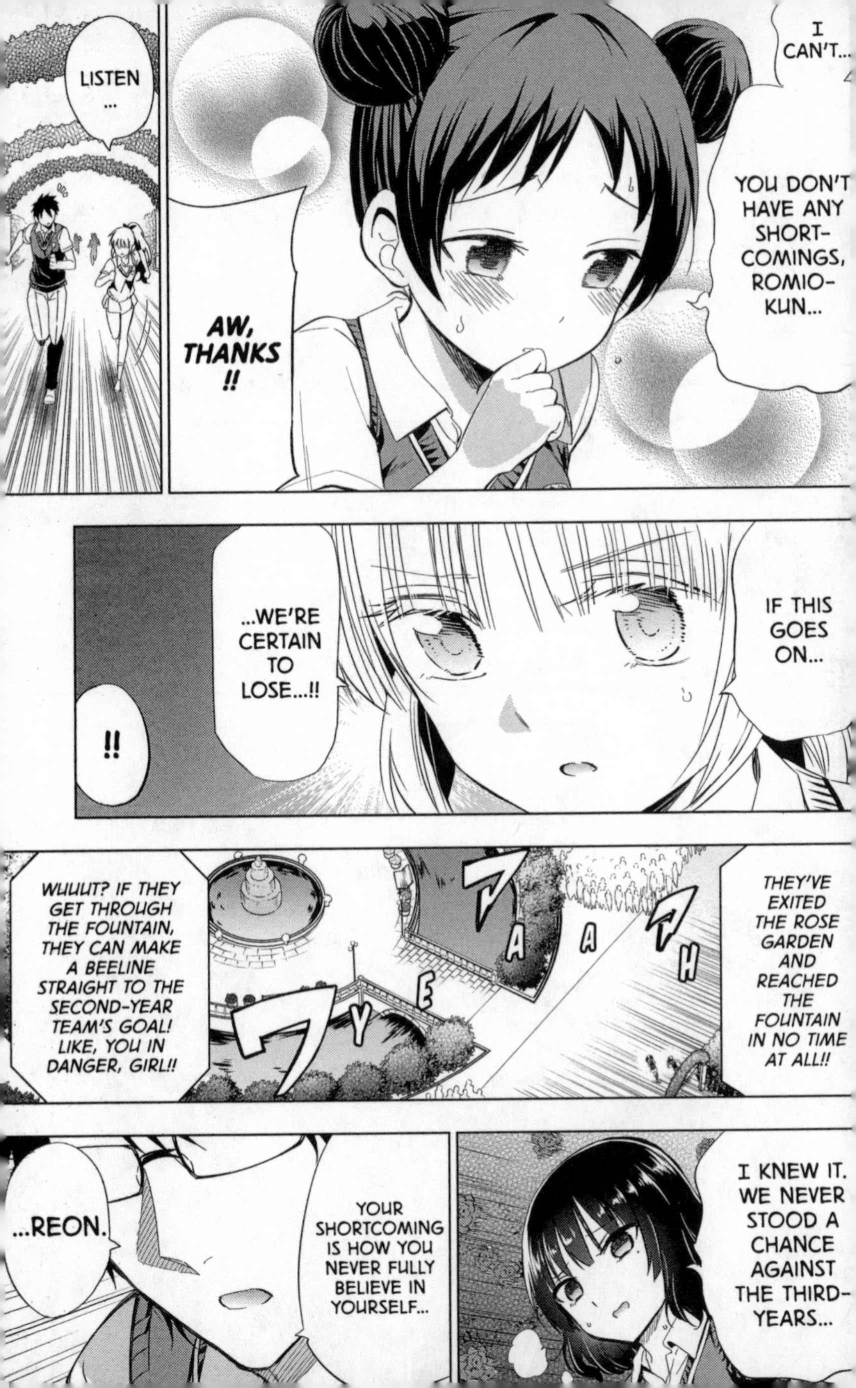
I CAN'T...
YOU DON'T HAVE ANY SHORT-COMINGS, ROMIO-KUN...
AW, THANKS!!
LISTEN ...
IF THIS GOES ON...
...WE'RE CERTAIN TO LOSE...!!
!!
THEY'VE EXITED THE ROSE GARDEN AND REACHED THE FOUNTAIN IN NO TIME AT ALL!!
YEAAH
WUUUT? IF THEY GET THROUGH THE FOUNTAIN, THEY CAN MAKE A BEELINE STRAIGHT TO THE SECOND-YEAR TEAM'S GOAL! LIKE, YOU IN DANGER, GIRL!!
I KNEW IT. WE NEVER STOOD A CHANCE AGAINST THE THIRD-YEARS...
YOUR SHORTCOMING IS HOW YOU NEVER FULLY BELIEVE IN YOURSELF...
...REON.

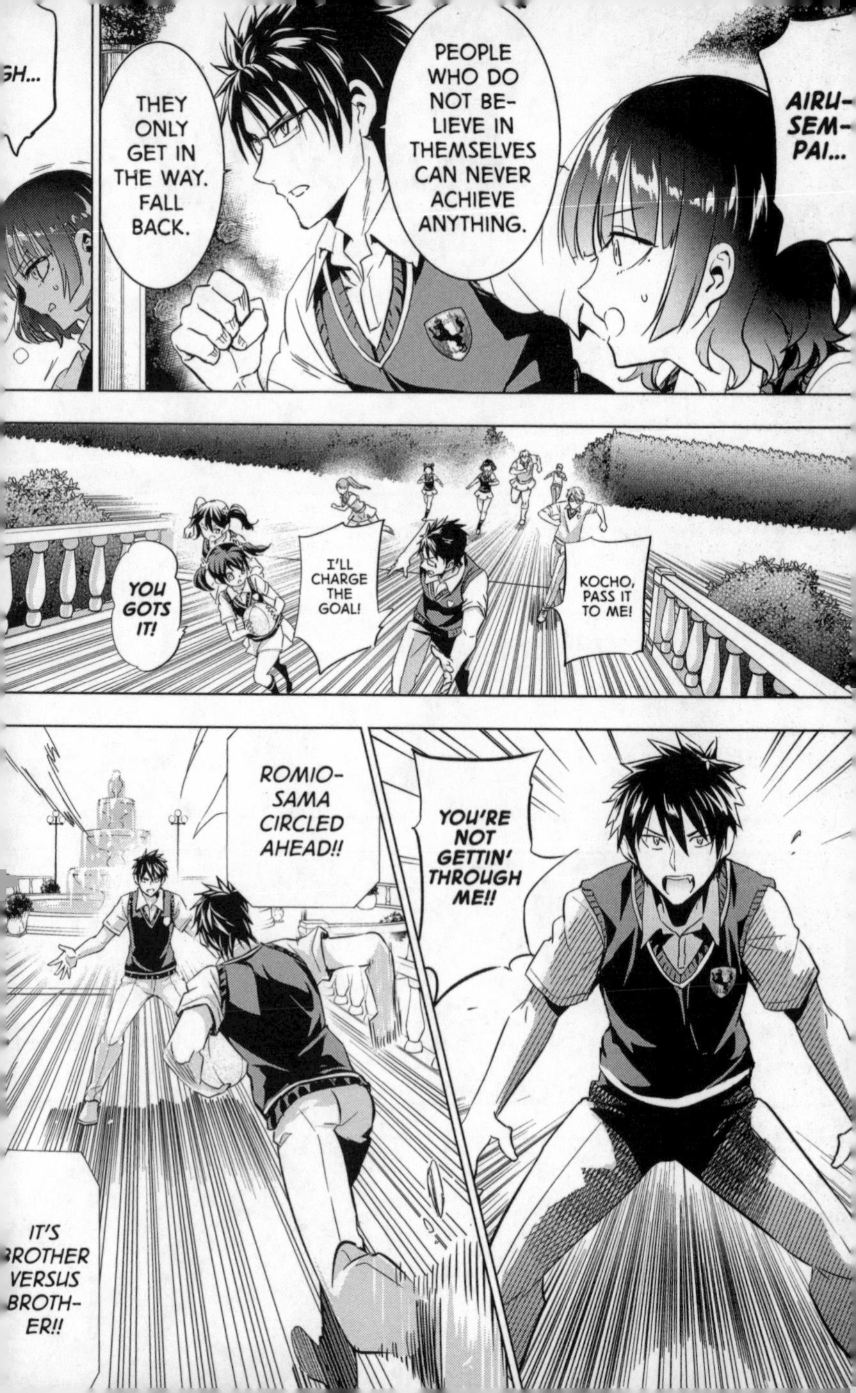

AIRU-SEMPAI...
PEOPLE WHO DO NOT BELIEVE IN THEMSELVES CAN NEVER ACHIEVE ANYTHING.
THEY ONLY GET IN THE WAY. FALL BACK.
GH...
KOCHO, PASS IT TO ME!
I'LL CHARGE THE GOAL!
YOU GOTS IT!
YOU'RE NOT GETTIN' THROUGH ME!!
ROMIO-SAMA CIRCLED AHEAD!!
IT'S ROTHER VERSUS BROTHER!!

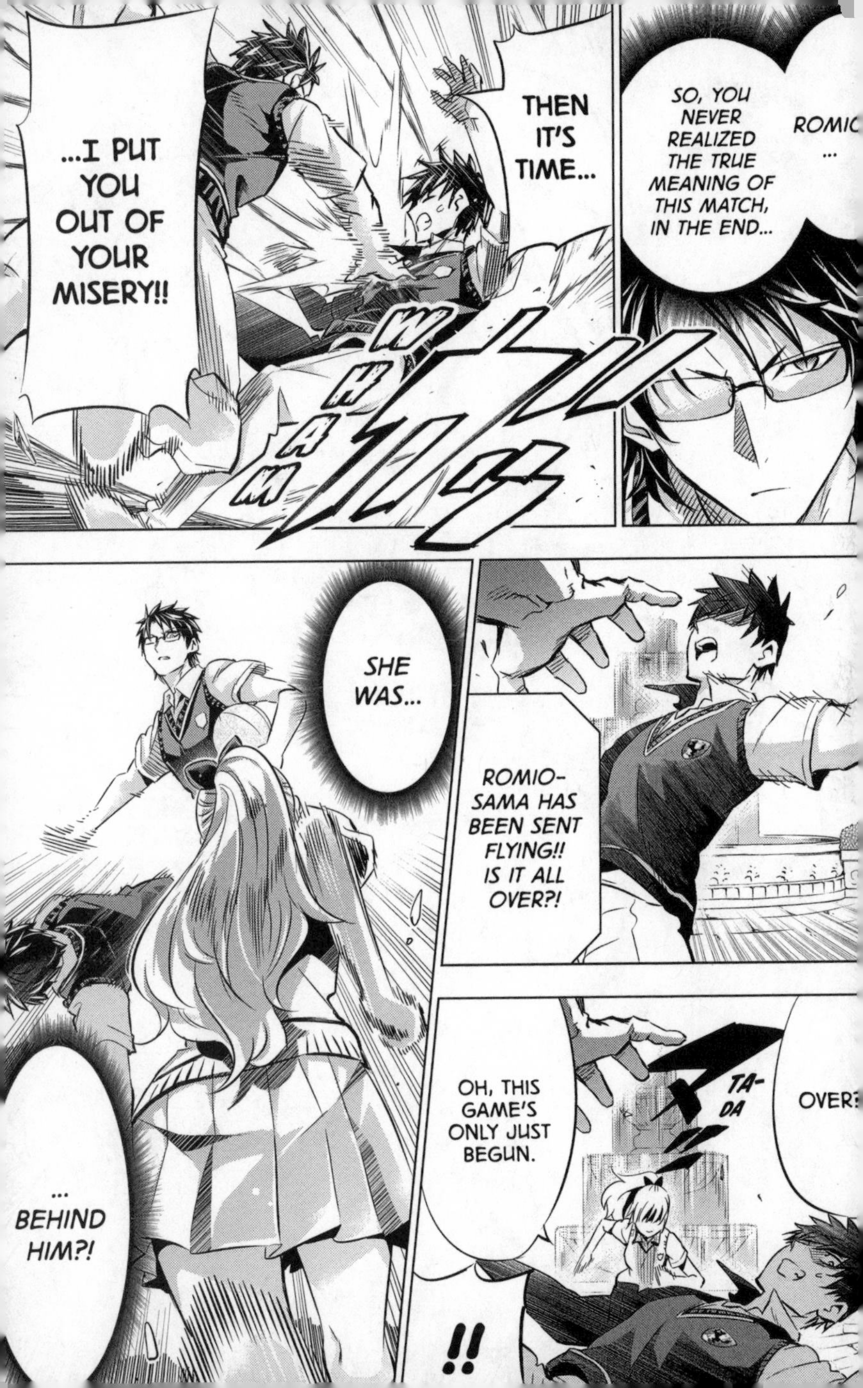
ROMIO ...
SO, YOU NEVER REALIZED THE TRUE MEANING OF THIS MATCH, IN THE END...
THEN IT'S TIME...
...I PUT YOU OUT OF YOUR MISERY!!
WHAM
ROMIO-SAMA HAS BEEN SENT FLYING!! IS IT ALL OVER?!
OVER
TA-DA
OH, THIS GAME'S ONLY JUST BEGUN.
!!
SHE WAS...
... BEHIND HIM?!

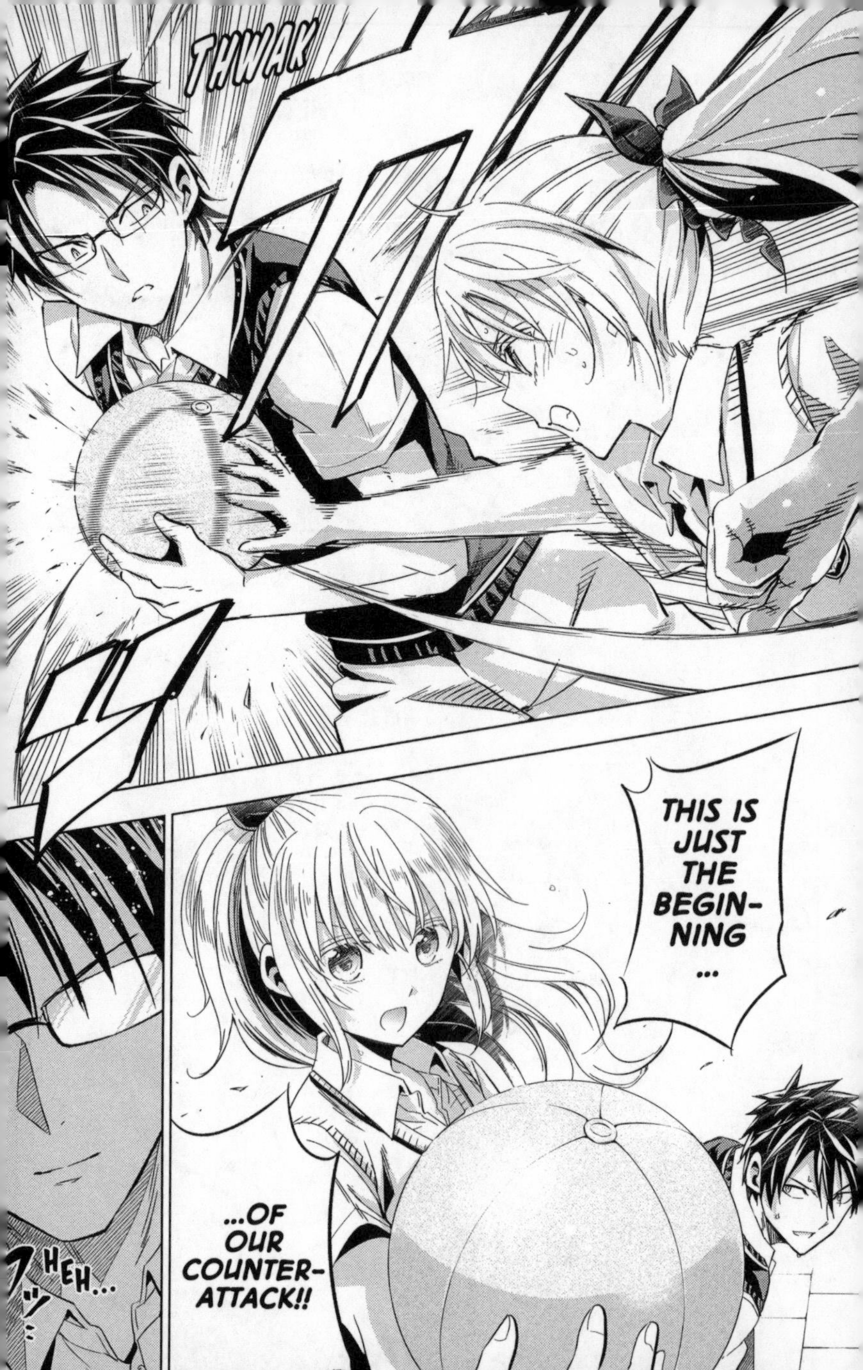
THWAK
THIS IS JUST THE BEGINNING...
...OF OUR COUNTER-ATTACK!!
HEH...

CONTINUED IN VOLUME 14

# BONUS COMIC STRIP: MATCHING

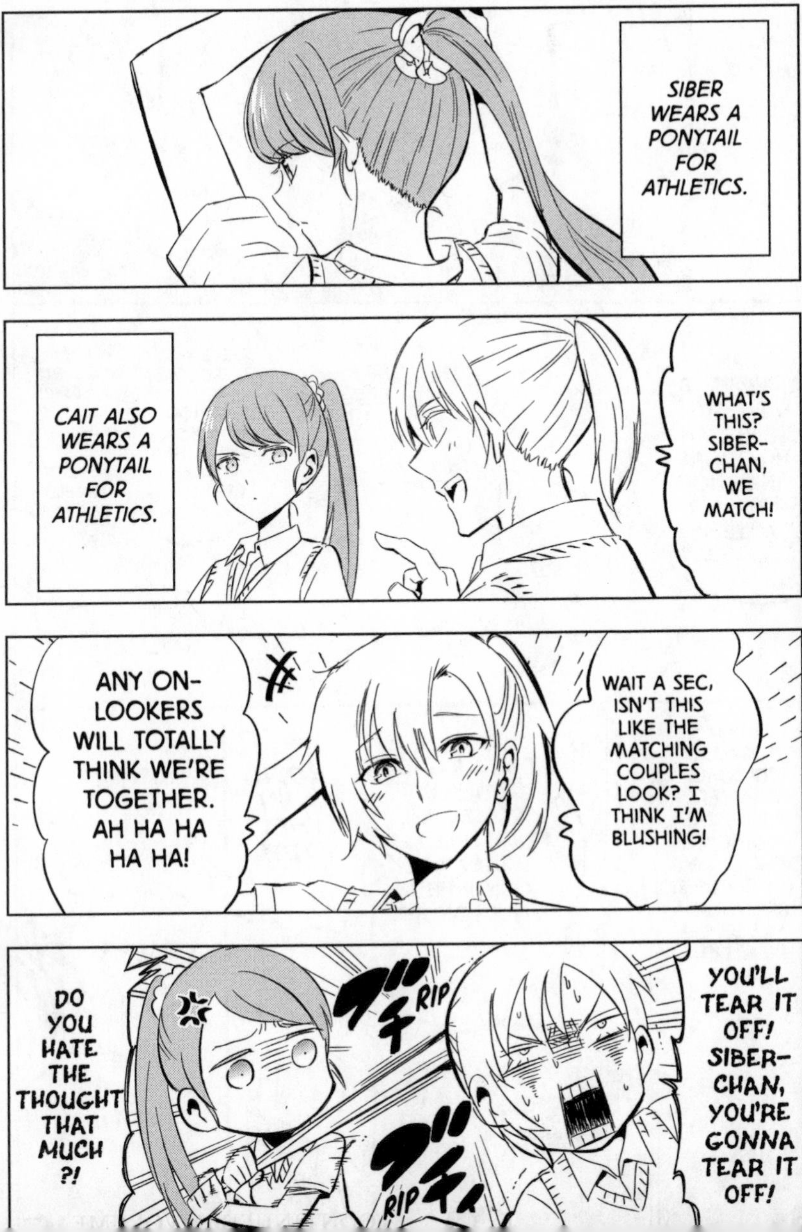
SIBER WEARS A PONYTAIL FOR ATHLETICS.
WHAT'S THIS? SIBER-CHAN, WE MATCH!
CAIT ALSO WEARS A PONYTAIL FOR ATHLETICS.
WAIT A SEC, ISN'T THIS LIKE THE MATCHING COUPLES LOOK? I THINK I'M BLUSHING!
ANY ON-LOOKERS WILL TOTALLY THINK WE'RE TOGETHER. AH HA HA HA HA!
YOU'LL TEAR IT OFF! SIBER-CHAN, YOU'RE GONNA TEAR IT OFF!
RIP
RIP
DO YOU HATE THE THOUGHT THAT MUCH ?!

# AFTERWORD

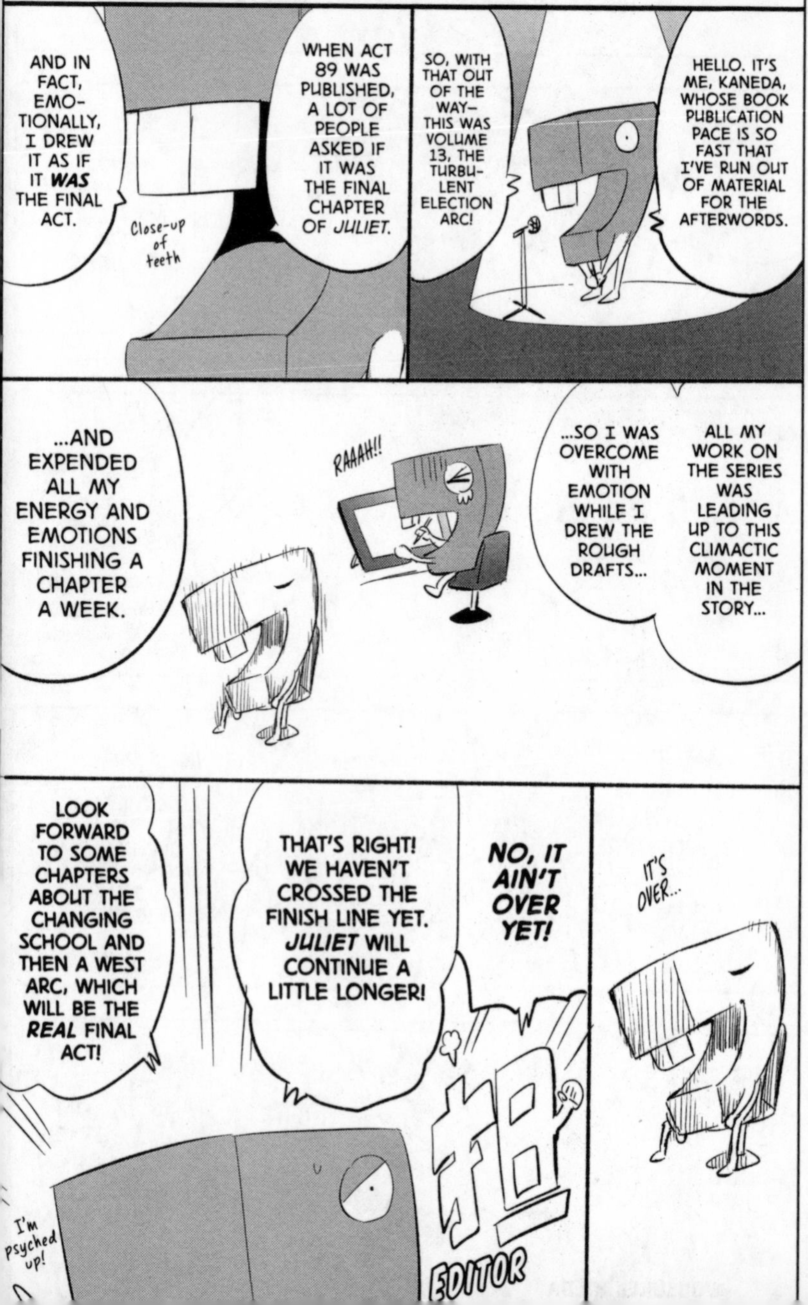
HELLO. IT'S ME, KANEDA, WHOSE BOOK PUBLICATION PACE IS SO FAST THAT I'VE RUN OUT OF MATERIAL FOR THE AFTERWORDS.
SO, WITH THAT OUT OF THE WAY— THIS WAS VOLUME 13, THE TURBULENT ELECTION ARC!
WHEN ACT 89 WAS PUBLISHED, A LOT OF PEOPLE ASKED IF IT WAS THE FINAL CHAPTER OF *JULIET*.
AND IN FACT, EMOTIONALLY, I DREW IT AS IF IT ***WAS*** THE FINAL ACT.
Close-up of teeth
ALL MY WORK ON THE SERIES WAS LEADING UP TO THIS CLIMACTIC MOMENT IN THE STORY...
...SO I WAS OVERCOME WITH EMOTION WHILE I DREW THE ROUGH DRAFTS...
RAAAH!!
...AND EXPENDED ALL MY ENERGY AND EMOTIONS FINISHING A CHAPTER A WEEK.
IT'S OVER...
***NO, IT AIN'T OVER YET!***
EDITOR
THAT'S RIGHT! WE HAVEN'T CROSSED THE FINISH LINE YET. *JULIET* WILL CONTINUE A LITTLE LONGER!
LOOK FORWARD TO SOME CHAPTERS ABOUT THE CHANGING SCHOOL AND THEN A WEST ARC, WHICH WILL BE THE ***REAL*** FINAL ACT!
I'm psyched up!

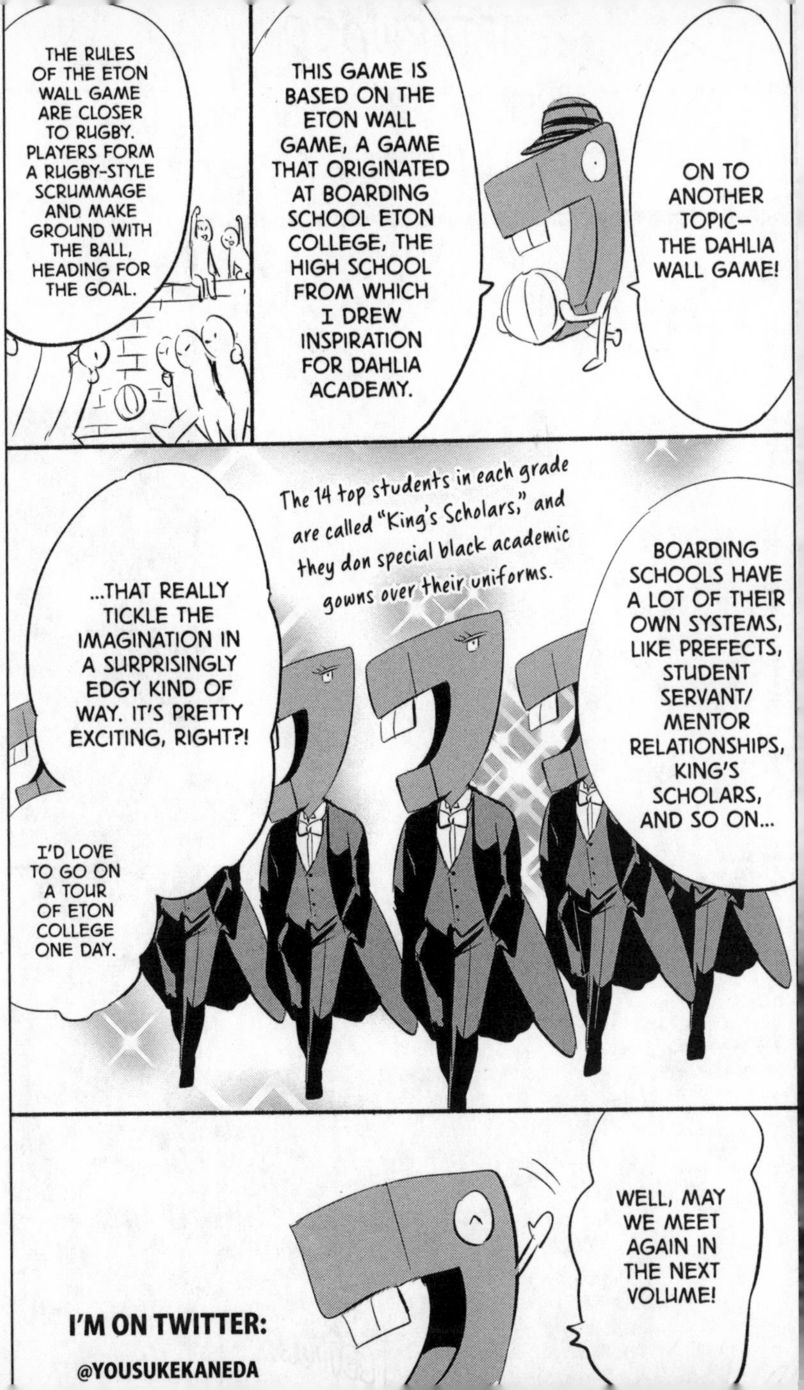
ON TO ANOTHER TOPIC— THE DAHLIA WALL GAME!
THIS GAME IS BASED ON THE ETON WALL GAME, A GAME THAT ORIGINATED AT BOARDING SCHOOL ETON COLLEGE, THE HIGH SCHOOL FROM WHICH I DREW INSPIRATION FOR DAHLIA ACADEMY.
THE RULES OF THE ETON WALL GAME ARE CLOSER TO RUGBY. PLAYERS FORM A RUGBY-STYLE SCRUMMAGE AND MAKE GROUND WITH THE BALL, HEADING FOR THE GOAL.
BOARDING SCHOOLS HAVE A LOT OF THEIR OWN SYSTEMS, LIKE PREFECTS, STUDENT SERVANT/ MENTOR RELATIONSHIPS, KING'S SCHOLARS, AND SO ON...
The 14 top students in each grade are called "King's Scholars," and they don special black academic gowns over their uniforms.
...THAT REALLY TICKLE THE IMAGINATION IN A SURPRISINGLY EDGY KIND OF WAY. IT'S PRETTY EXCITING, RIGHT?!
I'D LOVE TO GO ON A TOUR OF ETON COLLEGE ONE DAY.
WELL, MAY WE MEET AGAIN IN THE NEXT VOLUME!
I'M ON TWITTER:
@YOUSUKEKANEDA

# A SMART, NEW ROMANTIC COMEDY FOR FANS OF *SHORTCAKE CAKE* AND *TERRACE HOUSE*!

LIVING ROOM

MATSUNAGA-SAN

*Keiko Iwashita*

KC KODANSHA COMICS

A romance manga starring high school girl Meeko, who learns to live on her own in a boarding house whose living room is home to the odd (but handsome) Matsunaga-san. She begins to adjust to her new life away from her parents, but Meeko soon learns that no matter how far away from home she is, she's still a young girl at heart — especially when she finds herself falling for Matsunaga-san.

*Boarding School Juliet* 13 copyright © 2019 Yousuke Kaneda
English translation copyright © 2020 Yousuke Kaneda

All rights reserved.

Published in the United States by Kodansha Comics, an imprint of Kodansha USA Publishing, LLC, New York.

Publication rights for this English edition arranged through Kodansha Ltd., Tokyo.

First published in Japan in 2019 by Kodansha Ltd., Tokyo as *Kishuku Gakkou no Jurietto*, volume 13.

Original cover design by Seiko Tsuchihashi (hive & co., Ltd.)

ISBN 978-1-63236-977-2

Printed in the United States of America.

www.kodanshacomics.com

9 8 7 6 5 4 3 2 1
Translation: Amanda Haley
Lettering: James Dashiell
Editing: Erin Subramanian and Tiff Ferentini
Kodansha Comics edition cover design by Phil Balsman

Publisher: Kiichiro Sugawara

Director of publishing services: Ben Applegate
Associate director of operations: Stephen Pakula
Publishing services managing editor: Noelle Webster
Assistant production manager: Emi Lotto, Angela Zurlo